THE UNIVERSITY OF NORTH CAROLINA
SESQUICENTENNIAL PUBLICATIONS

THE CAMPUS
OF THE
FIRST STATE UNIVERSITY

OLD EAST
The first building to be erected on the campus of any state university in
the United States.

The Campus
of the
First State University

BY

ARCHIBALD HENDERSON
KENAN PROFESSOR OF MATHEMATICS

CHAPEL HILL
THE UNIVERSITY OF NORTH CAROLINA PRESS
1949

FOREWORD

THE CAMPUS of the first State University in the United States to open its doors to students connotes vastly more than the word "campus" ordinarily signifies. Campus here implies University lands as well as the grounds upon which the institution is located: buildings, athletic fields, gymnasium, stadium, arboretum, forests, plants and flora, landscape gardening, architecture, and innumerable other aspects of the University's life throughout the entire course of its material growth and physical development for one hundred and fifty years. Interesting, humorous, and bizarre features of Campus life are mirrored, so far as restrictions on space would permit, in a narrative which purports to be something richer than a mere catalog of properties and services. Subjects hitherto neglected or overlooked in accounts of the University are treated in some detail: the Preparatory Department and Grammar School; Steward's Hall; the first infirmary, known as "The Retreat"; the development of athletics including both outdoor and indoor sports; University architecture; the Arboretum; the astronomical observatories; landscape gardening; and the decline, suspended animation, and revival during the crucial years, 1861-1875, of the University's life.

The writing of this volume of the Sesquicentennial Publications, undertaken with no little diffidence at the invitation of the Committee on Grounds and Buildings, has been a labor of love and of far-ranging research, both extensive and intensive. Invited contributions, "The Arboretum" and "The Forests" by William Chambers Coker, for many years Chairman of the Committee on Grounds and Buildings, and "The Architecture of the University" by Arthur C. Nash, Consulting Architect, are incorporated without change in the present volume. Voluminous data on athletics here have been compiled and kindly placed at my disposal by the present chairman of the Committee on Grounds and Buildings, Richard J. M. Hobbs. Free use has been made of a perceptive critical study of Campus architecture here, generously prepared at my request by Fiske Kimball, Director of the Philadelphia Museum of Fine Arts. Supervision of maps has been efficiently performed by Paul W. Wager of the Committee on Grounds and Buildings; and new maps or revisions have been faithfully executed by Gray Culbreth, University Engineer, and Thomas D. Rose, City Engineer. Survey of illustrative materials has been entrusted to the artist, William Meade Prince, of the Committee on Grounds and Buildings.

For helpful information and access to official files, I am indebted to the following University officers: President Frank P. Graham, Chancellor R. B. House, P. L. Burch, Supervisor of Buildings, L. B. Rogerson, University Research Officer, J. S. Bennett, Supervisor of Operations, and C. E. Teague, Assistant Controller and Business Manager.

Thanks for exceptional aid are·extended to Lucile Kelling in matters of research, reference, and transcription; and to my sisters: Mary Ferrand Henderson for extended researches in the Swain and University MSS., in the original minutes of the Trustees, and in newspaper files; and Elizabeth Brownrigg Henderson (Mrs. Lyman A. Cotten), Curator of the Southern Historical Collection, for making available and furnishing typescripts of letters and documents in that very extensive collection of historical manuscripts.

Acknowledgments for assistance of various kinds are gratefully extended to: Mrs. Edwin A. Alderman, the late Alexander B. Andrews, William J. Battle, the late John M. Booker, M. S. Breckenridge, Mrs. S. J. Brockwell, Carrie L. Broughton, William D. Carmichael, Mrs. Hope S. Chamberlain, Harry W. Chase, Albert and Gladys Coates, Mrs. Collier Cobb and Miss Mary Cobb, Oscar J. Coffin, Harry F. Comer, R. D. W. Connor, Z. V. Council, Mrs. Ethel T. Crittenden, Vernon L. Crook, George B. Cutten, Preston H. Epps, Robert A. Fetzer, Mrs. Sam Fisher, W. Critz George, Louis and Mildred Graves, Karl P. Harrington, T. Felix Hickerson, Robert B. Lawson, J. Burton Linker, Robert W. Linker, Mr. and Mrs. Lacy LeGrand Little, Lawrence London, Augustus W. Long, James Lee Love, William de B. MacNider, the late A. W. McAllister, Robert W. Madry, William Starr Myers, Arthur S. Nash, Alice Noble, the late Haywood Parker, Mrs. A. H. Patterson, Mrs. Mary Graves Rees, Phillips Russell, Mrs. Lucy Phillips Russell, J. Maryon Saunders, Samuel Selden, Charles Lee Smith, Joe Sparrow, the late George G. Stephens, Mary L. Thornton, H. Raymond Weeks, A. L. M. Wiggins, and Louis R. Wilson.

For aid and courtesies extended, cordial thanks are offered to the staffs of the University of North Carolina Library, North Carolina State Library, Library of Congress, Avery Library of Columbia University, New York Historical Society, Maine Historical Society, North Carolina Department of Archives and History, University of North Carolina Alumni Association, Metropolitan Museum of Art. The index of this work was made by Agatha Boyd Adams.

For helpful suggestions and criticism, I am indebted to the editor-in-chief of the University's Sesquicentennial publications, Louis R. Wilson.

ARCHIBALD HENDERSON

Chapel Hill, N. C.
October 12, 1947.

ABBREVIATIONS USED IN THE FOOTNOTES

Barrier—Henry Smith Barrier, *On Carolina's Gridiron, 1888-1936; a History of Football at the University of North Carolina.* (Durham, N. C., Seeman Printery, 1937.)

Battle—Kemp Plummer Battle, *History of the University of North Carolina. I. 1789-1868; II. 1868-1912.* (Raleigh, Edwards & Broughton Printing Company, 1907-1912.)

Chamberlain—Hope Summerell Chamberlain, *Old Days in Chapel Hill, Being the Life and Letters of Cornelia Phillips Spencer.* (Chapel Hill, The University of North Carolina Press, 1926.)

E. C. T. M.—University of North Carolina. Trustees. Executive Committee. *Minutes.* Manuscript in the University of North Carolina Library.

Hooper—William Hooper, *Fifty Years Since; an Address before the Alumni Association of the University of North Carolina, June 7th, 1859.* (Raleigh, Holden & Wilson, "Standard" Office, 1859.)

J. S. H. S.—*James Sprunt Historical Monographs,* vols. 1-8; *The James Sprunt Historical Publications,* vols. 9-18; *The James Sprunt Historical Studies,* vols. 19— (Chapel Hill, The University of North Carolina Press.)

Link—Arthur Stanley Link, *A History of the Buildings at the University of North Carolina.* A thesis . . . for the degree of Bachelor of Arts, with honors, in the Department of History. (Chapel Hill, 1941.) Typescript in the University of North Carolina Library.

Love—James Lee Love, *'Tis Sixty Years Since; a Story of the University of North Carolina in the 1880's.* (Chapel Hill, 1945.)

Murphey—Archibald DeBow Murphey, *Papers;* edited by William Henry Hoyt. Two volumes. Publications of the North Carolina Historical Commission. (Raleigh, E. M. Uzzell & Company, State Printers, 1914.)

N. C. B. H.—*The Biographical History of North Carolina;* editor-in-chief, Samuel A'Court Ashe. Eight volumes. (Greensboro, N. C., Charles L. Van Noppen, 1905-1917.)

N. C. C. R.—*The Colonial Records of North Carolina,* 1662-1776. Ten volumes. (Raleigh, P. M. Hale [etc.], State Printer, 1886-1890.)

N. C. S. R.—*The State Records of North Carolina,* 1776-1790. Sixteen volumes. (Goldsboro, N. C., Nash Brothers, Printers, [etc., etc], 1886-1906.) *Index to the Colonial and State Records.* Four volumes. (Goldsboro, Raleigh [etc.], 1909-1914.)

S. P. I.—Cornelia Phillips Spencer, "Pen and Ink Sketches of the University of North Carolina," *Daily Sentinel,* April 26—July 6, 1869. Typescript copy in the University of North Carolina Library.

S. U. M.—Cornelia Phillips Spencer, "Old Days in Chapel Hill," *University of North Carolina Magazine,* 1884-1890. Bound together in one volume, in the University of North Carolina Library.

Spencer—Cornelia Phillips Spencer, *The Last Ninety Days of the War in North Carolina.* (New York, Watchman Publishing Company, 1866.)

Swain—David Lowrie Swain, *Early Times in Raleigh; Addresses . . .* compiled by R. S. Tucker. (Raleigh, Walters, Hughes & Company, 1867.)

T. M.—University of North Carolina. Trustees. *Minutes.* Manuscript in the University of North Carolina Library. *Note.* The page references for the years 1789 (December 18) to 1835 (December 5) are to the typescript copies of the Trustees' *Minutes.* The page references for the years from 1835 to date are to the volumes of the original manuscript records.

U. N. C. C.—[Kemp Plummer Battle], *Sketches of the History of the University of North Carolina, together with a Catalogue of Officers and students, 1789-1889.* (Chapel Hill, University, 1889.)

U. N. C. I. 1791-1867.—Record book, *History of the University of North Carolina: Letters, etc., 1791-1867*, Carolina Room, University Library.

U. N. C. I. 1796-1835.—Record book, *University of North Carolina: From 1796 to 1835*, Carolina Room, University Library.

U. N. C. M.—*University of North Carolina Magazine*. Various titles.

Wheeler—John Hill Wheeler, *Reminiscences and Memoirs of North Carolina and Eminent North Carolinians*. (Columbus, Ohio, Columbus Printing Works, 1884.)

CONTENTS

xiii

ILLUSTRATIONS

MAPS AND PLANS

PART I
LAYING THE FOUNDATIONS

1

ESTABLISHMENT OF A STATE UNIVERSITY; SELECTION OF UNIVERSITY SITE; LAYING OF THE CORNERSTONE

IN ORDER to understand the story of the Campus of the first State University, to grasp its full meaning and deep rootage, it is necessary to anticipate the chartering of the institution in 1789 and the opening of its doors in 1795. This University was the end-product of ideas, ideologies, and events—social, political, and religious—which were born of evolving American democracy and the irrepressible thrust toward independence. It was not accidental that the constitutional provision for the establishment of a State University fell in the year of the national Declaration of Independence; and that the charter of the University of North Carolina was adopted in the year of North Carolina's ratification of the Federal Constitution. Independence and education, State Constitution and democracy, Federal Constitution and university, logically and harmoniously synchronized. The University of North Carolina, said Edwin Anderson Alderman, was chartered "by the legislative action of a pioneer people, in a primitive wilderness, to furnish impulse and light to an agricultural community of English people."[1]

The University of North Carolina stemmed directly from the popular impulse expressed in the Instructions to the Delegates from Mecklenburg County to the Provincial Congress at Halifax, November 12, 1776: to "endeavor to establish a free government" which should approximate to a "simple democracy." Waightstill Avery, who had worked so patiently and assiduously for the establishment of a college in Mecklenburg County, is generally credited with sponsoring Article 41 in the Constitution of North Carolina providing for the establishment of a state university:[2]

1. *The Inauguration of Edwin Anderson Alderman*, January 27, 1897 (Chapel Hill).
2. Battle, II, 779, citing Swain; S. A. Ashe, *History of North Carolina* (Greensboro, N. C., 1908) I, 565 n, 567.

A school or schools shall be established by the legislature for the convenient instruction of youth, with such salaries to the masters, paid by the public, as may enable them to instruct at low prices; and all useful learning shall be encouraged and promoted in one or more universities.[3]

The first movement in North Carolina toward implementing Article 41 of the State Constitution, in the establishment of a state university, originated in Rowan County. The leader of this movement was the Rev. Samuel Eusebius McCorkle, graduate of the College of New Jersey in 1772 and pastor of Thyatira Presbyterian Church near Salisbury since 1776. He was a trustee of Liberty Hall, founded in Charlotte in 1777; and in the summer of 1779, in company with Dr. Ephraim Brevard of Mecklenburg County, was sent north by the trustees to solicit funds for the academy and to invite Dr. Alexander McWhorter to accept the presidency. From its founding Liberty Hall had been supported by leading families in Mecklenburg and Rowan, and when it fell into a state of decline, McCorkle conceived the idea of having it transferred by law to Salisbury. One year having elapsed since the close of the Revolution, the moment seemed auspicious for endeavoring also to secure the passage of a bill chartering a state university. McCorkle prepared such a bill, to which, according to common report, the finishing touches were given by Spruce Macay, representative of the borough of Salisbury in the Assembly, and the legal preceptor of William Richardson Davie and Andrew Jackson.[4]

The person selected to present these two educational bills in the Assembly was William Sharpe, native of Maryland and representative from Rowan County, who had held many public offices in North Carolina and had served two terms as a delegate from North Carolina in the Continental Congress. The bill for establishing the Salisbury Academy, the new name of Liberty Hall, which required no appropriation by the State, was intro-

3. Comparison of Article 41 of the constitution of North Carolina with Article 44 of the constitution of Pennsylvania, adopted earlier, shows that the former is identical with the latter, except for the omission of the words "in each county" after the word "established" and of the word "youth" after the word "instruct." *N.C.C.R.*, X, 1003-13.

4. William R. Davie to Spruce Macay, Halifax, N. C., September 3, 1793. Papers of Judge Nathaniel Boyden, Salisbury.

duced by Sharpe and readily passed, November 23, 1784.[5] On November 8, Sharpe had introduced in the House of Commons a "Bill for Establishing a University in this State" to be designated the "North Carolina University." On the following day the bill was "read for information"; and on November 11 it was "read the first time and passed." It was then sent to the Senate and read the first time on November 11. The next day the bill was taken up and ordered to "lie over until the next Session of Assembly."[6] The confused condition of the times immediately following the Revolution, the western revolt of the State of Franklin, the fear on the part of the radical republicans that a higher institution of learning might be used as an engine of political propaganda and as a bulwark of aristocratic privilege, the excessive scarcity of "hard money," the innumerable claims against the State in consequence of the late war, and the depleted condition of the treasury, all united to compel postponement of the university bill.

In educational progress in North Carolina, the influence of the College of New Jersey (as Princeton was then called) from the first has been conspicuous. Seven of the trustees of the first Salisbury Academy were graduates of the College of New Jersey: Governor Alexander Martin, formerly a resident of Salisbury, Samuel Eusebius McCorkle, Spruce Macay, Adlai Osborne, David Caldwell, James Hall, and Samuel Spencer.[7] In explanation of the abandonment of further efforts, during the next five years, to obtain a charter for a state university, it should be noted that neither Sharpe nor Macay ever returned to the Assembly; and McCorkle was preoccupied with the direction and maintenance of the Salisbury Academy, of which he was head. Writing from Salisbury to the brother of Elizabeth Maxwell Steel, his wife's mother, McCorkle relates: "We are driving forward a little academy with as much expedition as the great scarcity of cash will admit. Time only can tell what it will rise to."[8]

5. *Laws of 1784*, first session, Chapter XXIX; *N.C.S.R.*, XIX, 479, 737.
6. *N.C.S.R.*, XIX, 447, 765, 781. The original "bill for establishing a University in the State," on eight large sheets of parchment, is preserved in the State Department of Archives and History, Raleigh.
7. *N.C.S.R.*, XXIV, 690-92, 754-56.
8. S. E. McCorkle, Salisbury, N. C., to Ephraim Steel, Carlisle, Pa.,

Almost nothing is known of the gradual and steady growth of public opinion during the next five years, doubtless due to recognition of the urgent necessity of the education of youth for leadership in public life, in favor of the establishment of a state university. Unlike McCorkle, Sharpe, and Macay, who were opposed in 1784 by an anti-Federalist Assembly during a period of great financial stringency, Davie in 1789 presented his bills for establishing and chartering a state university in an assembly strongly Federalist in complexion and reputedly "actuated by a spirit of unusual liberality."[9]

A great impetus to the projected University, arousing high hopes for its success, was the munificent gift by Colonel Benjamin Smith of 20,000 acres of land in western North Carolina (northwest Tennessee). This "liberal and generous donation," as phrased by the Secretary, was announced by Davie at the first meeting of the Board of Trustees, Fayetteville, December 18, 1789.[10]

At Newbern on January 2, 1792, the last day of many meetings, the Trustees appointed Judge John Williams, General Thomas Person, General Alexander Mebane, Colonel John Macon, Colonel Benjamin Williams, Colonel Joel Lane, and the

March 18, 1786. Original letter in the writer's possession. The attendance at the academy was about fifty by the end of 1786. Jedidiah Morse, *The American Geography* (1789), p. 417.

9. G. J. McRee, *Life and Correspondence of James Iredell*, II, 270-71. For the great skill and eloquence displayed by Davie in overcoming all obstacles to the university bills, consult F. M. Hubbard, *Life of William Richardson Davie*, Jared Sparks' *Library of American Biography* (Boston, 1848), XIV, 107; Archibald D. Murphey, *Oration at Chapel Hill, June 27, 1827* (1827, 1832), *passim*; N.C.S.R., XXV, 23-24.

10. *T. M.*, 1789-1791, p. 1. This special meeting of the Board was called for the purpose of announcing the gift of Colonel Smith. At the second meeting of the Board, James Hogg presented the patents for the 20,000 acres given by Benjamin Smith, as follows: No. 31, 3,000 acres; No. 84, 4,000 acres; No. 89, 5,000 acres; No. 122, 3,000 acres; No. 165, 5,000 acres; and also the deed therefor, signed by Benjamin Smith, and witnessed by J. Hamilton and W. Nash.—*Ibid.*, p. 3. At a meeting of the Board of Trustees, Fayetteville, November 24, 1790, the following resolution of thanks for the gift of 20,000 acres of land was unanimously voted: "Resolved that this board do accept the said grant of lands; and that they entertain a proper impression of the public spirit and liberality manifested by Colonel Smith in this his early and valuable donation." *State Gazette of North Carolina*, January 7, 1791.

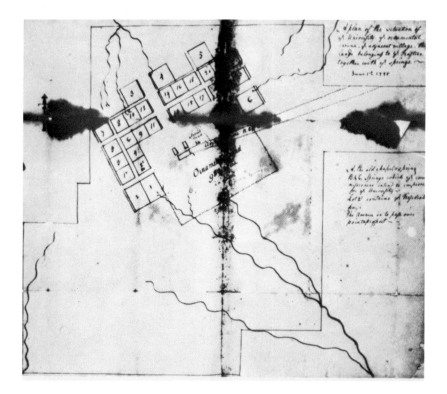

"A PLAN OF THE SITUATION OF Y^E UNIVERSITY—Y^E ORNAMENTAL
GROUND, Y^E ADJACENT VILLAGE. THE LANDS BELONGING TO Y^E TRUSTEES
TOGETHER WITH Y^E SPRINGS—

JUNE IST 1795"

This has been identified as the lost Harris map, made in 1795 by
Charles W. Harris. The legend in the lower righthand corner
reads:
"A. the old chapel-spring
B. & C. Springs which y^e commissioners intend to improve for y^e
University.
Lot 2 = contains y^e Presidents house
The Avenue is to pass over point prospect."

Honorable Alfred Moore or any three of them to "view and examine the most proper eligible situations whereon to fix the University in the counties of Wake, Franklin, Warren, Orange, Granville, Chatham, and Johnston; and ordered that they be requested to inquire of the general proprietors of such situation the lowest terms on which they will dispose, which they shall require in writing under their several hands, and make report thereof to the next stated meeting."[11] The familiarity of military leaders with geography and experience in location, as essentials of the business of waging war, doubtless explains why five of the seven committee members were officers of high rank. For reasons now impossible to determine, no report was forthcoming from this committee when the Trustees next met, seven months later, August 1, 1792, at Hillsborough. Two days later a committee consisting of William R. Davie, Alfred Moore, and Willie Jones, three of the most constructive thinkers in the North Carolina of that day, was appointed to prepare an ordinance for fixing the seat of the University. In this ordinance, unanimously adopted August 4, 1792, a new device for choosing the site was set up, it being ordained that

One person from each district be elected by ballot out of the body of the Trustees of the said University, and they or a majority of them are hereby authorized and directed to view the County within the limits aforesaid,[12] and determine on the spot or place most proper for the purpose above mentioned and to contract with, and purchase from owners the place they shall fix and determine on, together with not less than six hundred and forty acres of land thereto adjoining, and also one thousand four hundred acres so conveniently situated in the neighborhood thereof as to answer the purposes of a farm and a sufficient supply of firewood and timber for the University. . . .[13]

The plan was of large scope, with wise provisions made by men who were agriculturists on an extended scale and familiar with pioneer conditions.

11. *T. M.*, 1789-1810, p. 40.

12. Eight places were put in nomination for a geographical center, within fifteen miles of which the University was to be located. Cyprett's, later Prince's, Bridge, over New Hope Creek in Chatham County had been chosen by ballot on August 2 as the geographical center.

13. *T. M.*, 1789-1795, p. 48.

The eight commissioners were immediately chosen by ballot: William Porter, Morgan District; John Hamilton, Salisbury; Alexander Mebane, Hillsborough; Willie Jones, Halifax; David Stone, Edenton; Frederick Hargett, Newbern; William H. Hill, Wilmington; James Hogg, Fayetteville. At the place and time appointed, Pittsborough, November 1, 1792, a majority of the committee met and entered upon the performance of their important and delicate duties. During the period November 1 to 9, inclusive, the committee inspected various sites and received proposals in the form of offers of land and cash. The journal kept by the committee was presented at a meeting of the Trustees, Newbern, December 3, 1792, as its report.

All alumni of the University are familiar with the story that, on a warm summer day, exhausted by their searches for a suitable site, a group of Trustees headed by Davie sat down to rest upon the luxuriant grassy lawn beneath a giant poplar standing near the crest of the ridge popularly known as Chapel Hill. Beneath the poplar's umbrageous limbs the weary Trustees regaled themselves with exhilarating beverages; and after partaking of a picnic lunch and a refreshing nap, they unanimously decided that it was useless to proceed further, the eloquent Davie having convinced them that no more beautiful or suitable spot could be found elsewhere. It has been said that then and there was founded the first air-cooled cafeteria ever established in North Carolina. In commemoration of this apocryphal story, Mrs. Cornelia Phillips Spencer, it has been alleged, named the giant tree the "Davie Poplar"; and from that day to this, the beloved and "historic" tree has borne this honorable cognomen.

The true history of the influences which secured the location of the present site, while less romantic and entertaining than the "human interest story" of Davie and the tired Trustees reclining beneath the giant poplar, is rooted in individual service and economic logic. James Hogg, a native of East Lothian, Scotland, was persuaded by his brother Robert, prominent merchant of Wilmington, where he had settled in 1756, to emigrate to North Carolina. In 1774 James Hogg brought a shipload of 280 persons to America, a number of whom, including Strayhorns (Straughans), McCauleys, and Craigs, among others, settled in Orange

County. James Hogg sojourned first at Cross Creek, later re-named Fayetteville, where he conducted a mercantile establishment in partnership with his brother Robert. During the Revolution or just before, he settled in Hillsborough; and having many acquaintances in Orange County, especially among those who had come with him from Scotland, he soon acquired a wide and intimate knowledge of lands in that region.

During the year 1792, the sites of both the State capital and the State University were being chosen. It is interesting to note that Frederick Hargett was a commissioner on both boards. Of the seventeen sites under consideration for the location of the capital, the 1,000-acre plantation of Joel Lane, at Wake Court House, was chosen on March 30, 1792. The conviction prevailed that, consonant with suitable geographical conditions and physical environment, both capital and University should be located near the center of the State. It has been surmised that Cyprett's Bridge was chosen as the center of the 15-mile circle within which the University must be located as the result of the influence of Joel Lane, aided by Willie Jones and Davie; but Lane's own bid for the University site was unsuccessful.[14] Although he was not one of the commissioners, Davie was paid the compliment of having one of the streets of the capital named for him, perhaps through the influence of his fellow-townsman, Willie Jones, who was commissioner at large for locating the capital.[15]

James Hogg, canny Scotsman and expert realtor, determined to exert all his influence in favor of New Hope Chapel Hill, which he had often visited and regarded as the ideal spot for the University's location. He persuaded his friends in that neighborhood, prior to the meetings of the commission of which he was a member, to make generous offers of land and money.

14. Under the heading "Pittsboro, November 2, 1792," appears the following entry in the journal of the commissioners to select a site for the University: "Willie Jones handed to the commissioners an offer of Col. Joel Lane, of 640 acres near Nathaniel Jones's, at the cross-roads, in Wake County, provided the University was fixed at Nathaniel Jones's." *T. M.*, 1789-1810, p. 53.

15. Consult Battle, I, 24; *The Early History of Raleigh: A Centennial Address*, Raleigh, October 18, 1892 (Raleigh, 1893), pp. 19-29.

Although fourteen sites were put in competition, the commissioners unanimously recommended to the Trustees at Newbern, December 3, 1792, that New Hope Chapel Hill be chosen as the "seat of the University of North Carolina." The gifts, all "conditional that the University shall be established on New Hope Chapel Hill, in Orange County," totaled 1,386 acres of land and £798 or thereabouts.[16] In consideration of their donations, the donors were voted the "respective privilege of having one student educated at the said University free from any expense of tuition."[17]

It is abundantly clear that economic considerations and common sense, coupled with the beauty and "eligibility" of New Hope Chapel Hill, prevailed in the selection of a site, backed as the location was by the unanimous recommendation of the commissioners. Much the best and highest bid was made by the citizens and landholders of New Hope Chapel Hill and vicinity; and credit for the location is attributable both to the generosity of the donors, and to the shrewdness, assiduity, and indefatigable labors of James Hogg in personally soliciting the gifts.

James Hogg, an early American captain of industry, belonged to the family which produced the Scottish poet of the same name, known as "the Ettrick Shepherd"; and his wife, McDowal Alves, was second cousin to Sir Walter Scott. For thirteen years (1789-1802) he was a devoted and active member of the Board of Trustees, serving on many committees, including the Visiting Committee whose duty it was at that time to examine students at Commencement. Two of his sons, Walter and Gavin Alves, served as Secretary, and the former also as Treasurer, of the Board of Trustees.[18] His daughter, Helen, became the second

16. The figure given in the Trustees' Minutes is the round number of 1,390 acres of land, of which 840 "lie on Chapel Hill or adjoining thereto, and the remainder within 4 or 5 miles or thereabouts." For the donors and their respective gifts of land consult *T. M.*, 1789-1810, pp. 53-54. Also see map on p. 354 of present volume.

17. For some reason, not now ascertainable, this privilege was not extended to three donors, Alexander Piper, James Craig, and Thomas Connelly, whose gifts were respectively 20, 5, and 100 acres, the deed for the last mentioned not having been executed up to November 9, 1792.

18. When Walter Alves, brother of Mrs. James Hogg, was lost at sea, traveling from the West Indies to England, the family name of Alves became extinct. In 1786 James Hogg petitioned the legislature of North

wife of Joseph Caldwell, the University's first president.[19]

On August 2, 1792, the Trustees, in session at Hillsborough, on the motion of Davie, appointed a committee consisting of Richard Dobbs Spaight, Benjamin Hawkins, John Williams, Adlai Osborne, and Samuel Eusebius McCorkle to "report the plan of the buildings of the University and particularly such part of the said buildings as it may be proper to erect at present." The following day Davie, Alfred Moore, and Willie Jones were designated to "prepare an ordinance for fixing the seat of the University, for purchasing the necessary quantity of land, and for erecting the buildings." On August 4, Benjamin Hawkins from the committee appointed to offer a plan of the buildings of the University, reported that in their opinion

. . . the building should be 120 feet by 50, 3 stories high, 8 rooms on each floor, 18 by 16, a dining room on the first floor 40 by 30, 2 rooms 12 by 16 on each side of the entry. The entry 16 by 16, a passage through the center of the building 10 feet wide, a public Hall in the second and third story 40 by 30 with a gallery in front 40 by 10, a semi-octagon in the back, front to extend so far as to make the dining room 40 by 30—a passage through the second and third story 10 feet wide, the space for the entry and the two small rooms to be so apportioned in the second and third story as to admit of two large rooms, adjoining the stair case the one for a library. The first story 12, the second 10, the third 9 feet, 36 feet from the surface to the eves, 4 chimneys in the center of the partition dividing the room 16 by 18, 2 windows in each room to correspond with the pitch of the stories—windows on each side of the semi-octagon, —the foundation of stone, the remainder brick,—the doors to enter the rooms from the oblong entry,—a light over each doorhead in the passage.[20]

The description in detail is given here because of the historic character of this building: the first to be erected upon the campus of any state university within the present bounds of the United

---

Carolina to change the names of his sons Walter and Gavin Hogg to Walter and Gavin Alves. The act was passed on December 26, 1786. See *Private Acts of North Carolina*, 1786, Chapter CLV; also *Draper MSS.*, 2CC33.

19. James Hogg should not be confused with a Scotsman of the same name, father of the famous lawyer, Gavin Hogg, of Raleigh, who was long a resident of Chapel Hill.

20. *T. M.*, 1789-1810, pp. 42, 45, 46-47.

States. For lack of means, however, this ambitious plan for the first university building was not adopted.[21] The committee of eight, elected on this same day to "view and determine on the spot or place whereon to erect the buildings of the University," was instructed to "enquire into the prices whereat building materials may be procured at the place by them to be appointed" for a site, and given discretionary power to "contract for 300,000 brick to be delivered at said place." On November 9 the committee contracted with Colonel John Hogan, one of the original donors of land (200 acres) "to make and deliver 150,000 bricks at 40 c. per hund. as per contract."

On December 8, 1792, at Newbern the Trustees elected Alfred Moore, W. R. Davie, Frederick Hargett, Thomas Blount, Alexander Mebane, John Williams, and John Haywood to superintend the erection of the buildings; and by the ordinance voted on August 3 preceding, which was presented on this same day (December 8) by Davie, the above commissioners were "required to lay off and survey adjacent thereto [i.e., to the University site] a town containing 24 lots of two acres each and six lots of four acres each—and to sell and dispose of the said lots at public vendue on 12 months credit." They were furthermore "directed and impowered to cause to be built on the ground allotted for that purpose a house or houses sufficient if practicable from the sum appropriated for that purpose to accommodate fifty students. . . ."[22]

In those pioneer days in America, be it remembered, the professional architect had not yet emerged. All buildings, whether small or spacious, were erected by contractors who then bore the lugubrious name of "undertakers." Such men "undertook" the contract; and with the cooperation of handicraftsmen in carpentry, stone cutting, bricklaying, mortar making and plastering,

21. However, as Dr. Battle says, the "Old East was designed to be no ephemeral structure. . . . The mortar is of two measures of lime to one of sand. The sleepers are 3 by 10 inches and are only 14 inches apart. The timbers are of the best heart, the bricks carefully made on the University grounds and burnt hard as the imperishable rocks." "History of the Buildings of the University of North Carolina," address at Chapel Hill, October 12, 1883, in Wheeler, p. 346.

22. T. M., 1789-1810, p. 60. This proposal replaced Hawkins' more ambitious plan, given above.

erected structures which in stability, excellence and durability of materials, and appearance, often compare favorably with the architectural compositions of today. For the most part, esthetic considerations did not enter; economic and utilitarian objectives held full sway. The type of architecture was elementally "functional." The committee industriously went ahead, contracting with George Daniel of Orange County for the making and delivering of 350,000 brick at the rate of 40 shillings per thousand. On August 10, 1793, the commissioners met at New Hope Chapel Hill and laid off both the site for the University buildings, offices, avenues, and "ornamental grounds," and also the site, adjacent thereto, of a town. The survey and map of the lands were made by John Daniel, and the map is still preserved in the University archives. The "plan of the intended buildings of the University," for executing which he received £10, was drawn by John Conroy.[23] For the sum of £100 ($200) the commissioners most judiciously purchased 80 acres of land owned by Hardy Morgan which "ran up angularly" into the University tract.

On July 19, after considering a number of proposals by different contractors, the Trustees engaged James Patterson of Chatham County to build a two-storey brick building 96 feet 7 inches long and 40 feet 1½ inches wide, according to the plan submitted, for the sum of £2,500 ($5,000), the University to furnish the brick, sash weights, locks, hooks, fastenings, and painting. The building, to contain sixteen rooms and four passages, was to be finished by November 1, 1794; and, according to a master plan, was to be one (the north) wing of a larger building and was "placed by them accordingly."[24]

23. *T. M.*, 1789-1797, p. 96. This plan has disappeared. It seems evident that James Hogg used the John Daniel map to aid him in soliciting contributions of land for the University. Colonel Frederick Hargett writes from Newbern to James Hogg at Wilmington, December 22, 1792: "Both your letters came safe to hand with Col. McCawley's [*sic*] deed inclosed, I also Rec'd the platt drawn by Mr. Daniel, much to my satisfaction, which I Laid before the Board. . . ." *U.N.C.I. 1791-1867.*

24. John Haywood's Report, *T. M.*, 1790-1810, pp. 68-70. The drawing by a student, John Pettigrew, shows outside platforms, with double stairways, running north and south, before each of the two side entrances. Battle, I, illustration facing p. 60. The greater portion of the exterior,

The original design for buildings and grounds, proposed by John Conroy, indicates a preoccupation with oriental ideas, in consonance with Moslem *mores*. In the East, it was customary to bury the dead with head directed toward the east, to face toward the east in crying the *Muezzin* (call to prayer), and to build temples and mausoleums fronting toward the rising sun. This fashion of "Orientalization," as it was called in architectural circles in America, doubtless had its origin in the Masonic Order; and Conroy may well have been influenced in his design by Davie who became Grand Master of Masons in North Carolina in 1792.[25] On the plan sent by Charles W. Harris to his uncle, Dr. Charles Harris of Cabarrus County on June 1, 1795, a broad avenue was laid down to run N. 69°E., *i.e.*, perpendicular to the east front of the "main building," and to extend all the way to Point Prospect, a distance of almost a mile. Later on, according to the original conception, there was to be a "main building" at a distance of 180 yards from the main street of the village, flanked by two wings, to north and south respectively, also facing eastward; but this intention was not carried out.[26] The spacious Campus was to contain almost 100 acres; and certain springs in the area were valued for their "mineral tinctures." Harris speaks enthusiastically of the "University lands—the village—ornamental grounds, springs, &c. . . . But it would be unnecessary to enter into a Geographical description. . . . The general opinion is that the plan is most happily situated, . . . a

---

except some layers of brick at bottom and top, was evidently covered with stucco and painted white or some light color.

25. Marshall De Lancey Haywood, *The Beginnings of Freemasonry in North Carolina and Tennessee* (Raleigh, 1906). Davie served as Grand Master from December 14, 1792, until December 4, 1799.

26. An analog of the original design for the three central buildings of the University is that of the North Carolina Hospital for the Insane in Raleigh. Roger Hale Newton, *Town & Davis, Architects* (New York, 1942), Plate 30. This building, completed in 1850, was designed by the famous architect, Alexander Jackson Davis, who designed and remodeled a number of the buildings at Chapel Hill, as will appear in the sequel. The plan drawn by Harris, along with his letter, are preserved in the University archives. The plan bears the legend: "A plan of the situation of yᵉ University—yᵉ ornamental ground, yᵉ adjacent village. The lands belonging to yᵉ Trustees together with yᵉ springs." *U.N.C.I. 1791-1867*. This plan is reproduced in the present volume.

DAVIE POPLAR

At right is the famous Davie Poplar. According to legend, a group of
Trustees headed by Davie stopped here, and after rest and refreshment
declared that no more beautiful location could be found for the University. Mrs. Cornelia Phillips Spencer is said to have given the tree
its name.

TO THE PUBLIC.

THE fubfcribers having been appointed a committee of the Board of the Truftees of the Univerfity of North-Carolina, for the purpofe of receiving propofals from fuch gentlemen as may intend to undertake the inftruction of youth in that inftitution, take the opportunity of making known to the public their wifh that fuch gentlemen fhould fignify their inclination to the fubfcribers.

The objects to which it is contemplated by the Board to turn the attention of the ftudents, on the firft eftablifhment, are—The ftudy of Languages, particularly the Englifh—Hiftory, antient and modern—the Belle lettre—Logic and Moral Philofophy—the knowledge of the Mathematics, and Natural Philofophy—Agriculture and Botany, with the principles of Architecture.

Gentlemen converfant in thefe branches of Science, and Literature, and who can be well recommended, will receive very handfome encouragement by the Board. The exercifes of the inftitution will commence as early as poffible after the completion of the buildings of the Univerfity, which are to be contracted for immediately.

SAMUEL ASHE,
A. MOORE,
JOHN HAY,
DAVID STONE,
SAM. M'CORKLE.

ADVERTISEMENT FOR TEACHERS IN THE HALIFAX
NORTH CAROLINA JOURNAL, APRIL 10, 1793

delightful prospect, charming groves, medicinal springs . . . light and wholesome air . . . & inaccessible to vice."[27]

October 12, 1793, the date of the laying of the cornerstone of the "North Wing," later known as "Old East," is certainly one of the most significant dates in North Carolina's history. Seen in just perspective—in the light of its far-reaching consequences: educational, cultural, social, political, economic, and of the unpredictable future of widening effects upon North Carolina, the entire Southeast, and the nation—October 12, 1793 ranks in importance with April 12, 1776 and with November 21, 1789. The instructions of the North Carolina delegates in the Continental Congress to vote, in conjunction with the delegates of other colonies, for national independence; the provision in the state constitution for the establishment of one or more universities; the introduction of bills, by Sharpe in 1784 and by Davie in 1789, to create the University of North Carolina; and the adoption of the charter of the University and the ratification of the Federal Constitution in 1789—all find their culmination in the simple, yet momentous, ceremonies of the laying of the cornerstone of the first building upon this Campus.

On that bright autumn day, when the "maple trees flamed red in the eager air," a procession of dignitaries, stately in mien and conscious of the far-reaching importance of the occasion, wended its way eastward along the gently undulating slopes of New Hope to the spot destined to become eternally historic. Notable among the Trustees in that procession were the commissioners who located the site and laid off the town: Alfred Moore, small in stature, neat in his dress, and graceful in his manners, notable advocate and six years later to receive appointment as justice of the Supreme Court of the United States; John Haywood, able, genial and beloved, for forty years Treasurer of North Carolina and long devoted in service to the University; John Williams, founder of Williamsborough, judge of the highest court in North Carolina and representative in the Congress of the Confederation; William Henry Hill of Wilmington, grad-

27. H. M. Wagstaff, ed., "The Harris Letters," *J. S. H. S.*, Vol. XIV, No. 1 (1916), 17-18. Charles W. Harris to Dr. Charles Harris, June 1, 1795.

uate of Harvard who studied law in Boston, first District Attorney of the United States for North Carolina, and subsequently member of the United States Congress; General Thomas Blount, Commissioner to locate both the State capital and the State University and representative in the United States Congress; General Alexander Mebane, pronounced radical who vigorously opposed the ratification of the Constitution of the United States, and at this time a member of the United States Congress; and the venerable Frederick Hargett, competent and trustworthy, long a State senator from Jones County and a colleague of Abnèr Nash.

In this distinguished gathering, the two figures primarily instrumental in founding the University were most conspicuous. The orator of the day was Dr. Samuel Eusebius McCorkle, who was presumably given this honor and also elected to the Board of Trustees, the only minister so honored, in recognition of his pioneering labors for education in North Carolina. He was more than six feet tall, with light hair falling on his shoulders, and clear blue eyes, a living replica of Thomas Jefferson in his latter years.[28] At his side, the resplendent Masonic regalia of North Carolina's Grand Master contrasting with McCorkle's somber ministerial black, marched the handsome William Richardson Davie, one of the most gifted and cultured men on the continent. On this first University Day celebration, Davie's star was in the ascendant; and the laying of the cornerstone of the Old East Building was, in symbol, as well as in fact, the most significant and influential act of a memorable career.

To Davie's immediate rear in the procession came Judge Spruce Macay, distinguished jurist, especially honored along with McCorkle in being mentioned by name, in the account of the ceremonies prepared by Davie, doubtless because of their activities in the effort to secure the establishment of the University in 1784. The delegation of Masons, representing Eagle Lodge of Hillsborough, was headed by Absalom Tatom, captain

28. W. H. Foote, *Sketches of North Carolina* (New York, 1846), p. 361. An inexplicable and inexcusable blunder is the omission of the black-robed figure of Dr. McCorkle from the mural by Dean Cornwell on the west wall of the United States Post Office in Chapel Hill.

in the Revolution, sometime representative in the State legislature, and pronounced democrat.[29]

It is fortunate for posterity that a graphic and interesting account of the exercises was written by Davie and published in his home town of Halifax.

On the 12th inst. the Commissioners, appointed by the Board of Trustees of the University of this State, met at Chapel-Hill for the purpose of laying the corner-stone of the present building, and disposing of the lots in the village. A large number of the brethren of the Masonic order from Hillsborough, Chatham, Granville, and Warren, attended to assist at the ceremony of placing the corner-stone; and the procession for this purpose moved from Mr. Patterson's at 12 o'clock in the following order: The Masonic Brethren in their usual order of procession, the Commissioners, the Trustees not Commissioners; the Hon. Judge Macay and other public officers; then followed the gentlemen of the vicinity. On approaching the south end of the building, the Masons opened to the right and left, and the Commissioners, etc., passed through and took their place. The Masonic procession then moved on round the foundation of the building and halted, with their usual ceremonies, opposite the southeast corner, where *WILLIAM RICHARDSON DAVIE*, Grand-Master of the Fraternity, etc., in this State, assisted by two Masters of Lodges and four other officers, laid the cornerstone, enclosing a plate to commemorate the transaction.[30]

29. "The second anniversary of the institution of the Lodge, October 12, 1793, was observed by a delegation of the brethren, led by Worshipful Master Absalom Tatom, making a journey to 'Chappel Hill' to assist in the ceremony of laying the Cornerstone for the first building of the State University. From this cornerstone of 'Old East' building has arisen a great University dedicated to the services of God and the education of Youth." R. B. Studebaker, *History of Eagle Lodge* (Chapel Hill, 1937), p. 14.

30. The foundation was laid both wide and deep, the bottom wall being of stone and three feet thick. The brass plate here mentioned bore on face and reverse, respectively, the following inscriptions, the former in English, the latter in Latin. It may be noted that the phrase *Sit Aere Perennius* is not found in the inscription in English.

The
Right Worshipful
William Richardson Davie
of
The most Ancient and Honorable Fraternity
Of FREE MASONS, in the State of NORTH CAROLINA
One of the TRUSTEES of the UNIVERSITY
of the Said STATE,

The Rev. Dr. McCorkle then addressed the Trustees and spectators in an excellent discourse suited to the occasion. . . . He concluded with these observations:

"The seat of the University was next sought for, and the public eye selected Chappel-Hill—a lovely situation—in the center of the state—at a convenient distance from the Capital—in a healthy and fertile neighborhood. May this hill be for religion as the ancient hill of Zion; and for literature and the muses, may it surpass the ancient Parnassus! We this day enjoy the pleasure of seeing the corner-stone of the University, its foundations, its materials, and the architect for the building; and we hope ere long to see its stately walls and spire ascending to their summit. Ere long we hope to see it adorned with an elegant village, accommodated with all the necessaries and conveniences of civilized society."

This discourse was followed by a short but animated prayer, closed with the united *amen* of an immense concourse of people.

And a Commissioner of the Same
Assisted by
The other Commissioners, and the Brethren
Of the EAGLE AND INDEPENDENCE LODGES
on the 12th day of October
IN THE YEAR OF MASONRY 5793,
and in the 18th Year of American INDEPENDENCE
LAID THE CORNER STONE
of this EDIFICE

HUNC LAPIDEM
Honorariis Curatoribus hujus Academiae
nec non
FRATRIBUS MASONICIS HILLSBORIA aliundeque
RITE presentibus
GULIELMUS R. DAVIE, equestris praefectus
Carolinaque Septentrionalis ARCHE ARCHITICUS
Anno Lucis 5793°. Salutis 1793°
AMERICANAE LIBERTATIS 18
& 12.mo die Octobris
MULTO CUM ORDINE
LOCAVIT
SIT AERE PERENNIUS

This copper plate was engraved in 1792 by Roswell Huntington, of Hillsboro, who was born in Norwich, Conn., March 15, 1763, the son of Ebenezer, Jr., and Sarah Edgerton.

For the story of the recovery of this plate, see "The Presentation of the Plate," *Alumni Review*, V (November, 1916), 38-41. The plate, face and reverse, is reproduced on page 28 of this issue of the *Alumni Review*.

The Commissioners then proceeded to sell the lots in the village; and we have the pleasure to assure the public, that although there were but twenty-nine lots, they sold for upwards of one thousand, five hundred pounds, which shows the high idea the public entertain of this agreeable and healthful situation.[31]

31. *North Carolina Journal*, Wednesday, October 16, 1793. Perhaps the adjective "immense" should be taken with a grain of salt. In appreciation of McCorkle's oration, briefly quoted above, the University's historian fervently exclaims: "We thank thee for thy golden words, thou venerable father of education in our State." Battle, I, 40.

2

CHAPEL HILL: THE GEOGRAPHIC SETTING

MANY ATTRACTIVE locations within a circle of fifteen miles radius having its center at Cyprett's, later Prince's, Bridge might have been chosen for the site of the University of North Carolina. The location might have fallen in Chatham, Wake, or Orange counties—"from the highlands of New Hope to the hills of Buckhorn; from the Hickory Mountain to the eminence overlooking our beautiful capital on the west." Economic considerations in great measure, as already indicated, tipped the scales in favor of the site chosen. But it almost seems as if a benignant Providence arranged that the most generous offer afforded the most charming and suitable site. An excellent statement of the reasons for the choice of the site is given by Judge Williamson, historian and Governor of Maine:

The location itself was selected with much well-advised discretion. The ground on which the colleges stand is elevated and dry, and so formed by nature as to turn the water from them every way. On all sides stand numbers of lofty spreading oaks, ornaments of nature's producing, which rise as sylvan bowers beneath a summer's sun and form something like battlements to the attacks of tempests. But the principal considerations which united the minds of the trustees on this place were three-fold: the purity of the water, the salubrity of the air and the great healthfulness of the climate. Perhaps there can hardly be found a residence in the same latitude where these form a more happy coalescence. The place, however, is central to the territory of the State, and will ultimately be so to the population.[1]

Although the charter forbade the location of the University within five miles of any town where court was held, the Trustees were unquestionably influenced by considerations of accessibility.[2] Chapel Hill qualified under this test, as here crossed

1. W. D. Williamson, "The University of North Carolina," *Boston Recorder*, December 14, 1843; copied in the Raleigh *Register* in 1844; and reproduced in *U. N. C. M.*, I (1852), 372-84.
2. *Laws of North Carolina*, 1789, Chapter XX, § 21-25.

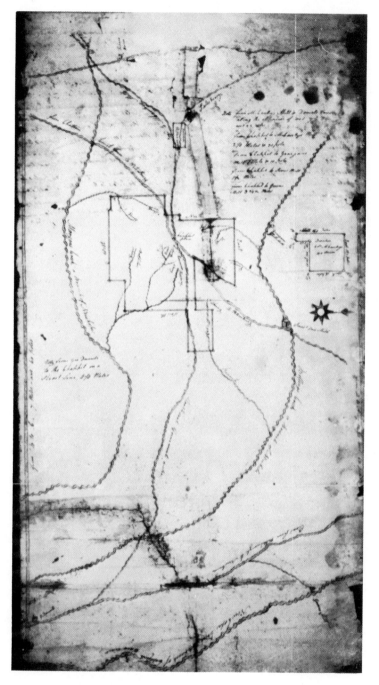

DANIEL MAP

This is a copy of the original map of Chapel Hill made in 1792 by John Daniel, surveyor for the Trustees of the University.

two great highways, main arteries of travel and trade. One was the road which ran from Petersburg, by Oxford, and on to Pittsborough, passing Chapel Hill to the south of the present President's lot, through the Campus between the Old West Building and Person Hall, and across the lot where the Peabody Building now stands. The other was the road from Newbern which ran by Wake Court House, where the capital was then being laid out, and on to Guilford Court House, near present Greensboro, passing through the Campus to the south of present South Building. The intersection of these two main highways was on present Pittsboro Street near the spot where in later years was erected the village schoolhouse.[3]

In the northeast corner of this intersection was located a small Chapel of Ease which, as well as St. Jude's in the Hawfields, St. Mary's, Williamsborough, in Edgecombe, later Granville, County, and perhaps other houses of worship, was one of the "ante-Revolutionary mission posts at which the Rev. George Micklejohn used to preach."[4] Micklejohn, graduate of the University of Cambridge, which later conferred upon him the honorary degree of Doctor of Sacred Theology, was assigned to St. Matthew's Parish, Orange County, shortly after his arrival in the

3. Consult original map of Chapel Hill made by John Daniel in 1792, at the instance of the Trustees, preserved in the archives, University of North Carolina, and reproduced in the present volume. Mr. Daniel was allowed eight pounds by the Trustees for surveying and drawing a plot of the University lands. *T. M.*, 1789-1797, p. 55. December 4, 1792.

4. Statement made in 1882 by Bishop William Mercer Green of Mississippi, long a resident of Chapel Hill, Professor in the University, and the animating force in the erection of the Church of the Atonement, later consecrated as the Chapel of the Cross. Considerably more than a century ago, remains of this "rough little edifice were still to be seen at a spot in the garden of the Graves place, according to the wife of the Rev. James Phillips, who became a professor in the University in 1826." K. P. Battle, "Historical Notes," archives, Chapel of the Cross. The "Graves place" was the spacious lot whereon the Carolina Inn and annexes now stand. The Chapel of Ease stood near the southwest corner of the Inn Annex quadrangle. It was still standing, although in a dilapidated condition, in 1792, according to the evidence of the Daniel map. Near the Chapel of Ease was a spring of considerable size, known as the Chapel Spring, from which flowed the "stream which winds its way through picturesque scenery, by the Meeting of the Waters to Morgan's Creek at Scott's Hole on the Mason plantation."

province in 1766, by Governor William Tryon. A man of marked eccentricities but genuine probity, Micklejohn exerted great influence throughout this entire region, although he was aggressively Royalist in sentiment. On November 23, 1776, after a discipline of seven months by the Halifax Congress of April, 1776, he took the oath of allegiance to the American cause. He lived for slightly more than a century (1717-1818).

The parent church, a large frame structure built a decade or more before the Revolution, was located in Hillsborough, where were held the courts of seven or eight counties. In this church building assembled the Revolutionary Congress on August 20, 1775, and in the summer of 1788 the State Convention, which resolutely declined to ratify the Federal Constitution. For many years after the Revolution, the Episcopal Church languished in North Carolina, since the Anglican Church, the state church of Great Britain, bore the brunt of animosities engendered by the Revolution. Nevertheless the pertinacious Micklejohn, according to tradition, continued to hold occasional services in New Hope Chapel on the Hill for many years after the Revolution.[5] In this way the eminence on which the University came to be located derived its name from this Chapel of Ease, being called the Hill of New Hope Chapel or more briefly Chapel Hill.[6]

This hill is an upheaval belonging to what geologists term the Laurentian system, being a portion of the coast line of a primeval

5. Parson Micklejohn, as he was universally called, was a man of tireless energy, constantly on the road to one of his chapels, keeping up his missionary ministrations until well along in the first decade of the last century. Although in his late seventies, he was mentioned for the post of first president of the University. General Thomas Person, one of the University's early ·benefactors, was a man of pronounced Regulating principles; and it was through the efforts of Parson Micklejohn that he was saved from condign punishment by Governor Tryon. For this service Person ever cherished toward Micklejohn the deepest gratitude, and gave him a home, known as "The Glebe," on his own plantation in Granville County, which bears to this day the name "Goshen."

6. In his "Historical Notes," archives, Chapel of the Cross, Battle remarks: "The word Hope in South Scotland means Haven; and most of the settlers in the neighborhood were Scotch-Irish." In the report of the commissioners to choose the site for the University, the eminence selected is termed "New Hope, Chappell Hill," November 5, 1792, and "Chappell Hill," November 6, 1792. *T. M.*, 1789-1797, p. 53.

arm of the ocean some sixteen miles wide. Durham, twelve miles distant, is situated on this ancient sea bottom. The bench mark on Memorial Hall shows an elevation above sea level of 503 feet. The late Professor Collier Cobb, for many years head of the Department of Geology, described the spacious depression east of Chapel Hill as the former bed of a "Triassic sea"; and local specimens from this primeval ocean bed, which once extended from New York to central Georgia, reveal "ripple marks of the waves, and of the prints of plants and animals found in its shallows." The promontory of granite, constituting the eastern end of the ridge, overlooks the site of the primeval sea stretching far away to the east. In prehistoric times the bed of this vast sea was elevated by some subterranean, presumably volcanic, upheaval, and so became dry land. It is upon this plateau, elevated some 250 feet above the gently rolling country on the east, that the University is situated.

William R. Davie, who had carefully inspected the University site and surrounding country, probably in August, 1793, drafted a vividly graphic and admirable description for the press, which bears the earmarks of his enthusiastic approbation.

We are authorised to assure the public that the cornerstone of the building of the University, undertaken by Mr. Patterson, will be laid on the 10th Oct. next; when the commissioners and a number of gentlemen will attend to assist at the ceremony. The sale of the lots in the village will take place on the same day. The town consists of one principal street, laid off in lots of two acres each, parallel with the North front of the buildings. There are also six lots of four acres each, located on the most elegant situations contiguous to the University.

The seat of the University is on the summit of a very high ridge. There is a very gentle declivity of 300 yards to the village, which is situated on a handsome plain considerably lower than the site of the public buildings, but so greatly elevated above the neighboring country, as to furnish an extensive and beautiful landscape, composed of the heights in the vicinity of Eno, Little and Flat rivers.

The ridge appears to commence about a half a mile directly east of the buildings, where it rises abruptly several hundred feet. This peak is called Point Prospect. The flat country spreads out below like the ocean, giving an immense hemisphere, in which the eye seems to be lost in the extent of space.

There is nothing more remarkable in this extraordinary place, than the abundance of springs of the purest and finest water, which burst from the side of the ridge, and which have been the subject of admiration both to hunters and travellers ever since the discovery and settlement of that part of the country. Several of the lots on the north side of the town have the advantage of including a spring.

The University is situated about twenty-five miles from the city of Raleigh and twelve from the town of Hillsborough, and is said to be in the best direction for the road. The great road from Chatham and the country in the neighborhood of that county, to Petersburg, passes at present directly through the village; and it is a fortunate and important circumstance both to the institution and the town, that the road from all the western country to the seat of government, will also pass through this place, being the nearest and best direction.

This town, being the only seat of learning immediately under the patronage of the public, possessing the advantages of a central situation, on some of the most public roads in the State, in a plentiful country, and excelled by few places in the world, either for beauty of situation or salubrity of air, promises, with all moral certainty, to be a place of growing and permanent importance.[7]

Within a mile or so, and south of the ridge runs the stream known as Morgan's Creek, famous for its two ancient mills, King's and Purefoy's. A hill on its western bank, above Purefoy's Mill, was pronounced by Professor Cobb to be the crater of an extinct volcano. About two miles southeast of Chapel Hill is the "Mason Farm," a rich plantation of some 800 acres bequeathed to the University in 1894 by Mrs. Mary Elizabeth Morgan Mason, granddaughter of Mark Morgan, one of the original donors to the University. One Laurel Hill, on the south side of Morgan's Creek, is located on this plantation; the other Laurel Hill is near King's Mill, which was built about 1800 by Christopher Barbee, the land on which it was located being owned in 1792 by John Daniel, one of the original donors to the University and surveyor for the Trustees.[8]

7. *North Carolina Journal*, Halifax, September 25, 1793. This letter was printed in *U. N. C. M.*, I (1852), 3. The erroneous date, October 10, is printed in the *North Carolina Journal*.

8. Consult John Daniel's map of 1792, reproduced in the present volume. King's Mill was successively known, from the names of the owners, as Barbee's, Cave's, King's, the Bennett and Oldham Mill, and finally the Henderson Oldham Mill, the latest owner being a worthy colored man. One of Christopher Barbee's granddaughters was married to Dr. Belfield W. Cave, which gave the mill its second name.

Purefoy's Mill, more than a mile above King's Mill on Morgan's Creek, was probably built later than Barbee's Mill; and in the first quarter of the last century Merritt's Mill, as it was then styled, became famous in Orange and in eastern counties for the excellent quality of its flour.

To the northwest of the ridge arises the elevation known as Iron Mountain wherefrom, at different periods, ore has been taken, although never with commercial success. Descending thence the valley of Bowlin's Creek, one enters a wild, romantic-looking defile termed "Glenburnie," a name still preserved in a well-known road. Here, before the Revolution, was erected the oldest mill known in this section, built by one of the first donors to the University, Benjamin Yeargin. On the right of the Hillsborough Road in the valley of the creek was the Valley Mill and a large pond much frequented by swimmers in summer and skaters in winter. Still further down the creek, where the valley widens, there arises on the north side a small eminence, once a volcano surmised by geologists to have been in active eruption in Triassic times. Credence is lent to this surmise by the vast numbers of rocks of granitic gneiss which thickly stud the surrounding country. The hill is known as Mount Bolus (an abbreviation of *Diabolus*), a name given this extinct volcano by the students in honor of President Caldwell because of his diabolic ingenuity in apprehending delinquents.

Through the spacious plantation of Benjamin Yeargin, later owned by Oregon Tenney, overrunning the steep slopes from the village to Bowlin's Creek, wound a main-traveled country road. In the valley to the west of this road stood an old farm house in the second decade of the last century where James K. Polk, William H. Battle, and other lusty youths who delighted equally in long walks and savoury fare, were served thrice daily by deft Afro-American practitioners of the culinary art. To the north of the main road to Durham were two cool and lovely springs often visited by habitual pedestrians: "Roaring Fountain," with its musical note of falling waters; and the "Mineral Springs," chalybeate with iron and sulphur tinctures, some twenty feet below the level of the "new road" to Durham, just where it turns sharply northward midway of Strowd's Hill. The beautiful dense woods east and southeast of the village came in time to bear the name of Battle Park for the nature-loving University president who labored so assiduously with his "little hatchet" to cut charming paths and reveal enchanting vistas through the massed foliage. These leafy bowers, picturesque havens, and flowery retreats he loved to endow with attractive, not seldom sentimental and romantic names: Trysting Poplar, Anemone Spring, Fairy Vale, Lion Rock, The Triangle, Over-Stream Seat, Vale of Ione, Glen Lee, Wood-Thrush Home, Dogwood Dingle, and Flirtation Knoll. It was often a pleasure to friends and visitors to accompany this Southern Thoreau, a sort of amateur, composite Burroughs and Muir, on long walks over the hills, down the valleys, and through the forests, listening delightedly the while to his naïve narratives, part history, part fancy, part legend, and reveling in visits to Dromgoole's Rock, Miss Fannie's Spring, the Meeting of the Waters, Lone Pine Spring, Otey's Retreat, the Judge's Spring, Love Rocks, and the Patriot's Grave.[9]

Viewed from various vantage points, Chapel Hill graciously invites the attention and interest of the approaching visitor. From the west one notes towering stark above the horizon tall chimneys and furling wisps of smoke lazily floating skyward; from the southeast the picturesque vision in granite of Gimghoul Castle with its rugged form and Gothic beauty; and from the east the "dreaming spires" of village churches and the sharply penciled outlines of the Italianate bell tower, whence fall pleasingly upon the ear the mellifluous chimes of some ancient dirge.

9. For charming accounts of attractive walks, scenes, and points of interest in and around Chapel Hill, see Battle, II, 764-75.

3

WILLIAM RICHARDSON DAVIE; PROVISION FOR FINANCIAL MAINTENANCE

THE TORCH of higher learning in North Carolina, lit by Waightstill Avery, carried by Dr. McCorkle, and unsuccessfully offered by William Sharpe to an unresponsive legislature in 1784, passed, as we have seen, into the hands of William Richardson Davie, whose youth and early manhood were spent in western North Carolina in association with many of the great figures of that region. At the age of thirty, Davie entered vigorously upon a public career, and, with magic touch, accomplished everything he undertook. He was a representative of the borough of Halifax in the House of Commons in 1786, 1787, and 1789; a delegate to the Constitutional Convention in 1787 at Philadelphia; and a member of the North Carolina Constitutional Conventions of 1788 and 1789. Davie was not an educator by profession; but he grasped the cardinal fact that the training of leaders in public life for solving the many and complex tasks in the new republic could be accomplished, in the long run, only through the establishment of first-class academies and a state university.

In the establishment of a university, with the attendant problems of location, lands, surveys, buildings, contractors, architects, ways and means had to be provided at the outset for construction, maintenance, and continuing support. Certain parts of the charter deal with these problems; and a sort of "golden book of remembrance" was proposed for the record of benefactors. Article 10 of the charter, soliciting contributions, provides

That the public hall, the library, and four of the colleges [college buildings] shall be called severally by the names of one or another of the six persons who shall within four years contribute the largest sums towards the funds of the University, the highest subscriber or donor having choice in the order of their respective donations. And a book shall be kept in the library of this University, in which shall

be fairly entered the names and places of residence of every benefactor to the seminary, in order that posterity may be informed to
whom they are indebted for the measure of learning and good morals
in the state.[1]

Like so many alluring promises of glittering rewards for worthy
service, these were kept for a time, and then forgotten. The
handsome gifts of Benjamin Smith, Thomas Person, and Charles
Gerrard were, sooner or later, recognized in buildings bearing
their names. Belated justice, not blind but clear-eyed, might
fittingly be rendered in the naming, according to legislative promise, of buildings for the three most generous donors to the subscription fund taken up in 1793: Alfred Moore, great jurist and
associate justice of the United States Supreme Court; Walter
Alves, Secretary and Treasurer of the Board of Trustees; and
William Cain, leading citizen of Hillsborough and State senator
from the County of Orange.[2]

Davie entertained spacious ideas for the projected university
in anticipating the early need for six essential buildings. Having
made no advance campaign to obtain contributions and with no
financial provision for implementing the charter, Davie at once
took steps to secure the passage of the requisite enabling legislation. This legislation, entitled "An Act for Raising a Fund for
Erecting the Buildings and for the Support of the University
of North Carolina," provided that the total of all monies and
arrearages due the State government up to January 1, 1783
(monies or certificates due for confiscated property which had
been purchased being excepted) "shall be and is hereby declared
to be fully and absolutely made, for the purpose of erecting the
necessary buildings, employing professors and tutors, and carrying into effect the act before cited. . ." For the carrying out of
this provision, attorneys for the University, one for each of the
judicial districts, were later appointed by the Board of Trustees;
and by indefatigable efforts on the part of various people the
sum of $7,362 was eventually obtained, from which only the

1. N. C. S. R., XXV, 24.
2. Person Hall, Gerrard Hall, and Smith Hall were all named long
after the donations which made them possible. See *infra*. With the erection of the new dining hall in 1939, belated honor was done to William
Lenoir, first president of the Board of Trustees.

interest could be used. The "saving clause" of the act, article 2 of Chapter 21, proved in the end to be highly significant and of appreciable financial benefit to the University. The clause provides

That all property that has heretofore or shall hereafter escheat to the State, shall be and hereby is vested in the said Trustees, for the use and benefit of the said University.[3]

The method of selection of a site for the University was safeguarded in the charter by the provisions: that the meeting of the Board of Trustees, at which the site should be determined, must be advertised in the *State Gazette* for at least six months in advance of the meeting; and that special notice of such meeting must be given to each Trustee. The Board of Trustees was composed of representative citizens, irrespective of social, political and religious affiliations; and from the very outset the affairs of the University were matters of general concern. Indicative of the strong interest in the University is the early meeting of the Board of Trustees in Fayetteville, December 18, 1789, only one week after the adoption of the charter. At this meeting William R. Davie and James Hogg were requested to prepare blanks for subscriptions. Prior to the second meeting of the Board (the first provided under the charter), at Fayetteville, November 5, 1790, the campaign for subscriptions had been actively prosecuted. Hogg interviewed many citizens of Orange County; and Davie, according to his biographer, was "vigilant and anxious in its prosperity." McCorkle rendered yeoman service from the pulpit and on trips he made for the purpose of raising funds for the University's support.

The Trustees were especially fortunate in having as president, in 1790, the recently elected governor, Alexander Martin, graduate of the College of New Jersey, class of 1756, one of the most popular men who ever lived in North Carolina. As a young man, after teaching school for a time in Virginia, he came to Rowan County in 1760, residing in Salisbury until his removal in 1772 to the part of Rowan County which is now Guilford. Martin was a colonel in the Revolution, member of the Society of the

3. *N. C. S. R.*, XXV, 24-25.

Cincinnati, many times member and Speaker of the House of Commons, United States Senator, and six times Governor of North Carolina, five times by election and once by succession. Over a period of years he proved himself to be a vigorous champion of popular and higher education. In his message to the legislature, April 20, 1784, Governor Martin said: "Let me call your attention to the education of our youth; may seminaries of learning be revived and encouraged, where the understanding may be enlightened, the heart mended and genius cherished; where the state may draw forth men of abilities to direct her councils and support her government." To the legislature which postponed to a subsequent session the bill, engineered by McCorkle and presented by Sharpe, for the establishment of a state university, Martin said in his message, October 26, 1784: "Your schools of learning . . . are great objects of Legislative attention which cannot be too often repeated and held up to your views, that the mists of Ignorance be dissipated and good morals cultivated. . . ." He threw the full weight of his influence in behalf of the State's financial support of the recently chartered University, addressing the legislature on November 2, 1790, in the following unequivocal language:

This institution, already stamped with importance, having the great cause of humanity for its object, might do honor to this and the neighboring States, had it an adequate support, where our youth might be instructed in true religion, sound policy and science, and men of ability drawn forth to fill the different departments of government with reputation, or be formed for useful and ornamental members of society in private or professional life.[4]

Pursuant to these beliefs and sentiments, he forthwith recommended a loan to the University for erecting buildings to "give it a more essential than a paper being."

During the prolonged sessions of the Board of Trustees, December 19, 1791 to January 2, 1792, report was made describing "how extremely ill the Resources of the Trustees are proportioned to their necessities." In view of the inconsiderable sum available for immediate use, a committee whose names are not recorded was appointed to memorialize the General Assembly. This memo-

4. *North Carolina Chronicle* or *Fayetteville Gazette*, November 15, 1790.

DOGWOOD IN BLOOM
One of many lovely scenes encountered in walks through the woods in and around Chapel Hill.

POINT PROSPECT

View eastward from Gimghoul Castle, showing the former bed of an ancient Triassic sea. William Richardson Davie said of this view: "The flat country spreads out below like the ocean, giving an immense hemisphere, in which the eye seems to be lost in the extent of space."

rial, adopted December 23, after adverting to the circumstances under which the endowment, provided by the Assembly of 1789, was not immediately available and the subscriptions were not adequate for erecting buildings and conducting a university, asserts that the President and Trustees

will, with the confidence, which becomes them as men, and as citizens zealous for the good of the Republic, and for the honor and dignity of the State, at once step forward and ask of the general assembly, the guardians and representatives of their common country, that they will be pleased to grant them a loan of Five Thousand Pounds or such sum and for such length of time as to them shall seem proper and adequate to the purpose of carrying into effect the intentions of the legislature in establishing the said Institution.[5]

The presentation of this memorial to the General Assembly was entrusted to Davie, who represented the borough of Halifax; and he gave the full force of his logic and eloquence to the University's cause. He rose to noble heights in reminding his attentive hearers of the honor and dignity of the State; stressed the low ebb, despite the growing success of the academy movement, to which useful learning had then fallen in North Carolina; accentuated the growing need in a rising democracy, confronted with many new and complex problems, for educated and informed leaders; and made a moving appeal for the sustention, through such loan, of the interest, the reputation, and the respectability of the State.

The request for a loan, one indeed of considerable size, to implement the bill for the University's establishment doubtless precipitated a lively debate; for many of the members, according to the University's historian, believed that "the people's money should not be expended for any purpose other than the prevention and punishment of crime, settling disputes among citizens, and other similar governmental functions."[6] Indeed, the vote may be regarded as close: 57 to 53 in the House, 28 to 21 in the Senate. It is creditable to North Carolina that the first appropriation to the University, originally made as a loan, was ultimately transformed into a gift.

5. *T. M.*, 1789-1797, pp. 31-33. The sum of £5,000 was then estimated at the rate of one to two for American currency, namely, $10,000.
6. Battle, I, 17.

PART II
BUILDING A STATE UNIVERSITY

4

THE PREPARATORY DEPARTMENT: THE GRAMMAR SCHOOL

HE FORMAL OPENING of the University of North Carolina was little more than a visit of inspection on the part of the chief executive of the State and interested Trustees, and an official announcement that the doors of the institution were open to receive ambitious youths eager to acquire a college education. The press of the State had carried advance announcement of the occasion, and interest was widespread.[1] Richard Dobbs Spaight, the first native of North Carolina to become its governor, had finished his education at the University of Glasgow; and was wholeheartedly concerned in laying broad and deep the University's foundations. Follows the account of the occasion, which was thirty-nine days in reaching the public:

HALIFAX, FEBRUARY 23.

Pursuant to a request of the Board of Trustees of the University of North Carolina, his Excellency Richard Dobbs Spaight, Esq. Governor of the State, and President of the Board, accompanied by several Members of the Corporation, and many other gentlemen, Members of the General Assembly, made a visit on the 15th of January last, to the seat of the University of this state, in order to be present at the beginning of the exercises in that institution: —The unfavorable state of the weather disappointed many of our fellow-citizens who wished to be present on that much desired occasion: —The Governor, however, with the Trustees who accompanied him, viewed the buildings, and made report to the Board, by which they are enabled to inform the public that the buildings prepared for the reception and accommodation of Students, are in part finished:—That the exercises of the institution have begun, and that youth disposed to enter at the University may come forward with an assurance of being received.

Students are to pay fifteen pounds per annum, North-Carolina currency, for their board:—Five dollars per annum for room rent, to be paid half yearly in advance:—They are to be furnished with tables and bed-steads, but they are to provide their own beds, &c.

1. For example, *North Carolina Journal*, November 24, and December 15, 1794.

37

They are also to provide wood and candles for their chambers, and pay for their washing.[2]

As the weather was inclement, the brief ceremonies were held indoors, in the North Wing (Old East). Aside from this building, which had just been completed, and the geographical setting, there was little to be seen from the North Wing on this drear morning of drizzling rain: the president's house, as yet unpainted, more than a hundred yards to the southwest; a pile of lumber for the building of a steward's house, a short distance to the east; and the staked-off area for the foundation of a chapel, some seventy-five yards due west.

The Faculty consisted of one man, Dr. David Ker, born in Ireland, February, 1758, who had emigrated to America in 1791, a man of high character, a learned classical scholar, educated at Trinity College, Dublin, Presbyterian minister at Fayetteville where he also conducted the high school, a violent republican who was destined to serve as presiding professor for only a year and a half.[3] As early as December 12, 1793, a committee to prepare an ordinance providing for the curriculum and the opening of the University had been appointed; a report was made on December 21, 1793; and the ordinance was adopted on January 10, 1794.[4] Owing perhaps to the uncertainty as to whether the buildings would be ready by January 15, 1795, for the reception of students, this ordinance was not released to the press for almost eleven months.[5] The slow rate at which news was disseminated gave little or no time, after the news of the opening was received, for parents to make up their minds and also their arrange-

2. *Ibid.*, February 23, 1795. President Swain, manuscript notes, Southern Historical Collection, records: "East Building, Stewards Hall & President's House completed prior to February 12, 1795."

3. At a meeting of the Board of Trustees, December 21, 1793, the Rev. Samuel Eusebius McCorkle, Dr. David Ker, Rev. George Micklejohn, then seventy-six years of age, Rev. Robert Archibald, John Brown, Andrew Martin and Rev. James Tate were put in nomination for the post of "Professor of Humanity." At the meeting of the board, January 10, 1794, with only eight Trustees present, Ker was elected. *T. M.*, 1789-1797, pp. 96, 98.

4. *Ibid.*, pp. 91, 94-96, 98-101. The committee who prepared this ordinance consisted of John Haywood, William R. Davie, John Louis Taylor, James Hogg, Adlai Osborne, and William Polk.

5. *North Carolina Journal*, December 1, 1794.

ments for sending their sons to college. Moreover, the restricted transportation facilities and the unbelievably wretched roads further delayed prospective students in reaching Chapel Hill. Under all the retarding circumstances, it is by no means surprising, however disappointing it may have been to Governor Spaight and his *entourage*, that not a single student appeared at Chapel Hill on January 15, 1795.

Like Napoleon, "grand, gloomy, and peculiar," Dr. Ker waited for exactly four weeks for the arrival of the first student. From that portion of New Hanover, which in 1875 became Pender County, came Hinton James whom Dr. Ker warmly welcomed. The ambitious Freshman of eighteen years, historic in primacy, trudged manfully more than 150 miles to reach the beckoning bourne of the State University on February 12, 1795. It is amusing to recall that this lonely boy who, for two mortal weeks in the worst weather of the year, as the University's historian says, held the unenviable distinction of being the entire student body and first honor man of his class, afterwards wrote, perhaps in satiric vein, prize essays on "The Pleasures of College Life" and "The Effects of Climate on the Minds and Bodies of Men." Of the seven members of the first graduating class (1798), he was the only one who had not received his preparatory training under Dr. McCorkle.[6]

Toward the end of February students began to arrive, in driblets, and by the end of the first term, July 15, forty-one boys were absorbed in their studies. It is doubtful if the makeshift curriculum, already mentioned, which was devised for advertising the opening of the University, was ever put into effect. As Dr. McCorkle was the most distinguished scholar among the Trustees, he was naturally looked to for the preparation of a suitably co-ordinated curriculum; and the plan of education which he submitted on January 13, 1795, was approved by the Trustees on February 6, 1795.[7] McCorkle's plan was incomparably

6. The six who prepared for the University under Dr. McCorkle were: Samuel Hinton, William Houston, Robert Locke, Alexander Osborne, Edwin Jay Osborne, and Adam Springs.

7. *T. M.*, 1789-1797, pp. 105, 122-27. The committee to prepare a plan of education, consisting of Messrs. McCorkle, Stone, Moore, Ashe, Hay, Williams, and Williamson, the last two named being subsequently (Jan-

superior to the original advertised curriculum, which was not greatly above the grammar school level.

During the course of the first academic year, a disquieting discovery compelled the preparation of a new curriculum. Although North Carolina led all the states in the chartering of academies down to 1800, not all of the two score or more established before 1795 were in operation; and some of those chartered had been open for only a very short time.[8] As the result of the disturbed conditions during the twelve years following the Revolution, only a comparatively small proportion of the educated youths of North Carolina had received adequate preparation for entering a college or, euphemistically styled, university. By the end of the second term at Chapel Hill, the number of students had increased from forty-one at the end of the first term to upwards of one hundred. At least one half of these were unprepared to enter the University classes. Furthermore there was a noticeable dearth of accommodations in room and board for students. Accordingly the Trustees were faced with the necessity of establishing a Preparatory Department of the University, to build a house for this "Grammar School" as it was called, and to provide limited accommodations in this building for the "preps." Owing to the scarcity of competent teachers, it was necessary to advertise, requesting professional teachers to apply.

---

uary 21, 1795) added, was appointed on December 4, 1792. *Ibid.*, pp. 55, 109. In a preliminary report, rendered on December 5, 1792, Dr. McCorkle recommended, among other subjects, the study of botany, the theory and practice of agriculture, the principles of architecture, and laboratory methods in natural philosophy. *Ibid.*, pp. 57-58.

8. Archibald D. Murphey was in error in the statement: "Before this University came into operation, in 1795, there were not more than three schools in the State, in which the rudiments of a classical education could be acquired." Oration at the University of North Carolina, June 27, 1827, Murphey, II, 355. In addition to Dr. David Caldwell's "log college," which is the only school mentioned by Murphey, there existed: New Bern Academy, Edenton Academy, Warrenton Academy, established by Davie, Williamsborough Academy, Pittsborough Academy, Zion-Parnassus Academy near Salisbury, established by McCorkle, Dr. James Hall's Academy of the Sciences, and a number of others of lesser distinction.

At the meeting of the Trustees, July 14, 1795, it was

Resolved, that the building commissioners be directed to contract with workmen for building and furnishing as quick as possible, on such spot as shall appear to them most eligible, a house for a grammar school of such dimensions as will best answer for that purpose containing three or more lodging rooms, and that they be authorized to draw on the treasury for a sum of money sufficient thereof.[9]

At the same meeting, it was resolved that "the professor and tutor [the Rev. David Ker and Charles Wilson Harris] be and they are authorized to employ a proper person as a grammar master for any time not exceeding one year on the best possible terms."[10]

A clear picture of the situation in midsummer, 1795, is presented by Charles W. Harris in a letter to his uncle, written from the "University":

The number of students in the commencement of orders [presumably new students registered for the second term] will amount to 54. Such numbers crowding in the trustees thought proper to make some further provision for their accommodation and instruction. They determined to proceed as soon as possible to the large building [Main, later called South, Building]—120 feet long—56 broad, 3 stories high. They are to receive proposals at the next general assembly. But as such a work could not be in any degree of readiness in less than two years, the building commissioners are ordered to build a two story wooden house with 6 large rooms and a school room, with a purpose to accommodate the younger boys and is to be termed the Grammar School. When this becomes no more necessary for its present purposes it is intended to be converted into a dwelling house for some future professor who may have a family. . . .[11]

Confronted with the necessity of providing a greatly enlarged plan of study, to include curricula and regulations for both a

9. *T. M.*, 1789-1797, p. 135. In a letter to John Haywood, written from Richard Bennehan's home in Orange County, July 22, 1795, Davie says: "They [the students] will soon suffer very much for want of rooms; and an expedient was adopted to give temporary relief from this mischief; by building a house for a grammar school with three or four lodging rooms." J. G. deR. Hamilton, "William Richardson Davie: a Memoir," *J. S. H. S.*, No. 7 (1907), p. 30.

10. *T. M.*, 1789-1797, p. 138.

11. Wagstaff, *op. cit.*, pp. 19-20. July 21, 1795.

Preparatory Department and the University proper, Dr. Ker, it appears, called upon General Davie to prepare such a plan of education. It was presented to the Board of Trustees by Davie on December 1, 1795; and the plan, together with a letter from Ker to Davie and a report by the former, were referred to a committee of five: John Williams, James Hogg, John Haywood, W. R. Davie, and Adlai Osborne. The plan as a whole was adopted on December 3, 1795, and was ordered to be put in force after the next vacation.[12] Tuition in the Preparatory Department was eight dollars a year. The two tutors were to receive one hundred dollars a year each and to get equal shares of the tuition money. Board at the University was set at twenty pounds per annum.

The building for the Grammar School, ordered by the Trustees on July 14, 1795, was not erected until seven years later. It was necessary to rent a building for the time being, owing both to the large number of boys packed into the North Wing, the only dormitory, and to the need for teaching the unprepared students in a separate institution. On April 12, 1796, there were eighty-six students at Chapel Hill, about half of whom belonged in a grammar school; and by June 1, 1797, there were sixty-two or sixty-three boys in the Grammar School alone. The Grammar School, not built until 1801-1802, stood in the Grand Avenue, between Franklin and Rosemary streets, and somewhat west of the subsequent site of the Union Church, known as the village chapel. This would place it somewhere between the present Presbyterian Church and the southeast corner of the intersection of Henderson and Rosemary streets. At the time of its erection it was located in a lonely spot surrounded by woods; and in the vicinity were "two never-failing springs of purest water," one of which was famous as the Vauxhall (corrupted into "Foxhall") Spring.[13] In some delightful reminiscences of 1804, too lengthy

12. *T. M.*, 1789-1797, pp. 146, 154-60. This plan was published in the *State Gazette of North Carolina* (Edenton), March 10, 1796, and doubtless in other state newspapers.

13. Battle, I, 71, 290. On August 19, 1801, Walter Alves and Richard Bennehan on behalf of the Trustees signed a contract with John M. Goodloe for building a house, 30 x 30 x 10 feet, to be known as the Grammar School, at a cost of £159 12s. 1d. *U.N.C.I. 1791-1867*.

for quotation here, by an "old grad," we are told that the Faculty consisted solely of President Caldwell, Professor Bingham, and Tutor Henderson, called by the students "Old Joe," "Old Slick," and "Little Dick," respectively. The Preparatory School was taught by Matthew Troy and Chesley Daniel.[14]

During the period of something more than the two decades of its operation, the Preparatory Department of the University was one of the most efficient and well-conducted classical schools in North Carolina. It was well patronized, and some of the ablest and most representative North Carolinians were prepared here for the University. The discipline was strict and rigorous, and corporal punishment was freely practiced. Early in the school's existence, the teachers were given authority over all the students, and admitted to membership in the University Faculty, first without, and a little later with, the right to vote. At the outset, the Preparatory Department was an integral part of the University, and its graduates were allowed without examination to enter the Freshman class. After a few years the two institutions became almost entirely separate. With the great increase in the number of academies in the State, the attendance in the Grammar School of the University steadily declined. It eventually became evident that the need for such a department no longer existed; and it was discontinued, on the resignation as headmaster of the Rev. Abner W. Clopton, in 1819.[15]

For some years, the Grammar School building remained unoccupied, and was neglected by the University authorities. Eventually a professional hunter, Peyton Clements, took possession of the house with the tacit consent of the Trustees; and continued to occupy it with his family for upwards of ten years.[16] On June

14. Hooper, p. 10. On June 2, 1813, the Trustees ordered that $98.40 be paid for repairs in and on the Preparatory House. *T.M.*, 1811-1822, p. 55.

15. Battle, I, 185, 283. Clopton entered the Junior class at Chapel Hill in 1808, and was appointed to a tutorship in 1809. The following year he left Chapel Hill; but in 1812 he returned to become headmaster of the University's Preparatory Department. Consult Jeremiah B. Jeter, *A Memoir of Abner W. Clopton, A. M.* (Richmond, Va., 1837), and R. Ryland, "A. W. Clopton," *Biblical Recorder*, January 7, 1946.

16. K. P. Battle, *Memories of an Old-Time Tar Heel* (Chapel Hill: The University of North Carolina Press, 1945), p. 86.

20, 1832, on motion of Col. William Polk, Dr. James Webb was "authorized & requested to make sale of the Preparatory School House together with an Acre of Ground attached upon a credit of one, two and three years, the proceeds of which are hereby appropriated towards the completion of the New Chapel."[17] Only a small sum was realized by the sale.[18] *Finis* is thereby written to the story of the Preparatory Department, often termed the University Grammar School.

17. Battle, I, 334.

18. Apparently no official records of the Preparatory Department have been preserved. The activities of the school are revealed chiefly in the records of the Trustees and Faculty, contemporary newspapers, correspondence and reminiscences.

5

STEWARD'S HALL

URING the protracted series of meetings at Fayetteville, December 9, 1793 to January 10, 1794, inclusive, the Trustees provided, as we have seen, for the erection of the north wing of the projected main university building. Fully cognizant of the dearth of boardinghouses in the little settlement of New Hope Chapel Hill and of the immediate need for a dining hall spacious enough to accommodate the full quota of students to occupy the North Wing, the Trustees on December 21, 1793 resolved:

A Steward's house containing a large dining room, kitchen, and such other rooms as may be deemed necessary shall be built and finished by the said 15th day of January [the date set at this meeting for the opening of the University]; the size and manner of the house shall be left to the commissioners heretofore appointed to carry on the buildings of the University.[1]

The contractor superintending the building of the North Wing, the steward's house, the Chapel, and the president's house was Samuel Hopkins of Albemarle County, Virginia. The builder was Martin Hall. The steward's house, which was soon styled Steward's Hall, was a wooden structure, at first painted white and later embellished with green blinds. The ground on which Steward's Hall stood was a lovely level lawn, covered with a carpet of natural verdure. It was in the center of present Cameron Avenue north of Carr Building, and fronted west.[2] As the cul-

1. *T. M.*, 1789-1797, p. 94. For a time, according to tradition, a boardinghouse on the north side of Franklin Street, almost opposite the site of the old Chapel of the Cross, was conducted by the University authorities until Steward's Hall was ready for use.

2. It is not possible to estimate the exact cost of each of the early University buildings. The amounts paid Patterson and Hopkins were: in 1793 and 1794, $6,896; in 1795, $4,164; in 1796-1799, $1,120. The total, $12,180, covered the cost of Old East, Person Hall, Steward's Hall, and the president's house. The cost of Person Hall was $2,826. The cost of the president's house is not known, but was probably about $2,000. The cost of Steward's Hall was presumably $700. The proposals of James Patterson and John Conroy were respectively £350 and $765. See original con-

inary facilities were soon found to be inadequate, a separate kitchen, of ample proportions, was built, for which on July 14, 1795, was paid to Hopkins the sum of £40 16s. 8d. On the same date Robert Creight was allowed the sum of £7 10s. 0d. "for the building of a cross wall and underpinning the Steward's kitchen."[3]

At the opening of the University, the price of board per year was fixed by the Trustees at $30 per student; and the steward was required to give bond with satisfactory security for the performance of his stipulated duties. The fare first supplied must have been far below the standard of living and eating to which young Southern aristocrats had been accustomed; but the steadily rising scale of prices over a period of almost half a century, as revealed by the records, probably indicates a gradual improvement in both the quantity and quality of the food furnished the students. The rate was $3 per month the first year (1795-1796) and $4 per month the next four years, when (1800) the rate rose to $57 per year of ten months. The ascending scale is thus recorded: beginning in 1805, $60; 1814, in a period of inflated war prices, $66.50; 1818, $95; and 1839, $76, when the record ceases. In 1843, Judge Williamson of Maine reports: "The annual expense of a student of the University will not exceed $200, though the tuition be $50, and the board of 40 weeks $100 of the amount. In fact, board may be had at the steward's hall at $8 by the month, equal to that 'furnished at the tables of the

---

tracts: Old East, to be finished by November 1, 1794, undertakers, James Patterson, George Lucas, and Patrick St. Lawrence; president's house, preliminary undertakers, Samuel Hopkins, William Cain, Daniel Ray, Henry Thompson, Will Lytle; final undertaker, Samuel Hopkins. *U.N.C.I. 1791-1867.* The contract with James Patterson for Old East was for $5,000; but he did not complete his contract. The Trustees expended $2,000 for brick for the first buildings.

3. *T. M.,* 1789-1797, p. 137. In the *North Carolina Journal*, September 7, 1795, James Patterson, "undertaker" for the North Wing (Old East), advertised for the apprehension of Robert Creight, bricklayer, and his wife, who had stolen considerable property, including two "waggon horses," and run away from the University. They were last seen at the Haw-Fields. Creight is described as an "old offender, much given to fighting and loitering when intoxicated." The advertisement carries the date of August 10, 1795. James Patterson uniformly used the spelling "Paterson."

most respectable boarding-houses in any of the neighboring villages.' "[4]

At a meeting of the Trustees in Raleigh, November 9, 1795, it was decided to appoint a steward for five years, to define specifically the "kind of diet to be furnished" and the steward's duties, and to make it a "part of the duty of the Faculty of the University to superintend the conduct of the Steward." In the event that charges grave enough to require a hearing should be preferred by the Faculty, such hearing should be publicly held and the Trustees should sit as a court upon the case. Should the conduct of the steward, however, continue so improper as to endanger the good of the institution, the Faculty was empowered to dismiss him, after three months' notice. The original committee, consisting of Messrs. Lenoir, Stone, Lane, Porter, and Haywood, at the Trustees' meeting, January 13, 1795, decided on a suitable diet with the express order that no "drink other than water be furnished"—a highly wise and commendable resolution in that day of free potations and the habitual imbibing of intoxicants.[5] At a subsequent meeting, January 21, 1795, the following additional duties were assigned to the steward: "to cause that the whole of the floors, passages and stair cases be washed at least once in every two weeks, that the student rooms be swept and their beds made once a day, and that a sufficient quantity of water be brought from the spring at least four times in the day, and placed in such situation as the professors shall think proper."[6]

John Taylor, a resident of Raleigh, was engaged as steward for one year by the Trustees on January 21, 1795. Taylor, commonly called Buck, a veteran of the Revolution, was a man of strong character and resolute will, of pronounced eccentricity and grim disposition. Under the contract, he was to be recompensed at the rate of $30 per person per annum; and was to give bond in the sum of $400, his securities being Walter Alves and William Lyttle, both of Orange County.[7] He was reappointed

4. Williamson, *op. cit.;* Battle, I, 274.
5. *T. M.,* 1789-1797, pp. 105-6.
6. *Ibid.,* pp. 108-9. The spring referred to is located near the northwest corner of the present Arboretum.
7. *Ibid.,* pp. 108-9; Battle, I, 52.

for the year 1796, the securities for his bond, $4,000, ten times the amount of the bond for the preceding year, being Messrs. Lyttle, Hunt, Mebane, and Patterson.[8] The steward was allowed the "use of eight or ten acres of the old field adjoining the Steward's House provided he shall enclose the same at his own expense." Moreover he was given permission to "cut up and use for fuel, such timber on the lands of the University as may be blown down by winds or shall be found lying on the ground; but shall in no case fell a tree, but with the express permission of the Trustees."[9]

The fare was editorially commended in the *North Carolina Journal* as having "exceeded the expectations both of students and of strangers," but this commendation does not accord with the reports of Davie's sons, Hyder Ali and Allen, who were accustomed at home to the best fare in the land.[10] The Davie boys were by no means unique in registering complaints of the fare. The letters of the Pettigrew boys, John and Ebenezer (1795-1797), for example, contain complaints against the steward for exorbitant prices charged for beds and for food not measuring up to exalted home standards.[11]

Although the redoubtable Buck Taylor was not easily stampeded by such complaints, and was prepared to put down any mass revolt with a strong hand, he gave up the stewardship after serving only three years of his five-year contract. He was succeeded, December 9, 1797, by another veteran of the Revolution, Major Pleasant Henderson.[12]

The new steward served one year longer than did Taylor;

8. *Ibid.*, pp. 139-41, 143. Meetings of November 9 and 12, 1795.

9. *Ibid.*, pp. 119, 140. Meetings of January 27 and November 9, 1795. At the latter meeting Mr. Haywood and Mr. Alves were "appointed and authorized to contract for the building a House containing a stable and granary under the same roof, for the use of the Steward." For the floor plans of Steward's Hall and two outhouses, consult old map (prior to 1812). *U.N.C.I. 1791-1867.* This map is reproduced in the present volume.

10. Hamilton, *op. cit.*, p. 30.

11. The Pettigrew Papers, Southern Historical Collection, Chapel Hill.

12. *State Gazette of North Carolina* (Edenton), January 12, 1798. Consult *U.N.C.I. 1791-1867.* This book contains the five-year contract and bond between the Trustees and John Taylor, pp. 167-70; and the bond given by Pleasant Henderson to the Trustees, pp. 171-74.

THE Lots in the village laid off at the seat of the University, in Orange County, will be sold, on the premises at public vendue, on Saturday the 12th of October next :—Confiderable time will be allowed for payment, the purchafers giving bond with approved fecurity.

July 22, 1793.

W. R. DAVIE,
A. MOORE,
A. MEBANE,
T. BLOUNT.

} Com'rs.

NOTICE IN THE EDENTON *STATE GAZETTE OF NORTH CAROLINA*, SEPTEMBER 21, 1793, ANNOUNCING THE SALE OF LOTS FOR THE PROJECTED VILLAGE OF CHAPEL HILL

WILLIAM RICHARDSON DAVIE

He was chiefly responsible for founding, locating, and providing for the future development of the University of North Carolina. From the oil painting by the famous artist, John Vanderlyn, owned by Dr. Charles Lee Smith.

but his incumbency falling during a period of disgraceful, indeed alarming student insubordination, he was more roughly treated than his predecessor. The first complaint against the fare supplied by Major Henderson was made by the students to the Trustees' Committee of Visitation. The committee made no inquiry as to the real facts but reported that the steward's "invariable service of mutton and of bacon too fat to be eaten had nearly starved the boys." The alleged "information" supplied by the committee the irate Major denounced as diabolically false, the record showing that there were served "only 11 muttons, about 500 pounds, 12 or 13 dinners, about seven pounds apiece for the whole session." He assigned the dearth of beef, shoats, and chickens as the cause for serving the boarders even so negligible an amount of mutton as he mentions. While admitting that the bacon was fat, he deplored the intimation that the middlings should have been discarded, and

> Insisted on the golden mean
> Of fat along with lean.[13]

During the first five years of the last century, the riots and disorders of the students steadily increased in violence, finally leading to the state-wide scandal known as the "great secession." While these disorders were at their height, the residence of Major Henderson was stoned, one of his outhouses overturned, and his gate taken from its hinges and placed upon the pulpit of the chapel. Perhaps in consequence of these acts of violence, Major Henderson did not apply for the stewardship in 1802.

On December 3, 1802, he was unanimously elected a member of the Board of Trustees, to succeed John Gray Blount; but he immediately declined, and William Gaston was elected to the vacancy.

Major Samuel Love of Virginia, then living near Chapel Hill, was appointed steward for 1802 by the Trustees on December 12, 1801.[14] He served with reasonable success for four

13. *U.N.C.I. 1791-1867.*

14. *T. M.,* 1798-1801, p. 11. The minutes for December 12, 1801, state that "Mr. Love has entered into bond with security, and has covenanted to furnish each student and other persons living at commons with diet agreeably to a bill of fare agreed on, at the rate of fifty-seven dollars, for the two sessions in the year, or thirty-three dollars, for the first ses-

years; but even the genial John Haywood, State Treasurer, wrote in mild protest to President Caldwell in 1803: *"In re* matter of having Mr. and Mrs. Love furnish butter at supper, we think with you that a supper of Tea and Bread, or Coffee and Bread, without either butter or meat, has few charms, and can be but illy [*sic*] fitted to gratify palates accustomed to better fare, but the contract has been made and published and cannot be changed."

Because of shoddy materials and inferior workmanship in the construction of the College (Old East) and Steward's Hall, the Board of Trustees, meeting at Chapel Hill, July 12, 1804, found it necessary to order extensive repairs: for the former, roof repaired and painted, new outside doors and window sashes, and four ladders made and installed; for the latter, new dining-room door, roof painted, small rooms next the dining room ceiled with completely seasoned plank, two kitchen chimneys replaced, new locks, new set of benches for the dining hall, and the passage to the Back House shingled and guttered, together with new steps. To supply the steward's expressed need for a pasture, the Board recommended that he be allowed to procure 4,000 rails from the college lands, at a suitable distance from the buildings and ornamental grounds, for fencing a pasture; and that the front yard of Steward's Hall be enclosed with a plank fence, with Lombardy poplar trees planted along the fence at regular intervals. The Board further recommended that "the Treasurer take an obligation in writing to act as custodian of the [Steward's] House, garden & other property under his charge, to keep them in good order."[15]

At the outset of his second term of service as steward, 1805-1810, which lasted for more than five years, Buck Taylor, Love's successor, was heartily praised by a resolution of the Trustees, which constituted a vindication of the charges brought against him by the students during his first term.[16] He was in-

---

sion and twenty-four dollars for the second session; and the trustees to have the liberty, in case they judge it best, to deduct one dollar out of the fifty-seven, for the purpose of employing a baker."

15. *T. M.*, 1801-1810, pp. 69-70. Perhaps the buildings were rushed too rapidly to completion.

16. *Ibid.*, p. 145. At this meeting of the Trustees, held July 11,

structed to have the tables and benches properly repaired, and to "employ some fit person to trim the trees in the Grove and adjoining to the public buildings." This is the first indication, in the records, of the need for a superintendent of buildings and grounds. Five or six years later the office of "Superintendent of Buildings and Grounds" was established with Taylor as the first incumbent. In 1808, Taylor was the target of a fierce attack launched by thirty-eight students, among whom were a number afterwards distinguished. This petition to the Faculty, which the latter regarded as offensive and rebellious, contained such bold language that the students were rebuked by the Faculty and instructed to modify the petition. Some amendment of conditions at Steward's Hall resulted, but before a great while, Taylor, possibly as the consequence of this vigorous protest, was superseded.

William Barbee, son of Christopher Barbee, one of the original donors, next held the position of steward for ten years until 1819, when Steward's Hall was abandoned as Commons conducted by the University. With Barbee as with his predecessors, the stewardship was not all "beer and skittles." In 1814 prices, including the cost of board at Steward's Hall, took a sharp rise as the result of the war then in progress. In consequence, the Trustees authorized the Committee on Appointments to abolish Commons and to rent out the building, if they saw fit. After investigation, the committee decided not to abolish Commons, but to attempt a betterment of conditions. Improvements were added to the building, for which Bennett Partin, carpenter, was paid the sum of $456. In November, 1815, the Faculty reported irregularities originating at Steward's Hall; and declared it essential to the growing prosperity of the University that further improvements be made in respect to the management. According to President Swain, the use of Steward's Hall as University Commons was discontinued by the Trustees in December, 1816.

1805, it was resolved that the "thanks of this Board be and they are hereby given to John Taylor Esquire for the faithful and proper manner in which he has fulfilled the duties attached to the office of Steward of the University, and the Trustees entertain no doubt of a continuance of his exertions to fulfill the duties of that office and to promote the welfare of the institution."

In 1819 Steward's Hall was rented to a Mrs. Burton, whose husband had died the year before; and she occupied the house and took boarders. Mrs. Burton accepted the condition, imposed by the Trustees, of supplying food to student applicants at not exceeding $9 per month for the first year and $10 afterwards. She also agreed that the practice of holding the Commencement ball in the dining room, which for a quarter of a century had prevailed, should be continued. After being maintained on this basis for several years, Steward's Hall was given up by Mrs. Burton, and remained empty for some time. It was rented in 1825 for six months by a Mr. Moore. About that time, Dr. Elisha Mitchell installed his laboratory in a portion of the building. Steward's Hall was repaired under the superintendency of the contractor and builder, William Nichols, in 1827.[17] Two years later, December 15, 1829, the Trustees ordered that $111 be paid to Bryant Kittrell for further repairs.[18]

In 1835 Dr. Mitchell, while serving as acting president, pointed out that Steward's Hall had been a source of vexation here, as were commons at all other colleges. He was half a century ahead of his time in advocating the establishment, with funds accruing from tuition, of an eating house for poor students, presumably on the basis of "plain living and high thinking." Unfortunately his sensible recommendation to the Trustees was not carried into effect. Steward's Hall continued for some years to be rented to persons willing to charge the students reasonable rates, although boarding there was not made compulsory by the Faculty. Among those who conducted dining rooms under this University regulation were John B. Tenney, Mrs. William McCauley, Mrs. John (Caroline) Scott, and Miss Sally Mallett. In 1844 Steward's Hall ceased to be conducted under University control; and the following year the building was rented as a private residence. In 1847 the main building of Steward's Hall was dismantled; and the well in the yard, the water of which had been reported muddy as early as 1825, was filled up. The wings were given to President Swain to be used in erecting a servant's house; and the main structure was sold to form a part of the village schoolhouse.[19]

17. Battle, I, 297.
18. *T. M.*, 1823-1840, p. 148.
19. Battle, I, 431, 614.

6

THE BEGINNINGS OF CAMPUS
CONSERVATION

THE HISTORY of the University Campus and its development throughout a century and a half dates from August 10, 1793. On that date, as we have already seen, the commissioners appointed by the Trustees met at New Hope Chapel Hill and laid off the bounds of the University Campus and of the town of Chapel Hill. With vision and insight, these founding fathers utilized to best advantage the natural beauties of the landscape; and exhibited wise judgment in locating the sites for proposed buildings and offices, and comprehensive scope of view in mapping out the Campus, broad expanses of territory for park areas, and contiguous land for a town. The central plan embodied two wide and spacious strips of land at right angles to each other: one running N 21° W, the other N 69° E. These strips of land, curiously termed "avenues," were not intended for vehicular traffic; but were designed for park areas, being for the most part dense with natural growth of noble trees and shrubbery. The "avenue" running eastward was "controlled" by Point Prospect, its destination, whereas the "avenue" running northward established the primary axis for the Campus proper. These broad bands of forest land, given the name of "ornamental grounds," were designed to be the happy hunting grounds, in some problematical future, of the botanist and the landscape gardener. Our forefathers, pioneering in virgin regions, were actuated by the same type of esthetic considerations as inspired such contemporaries as Thomas Jefferson and the two gifted French botanists, André and William Michaux. Practical and esthetic conceptions went hand in hand in original University planning and Campus development; but proposals for an extensive farm and a botanical garden, which early were brought forward, had long to await successful realization. Our ancestors happily conceived in comprehensive design and massive proportion: a huge main building with wings commensurate in size, and a Campus twice the size of the Campus of today.

A study of the original map of the University and Chapel Hill will clarify the designs and proportions of the various features of the plan. The strip of land gently sloping northward from the crest of the ridge extended across present Franklin Street and penetrated deeply into the forest, now the urban development known as Cobb Terrace. This expanse of forest land thickly studded with superb oaks and poplars was two hundred and ninety feet in width; and the bounding lines of the strip were the extensions of the east wall of the Old East and the west wall of the Old West buildings. This mighty sylvan esplanade, given the imposing sobriquet of "Grand Avenue," seemed designed as a stage for some "Peripatetic School" of nature lovers and devotees of meditation, and even as camping grounds for picnics. These were the so-called "ornamental grounds"; but the southern extension of the Grand Avenue was apparently to remain, for the time being, undeveloped.

The "Campus" proper was originally laid off as a square, extending eastward to the west line of the Andrew Burke, later William Horne Battle lot, and westward to the east line of the lot on which the president's house (later site of Swain Hall) stood. From present Cameron Avenue the other dimension of the square ran N 21° W to Franklin Street and southward almost to the present Raleigh Highway passing just north of the Bell Tower.[1]

Dr. McCorkle, the moralist, desired a location for the University remote from centers of population in order that it might be, as Charles W. Harris expressed it, "inaccessible to vice." Deeply fixed in McCorkle's mind, as indicated in his dedicatory sermon on October 12, 1793, was an institution of learning with a duplex role, uniting the philosophy of Hebraism with the esthetics of Hellenism. So obsessed was he with this thought that when he opened his own school at Thyatira near Salisbury some three months later he endowed it with the quaint joint title of Zion-Parnassus. Indeed, in its then native beauty and picturesque wildness, the primitive "ornamental grounds" and plotted "Grand Avenue" might well have been a late eighteenth-century reproduction of a composite of academy of Hebraic theology and

1. Battle, I, 44-47.

haunt of the Muses. Our ancestors seemed to hope that here if anywhere in the Western world, amid towering trees, fragrant flowers, velvety turf, and crystal-clear, bubbling springs, might perhaps be realized the dream of an American Academe.

At the sale of lots for the projected village of Chapel Hill contiguous to the University, on October 12, 1793, the several scores of people assembled on the spot saw few tangible evidences of communal life.[2] Near the southwest corner of the intersection of present Franklin and Columbia streets stood an inn which is believed to have stood there in Revolutionary days; and this was acquired in 1795 of James Patterson by a Revolutionary soldier and his wife, William and Elizabeth Nunn, and conducted as combined tavern and boardinghouse for more than half a century. The Nunns gaily described their inn as a "house of Entertainment" in a contemporary gazette:

ENTERTAINMENT

The subscriber wishes to inform his friends and the public in general, that he is now living at the University of North Carolina, and keeps a house of Entertainment, where James Patterson lately lived. He assures those who may think proper to call on him, that every attention which may be in his power to give, shall be used to make their time easy and agreeable while with him.

Wm NUNN

Orange county, October 23.[3]

Some fifty yards to the east of this tavern stood the blacksmith shop of Christopher Barbee, an early settler who had an undisputed monopoly of the farrier's trade. To the northeast of the intersection of the two great highways, one to Raleigh, the other to Petersburg, Virginia, near the site of the later village schoolhouse on present Pittsboro Street, stood the neglected little Chapel of Ease which gave the name to the eminence.[4] The

2. "The price for all the lots sold, about £3000," was, says Dr. Battle, "considered highly satisfactory." Wheeler, p. 347.
3. *The North-Carolina Journal,* November 9, 1795.
4. Consult the earliest known map of the Chapel Hill area, executed by John Daniel and reproduced in this book. On this map are located certain mills and houses in the vicinity, notably the homes of George Daniels, Alexander Piper, Christopher Barbee, and "Col." Matthew McCauley, McCauley's, Yeargin's and Green's grist mills, and Jones' saw mill on

Raleigh highway cut diagonally across the Campus, running through fields and dense forests; and the road to Petersburg ran from the intersection of present Cameron Avenue and Pittsboro Street in a general northeasterly direction.

It is worthy of note, at this point, that the village maintained a mere snail's pace in development. In 1853, William Dunn Moseley, of the class of 1818, fortunately for the historian, has described the University and the village as it existed in his college days, and has included in his letter a map showing the streets and houses. A quotation from his letter follows:

I would like to look into the room occupied by President Polk and myself; where we spent many pleasant hours, in reading together the latin & greek authors; and in demonstrating the propositions, Conic Sections; and being the first class that ever studied that branch of mathematics—Our room was in the S° West Corner of the 3rd Story of what was then called the new-College—I would like too, to see the libraries; and to take a stroll through the village; beginning at Mrs Nunn's, and going eastwardly down the main Street, first by Mrs Mitchell's on the right; Trice's store on the left; Then Major Hendersons, Then James Hogg's immediately opposite; then the tavern occupied by Hilliard; Then Tom Taylors store, on the left, Then Edmund Pitts dwelling, Then Tom Taylors, Then (East of the Raleigh road), Dr. Caldwells residence, Then Mr Hooper's; immediately opposite to the latter was Mrs Puckets—This was then the principal Street; South of Mrs Nunn's was Wm Barbee's, Then the President's house, occupied by yourself. Then, S° West, Mrs Pannell's and Watson's—These I believe, were at that time the houses composing the village; with two college buildings; and Person Hall-Chapel.

I would like too, to visit the graveyard, then containing some half dozen graves; and the rock-spring, and the twin-sisters, and the bath. I would like too, to visit the old poplar, on the right of the path, leading from the Chapel to Dr Caldwell's—Is it still living?[5]

Major Pleasant Henderson with his large family removed from Rockingham County to Chapel Hill in 1797 and built a spacious

---

Bowlin's Creek (not named on the map) at the crossing of the Petersburg Road, 60 rods more than 1½ miles from the chapel. It is to be noted that neither the home of James Patterson, contractor for the Old East Building, nor the blacksmith shop of Christopher Barbee on the north side of Franklin Street, is shown on the map.

5. W. D. Moseley to Elisha Mitchell, Tallahassee, Florida, August 13, 1853. *U.N.C.I. 1796-1835.*

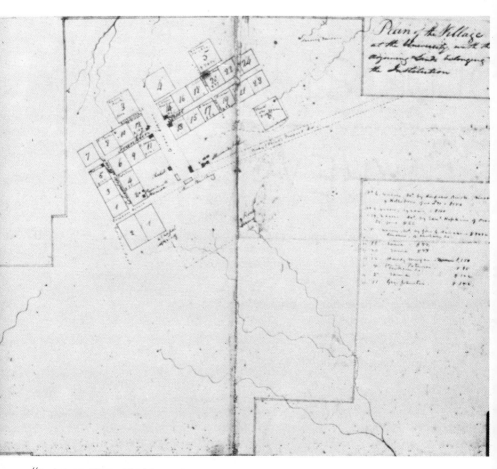

"PLAN OF THE VILLAGE AT THE UNIVERSITY WITH THE ADJOINING
LANDS BELONGING TO THE INSTITUTION"

This map was drawn some time between 1797 and 1812 by an unknown person. This is doubtless the map which W. D. Moseley
enclosed in his letter of August 13, 1853, to his uncle, Elisha Mitchell. At lower right is a partial list of the purchasers at the sale of
1793. A complete list may be found in Battle, I, 46-47.

dwelling on the site of the present U. S. Post Office, together with a store on the same lot, conducted under the firm name of Henderson and Searcy.[6] Mrs. Elizabeth Puckett's house (the present home, with additions and enlargements, of Chancellor and Mrs. House) is said, on doubtful authority, to have been built prior to 1796. She was certainly taking students as boarders in 1796. Mr. and Mrs. James Hogg, the parents of Gavin Hogg, famous lawyer, removed to Chapel Hill from Wilmington about 1800, and resided on the lot where Battle-Vance-Pettigrew dormitories now stand. Thomas H. Taylor, merchant, and later superintendent of the property and finances of the University, owned the house on the Spencer Hall lot which was later occupied (1837-1844) by President Swain and in the 1890's and later was occupied successively by Professors Alexander and Bain. His store, on the north side of Franklin Street, was located just east of the present Village Apartments. "Edmund" Pitt (whom Dr. Battle identifies as William Pitt) lived on the northwest corner of Franklin and Hillsboro streets, on the lot where Mrs. A. H. Patterson now resides. This house was sold shortly after 1818 to Henry C. Thompson who was taking boarders the following year. Places overlooked by Governor Moseley were the homes of: Abner W. Clopton, Headmaster of the Grammar School; and of Mrs. Burton, who took boarders and rented Steward's Hall after it was given up as commons by the University in 1819. Houses outside of the town, where roomers were taken, were the homes of Messrs. Kittrell, Moring (commonly called "Moreen"), and Strayhorn (pronounced Strain), and of Mrs. Craig. The antiquity of Davie Poplar is attested by Governor Moseley's reference to it, 129 years ago, as the "old poplar." Rock Spring is shown on the John Daniel map. The Twin Sisters, two small brooks arising in springs, located on present Cobb Terrace, were canalized by troughs and delightedly used by the University students as an open-air shower bath.

6. The street running north and south past the Post Office was named Henderson Street in honor of Major Pleasant Henderson. The firm of Henderson and Searcy furnished both building materials and skilled service to the University. *T.M.*, 1801-1810, p. 157.

Once the University was well under way, with a satisfactory Preparatory Department, well-organized curricula, and an adequate number of buildings for successful operation, the minds of the Trustees naturally turned toward the problem of the care and conservation of University property. The 1,400 acres owned by the University, virgin land chiefly forests, needed to be safeguarded; for pioneer settlers usually regarded forests as free domain and timber available to any man with an axe. It was too soon for artificial adornment, in the forms of planting, terracing, and landscaping. As for the Campus, the *genius loci* was native and sylvan, without the need of titivation. The primary need was the clearing away of brush and the trimming of the splendid trees, in the interest of improvement and beautification. We need not be surprised then that the first recorded action of the Board of Trustees, July 11, 1805, dealing with conservation, reads as follows:

Resolved, That John Taylor Esquire [the University Steward] be and is hereby requested to employ some fit person to trim the trees in the Grove and adjoining to the public buildings, in a proper and judicious manner; and when done, to certify to the Treasurer what sum ought to be paid to the [one] performing such duty, which the Treasurer shall pay out of the funds in his hands.[7]

At this same meeting, Archibald D. Murphey, thus early displaying his broad vision and constructive power of long-term planning, introduced a series of important resolutions, concerning the preservation of buildings; and these were adopted *in toto*. The preamble and first resolution are given below:

This Board being impressed with the necessity of adopting such measures as appear to them necessary to preserve the Buildings of the University in constant repair, have come to the following Resolutions, viz.,

Resolved, That a superintendent of buildings shall be immediately appointed, whose special duty it shall be to examine the state of the buildings of the University from time to time and at all times, and to cause all repairs to be properly made without further delay whensoever the same shall become necessary.[8]

7. *T. M.*, 1801-1810, p. 145.
8. *Ibid.*, pp. 145-46.

The Steward of the University, John Taylor, was appointed, in the final resolution, "Superintendent of the Buildings of the University of North Carolina." The emoluments of this position of imposing title amounted to the princely sum of "twenty dollars annually as a full compensation for all services to be by him performed in executing the duties of his appointment."[9]

After the expiration of five years, experience clearly indicated that the lands, as well as the buildings, should be placed under the supervision of some responsible official; but the Trustees again failed to provide an adequate salary for such official. On December 20, 1810, the Trustees appointed John Taylor to the enlarged post of "Superintendent of the Buildings and Lands of the University," at the same pitiful salary of ten pounds per annum "as a compensation in full of all the duties by him performed." The ordinance regarding the conservation of University lands reads in part as follows:

> Be it further ordained that it shall be the duty of the said superintendent to take care of the lands belonging to the University in the vicinity of Chapel Hill and see that no waste is committed thereon. . . .[10]

Following the resignation of Taylor both as steward and superintendent of buildings and lands, the Trustees on November 23, 1811 appointed as his successor a worthy citizen and competent man of affairs, William Barbee.[11] Three weeks later, on account of the niggardly annual compensation of £10 or $20, William Barbee resigned the post of superintendent of buildings and lands; and on December 18, 1811, John Close, a local contractor, was elected his successor.[12]

During the next fifteen years, the work of conservation of forests, grounds, and property was of a routine nature. Cameron Avenue stopped at the present Pittsboro Road; and to the west was a field adjoining thick woods. In 1814, President Chapman was granted the use of this field and permission to cut firewood from the woods adjoining it.

9. *Ibid.*, p. 146.
10. *Ibid.*, p. 311.
11. *T.M.*, 1811-1822, p. 3.
12. *Ibid.*, p. 27.

In 1815, because of high prices due to the war, a plan was developed which had the two-fold purpose of advantaging the Faculty financially and improving University property. There were two roads from Chapel Hill to Raleigh, one traversing the summit of the Point Prospect ridge, and the other running about one hundred yards to the north. With the ostensible purpose of affording a "full view of the distant horizon over Point Prospect to the east," the Trustees authorized the Faculty to clear out the land along these roads; and in this way many charming views and vistas were obtained. The Faculty thereby acquired the excellent oak and hickory wood of the trees which they cleared off from twenty acres of land. Two years later, turbulent and lawless students, perhaps in protest against the British proclivities of President Chapman, ran amuck and did much damage to the buildings and the Grove, as the Campus was then called. So incensed were the Trustees by this callous disregard of property rights that they instructed the President to "invoke the aid of the criminal laws to punish the perpetrators" of these outrages. The damage then done to the trees in the Grove may well have proved lasting; for in 1825 Elisha Mitchell reports that "the oak trees in the Campus were failing, and that there was no undergrowth from which a supply of new trees was obtainable." In view of these discouraging conditions he recommended extensive replanting.

Doubtless a realization of the consequences of sustained neglect of University property, brought home to the Trustees by the reports of Mitchell and others, led to a much needed reform. In 1825 provision was made by the Trustees for the appointment of a "Superintendent of the property and financial concerns of the University," with carefully prescribed duties. The incumbent must reside in Chapel Hill, give bond in the sum of $10,-000, and receive an annual salary of not more than $500. The appointee was Thomas H. Taylor; but his services soon proved to be unsatisfactory. In May, 1826, the Faculty, it appears, passed regulations for better preservation of the college buildings and grounds. Taylor's post was taken by Dr. Mitchell, who ever since his arrival late in 1818, had informally served as University bursar, with no clearly prescribed definition of his duties.

On December 15, 1826, Mitchell reported to Charles Manly, Secretary of the Board of Trustees, that "there is a balance in my favour [on the bursar's books] of some 300 dollars and more, on the several scores of Salary, as professor and Superintendent of the Public Buildings, Repairs, expenditures by the direction of the Committee for trimming and Improving the Grove, etc."[13] The deplorable consequences of the niggardly policy of paying the superintendent only $20 a year are revealed in the Report of the Committee of Visitors, June, 1827. After pointing out that Dr. Mitchell as bursar had kept no detailed and itemized accounts since 1818, which he could scarcely have been expected to do under the circumstances, the Report continues, anent the condition of the buildings:

They found the East wing in good order, the plaistering sound & the rooms neat & comfortable, the west or new building is considerably dilapidated in its walls, and needs repairs. The main building is in a wretched state, the plaistering tumbling down & the walls apparently rotting. Was the institution free from debt and its [property] unincumbered, your committee would have no hesitation in recommending its demolition & reconstruction. As it is it will continually prove a source of burthensome expense—the materials of which it is built are worthless & the workmanship wretched.

Your Committee would call the attention of the board to the situation of the new Chapell—it is at present in a very exposed situation & should either be finished without delay, or steps taken to secure it against the weather.

From a conversation with Mr. [Bryant] Kittrell, the present occupant of the Steward's hall, they learn that that building needs repairing.[14]

It must have come as a shock to the Trustees, both to hear this depressing report and on December 17, 1827, the even more discouraging report of President Caldwell, stating that the Main [South] Building, the materials of which were worthless and the workmanship wretched, was in ruins; and that in consequence it had actually not been occupied for some years! Caldwell recommended a change in the superintendency of buildings; and for the time being Dr. Mitchell voluntarily continued to perform

13. University Papers, Southern Historical Collection.
14. *Ibid.*

the duties of that office. On December 27, 1827, the Trustees re-appointed Thomas H. Taylor as "Superintendent," without speci-fication of duties, for the year 1828, at an annual salary of $400. During that year Dr. Mitchell presented a memorial to the Trus-tees in which, among other recommendations and suggestions, he registers a complaint against the Superintendent to the effect that he "had departed from the old custom of paying the Faculty from time to time sums out of the tuition money, that he retained all his own salary and otherwise appropriated the funds, leaving little for other members of the Faculty."[15] Owing to the grow-ing dissatisfaction with Taylor, the Board of Trustees on Jan-uary 2, 1829, empowered the Faculty to choose the superin-tendent from among their own members, at an annual salary of $200; and the Faculty chose Dr. Mitchell.[16]

Eternal vigilance is the price of maintenance and conservation, no less than of liberty. On June 21, 1830, an "emergency" meet-ing of the Board of Trustees was held. So desperate were the financial straits that the University seemed to be on the brink of ruin. Mr. James Iredell reported on the University's financial status, and a committee, consisting of Thomas Ruffin, Duncan Cameron, and William Gaston, was appointed to draw up a memorial to the General Assembly. This eloquent and exhaus-tive report, drafted by Judge Ruffin, was presented to the Trus-tees at their meeting on November 24, 1830.[17] So alarming be-came the pressure of debt that a committee consisting of Wil-liam Polk, James Mebane, and James Webb was appointed by the Trustees to offer for sale the unimproved lands of the Uni-versity in the vicinity of Chapel Hill. Fortunately other remedies were resorted to; and only the Preparatory School house and its one-acre lot were sold, for an insignificant sum.[18]

In 1832, President Caldwell was so outraged by the depreda-tions of the villagers on the woodlands of the University that, in anticipation of modern practice, he recommended, but without avail, the employment of a forest ranger to put a stop to the

15. Battle, I, 308.
16. *T. M.*, 1822-1835, p. 115.
17. *Ibid.*, pp. 141-59.
18. Consult Chapter 4.

abuse. The Trustees did make a contract of sale with Professor William Hooper for fifty acres of the forest lands east of the Campus, now known as Battle Park. Under this contract the large trees, with the exception of white oaks, were cut down. Upon the resignation of Professor Hooper in 1836, the contract was canceled.[19]

19. Battle, I, 366-67. Presumably this tract was enclosed, in whole or in part, for Dr. Battle states: "There are remnants of a stone wall enclosure extending into the Park."

7

THE OLD CHAPEL: "AULA PERSONICA"

FROM THE very beginning of the University, concern for the development of the character of the students and the safeguarding of their morals was a prime objective of Faculty and Trustees. Dr. McCorkle, eminent divine, Presbyterian minister, moralist and theologian, exerted a great influence upon the young University. In the charter, it is expressly set forth that the Trustees "shall have the power to make all such laws and regulations for the government of the University and preservation of good order and morals therein, as are usually made in such seminaries, and as to them may appear necessary. . . ."[1] During the early years of the University's history, a period when Tom Paine's *Age of Reason* exercised a blighting influence upon the people of the young republic, the Faculty was not immune to or unaffected by this demoralizing philosophy which flowed directly from the French Revolution. Indeed the first "presiding professor," David Ker, was a pronounced infidel, Professor Charles W. Harris was strongly influenced in the same direction, Professor Samuel Allen Holmes, according to President Caldwell, "embraced and taught the wildest principles of licentiousness," Nicholas Delveaux, Headmaster of the Preparatory School, was a recusant Roman Catholic monk, and even Davie, the founder of the University, was not a church member, had imbibed something of the prevalent scepticism, and entertained a strong antipathy to priests and pulpit influence. In western North Carolina, a library of works of deistic philosophy and rationalistic criticism of the Bible was established during the last decade of the eighteenth century; and to counteract such tendencies the Rev. James Wallis in 1797 published an able pamphlet, entitled "The Bible Defended," against the "misrepresentations and falsehoods of Thomas Paine's *Age of Reason*."

The battle against infidelism was quickly won after the com-

1. *Laws of North Carolina*, 1789, Chapter XX, § 21-25.

FIRST PRESIDENT'S HOUSE

For a time the home of President Joseph Caldwell, it was also the residence of Professor Elisha Mitchell for many years. Later, Professor Joshua W. Gore lived here, and, still later, Andrew H. Patterson. The house was on the site of Swain Hall. The drawings on this page were made by Hope Summerell Chamberlain.

SECOND PRESIDENT'S HOUSE

Located on the lot where the President's Mansion now stands, it was the home of President Joseph Caldwell during the latter part of his administration. President David L. Swain also lived here from 1849 to 1868. The house was destroyed by a fire on Christmas morning, 1886, just one day after Dr. Thomas Hume had moved into it.

THE BUILDING COMMISSIONERS of the UNIVERSITY of North-Carolina, will attend at the town of Hillsborough, from the 6th until the 16th of April next, for the purpose of receiving proposals from any person disposed to undertake the building of a House at the seat of the University, of the following dimensions and description, viz.

It is to be of Brick, one hundred and twelve feet six inches in length—forty-six feet three inches in width, clear of the outside walls, and three stories high. A Plan of the Building, with a particular description of the manner in which it is to be executed, may be seen by applying to the Commissioners at the time and place above-mentioned.

Reasonable advances will be made from time to time, and satisfactory security will be required from the undertaker for the performance of the contract.

JOHN HAYWOOD, Chairman.

Hillsborough, North-Carolina, }
January 12, 1796. }

ADVERTISEMENT IN THE HALIFAX *NORTH CARO-LINA JOURNAL*, MARCH 21, 1796
The building described is Main Building, later known as South Building.

ing of Joseph Caldwell on October 31, 1796. One of the first features of the Campus which met his eye was the foundation of the Chapel. During the ante-bellum era (1795-1861) of the University's history, the influences of the Presbyterian Church, Princeton, and, through Dr. John Witherspoon, the Scotch universities were paramount. Princeton was a powerful focus of radiating missionary influence; and in the policy of the Scotch-Irish Presbyterians religious and secular instruction went hand in hand. In pioneer communities, the erection of the meeting house and of the schoolhouse were contemporaneous, the same building often serving for both purposes. This statement is confirmed in the case of Chapel Hill, which was a settlement carved out of the forests. Soon after contracts were given for the erection of the North Wing (the first dormitory and lecture hall), Steward's Hall (the first Commons), and the president's house, the erection of a chapel was determined upon; and Absalom Tatom, head of Eagle Masonic Lodge, and Walter Alves, the Treasurer of the University, prominent citizens of Hillsborough, were added to the Committee on Buildings on January 10, 1794, to contract for and oversee the erection of the proposed chapel and other buildings, probably because of the nearness of Hillsborough to Chapel Hill.[2] There was then in use no church in the neighborhood; and the little Chapel of Ease of the Anglican Church, called New Hope Chapel, although still a conspicuous landmark, was in a dilapidated condition.

The University Chapel, originally designed to be about 40 by 50 feet and one storey in height, was located somewhat erratically. The eastern bar of the letter I, in which design the present Person Hall is constructed, was the original Chapel. In 1794, whereas work on the North Wing, the president's house, and Steward's Hall was pressed by order of the Trustees, the work on the Chapel lagged behind. By the date of the opening of the University, January 15, 1795, a rainy, foggy day, the ground had only been broken for the foundation; and in con-

2. *T. M.*, 1789-1797, p. 101. The other seven commissioners, who had been elected December 8, 1792, were Alfred Moore, W. R. Davie, Frederick Hargett, Thomas Blount, Alexander Mebane, John Williams, and John Haywood. *Ibid.*, p. 60.

sequence Governor Richard Dobbs Spaight, who attended this student-less "opening," beheld only a pile of yellow earth where the Chapel was to stand. When the bills for the other buildings were presented in midsummer, 1795, by James Patterson, contractor for the North Wing, and by Samuel Hopkins, contractor for the president's house and Steward's Hall, and for certain extra work such as painting, etc., Davie expressed the belief that Patterson "charged six or seven prices" and that "Hopkins' bill . . . was almost as bad." He further claimed that Patterson's charges were "excessively exorbitant" and his work "infamously done."[3] The funds being very nearly exhausted as the result of these exorbitant charges, work on the Chapel was proportionately retarded; and Joseph Caldwell, shortly after his arrival, October 31, 1796, commented, with a certain sense of dismay over the primitive setting and slow progress of building operations: "The University is almost entirely in infancy, cut out of the woods, one building of the smaller kind is finished. . . . The foundation of the Chapel is laid but the completion is uncertain, as the mason and his negroes have spent the favorable autumn in raising the foundation [only] to the surface of the ground. According to agreement it must be finished by the first day of July next."[4]

On April 20, 1796, Thomas Person of Granville County, one of the Trustees under the charter, having learned that the funds for the erection of the University buildings were dwindling and that the prospects for the continuation of the work were not encouraging, notified the Trustees of his willingness to subscribe the sum of £500 to "be applied towards the finishing a Chapel." A year later, at the suggestion of William R. Davie, Person contributed an additional sum of £25 to provide for the cost of a memorial tablet.[5] The concluding clause of the acknowledgment of the Trustees eminently deserves quotation:

3. Hamilton, op. cit., p. 29. W. R. Davie to John Haywood, July 22, 1795. On December 17, 1807, the Board of Trustees directed the Superintendent of Buildings to build a porch on the president's house. T. M., 1801-1810, p. 244.

4. Battle, II, 113.

5. For the acknowledgment of the receipt from Thomas Person of £525, consult Report of the Treasurer, Gavin Alves, to the Board of

Resolved that the Board have a proper sense of the liberality of General Person in the important and benevolent donation by him made as above mentioned; and that they offer him their thanks for the same; assuring him likewise that proper mention shall be made of such his bounty in the records of the University.[6]

In that day of the almost unbelievable scarcity of "hard money," Person's gift of $1,050 particularly impressed the Trustees, as it was "said to have been paid in shining silver dollars. . . ."[7]

Person Hall was built by Philemon Hodges under the superintendency of Samuel Hopkins. In a letter to Caldwell, July 24, 1796, Charles W. Harris, the first tutor, says: "The Chapel is already contracted for & it will cost near 3,000 dollars."[8] The actual figure is $2,826.

This compact little one-storey brick building 54 feet by 36 feet was once described by Elisha Mitchell as "not a splendid, but . . . a very neat edifice." Until supplanted for this purpose by Gerrard Hall in 1837,[9] Person Hall was and remained for almost forty years the College Chapel, wherein the students congregated for morning prayers at sunrise and evening prayers at five o'clock. This hall was given over, particularly after 1837, to every variety of public occasion and assemblage, religious and secular, sacred and profane: twice-daily prayers on weekdays, Sunday School and church services on Sunday, animated debates of the Literary Societies, boisterous mass-meetings of the students, and dignified Commencement exercises whereat were gathered, it was said, "more distinguished men and beautiful women" than

---

Trustees, July 14, 1797: *T. M.*, 1789-1797, July 17-18, 1797. The record reads, in part, as follows: "Gen'l Person being desirous to have the direction of the appropriation of this last mention'd sum [£25], the Treasurer gave him a receipt to that effect." S. B. Weeks, "Thomas Person," *N. C. B. H.*, VII, 396-97. The foundation of Person Hall was laid by November 1, 1796. The building was completed in 1797 and the whitewashing in October, 1799.

6. *T. M.*, 1789-1797, pp. 198-99. December 17, 1796. Public announcement of the gift was made in the gazettes of the day. See *State Gazette of North Carolina* (Edenton), May 19, 1796.

7. Battle, I, 122.

8. Wagstaff, *op. cit.*, p. 31. The contract called for completion of the building by July 1, 1797.

9. Gerrard Hall was begun in 1822.

at any other spot in North Carolina. Bleak indeed must have been the meetings of the Literary Societies during the winter months, held in the single large room, which was without heat and swept by icy winds blowing in through many a broken window-pane. Only reluctantly had the Faculty and Trustees, alarmed over the likelihood of fire from guttering tapers, granted the Societies the privilege of meeting in Person Hall; and then only on the strict understanding that "the clerks of each society carefully . . . extinguish every candle, fasten the windows and lock the door upon the adjournment of the society." There is a vague tradition that even Commencement balls were held here, but it seems unlikely. It was not, however, for lack of desire on the part of the students, for on November 4, 1833, a group of three drafted an elaborate and flowery petition to the Board of Trustees in which they stated that, were the new Chapel completed, they would have asked to fit up the Old Chapel at their own expense for "the gratification and pleasure of the adored Fair who honor us with their company on that universal jubilee."[10]

To that "Old Chapel," says Mrs. Spencer in reminiscent mood, "all itinerant preachers, lecturers, showmen, ventriloquists, Siamese twins, and the like wended their way, and all Chapel Hill followed them, and spent their money, just as their successors do these days when 'Blind Tom' is the attraction. There I once saw a conjurer slip a glass pepper-castor into his mouth and proceed to chew it up. I have not got over it to this day."[11]

This hall was memorable for orations delivered by distinguished guests at the invitation of the Literary Societies. The custom was inaugurated by the most famous of the orations, one delivered by the ripe scholar, Archibald DeBow Murphey, on June 27, 1827. Intense excitement on the Campus was evoked by the coming of William Gaston, the most admired man of his day in North Carolina, to the Commencement of 1832, when he startled and stirred his audience to the depths by his historic

10. S. U. M., VIII (1889), 213-19. The three rising juniors who signed this petition were Christopher C. Battle, Jno. H. Watson, and William P. Webb.

11. S. U. M., II (1884), 394-98.

plea for the abolition of slavery, almost three decades before the firing of the first gun at Fort Sumter.[12] The most significant proof of the place in the affections of the administration held by Person Hall is that, although beginning in 1837 Commencements were held for more than thirty years in Gerrard Hall, the diplomas, inscribed in orotund Latin phrases, continued to record that the degrees were conferred *In Aula Personica.*

Before Gerrard Hall superseded the Old Chapel in many of its uses, a day came when the Trustees seriously considered the latter's demolition and the use of its durable bricks, then not easily duplicated, for other structures. A troubled Faculty, narrates Gladys Hall Coates in her diverting "Story of Person Hall," wrote the Trustees imploring that it be spared:

> We understand that it has been proposed to demolish the Old Chapel so soon as the new building shall be completed. It has doubtless been supposed it would then be of no use whatever. But for reasons which we could mention at length if it were necessary the place where we now assemble for morning and evening prayers is much more convenient for that purpose than the new building will be and we should give it up with extreme reluctance. We believe it will hardly be destroyed for the sake of materials.
>
> It is not a splendid but it is a very neat edifice and we hope that unless there are strong reasons for pulling it down, it may be suffered to remain. The New Chapel will be in a better state of neatness and preservation for public worship on Sunday and for Commencement.[13]

This precious relic of an historic beginning, the second permanent building to be erected upon any state university campus in North America, was fortunately spared, "as this Edifice was erected by the bounty of the Patron whose name it bears & as it is more conveniently situated than any other building for public prayer, & will by such use save the new chapel."[14]

Of all the buildings upon the Campus, with respect to the uses to which it has been put, as will be seen later on, Person Hall

12. W. J. Peele, ed., *Lives of Distinguished North Carolinians* (Raleigh, 1898), pp. 161-80; R. B. Creecy, *Grandfather's Tales of North Carolina History* (Raleigh, 1901), pp. 84-87.

13. *Bulletin of Person Hall Art Gallery,* Vol. III, No. 2 (April, 1943). Dr. Elisha Mitchell drafted this petition.

14. *T. M.,* 1823-1833, pp. 14-15. December 11, 1824.

has experienced, mathematically speaking, the greatest number of permutations and combinations. In view of Dr. McCorkle's dream of the University as a happy union of the Hebraism of Zion with the Hellenism of Parnassus, one might well surmise that if any hall on the Campus deserves the title Zion-Parnassus, it is Person Hall, which began as a chapel and ended as a school of fine arts.

It is somewhat humiliating to recall that still lacking of fulfillment is the pious resolution of the Trustees to place upon the front of the Old Chapel a tablet bearing the following inscription:

BY THE TRUSTEES
OF THE UNIVERSITY OF NORTH CAROLINA
THIS MONUMENT IS ERECTED
TO THE MEMORY OF
BRIGADIER-GENERAL THOMAS PERSON,
WHO EVINCED HIS PATRIOTISM
AND LOVE OF LEARNING
BY A PECUNIARY DONATION
WITH WHICH THIS CHAPEL WAS COMPLETED
IN THE YEAR 1797
IN HONOUR OF WHICH MUNIFICENCE
IT IS DISTINGUISHED BY THE NAME OF
PERSON HALL
OBIT AN. 1
AET.[15]

15. *T. M.*, 1801-1810, p. 291. December 7, 1810. The dates were left blank, as they were unknown to the authors of the resolution. A fragment of a letter from William R. Davie to John Haywood, of late 1810 or early 1811, in the Ernest Haywood Collection, Southern Historical Collection, gives interesting details regarding the tablet: "When Judge ₍Alfred₎ Moore and I prevailed upon General Person to make the cash donation for the purpose of building the chapel at the University, we gave him to expect that we would use our endeavours to have his munificence properly commemorated, and upon some observation made by the General evidently to ascertain *the manner* in which we supposed such a thing would be done, we suggested that the Trustees would after his death erect in the chapel some monument of marble to his memory; and afterwards in an enquiry what would be the cost of such a memorial of him, I remember to have told him that a neat marble slab set into the wall and surmounted by an urn or some ornament of that kind would not cost more than £40 or £50; I think he added that sum to the original

Some day, let us hope, this promised tablet may adorn the front of a massive colonial structure of which the original Person Hall shall form an integral part, properly balancing Alumni Hall, and strengthening the majestic dignity and bold sweep of that "Grand Avenue" so happily conceived by our ancestors.

---

donation:—and if I am not greatly mistaken you will find by the Treasurers books that such was the fact. Now I reproach myself exceedingly for not having stated this matter to the Board of Trustees while [end of fragment]." A sheet bearing the above inscription for the tablet has on the reverse side the date "January 17, 1811." On this date John Haywood may have read to the Board of Trustees the above quotation from Davie's letter. The minutes of the Trustees for a period in 1811 covering the date January 17, 1811, are missing.

8

"THE TEMPLE OF FOLLY": MAIN BUILDING

As EARLY as midsummer, 1796, a comprehensive plan, along sound lines of architectural planning and landscape gardening, had been outlined by the commissioners on buildings. "The Buildings which are to be erected" (in addition to the North Wing [Old East], the president's house, the steward's house, kitchen, and small outbuildings, all of which were then completed), optimistically wrote Charles W. Harris, July 24, 1796, "are a large house 115 feet long 56 broad & 3 stories; a wing exactly similar to the one above mentioned; a chapel 50 feet long & 40 broad. . . . The Trustees can at pleasure realize 15,000 dollars more with which they have determined to commence the large building as soon as they can procure an undertaker. It would be difficult to give any correct statement of the funds. I requested the Treasurer to make out a small account of them . . . he assured me that they could not be stated at less than 30,000 Dollars, tho' some of the property was such as could not be immediately productive."[1] The land warrants to Tennessee lands, given in 1790 by Col. Benjamin Smith, proved not to be readily salable, despite Harris' roseate outlook; and nothing was realized from them for almost twenty years. So the plans for erecting the Main Building were necessarily delayed for lack of funds.

Meantime, the attendance at the University began to increase; and the congestion became alarming when the North Wing and the Grammar School were taxed to the utmost, and the students were obliged to overflow into Steward's Hall where rooms were to be had only at exorbitant rates and into lodging rooms in private homes in the tiny village. At a meeting, July 14, 1795, the Trustees "Resolved that the President give notice by public advertisement in the several Gazettes in this State, that the Board will receive during their next annual meeting proposals for build-

1. Wagstaff, *op. cit.*, p. 31.

ing a house about 120 feet long, fifty feet wide, and three stories high of brick upon a plan that will then be shown by the board."[2] Advertisements requesting bids for erecting the building at the University continued to be inserted in the newspapers; but good "undertakers" were neither easy to find nor moderate in their charges.[3] There were only fourteen bedrooms in the North Wing; and, to the entire destruction of comfort and proper hygiene and at grave risk to health, six students were crammed into a room with only two windows—in pathetic contrast to conditions at Princeton, where only two students were then permitted in a room having three windows. So desperate were these conditions that, emboldened by the gift by Major Charles Gerrard of 2,560 acres of land near Nashville, Tennessee, the Trustees in 1798 resolved to authorize the erection of the Main Building. Only four, instead of six, students per room were to be permitted in future by order of the Trustees, in the North Wing. In a public defense of the University against attacks for commissioning the erection of so huge a structure as the Main Building, Caldwell, referring to the North Wing, firmly retorts: "Here are fifty-six persons huddled together with their trunks, beds, tables, chairs, books and clothes into fourteen little rooms, which by the excessive heat of summer are enough to stifle them, and in the winter scarcely admit them to sit around the fireplace. When the weather permits they fly to the shade of the trees, where they find a retreat from the burr and hurry and irrepressible conversation of a crowded society."

As Davie, with the passage of time, continued to take an ever deepening interest in the University, its development and welfare, the institution began to provoke, even thus early, severe attacks from the more radical of the democrats as a political engine of Davie and the Federalists who, constituting a majority of the first Board of Trustees, a self-perpetuating body, could thus retain control of the University indefinitely. Despite his lofty bearing and aristocratic manner, Davie's splendid talents and wide influence won him the governorship of North Caro-

2. *T. M.*, 1789-1798, p. 135.
3. See advertisements in the *North Carolina Journal* (Halifax), March 21 and April 4, 1796 (same), and another, August 8, 1796. The first of these advertisements is reproduced in this book.

lina, to which he was elected, December 4, 1798. But Federalism was on the decline; and the time was rapidly approaching when rabid democrats, under the cover of anonymity, were declaring in the public prints that the University was a hotbed of Federalism and that there "every effort is made to give direction to the minds of the students on political subjects, favorable to a high-toned aristocratic government." Many times during the past century and a half, the University has been charged with being a "hotbed" of some "ism" detested by the majority or the masses or both: a hotbed of infidelism at various periods, a hotbed of secessionism before and after the Civil War, a hotbed of Unionism afterwards, a hotbed of Communism in recent years.

It was history repeating itself after a lapse of thirty years. During the period of the Regulation, the common people, the "mob" or the "banditti," as they were indiscriminately called, revolted against excessive taxes, including a poll tax and a special tax to build a "governor's mansion" for William Tryon at Newbern. Incensed by the extravagance of building such an expensive structure, the Regulators dubbed it "Tryon's Palace"; and went to war against this and other excesses. So, during the early years of the University's precarious struggle for existence, the democrats or anti-Federalists protested against the wastefulness and extravagance of building another "palace" (Main Building) for another regal figure, William Richardson Davie, the Federalist leader. In an anonymous article signed "Citizen," this building is characterized as "the palace-like erection, which is much too large for usefulness, and might be aptly termed the 'Temple of Folly,' planned by the Demi-God Davie." Thus political frenzy was publicly displayed in denunciation of Davie as the real head of the University; and fear was expressed that "the country will be imbued with aristocratic principles because an aristocrat is at the head of it." [4] As a matter of fact, the man who designed or adapted the design for the Main Building was not Davie, but Governor Richard Dobbs Spaight, who was appointed one of the commissioners on buildings by the Trustees,

4. This may refer to President Caldwell; but it seems more likely that the reference is to Davie, who was generally thought of as the University's founder and leader.

on December 13, 1796. It is fortunate that the designs for the buildings were not left to the tender mercies of the "undertakers" but were executed or adapted by talented members of the Board of Trustees.[5] These early buildings, notably South, Old East, and Old West, reveal the influence of Princeton, and other collegiate buildings to the northward in their simple type of colonial style, rather than the influence of Sir Christopher Wren as exhibited in the main building of the College of William and Mary at Williamsburg, Virginia.

To the charge that the projected Main Building was "much too large for usefulness," Caldwell convincingly replied, with reference to the "twenty-three habitable rooms" it was to contain: "These with the rooms in the East Building will amount to 38, holding 76 students. We have more than once had over 70. The excess above 56, i.e., four to a room, lived in the village." Caldwell was determined to allow no more than two students to a room in future; and ventured upon a brief flight of eloquence: "If rooms sufficient were here we would have 100 students and our nation would have, not a Temple of Folly, but a monument of glory to herself and a pledge of utility and worth to all succeeding generations."

It is interesting to recall that, after the fashion of the English universities of Oxford and Cambridge, each of the principal buildings at the University was thought of, and referred to, in the early days as if it were a separate college. A brief excerpt from the records of the Raleigh Grand Lodge of the Masonic Fraternity, indicates this practice; and may further serve in lieu of any extant newspaper account to commemorate the laying of the cornerstone of the Main Building: "On the 14th of April, 1798, by order of its most worshipful Grand Master, a special Grand Lodge was called at the University of North Carolina for the express purpose of laying the foundation and cornerstone of the principal college of that seminary and to join the Trustees of the University in one ejaculation to heaven and the Great Architect of the Universe for the auspices of his eternal

5. See the resolution of the Board of Trustees, July 14, 1795, quoted above. Battle is authority for the statement that the Main Building was designed by Spaight.

goodness and for the prosperity of learning, wisdom and virtue of that college."[6]

One year before the opening of the new century, Joseph Caldwell's urgent representation of the needs for a large new building prevailed, despite grave misgivings expressed by some of the Trustees regarding their ability to finance the undertaking. It was probably on the suggestion of Walter Alves, Treasurer of the Trustees for five years (1795-1799), that Samuel Hopkins was appointed by the Trustees in 1799 to the office of "Superintendent of the Principal Buildings."[7] On July 12, 1799, the Trustees resolved that Hopkins be "required to have the earth around the walls of said building (Steward's Hall) rendered and deposited between the College and Chapel"; and further resolved that he "receive a warrant on the Treasurer for the sum of £275 for the purchase of 110,000 bricks; and whereas it has been suggested by Mr. Hopkins that the price of bringing 1000 bushels of shells purchased and lying at Fayetteville has not been allowed him in the last settlement of his accounts, Resolved that a further sum of £125 be advanced to him by the Treasurer towards carrying on the Building to be by him hereafter accounted for."[8] The allusion to "shells" sounds somewhat warlike; but the shells were not explosive, being marine deposits used in those days in making mortar for the building of brick structures. These shells were hauled in wagons over the great highway from Fayetteville to Chapel Hill.

As long as funds were available, Hopkins steadily pushed forward building operations; and for the year 1800 the sum of £4,900 ($9,800) was paid him. Work was discontinued after

6. Masonic Records, archives, Grand Lodge, Raleigh, N. C. See *North Carolina Journal*, No. 303, cited by D. L. Swain.

7. The connection of Samuel Hopkins with the University began on October 12, 1793, when, at the sale of the lots of the projected town of Chapel Hill, he purchased lot No. 14 for $66. Walter Lee Hopkins, *Hopkins of Virginia and Allied Families* (1931), *passim*. In 1794, Patterson, the contractor for the construction of the North Wing and the president's house, had fallen far behind in his contract, and Hopkins was engaged in his place to push these buildings to completion for the University's opening, scheduled for January 15, 1795.

8. *T. M.*, 1798-1801, p. 20. The minutes of this meeting are undated; but the meeting certainly occurred either on July 11 or 12, 1799.

the brick structure was raised to the height of one and a half storeys. In this unfinished state, exposed to all the rains that fell and winds that blew, the bare skeleton of a roofless building stood for more than three years. On July 12, 1804, alarmed by the report of damage the walls had already suffered from exposure to the weather, the Trustees recommended that the "walls be covered with rough planks."[9]

When the State of North Carolina in 1784 granted Science Hall at Hillsborough the privilege of raising funds by lottery, it was the "first instance in the history of the free State in which the aid of Government to schools extended beyond the mere formal granting of charters."[10] A committee of the Trustees, appointed June 25, 1801 and consisting of Walter Alves, William Polk, John Hill and Henry Potter, had investigated the funds of the University, the scale of expenditure, and the probable amount needed to finish the walls and cover the Main Building. As a result of its report and with the example of Science Hall in mind, another committee, consisting of Richard Dobbs Spaight and Joshua Grainger Wright, was appointed on December 9, 1801, to prepare and introduce into the General Assembly a bill to authorize the Trustees of the University to raise annually by way of lottery the sum of two thousand pounds, to defray the annual expenditure of the institution.[11] No difficulty was experienced in securing the passage of the requisite legislation.[12] Two lotteries were drawn, 1801-1802 and 1802-1803, which netted the sums of $2,215.45 and $2,865.36 respectively. It was only the University's dire need which impelled the Trustees to resort to the aid of the Goddess Fortuna, although at that time no moral obliquity was publicly attached to such a course. The day was to come, some three decades later, when the North Carolina legislature summarily rejected Archibald D. Murphey's second bill which would permit him to conduct a lottery to raise funds for financing a proposed history of North Carolina, on the ground of the alleged ill effects of games of hazard upon the

9. *T. M.*, 1801-1810, pp. 109-10.

10. Eugene Davis Owen, *Secondary Education in North Carolina*, (MS.) Doctoral Dissertation, George Washington University, 1934.

11. *T. M.*, 1798-1801, p. 54; 1801-1810, p. 8.

12. *Public Laws of North Carolina*, 1801, Chapter VIII, §7.

morals of the people. The high hopes entertained by the students of the completion of the Main Building through the use of the funds obtained from the two lotteries were frustrated. The provident and cautious Trustees voted not to expend the money in finishing the structure but to invest the entire sum realized, $5,080.81, in United States Bank stock![13]

The lotteries were conducted with scrupulous honesty, the Trustees offering tickets to the public with the solemn assurance that the "interests of the University of North Carolina, and of Learning and Science generally throughout our State are concerned in the immediate sale of the tickets." This statement was accompanied by the somewhat questionable assertion that the lottery was "calculated to promote the prosperity and happiness of our country." In view of the fact that none of the proceeds realized from the lotteries was applied to the completion of the Main Building, this pious sentiment was not shared by the luckless students who frequented the unfinished shell of the huge structure for years to come thereafter.

The students quartered in the North Wing [Old East], "cabined, cribbed, confined" from four to six to a room, were driven out of doors to seek sylvan retreats where, like Robinson Crusoe, they erected umbrageous huts, Hudsonian "green mansions," for shelter. But these pioneering undertakings in leafy home-building proved inimical to discipline, and were finally prohibited by University regulation. The curious use made by the students, over a period of years, of the skeletal Main Building, roofed over with rough boards, has been amusingly described by one of them, resident in the village, who attended both the Preparatory School and the University, 1804-1809. After assuring his hearers that the "South building" was inhabited, not by "toads and snails and bats" but by students, the witty speaker continues:

"As the only dormitory that had a roof was too crowded for study, and as those who tried to study there spent half the evening in passing laws to regulate the other half, many students left their rooms as a place of study entirely, and built cabins in the corners of the unfinished brick walls, and quite comfortable

13. *T. M.*, 1801-1810, pp. 60, 64-67. July 9, 1803.

cabins they were; but whence the plank came, out of which those cabins were built, your deponent saith not. Suffice it to hint that in such matters college boys are apt to adopt the code of Lycurgus: that there is no harm in privately transferring property, provided you are not caught at it. In such a cabin your speaker and dozens like him hibernated and burned their midnight oil. As soon as spring brought back the swallows and the leaves, we emerged from our dens and chose some shady retirement where we made a path and a promenade, and in that embowered promenade all diligent students of those days had to follow the steps of science, to wrestle with its difficulties, and to treasure up their best acquirements:

> Ye remnants of the Peripatetic school!
> Ah! Ye can tell how hard it is to climb
> The steep where fame's proud temple shines afar!

"They lived *sub divo*, like the birds that caroled over their heads. 'But how,' you will say, 'Did they manage in rainy weather?' Aye, that's the rub. Well, nothing was more common than, on a rainy day, to send in a petition to be excused from recitation, which petition ran in this stereotyped phrase: 'The inclemency of the weather rendering it impossible to prepare the recitation, the Sophomore class respectfully request Mr. Rhea to excuse them from recitation this afternoon.' To deliver this mission to the Professor I was appointed envoy ordinary (not extraordinary) and plenipotentiary, being a little fellow hardly fifteen, and perhaps somewhat of a pet with the teacher. The professor, a good-natured, indolent man, after affecting some vexation (though he was secretly glad to get off himself), and pushing the end of his long nose this way and that way some half a dozen times with his knuckles, concluded in a gruff voice with: 'Well, get as much more for tomorrow.' The shout of applause with which I was greeted upon reporting the success of my embassy resembled, if we may compare small things with great, the acclamations with which Mr. Webster was hailed by the nation upon happily concluding the Ashburton Treaty in 1842, by which war with Great Britain was prevented. Mr. Webster may have been greater, but he was not prouder than I was at the successful issue of my negotiations. Who knows but I might now have been a first rate diplomat, if I had followed up these auspicious beginnings!"[14]

Alexander Martin, who had repeatedly served as governor of North Carolina, was always an outspoken and forthright advocate of education, and in particular of the support of the University. Although some years earlier he had retired from public life, in 1803 he characteristically took the lead among the Trustees in drafting a strong appeal to the citizens of North Carolina for funds to complete the projected University buildings. Reporting for a committee of the Trustees, of which he was chairman, on July 9, 1803, Martin presented an extended paper in his somewhat florid style, recommending that it be transmitted to the people of North Carolina; and it was so ordered by the Trustees. After stressing the importance of "literary institutions" as the "grand security of our liberties founded on a republican form of government," from which in great measure "all civil and religious information flows," he adverted realistically to the "want of resources and funds to complete the principal building, the walls of which are yet incomplete." In this connection, let us recall that in 1801, animated by the violent spirit of the "new democracy," expressing itself in the forms of anti-Federalism and anti-aristocracy, the General Assembly gave the struggling infant University two body blows which might easily have proved mortal: repealing the act of 1794 granting all unsold confiscated land, and the act of 1789, granting escheated property, to the Trustees. In reference to these severe losses, Martin impressively outlined the views of the Trustees:

They flattered themselves from the funds with which they supposed they were amply supplied, by the acts for establishing and endowing the University, they would never have occasion to call upon their fellow citizens for aid but unfortunately being deprived of those aids solemnly guaranteed by the Legislature, they were reduced to the disagreeable necessity to raise money by way of lottery, a mode not the most honorable of raising money for an institution of which

14. Hooper, pp. 18-20. Andrew Rhea, a native of Virginia, was professor of ancient languages here from 1806 to 1814.

GERRARD HALL, *circa* 1890

The Greek portico, designed by Alexander Jackson Davis and completed
in 1844, has since been torn down.

ANNEX OF THE EAGLE HOTEL

This addition to the old Eagle Hotel was erected by Miss Nancy Segur
Hilliard, proprietor, in honor of President Polk's visit to the University
in 1847. Note the metal plate over the arch, described on pp. 95-96.

UPPER LEFT: MERIDIAN PILLARS. Built by Dr. Joseph Caldwell, these pillars were restored through a gift of James Lee Love, class of 1844. They are standing in the rear of the President's yard. UPPER RIGHT: ASTRONOMICAL OBSERVATORY AND METEOROLOGICAL LABORATORY. This barn-like structure, located south of present Phillips Hall, was the second astronomical observatory on the University Campus. It was used in Dr. Elisha Mitchell's time, and was torn down about the beginning of the present century. BELOW: "THE RETREAT." This two-room cottage, designed by Alexander Jackson Davis and built in 1858, was located on the lot where Spencer Hall now stands. It served as the University infirmary for thirty-six years.

the constitution of our government hath enjoined a different and liberal support . . . in the meanwhile trusting to liberal and enlightened fellow citizens to complete the principal building that must soon fall to ruins unless supported by their aid. The Trustees therefore request such donations of money [as] you may think proper generously to grant. . . .[15]

Two years later, heartened by the action of the legislature in repealing the act of 1801 which had repealed the former grant of all escheated property to the University, the Trustees resolved to continue the work upon the Main Building in the event the University's funds permitted, and even authorized the commissioners to contract for the carrying forward of the building program, payment for such work to be "made partly in cash, and partly in lands belonging to the University in the State of Tennessee. . . ."[16] Little or no advancement in the matter was accomplished during the next four years; and finally, in desperation, the Trustees on July 8, 1809, appointed a committee, consisting of Joseph Caldwell, John Haywood, and William Gaston, to solicit donations to the University, pledging the faith of the Board that the donations thereby received "shall be applied to the completion of the Main Building of the University."[17] In furtherance of this decision, the devoted and energetic Caldwell in 1809, and again in 1811, mounted his "stick-back gig," "visited the more opulent parts of the State and secured about $8,220."[18] In 1812, operations were resumed under a contractor who, being rather "near" in his calculations, bore, as Battle remarked, the "fitting name" of John Close. The completion of this building, in 1814, so long delayed, deeply gratified the devoted Trustees, gave Caldwell the assurance that his heroic labors had not been in vain, and delighted the students because at last they had suitable accommodations, a roof over their heads, and the Dialectic and Philanthropic Society Halls, their pride and glory, beneath that selfsame roof. The excited students expressed their jubilation by the firing of a cannon, for the first, last and only time in

15. *T. M.*, 1801-1810, pp. 64-67.
16. *Ibid.*, p. 172. December 19, 1805.
17. *Ibid.*, p. 251.
18. Battle, I, 134.

the town's history. The roar of that single gun, upon the completion of Davie's "Temple of Folly," was the annunciation of the University's permanence and stability.[19]

19. In 1812, 1814, and 1815, the sums paid John Close, the contractor, totaled £4,513 or $9,026. In 1816-1817 the expenditures on unpaid debts and contracts amounted to $7,863, giving a total of $16,889. For further details regarding the history of the South Building, see *infra*.

9

OLD WEST AND THE NEW CHAPEL;
PRESIDENT POLK'S VISIT

OR SOME YEARS after the completion of the Main Building, the number of students remained around one hundred. The University, having weathered the storm of anti-Federalist obloquy and abuse of aristocracy, began to endear itself to the people. During the five-year period, 1818-1823, the enrollment increased from 120 to 173, although the lack of facilities and accommodations, which was well-known throughout the State, may have been the cause of a decline in attendance to 157 the following year.[1] When the number began to rise the Trustees on December 22, 1818, took account of the shortage of rooms by authorizing the erection of the "second or remaining wing" of the University "as soon as possible," this building to be a duplicate of the other wing (Old East).[2] This second wing came in time to be called Old West. As building operations progressed but slowly, in part because of shortage of funds, the Trustees on December 11, 1819, gave the Building Committee the privilege of altering the plans and materials at their discretion and authorized them to borrow, when necessary, a "sum not to exceed $10,000 to be applied to the building."[3] Under President Caldwell's continued pressure, John Haywood for the Trustees recommended, December 14, 1821, a petition to the legislature to authorize with adequate security a "Loan or the borrowing of the Bank of this State to the Amount of Forty Thousand Dollars, for the purposes aforesaid."[4]

A serious objection to the execution of these plans was now made by the scientists recently (1818) imported from Yale College, Elisha Mitchell and Denison Olmsted, who pointed out that the facilities for the study of the physical sciences were virtually non-existent. With the support of the Faculty,

1. *T. M.*, 1841-1868, pp. 12-21.
2. *T. M.*, 1811-1822, p. 189.
3. *Ibid.*, pp. 202-3.
4. *Ibid.*, pp. 221-24.

Mitchell made an eloquent plea in behalf of an addition to the "South Building," the first storey of which might be given over to lodging rooms to be used also as recitation rooms, and the second storey used for a "Library and Philosophical Chamber."[5] Despite this petition the Trustees were not to be diverted from the responsibility of providing for the even more urgent needs in the matter of living space.

The old Capitol at Raleigh, built by Rodham (called and spelled "Rhody") Atkins, was found to be sadly in need of repairs in 1820; and Captain William Nichols of New York was appointed state architect, to supervise the work, and to add handsome porticos to east and west and a stately dome to the building. Nichols was a skilled architect; and he is best remembered today for the old Alabama State Capitol in Tuscaloosa, the Mississippi State Capitol, in which he collaborated with David Morrison and John Lawrence of Nashville, and the "elegant and sophisticated" Mississippi Governor's Mansion with its "unusually graceful Greek Corinthian porch."[6] The State Capitol was completed in 1822.

The University Trustees were much encouraged by the prospect of further sales of Tennessee lands; and on May 13, 1822, authorized the Building Committee to borrow $20,000 "for repairing the present & erecting new Buildings."[7] On July 24, 1822, the cornerstone of Old West Building was laid. On December 20, 1822, Duncan Cameron reported to the Board that the Building Committee had entered into various contracts, with William Nichols and others, for the erection of "said Building [Second Wing] & for repairing and enlarging the Old College Buildings & for other improvements. . . ."[8] In this same year the

5. *Ibid.*, p. 281. The Main Building is here for the first time termed "South Building" in the minutes.

6. Talbot Hamlin, *Greek Revival Architecture in America* (New York: Oxford University Press, 1944), pp. 256-57; David L. Swain, *Early Times in Raleigh* (Raleigh, 1867), pp. 8-9; K. P. Battle, *The Centennial Celebration of Raleigh* (Raleigh, 1893), pp. 36-37; Hope S. Chamberlain, *History of Wake County, N. C.* (Raleigh, 1922), pp. 106-9.

7. *T. M.*, 1811-1822, pp. 238-39. The Trustees later on borrowed $10,000 more, making a total of $40,000, as originally contemplated. Battle, I, 281.

8. *T. M.*, 1811-1822, p. 272.

Building Committee authorized Nichols to proceed with the building of a new chapel. Old West was occupied in July, 1823.

For the erection of Old West, the Trustees paid Nichols $26,-587.54, which included his fee of $1,000 and the costs of surveying and laying off some lots in Chapel Hill.[9] Unable to adopt a "pay as you go" policy, the Trustees made a contract with Nichols under which he assumed all the responsibility and the Trustees paid at their convenience. Probably because of the panic of 1825 Nichols was unable to fulfill his part of the contract; and eventually the Building Committee caused the work to be discontinued. The amount paid Nichols during the years 1826 and 1827 totaled $22,017.88.[10] In the final settlement, the payments were recorded as specifically for "Labor and material in repairing President's House, Steward's Hall, getting timber, making bricks and building new Chapel, taking down cupola from the South Building, repairing roof and building belfry."[11] The cupola was not replaced for over thirty years. The bricks for these buildings erected under Nichols' supervision were burnt at the old brickyard which was located south of the old athletic field, near Rock Spring, later known as Brickyard Spring, which was on Brickyard Branch. The large room in the middle of the south side, first floor South Building, was designed for a chapel and called Prayer Hall. A floor was thrown above Prayer Hall, which was converted into a chemical laboratory, and the rooms above made into a library and lecture-room, called the Philosophical Chamber, for the President and Professor of Rhetoric.[12]

During the five-year period, 1827-1832, the new Chapel remained unfinished and unused. In despair over raising funds from any source other than public subscription, the Trustees

9. Battle, I, 282, 297-98.
10. *Ibid.*, I, 826.
11. The belfry, a slender wooden structure, stood some forty yards north of the South Building and half-way between the Old East and Old West buildings. It was burned down in 1856; and the question, "Who burned the belfry?" in later years often put in solemn and menacing tones to the Negro janitors, remains unanswered satisfactorily to this day. The burning of the belfry was generally regarded as a prank of the students. This slim structure may be discerned in the view of the Campus in Battle, I, facing p. 632. See Battle, I, 653, for description of the incident.
12. Battle, I, 281-82, 555.

on June 20, 1832, appointed a committee to raise the necessary money to complete the building; and Professor William de B. Hooper was designated to receive contributions. The preparatory house, or Grammar School, which had been abandoned for thirteen years, was ordered to be sold, the proceeds to go toward the completion of the new Chapel.[13] Other possible sources of income were looked into, especially the Gerrard bequest. Major Charles Gerrard of Edgecombe, a native of Carteret, in 1797 bequeathed to the University upwards of 14,000 acres of land, specifying that one tract to which he attached a sentimental consideration should forever remain the property of the University. This tract of 2,560 acres which as a lieutenant he received as a grant from North Carolina was located by him in 1783 at the junction of Yellow Creek with the Cumberland River, not far below the city of Nashville. The tract lay within the claim purchased of the Cherokee tribe of Indians by the Transylvania Company at the Sycamore Shoals of the Watauga River in Tennessee, March 14-17, 1775.

Charles Gerrard was a member of the North Carolina Society of the Cincinnati. The title of major he acquired after the Revolution. In a published obituary occurs the following characterization: "He served in the revolutionary war against Great Britain from beginning to end, and as a soldier was brave, active, persevering. His character as a citizen, husband, father, friend and neighbour was justly admired by all who knew him; and it may truly be said that he carried with him to his grave the regard of all his acquaintances."[14]

For thirty-five years the Trustees regarded the wish expressed by Gerrard in his will as sacred; but when the appeal for funds

13. *T. M.*, 1823-1840, p. 221. See Chapter 4.

14. *The North-Carolina Journal* (Halifax), October 16, 1797. Charles Gerrard died October 4, 1797, at the house of William Arrington, near Nash County Court House. During his last three years he was "most dreadfully afflicted with a dropsy." He bequeathed 640 acres of land in Carteret County "to be rented annually for the benefit of the poor in that county." It appears that he was married but childless at the time of his death. The greater proportion of his lands, 11,364 acres, was left to the University of North Carolina with the proviso that "the Trustees will be at liberty to sell [said lands] at the end of seven years, when they [said lands] will very probably command 40,000 dollars."

to complete the new Chapel yielded inconsiderable results, a committee was appointed by the Trustees to examine into the legal status of Gerrard's wish, in order to discover whether they were compelled to abide by it. In 1833 two able lawyers and judges, William Gaston and George E. Badger, rendered the opinion that the Board had the right to sell this "service tract," despite the testator's wish. The Trustees, as Battle puts it, "after losses from the neglect and perfidy of agents and the onerous charges of taxes, while the black cloud of debt hung over the institution . . . concluded with sorrow to authorize its sale."[15] The resolution adopted by them and subsequently carried into effect reads as follows:

WHEREAS, The Trustees of the University of North Carolina have been compelled to direct a sale of a valuable tract of land, bequeathed by Major Charles Gerrard, with the request that the same might be perpetually retained by the University; and

WHEREAS, they are solicitous not only to manifest their own sense of the liberality of the donor, but as far as may be practicable to perpetuate its remembrance;

Resolved, Therefore that $2,000, part of the purchase money of said land shall be applied to the finishing of the new Hall at the University, and that the same shall be called by the name of "Gerrard Hall."[16]

The tract of 2,560 acres, particularly valued for its supposed fertility, brought only $6,400, the sale being effected by Colonel William Polk; and the iron deposits upon it, thought to be rich, proved to be of slight value.[17]

It was not until 1835 that the Trustees had the necessary funds in hand to justify further building operations. On May 22 of that year, the Executive Committee of the Board ordered that immediate steps be taken for the completion of Gerrard Hall.[18] On January 6, 1836, Professor Elisha Mitchell was directed by the same committee to order lumber to be delivered in Chapel

15. *U. N. C. C.*, p. 24.
16. *T. M.*, 1823-1840, p. 230. No report from Professor W. de B. Hooper of the results of the campaign to raise funds is available.
17. Battle, I, 350-51.
18. *E. C. T. M.*, 1835-1873, p. 13.

Hill for this purpose.[19] The structure was completed in time for the holding within its walls of the Commencement exercises of 1837, May 31, June 1-3; and it was described in the *Raleigh Register*, by a correspondent covering the story of that event, as a "commodious building, with large galleries, just completed with becoming taste and good style." In the flowery language of the period the reporter continues: "It is the first young budding of fame to a collegian, to see an ocean of bonnets and ribbons, and the banks of snowy gauze waving and rustling at his appearance, as if the gentle south wind had breathed on a wheat field; but it is the full bloom of popularity, if, when he retires, he shall see the ocean toss with emotion that rolls beneath its surface."

According to the original design, Gerrard Hall was to be a very simple, rectangular brick building, with no portico or ornamental doorways. While the building was in course of construction, Elisha Mitchell, an amateur road builder very proud of his engineering talents, had a prophetic vision of the University's development. He proposed to the Trustees that the road from Raleigh enter the Campus through present Emerson Field and then divide, one branch running south of Gerrard Hall and entering Cameron Avenue between present Phillips and Peabody buildings, the other passing by Old East in a northwesterly direction and entering present Franklin Street somewhat to the west of the present Battle-Vance-Pettigrew dormitories. With the engineer's "eye for ground" and perhaps a prevision of the South Quadrangle development three-quarters of a century later, Mitchell presented his plan so forcefully that it was endorsed by the Trustees.

Gerrard Hall was the plainest of brick structures, with an unattractive hip-roof, the eaves barely projecting beyond the walls, plain rectangular windows, and doors at the east front which were mere openings in the wall. Because of the proposed new highway, the Trustees decided to have Gerrard Hall face to the south; and the services of a skilled architect were required to draft plans for a remodeled structure with southern exposure. At this time the beautiful (second) State Capitol in Raleigh, designed by Alexander Jackson Davis, partner of Ithiel Town in

19. *Ibid.*, p. 33.

the great New York architectural firm of Town and Davis, and erected under the direction of David Paton, a young Scotsman, draftsman and architect, was nearing completion.[20] Davis, a meticulous and talented draftsman, a versatile designer, and already famous as a leading spirit in the Greek Revival of architecture in the United States, was engaged to undertake the work of remodeling Gerrard Hall. Beauty, simplicity, even austerity characterized the tetrastyle Greek portico, constructed on the south side of the severe assembly hall, with its massive Ionic columns and a hip-roof of the same height as that of the building itself. There were four doors, one each at east and west ends; and larger doors in the middle of north and south walls. The portico, according to Davis, was completed in 1844.[21]

Singularly enough, Mitchell's plan "back-fired" and had unfortunate consequences, architecturally, more than half a century later. The merchants of Chapel Hill, few in number though they were, together with the wagoners who engaged in a cross-country trade and dealt directly with the business houses on Franklin Street, did not petition the Trustees against the proposed roads; but they engaged in a quiet campaign of opposition, on the ground that their trade would be seriously impaired if traffic were diverted from Franklin Street to a large avenue designed to run south of Gerrard Hall. This unobtrusive but vigorous campaign proved effective, and Mitchell's road-making

20. Unquestionably the designs for the second North Carolina State Capitol were the work of A. J. Davis, although almost exclusive credit is erroneously attributed by Ashe to Paton, who superintended the execution of the work (1834-1839). Consult Talbot Faulkner Hamlin, "Alexander Jackson Davis," *Dictionary of American Biography* (New York, 1930), V, 103-4; S. A. Ashe, "David Paton: Architect of the North Carolina State Capitol," Bulletin No. 4, *Publications of the N. C. Historical Commission* (Raleigh, 1909).

21. Battle makes no mention of Davis as the designer of the portico. A picture of Gerrard Hall showing the portico may be found in this volume. Gerrard Hall still bears upon its east face a marble tablet with the inscription:

GERRARD HALL

1822

To do justly and to love mercy and to walk
humbly with thy God

plans were discarded. But by this time the Greek portico was already a *fait accompli;* and visitors were astonished to observe that Gerrard Hall was "facing the wrong way."[22]

In 1878-1879, through the generosity of David G. Worth of Wilmington, the interior of Gerrard Hall was remodeled, numbered pews replacing uncomfortable benches; and the nave, called the "bull-pen," passed into the limbo of the forgotten. In 1900-1901, Gerrard Hall was re-roofed and renovated, and the portico removed. The building was condemned for public use in 1935; but in 1938-1939 it was remodeled to serve the purposes of a small auditorium, seating 476 people. The cost of remodeling, part of a grant secured from the United States Government, was $24,534.35; and the general contractor was H. F. Mitchell, Jr.[23]

Prior to 1900-1901 the north and south doorways of Gerrard Hall had been walled up. An intention to erect a new portico at the east end was voiced by some of the Trustees; but this intention was never carried into execution. Viewed in the perspective of later plans for Campus development and the opening of the South Quadrangle and contiguous areas as a new building zone, a plan suggested by A. J. Davis as long ago as 1847, it appears that actually Gerrard Hall was "facing the right way," as is also the South Building, with its massive portico added in 1926.

Architectural fitness and landscape requirements dictate the restoration of the portico in precise replica of the original. The miniature scale of the Old Chapel (Person Hall) and its unsuitable location were the first architectural blunders of the University's early planners. In the light of present-day plans for future Campus development, the removal of the portico of Gerrard Hall now appears as another blunder. The restoration of the portico, the extension of the roof eaves, and the addition of artistic doorways at east and west would transform the build-

22. Mrs. Spencer, mistakenly it seems, attributed the facing of Gerrard Hall towards the south to President Caldwell. S. P. I., May 21, 1869.

23. Battle, II, 178-79, 595-96; *T. M.*, 1931-1938, pp. 274 ff.; 1938-1941, p. 62. The grant referred to was made to aid in financing the construction of additions, alterations, and repairs to Bynum Gymnasium, Alumni Building, Gerrard Hall, and Caldwell Hall.

ing into a memorable structure worthy of indefinite preservation.[24]

During the past century and more, Gerrard Hall has been the
scene of almost every conceivable type of public occasion and
celebration: Commencements; college prayers and religious services, including baptisms; speeches and orations by famous per-
sonages and orators, including Presidents Polk, Buchanan, and
Woodrow Wilson (before becoming president), Secretaries
Jacob Thompson, William H. Seward, John Y. Mason, Post-
master-General Alexander W. Randall, and others too numerous
to mention; academic lectures, single and in series, by scholars
great and not so great; humorists and public entertainers of all
sorts, musical, dramatic, and what not; Phi Beta Kappa orations;
student mass meetings and "pep rallies"; Faculty, alumni, and
Trustees' meetings; college classes; Summer School gatherings;
teachers' institutes; etc., etc. Gerrard Hall yielded place, as the
scene of Commencement exercises, to the combined gymnasium
and commons hall after its erection in 1885.[25]

Early in 1841, prior to entering upon the campaign for re-
election, Governor James Knox Polk of Tennessee, class of
1818, who entertained the warmest affection for his alma mater,

24. In the original building, the pillars supporting the galleries were
too spindling and too far apart; and following an alarm during the 1846
Commencement that the galleries were falling, which proved to be false,
these pillars were replaced by more substantial supports. The acoustic
properties of Gerrard Hall are as nearly perfect as possible. In the original seating arrangement, there was located in the centre of the hall a
nave about 18 feet square which the students irreverently called the
"bull-pen." This consisted of a semi-circular row of benches with backs
so high that only the heads of the persons seated therein could be seen
from the rear. Distinguished guests and speakers were seated in the "bull-
pen," which accommodated about forty persons. A narrow passageway
connected the "bull-pen" with the speakers' stand, located at the west
end of the hall. Occasionally the students would fasten a patient bull
yearling in the nave; and perhaps from such incident the nave derived
its common name. Link, p. 39; Battle, I, 454, 468.
25. During more recent years such exercises have for the most part
been held in Memorial Hall, alternating with open-air exercises, both
University Day and Commencement, weather permitting, held in Kenan
Stadium. In the latter were held many public exercises and military
reviews during the second World War.

announced his intention to attend the Commencement exercises the coming June. Mr. Polk's plan for attending the 1841 Commencement was not realized, doubtless because of his activity in the gubernatorial campaign. Following his inauguration on March 4, 1845, as President of the United States, the Trustees voted to confer upon James Knox Polk and his Secretary of the Navy, John Young Mason, a Virginian and graduate of the University of North Carolina, class of 1816, the honorary degree of Doctor of Laws; and these degrees were conferred *in absentia* at the Commencement in 1845. In his urgent invitation to President and Mrs. Polk and Mr. John Y. Mason to be his house-guests at the Commencement of 1847, President Swain observed:

Although we have never met on any occasion, your whole course of life from the time you entered college has been known to me with a particularity that you would scarcely have anticipated even from a native of North Carolina, nurtured upon the borders of Tennessee, five and twenty years ago the room-mate in college and in after years the familiar friend of your brother Marshall. Under such circumstances I feel that I have almost a right to consider you an acquaintance and friend, and at all events venture to hope that in the course of a few weeks there will exist no reasonable doubt on either hand.[26]

On learning of the coming visit of President Polk and his party to Chapel Hill, the Trustees were thrown into quite a dither on account of manifest unpreparedness to receive such distinguished guests and the dingy appearance of University buildings and residences. The following resolutions were accordingly passed by the Executive Committee of the Board of Trustees, April 21, 1847:

1. That the college buildings be rewashed with a coat of Hydraulic cement and the doors, windows, posts and sills be repainted.
2. That Girard Hall be enlarged by the construction of additional Galleries, Pews, and Seats according to the plan proposed by the faculty.

26. David L. Swain Papers, Southern Historical Collection, University of North Carolina. Swain to Polk, April 24, 1847. In the Swain Papers also is a long letter concerning plans for President Polk's reception from Governor William A. Graham to Swain, Raleigh, March 27, 1847.

3. That the 4 dwelling houses owned by the University and occupied by the President and 3 professors be repainted.

4. That President Swain and Professor Green be appointed a Committee to cause the improvements to be made.[27]

The visit of President Polk rendered the Commencement exercises of 1847 the most notable up to that time in the University's history. To this day it remains unique as the only occasion of the visit of a University alumnus who had attained the office of the nation's chief magistrate. Excerpts from President Polk's diary give a graphic picture of the scenes and events of that occasion.[28]

Monday, 31st May, 1847. At nine o'clock this morning I set out [from Raleigh] with my family and suite for Chapel Hill. . . .[29] At about six [five] P. M. I reached the village of Chapel Hill. On approaching the hotel at which quarters had been provided for me, I was received by a procession comprised of the faculty and students of the college and citizens. I was conducted into the hotel by Professor Green and the committee of students who had met me at Raleigh, and after a few minutes was conducted on foot to the college chapel [Gerrard Hall], where a large assembly of ladies and gentlemen were collected. I was addressed by the Hon. D. L. Swain,

---

27. *E. C. T. M.*, 1853-1873, p. 133. Over a period of years the name "Gerrard" was misspelled "Girard" by the University authorities, owing to the confusion of the identity of Major Charles Gerrard of North Carolina with Stephen Girard, the Philadelphia philanthropist who endowed and gave the name to Girard College. A legend that Gerrard Hall was originally built to be a temple of free speech and a forum of free discussion still survives. Its origin was perhaps due to the same confusion of names, Stephen Girard being notorious as a free thinker. For a considerable period, printed programs, fly-sheets, and catalogues displayed the spelling: "Girard Hall."

28. Quaife, Milo Milton, ed., *The Diary of James K. Polk, during his Presidency, 1845 to 1849* (Chicago, McClurg, 1910), 4 vols. Published for the Chicago Historical Society, in whose collections the original manuscript is preserved.

29. President Polk was accompanied by his wife, her niece, Miss Rucker, Colonel Walker, his private secretary, Judge Mason, his son, John Y. Mason, Jr., his daughter Betty, and Lieutenant Matthew F. Maury of the United States Navy. The delegation from Faculty and students which met President Polk and party at Raleigh and accompanied them to Chapel Hill consisted of Professor William Mercer Green and students William M. Howerton, William H. Manly, Robert H. Winborne, and John Pool.

the President of the College, tendering to me a cordial welcome on my return to the classic shades of the University. I briefly responded to his address. President Swain also addressed Judge Mason, who made a short reply. I was then introduced to the Trustees who were present, to the faculty and many of the students, as well as to many others, ladies and gentlemen. . . . After supper I attended the chapel and heard a sermon preached by Bishop Levi Silliman Ives of the Episcopal Church to the students.

The story continues with further extracts from President Polk's diary:

Tuesday, 1st June, 1847. . . . As soon as I rose this morning I found a large crowd at the hotel desiring to see me. After breakfast I visited the college buildings. They have been greatly enlarged and improved since my days at college. . . . The old chapel [Person Hall] I found had been converted into recitation rooms, and for the use of Trustees when they attended the University. . . . After night I attended the Chapel and heard several members of the sophomore and freshman classes recite speeches which they had committed to memory. . . .[30]

Wednesday, 2nd June, 1847. . . . At eleven o'clock A. M. I attended the chapel and heard Mr. [James W.] Osborne of Charlotte deliver a literary address to the two societies of the college. . . .

Thursday, 3rd June, 1847. . . . This was the commencement day of the college. . . . Hundreds from the adjoining country had come in. As soon as I left my room in the morning I was surrounded by them, and except while at breakfast, continued to receive them and to shake hands with them until the hour at which the commencement exercises commenced. . . . between ten and eleven o'clock. About one o'clock the President announced there would be a recess of one and a half hours. I returned to the hotel and took dinner. The crowd in waiting to see me was so great that it was impossible that they could all see me if I remained in the house. Several of my friends who thought the people present, many of whom had come a considerable distance, ought to be gratified, insisted that I should go out to the grove, and I did so. I was soon surrounded by hundreds of persons, and for an hour or more was constantly engaged in shaking hands with them. At the appointed hour the commencement

30. Before leaving the University in 1818, Polk voiced his condemnation of platform speakers who failed to make adequate preparation, and pointed out the injurious effect of delivering by rote speeches written and memorized in advance of delivery. "Eloquence," *U. N. C. M.*, XXXIII (1902), 1-10.

exercises were again commenced. I attended. They were concluded and the degree of bachelor of arts conferred on thirty-seven young gentlemen, and the whole ceremony closed about half past five o'clock P. M.

Saturday, 5th June, 1847.—Proceeding on our journey [from Richmond] we arrived at Washington about 5 o'clock P. M. and thus ended my excursion to the University of North Carolina. It was an exceedingly agreeable one. . . . My reception at the University, and the attentions paid me on the route going and returning, was all that I could have desired it to be.

My visit was wholly unconnected with politics, and all parties greeted and welcomed me in the most cordial manner.[31]

During his college days, according to reliable testimony, Polk performed all the upwards of five thousand duties required of him: "never missed a recitation nor omitted the punctilious performance of any duty." He was an assiduous student; and on graduation achieved the rare distinction of winning first honors in both mathematics and the classics. During his stay in Chapel Hill in 1847, as he records in his diary, he revisited the room which he occupied while a student here, in the southwest corner, third floor, South Building. The Negro servant, Benny Booth, nicknamed "Brick Top" because of the hardness of his cranium, waited upon him during his student days. At the commencement of 1847 it was observed that the President's countenance was lined by labor, strain, and suffering. He was universally applauded for his "total absence of ostentation, his sincere and unassuming courtesy." Mrs. Polk was "pronounced by all classes to be peculiarly fascinating."

The greatest tribute to President Polk upon this visit was that paid by the proprietor of the Eagle Hotel, a woman of striking personality, warm heart, and wide popularity, Miss Nancy Segur Hilliard. She erected an addition to her hotel for the express purpose of entertaining and accommodating President Polk and his cortège. Over the entrance facing on Franklin Street was a metal plate with the following hospitable inscription which

31. Quaife, *op. cit.* Cf. also Allan Nevins, ed., *Polk: The Diary of a President, 1845-1849* (New York, 1929). Polk's diary was not consulted by Battle nor did he print the speeches of Swain and Polk.

upon his arrival greeted the eye of the chief officer of the Republic:

Erected To Receive

Pres. Polk

On The Occasion of His

Visit To His Alma Mater.

This plate remained in place until the burning of the University Inn, November 30, 1921. It is jealously preserved in the University archives.[32]

32. For a picture of the burning building see *Alumni Review*, X (1922), 134.

DAVID LOWRIE SWAIN

President of the University, 1835-1868. During his administration he sponsored an active program of Campus beautification. At his recommendation the Trustees in 1839 appropriated $3,000 for the improvement of Campus and buildings. He was the first to conceive of the idea of using the plentiful rocks in Chapel Hill to construct rock walls around the Campus. It was he who was responsible for the University's obtaining the services of Alexander Jackson Davis as supervising building and landscape architect. And during Swain's presidency the University for the first time employed a landscape gardener as a University official. After the oil portrait by William Garl Browne owned by Mr. Tyn Cobb, Orlando, Florida.

ELISHA MITCHELL

For forty years (1818-1857) he served the University in such varied
capacities as mathematician, physicist, botanist, chemist, mineralogist,
geologist, surveyor, engineer, road-builder, agriculturist, professor, preacher, acting-president, bursar, and superintendent of buildings and
grounds. He worked closely with President Swain in the latter's program
of Campus beautification, making valuable suggestions as well as taking
an active part in the work. From the portrait by Nathaniel Jocelyn.

10

THE ASTRONOMICAL OBSERVATORIES

P RESIDENT CALDWELL, who was well abreast of the scientific progress of the age in mathematics, engineering, and astronomy, deserves to rank high as a pioneer in astronomical science in America. In a report addressed to the Trustees in February, 1823, a document of the first importance in the history of higher learning in America, Caldwell recommended first, the purchase of standard works and classic treatises to furnish the nucleus of a great collection of books for a university library. "A Professor in a college without books in tolerable supply," he sagely observed, "is analogous to the creation of nobility, which for want of estate is obliged to live in rags." In the second place, he recommended the purchase of scientific instruments without which it was impossible to carry on effectively study and research in Natural, sometimes called Experimental, Philosophy. In particular he mentioned the need for "an Astronomical Clock, a Transit Instrument, and an Astronomical Telescope." In view of the relative cheapness of books in England and on the Continent as compared to the same works purchased in America, and the necessity for careful inspection of scientific apparatus at the makers' establishments, he generously proposed the making of a trip to Europe for these purposes, at his own expense. He considered that he would be adequately compensated for the expense and labors of such a trip, by "personal improvement and accession of strength in regard to the affairs of the University." Although funds for such a purpose were not available, the Trustees were fired by Caldwell's fervor and enthusiasm to borrow "on the credit of the University Six Thousand Dollars to be placed at the disposal of the President of the University for the purchase of Philosophical Apparatus and additions to the Library."[1] No provision was made for paying Caldwell's expenses; but the decision taken by

1. *T. M.*, 1823-1835. December 13, 1823.

the Trustees was a long step forward towards assuring the progress of University studies.[2]

President Caldwell left Chapel Hill in the late spring of 1824, and was gone for almost a year, visiting the British Isles and making a tour of the Continent. In London he devoted almost a month to visiting libraries and educational institutions, booksellers and instrument-makers. The astronomical instruments purchased by Caldwell were: a Meridian Transit Telescope and an Altitude and Azimuth Telescope, both made by Simms of London; a Telescope "for observations on the earth and sky," made by Dollond of London; an Astronomical clock with a Mercurial Pendulum, made by Robert Molyneux of London; a portable Reflecting Circle, made by Harris of London; a sextant and a Hadley's quadrant, both made by Wilkinson of London.[3] The total amount expended for philosophical apparatus, which included electrical instruments,[4] was $3,361.35; and the sum expended for books, 979 volumes, was $3,234.74. Additional expenditures were: $9 for minerals, and $632.92 for boxing, packing, transportation, and exchange. The sum total of expenditures exceeded the amount appropriated by $1,238.06; and this extra cost, which Caldwell paid, was refunded by the Trustees.

2. It should be recalled that more than thirty years earlier the committee of the Trustees consisting of Samuel Eusebius McCorkle, chairman, David Stone, Alfred Moore, Samuel Ashe, John Hay, and Hugh Williamson, appointed to report a plan of education, recommended the purchase of "apparatus for Experimental Philosophy and Astronomy," enumerating among scientific instruments a telescope and quadrant. T. M., 1789-1810, p. 58. December 3, 1792.

3. "Astronomical Observatory at the University of North Carolina," The University Monthly, IV (October, 1884), 4-7. This article, unsigned, was written by Professor Charles Phillips. It is historically important to recall that twenty years earlier, sixteen ladies of New Bern presented to the University, "for the use of the Philosophical Class, a Quadrant, the best we could procure," as stated in a letter to President Caldwell, November 26, 1803. Battle, I, 131-32.

4. The philosophical apparatus, in addition to the items mentioned above, were: "a 3-foot plate electrical machine, a joint discharger, a powder house, a diamond spotted jar, one universal discharger, and a 12-inch convex mirror in blackened frame." The "diamond spotted jar" was a Leyden Jar covered with tin foil cut in diamond shape. There actually are preserved here two mirrors, one convex, the other concave; and these bear a paper label with the name: "W. & S. Jones, No. 30, opposite Furnival's Inn, Holborn, London."

Caldwell's services in the cause of science and literature were highly appreciated by the Trustees; and the students resolved to give him a rousing welcome upon his return. The scene has been graphically described by an eye-witness. "A brilliant illumination—the first and only one ever made in these buildings—was resolved on and it was an entire success. Well do I recall the splendor of that night and the procession of the students to his residence and his stepping out upon the floor of the back piazza —the cheer after cheer that was given to the dear old man. Falling into line, the march back to the college was commenced, and on our arrival at the front door of the South Building the President was escorted to a stand near the well, from which he addressed the students and the entire village population with the affection of a long-absent father, for he was indeed full of feeling, and it was with difficulty he could give utterance to his words. He was escorted back to his modest home, and the impression prevailed that it was the happiest day of his life—the consummation of his supreme joy."[5]

Upon the roof of his modest dwelling, which stood east of the present president's house and on the same lot, Caldwell built a platform, surrounded by a railing, and "here he would sit, night after night, pointing out to the Seniors, taken in squads of three or four, the outlines of the Constellations and their principal stars, and the highway of the planets and the moon."[6] Still standing, in the rear of the lot on which the President's house now stands and to the east of the residence, in a fair state of preservation, are the two brick pillars which he built in his garden, the "east and west faces carefully ground into the same plane," marking the true meridian.[7] Nearby stood a stone pillar, about

5. Address of Paul C. Cameron at the Alumni Banquet, June 5, 1889, *Centennial Celebration* (published by the Alumni Association, 1889), pp. 30-31.

6. Charles Phillips, "Astronomical Observatory at the University of North Carolina," *loc. cit.*, p. 7.

7. Through the generosity of James Lee Love, class of 1884, these pillars have been fully restored, and a tablet placed nearby, bearing the inscription: "Meridian pillars built by Joseph Caldwell, President of the University of North Carolina, 1804-1812, 1816-1835, shortly after his return from a trip to England in 1824-1825 for the procurement of Astronomical Instruments and Books."

five feet high, bearing upon its top a sundial; but this sundial was appropriated by Sherman's "bummers" during their occupation of Chapel Hill in April–May, 1865.

The Library of the University, which was also President Caldwell's study, was on the second storey of the South Building. In this room, Caldwell installed following their arrival from London during the years 1825 and 1826, the astronomical clock and meridian transit; and here, during the period, 1827-1831, began the "first systematic observations upon the heavens made in the United States."[8] Says the son of one of the observers: "With this Clock and this Transit in this room, Dr. Caldwell, assisted by Professors Mitchell and Phillips, attained the first approximate values for the Longitude and the Latitude of the South Building—values still [1884] used in all Geographical and Meteorological observations at the University. The writer of this paper well remembers seeing the manuscript records of these earliest observations, containing their dates and the calculations based on them. . . . An end of the wooden beam that supported the telescope can still be seen, embedded in the southern wall of that room. . . ."[9]

The astronomical instruments could be of only limited usefulness in the Library, because of the lack of slits in the wall, to permit of a large arc for the revolution of the telescope in a vertical plane. As the Trustees took no steps to house the instruments, Caldwell in 1830 decided to build an observatory for the University at his own expense.[10] The foundations were laid in April,

8. Collier Cobb, "Some Beginnings in Science," *Appleton's Popular Science Monthly*, XLIX (1896), 763-71. But see *infra*.

9. Charles Phillips, "Astronomical Observatory," *loc. cit.*, p. 5. Professor James Phillips determined the latitude of Chapel Hill, giving it to be 35° 54′ 22″. "Meteorological Observations at Chapel Hill (1844-1859)," *Journal Elisha Mitchell Scientific Society*, I (1884), 35-37. With instruments borrowed from the United States Geological Survey, namely a portable transit, Zenith telescope and a chronometer, Professor J. W. Gore in 1884 determined the latitude to be 35° 54′ 18″. 57 north. "Latitude of Chapel Hill," *ibid.*, II (1885), 32-33.

10. Battle, I, 336. See also *T. M.*, 1823-1835, p. 254. December 5, 1835. On January 10, 1835, the Executive Committee of the Board of Trustees resolved "that the Treasurer of the Board be authorized and directed to pay to Dr. Joseph Caldwell the sum of Four Hundred and Ninety-four dollars and seventy-one cents ($494 71/100) to reimburse him the Cash

1831; and the building, which began to be erected in March, 1832, was completed in August of that year.[11]

The observatory erected by President Caldwell stood north of the village cemetery, less than 200 yards northwest of the entrance.[12] It was located in a grove of cedars, on the highest spot in the immediate neighborhood. The trees all around were cleared away, to enable the telescope to have a complete sweep of the horizon. The building was 15 by 23 feet and 25 feet high with a door at the northern end of its eastern face and a window in each of its eastern and western faces. "The house had a high basement of stone on which rested walls of brick, ending in a low parapet. . . . Through the center of this single-roomed building arose a pillar of masonry which rested on an independent foundation, and bore on its top the Altitude and Azimuth

---

expended in the erection of the Observatory and in enclosing the said Grave Yard [burying grounds at Chapel Hill]." The cost of enclosing the graveyard was $64.41½, leaving $430.29½ for the observatory.

11. James Lee Love, "The First College Astronomical Observatory in the United States, at the University of North Carolina; and its Founder, Dr. Joseph Caldwell." This article, written after June 25, 1888, was never published; but it furnished the basis for a printed article by Dr. Love, "The First College Observatory in the United States," *The Sidereal Messenger*, VII (1888), 417-20. The use of this manuscript by the writer was permitted by Dr. Love, who derived his information from Professor Charles Phillips, President K. P. Battle, and others. The printed article, cited above, bears the legend: "Chapel Hill, North Carolina, October 31, 1888." The first known historical account of the astronomical observatory was prepared by Professor William B. Phillips; and, in his absence, was read by President Battle before the Elisha Mitchell Scientific Society on May 3, 1884. This paper gave an "account of the observations taken there by Drs. Caldwell, Mitchell and [James] Phillips during the few years that the building was in existence." No trace of this paper has been discovered. At this meeting Dr. Charles Phillips, according to a contemporary newspaper account, "told a racy anecdote about Dr. Caldwell's astronomical instructions"; and the loss of this anecdote, as the only "racy" one ever told of Dr. Caldwell, is particularly regrettable. For contemporary accounts of this meeting of the Elisha Mitchell Scientific Society, consult correspondence of the *News and Observer*, Raleigh, May 6 and 8, 1884.

12. As late as 1907, long before the hill was leveled for the tennis court area, the site of the observatory was readily identified, from the weathered brickbats and the sunken basement, surrounded by a fringe of cedars.

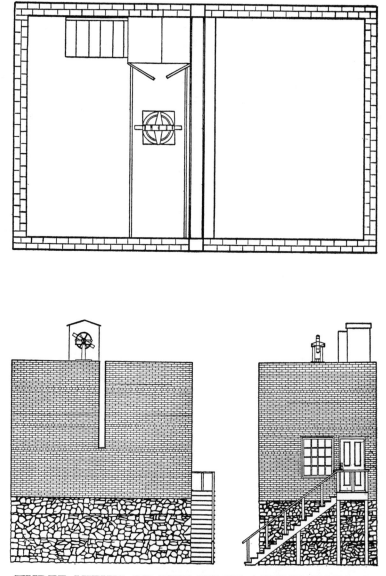

THREE VIEWS OF THE FIRST ASTRONOMICAL OBSERVATORY

Upper drawing is top view of the observatory, looking down upon the altitude and azimuth telescope. At lower left, south side of observatory, showing the telescope with pillar beyond. At lower right, east side of observatory, pillar to right of telescope. From drawings by Professor Ralph M. Trimble. For a description of the observatory, see pp. 101-4.

Instrument. The slit through the northern and southern faces and through the flat top of the house afforded a vertical range of 180 degrees for the Transit [which stood on a pillar inside the building]. The Altitude and Azimuth Telescope stood on a circular disk of sandstone which capped the [another] pillar. It was protected from the weather by a slight structure of wood which was drawn forwards and backwards, on a railway in the plane of the Meridian by a windlass and rope. . . . The pillar which supported it was built so that in the main and only room of the Observatory, it afforded a shoulder on which stood the supports of the Transit. The Astronomical clock was fastened to the eastern wall of this room."[13]

The pillar of masonry, referred to above, extended above the flat roof which served as an upper floor. At one side of the room rose a steep stairway which led through a trap door to the

13. Charles Phillips, "Astronomical Observatory," *loc. cit.*, p. 6.

INTERIOR OF THE FIRST ASTRONOMICAL OBSERVATORY

In the center, resting on the shoulder of the brick pillar, is the transit telescope. At right is the astronomical clock, which is now standing in the President's office in South Building. From a drawing by Professor Ralph M. Trimble.

top of the house. The first eight feet of the walls of the observatory were of stone, plastered inside and out, and enclosed a low basement slightly excavated. Above this the walls were of brick, terminating in a low parapet around the top. Another pillar rose up through the interior, terminating just above the first floor and bearing the transit instrument. Shutters were constructed to close up the slit, which afforded a wide range for the transit, when the latter was not in use.[14]

The transit instrument had a 3-inch aperture and a 44-inch focal length. The altitude and azimuth instrument had a 2½-inch aperture and a 33-inch focal length. Its horizontal and vertical circles were 20 and 24 inches in diameter, respectively, with two verniers and reading microscopes to each. These circles were graduated on platinum bands to five minutes of arc. The telescope was a small portable one of 2¾-inch aperture and 52-inch focal length. It had a 46-inch wooden barrel, painted red. The Hadley's quadrant had a scale of only 45° and a simple line of sight. The astronomical clock, with mercurial pendulum, is made of brass, with cabinet of mahogany, 6½ feet high with a 20-inch base, a 14" x 20" hood, and a 12-inch painted face. There was also an Armillary Sphere manufactured by W. & S. Jones, makers of Philosophical, Mathematical, and Optical Instruments, at the Archimedes, No. 30, Lower Holborn, London, nearly opposite Furnival's Inn.[15]

14. Two early efforts to represent pictorially the observatory have been made. The little sketch, drawn from a description by John H. Watson, Mayor of Chapel Hill, and reproduced in Collier Cobb's article, cited above, clearly does not conform, in fundamental details, with the descriptions by eye-witnesses, quoted above. The drawings, preserved here in the Physics Department, are somewhat nearer to an actual representation of the observatory; but the designs are conjectural rather than authentic reproductions of the interior and exterior of the building. The drawings executed by Professor R. M. Trimble of the Department of Mathematics are based on the description of the observatory by an eye-witness, Dr. Charles Phillips.

15. It is presumed that the instruments lost in transit from London to Chapel Hill, which are enumerated in the original order, were the sextant and the portable reflecting circle. The instruments mentioned above are still owned by the University and in a good state of preservation, except that the lenses of the transit are missing, having been carried off in 1865, it is said, by Sherman's "bummers." The astronomical clock stands in the President's office; and a sketch of it, by E. L. Harris,

The first astronomical observations were conducted, as already seen, in the Library, which served as President Caldwell's study, on the second floor of the South Building. It is known that the observers obtained the latitude and longitude of the South Building, the figures being 35° 54′ 21″ N. and 79° 17′ W., respectively. During the period from August, 1832, until President Caldwell's death, January 27, 1835, observations were made at the observatory. Owing to the declining health of the President, little was accomplished during the latter part of the time. "Observations were made at this place, with these instruments," records Dr. Charles Phillips, "by Dr. Caldwell and Dr. [James] Phillips, and Dr. Mitchell, observations for Longitude and for Latitude, and on Eclipses, and on Comets."[16] Not long before his death, President Caldwell urged the purchase of a large telescope costing about $1,200, in order to make astronomical observations more precise and permanently valuable than those afforded by the telescope then owned by the University; but his death ended these ambitious plans.[17] As a child Charles Phillips was frequently present when his father, Dr. James Phillips, made observations; and he is the principal source of information regarding the observatory and the work done there.[18] Unfortunately the records of these observations have been lost; and there is little likelihood that they escaped destruction during the investment of the village by Federal troops in 1865. An amusing story is narrated by Dr. Charles Phillips in this connection:

The last observation in which old Meridian Transit was used was made by the Yankee soldiers. . . . The old telescope was lying on a shelf in what was then "The Philosophical Room," now [1884] Professor Hooper's Greek room. It was covered thickly with dust,

---

is found in Cobb's article, *loc. cit.*, p. 7. The other instruments are in the custody of the Physics Department. Professor Otto Stuhlman supplied the description of the instruments and their condition at the present time. See also J. L. Love, "The First College Observatory in the United States," *The Sidereal Messenger;* Battle, I, 291-95, 334-36.

16. Charles Phillips, "Astronomical Observatory," *loc. cit.*, p. 6.

17. James Lee Love, "The First College Observatory in the United States," *The Sidereal Messenger.*

18. James Lee Love, "The First College Observatory," under "Correspondence," *The Nation,* XLVII (August 16, 1888), 131-32.

the accumulation of many years of repose. So it was thought to be a safe refuge for valuables from the curiosity of those northern marauders. My father and I unscrewed the object glass so carefully as not to leave a mark on the dust, and slipped our watches into the tube and thought ourselves smart and secure. But those curious, prying creatures were not respectful of that sacred dust. They found those watches, confiscated them and so thought to mark time with them in other Latitudes and Longitudes. But their commanding officer marred their calculations, and by restoring them, enabled me to time the transit of many a young astronomer across the blackboard.[19]

After President Caldwell became too ill to continue the observations, Professors Mitchell and James Phillips attempted to carry on the work; but the materials of which the observatory was constructed began to deteriorate. The bricks in the wall were porous and gradually crumbled. "The planks in the flat floor of the roof swelled and shrank, so that water-tight joints were nearly impossible. Weather boarding was tried to protect the walls, and tin and tar to shed the water from the roof; but in vain." Despite every effort, the deterioration had progressed so rapidly that it became necessary to remove the instruments from the observatory. The building, a mere hulk, was burned, presumably by mischievous students, in 1838; and this date marks the end of the first astronomical observatory ever erected at any State University in North America, and the second at any college or university within the present bounds of the United States.[20] Ten years before Professor Albert Hopkins of Williams

19. Charles Phillips, "Astronomical Observatory," *loc. cit.*, p. 7.

20. There was an astronomical observatory, at which observations were made, at the College of William and Mary in Virginia as early as 1780. The instruments used there, it is inferred, were a transit telescope, a sextant, and a clock. President James Madison, uncle of the President of the United States of the same name, was elected a member of the American Philosophical Society, January 27, 1780; and in November of the same year he sent to David Rittenhouse, President of the Society, in Philadelphia observations of the eclipse of Jupiter's satellites and the value of the longitude from Paris derived therefrom. The observatory was still standing on November 2, 1789; but it was destroyed, from some cause now unknown, prior to February 4, 1791. Compare Samuel Alfred Mitchell, "Astronomy during the Early Years of the American Philosophical Society," *Proceedings*, LXXXVI (1942), 13-21; *Transactions of the American Philosophical Society*, III (1793), 150.

College, a brother of Mark Hopkins, went to Europe to purchase philosophical apparatus, Joseph Caldwell went abroad for the same purpose. The astronomical observatory at Chapel Hill was completed six years before that at Williams College.

President Caldwell was a true scientist, an engineer of eminence and a competent astronomer. He had no successors here, as neither Professor Mitchell nor Professor James Phillips, his assistants in making observations, was a professional astronomer. President Swain, whose interest was enlisted in the subjects of history, law, and government, betrayed no concern for astronomy or the maintenance of an observatory. When it was burned the unsympathetic Swain cavalierly said in his report on student disturbances, December 4, 1838: "This ill-starred building has from the period of its creation been a nuisance rather than a benefit to the institution. The instruments were removed and the house abandoned two years since; and on examination, more than a year ago, the wall being found partly dilapidated and wood work wrotten [sic], the Faculty advised that it was not considered worth repairing."[21]

After the burning of the observatory, Professor Mitchell used (primarily as a chemical and metallurgical laboratory) a large wooden, barn-like three-storey structure. On the top storey were placed the astronomical instruments; and for their use, four large windows were cut in each sloping roof, and there were two vertical windows in each end wall. Astronomical observations were intermittently conducted here for some twenty years, until Dr. Mitchell's untimely death, June 27, 1857, on an expedition to check his former findings as to the highest peak east of the Mississippi River, later named in his honor, Mt. Mitchell. The building was on the lot known as the "old Richard J. Ashe place," to the south of present Phillips Hall.[22] In 1857 Dr.

21. Battle, I, 444.
22. This building, which is located on the Charles Phillips map (1852), was still standing in 1898. The lot on which it stood belonged to Dr. Mitchell; and the dwelling house, where the Carolina Inn now stands, was occupied for some years by Mr. Richard J. Ashe and family. Mr. Ashe was the husband of Dr. Mitchell's daughter, Mary. A picture of the second observatory is in this book. For many years, this building was used by Kendall B. Waitt, the college carpenter, and his successor, Foster

Charles Phillips recommended to the Trustees the purchase of additional scientific instruments and apparatus, and the erection of an observatory to house a telescope "of greater or less dimensions"; but no action was taken on this recommendation.[23]

The promising beginnings in the study of astronomy initiated through the energy and devotion of Caldwell were not implemented; and the notable historical position as pioneer in the field of astronomical science, won by this University, is today a mere memory. There is irony in the incident that President Swain, not wishing to waste the brick and stone in the ruins of the observatory, built them into a kitchen at the rear of his home, on the lot now occupied by Spencer Hall.[24] One may venture the hope that, at some not far distant day, a wealthy philanthropist and patron of science among our alumni will realize here, in the form of a great astronomical observatory, the pious hopes and earnest efforts of Joseph Caldwell.

Utley, as combined carpenter's shop and undertaking establishment. In *U. N. C. M.*, X (1861), 448, Kendall B. Waitt advertises the superlative merits of "Fiske's Metallic Burial Cases." The building was taken down about the beginning of the present century.

23. Battle, I, 679.
24. S. U. M., III (1884), 395.

11

ATHLETICS OF THE OLD-TIME
UNIVERSITY: 1795-1861

DURING THE FIRST ERA of the University's history, from its opening until the outbreak of the Civil War, athletics in the modern sense had no existence and hence have no history. Mass participation of students with coaches in sports of various kinds, intercollegiate contests, financial support of athletics as administrative policy, commodious gymnasiums, extensive playing fields, costly stadiums—these and their accompanying phenomena were wholly unknown. It is a mistake to infer, however, that the thousands of vigorous, lusty, active, hot-blooded and excitable Southern youth were inconceivably sluggish or cherished an invincible aversion from athletic exercise. From the University's beginning the students with the approach of spring or autumn invariably have proceeded, without asking leave, to utilize all available open spaces on or near the Campus for playgrounds.[1] In connection with this perennial nuisance, a natural concomitant of thoughtless and restless youth, it is interesting to recall one of the regulations passed by the Board of Trustees only four years after the University's opening:

And whereas the windows and other parts of the buildings are often injured while the students are at play near the same; be it therefore ordained that it shall not be lawful for any student to play at bandy or any other sport within fifty yards of any of the public buildings, under penalty of being punished for the same by admonition or otherwise in proportion to the aggravation of the offence.[2]

In a relativistic universe, human nature appears to be a fixed quantity in a ceaselessly changing world.

1. As illustrations of the contemporary Carolina method of cooperative democratic enterprise in Campus government as compared with the rules, inhibitions, and "punishments to fit the crime" devised by both Faculty and Trustees during the University's earlier days, see letters from Chancellor House to the Order of the Grail, and President Graham to the student body, *The Daily Tar Heel*, April 17 and 24, 1945.
2. *T. M.*, 1798-1801. Ordinance, pp. 38-39. December 20, 1799.

From the outset, ball games of various sorts, notably bandy, as well as such elementary forms as "single cat" and "Anthony over," were popular. These games were played anywhere on the Campus; but the favorite playing fields were on the open space to the east, and the park-like area, not too densely wooded for play, to the south of the Main Building. During the latter half of Swain's administration, after sustained steps were taken toward the beautification of the North Quadrangle by the English gardeners, Loader and Paxton, this area was banned for playing fields, and given the impressive name of the "Forbidden Ground." The Literary Societies by the imposition of fines assumed the responsibility for enforcing the ban, which was extended to pedestrians as well as to players. Occasionally considerable sums were thus realized when the students in numbers yielded to the temptation to pursue some terrified rabbit blindly fleeing across carefully tended lawns.[3]

For almost a century, the game of bandy, or, as it was called in later years, shinny, held first place in the students' affection. There is a three-fold explanation of the popularity of bandy: the cheapness and ease of acquisition of the equipment; the simplicity of the rules; and the excitement, violence, and danger of the matches. A shinny stick with a curved knob at the end, resembling a wooden golf club, was readily procurable in the woods adjoining the Campus; and a hard ball or even a rounded egg-size stone would serve. The impact of such a ball hurtling through the air at high velocity and blows from seasoned wooden clubs violently and often wildly wielded constituted hazards of unusual severity. Not infrequently players were knocked insensible; and broken jawbones, fractured arms, and cracked skulls were not unknown. So enshrined was this exciting and dangerous game in the hearts of the students that neither Faculty nor Trustees ever banned it. Shocked by an exceptionally severe casualty, the students themselves once voluntarily abandoned the game, only to resume it later on.[4] During the 1840's, Leonidas Taylor of Oxford, 1849, was reputedly the most expert player of this dangerous game, originated by and dear to Scotch

3. Battle, II, 198.
4. *Ibid.*, I, 193, 358, 590-91.

Highlanders. Dr. Battle praised bandy as one of the best college games.

Favorites with the students among semi-stationary and fairly harmless sports were various games of marbles. These included games in which marbles were skillfully rolled from hole to hole, or placed in a ring to be shot out, with the penalty of having one's knuckles painfully struck by large marbles, in the event "you" (your marble) were left in the ring. In a clever parody of Byron's "The Bride of Abydos," Samuel Field Phillips in 1853 described Chapel Hill as the paradise of devotees of the game of "knucks."

> 'Tis the land where the Junior, sworn foeman to books,
> Beats College all hollow in playing for knucks,
> From supper till sundown still kneels at his taw,
> Where students and shaving are done by Dave Moore.[5]

Another favorite stationary sport or pastime was "mumbledy-peg" (mumble the peg) in which a heavy pointed stick or pocket knife was dexterously flung, from many points of the head and body, with the object of sticking the point of peg or knifeblade into the turf.

For those addicted to walking, fond of markmanship, and intent upon capturing wild game, Chapel Hill afforded abundant opportunities. The surrounding country was well stocked with quail and rabbits, the adjoining county of Chatham being proverbial for the number and agility of its hares. An arduous and exciting nocturnal sport was opossum hunting with packs of hounds by moonlight, pine torches being employed when the moon was obscured, and a sharp axe proving indispensable for felling the tree whereon the fat marsupial had taken refuge. Long walks were the fashion, from Couchtown to Barbee's blacksmith shop, from the iron mine to the Mason Farm, across the broad acres of Major Pleasant Henderson and Professor William Mercer Green. A popular diversion was to escort professors' daughters and village belles to beautiful spots in the surrounding area, such as the "Roaring Fountain," the mineral spring on Strowd's Hill, "Laurel Hill" luxuriating in brilliantly flowering rhododendron,

5. *Ibid.*, I, 583-84. Dave Moore was the popular colored barber.

"Point Prospect" with its magnificent panoramic view, "Otey's Retreat," the gentle slopes of "Glenburnie," the remote site of the "Patriot's Grave," the "Lone Pine Spring," and the forest-girt "Meeting of the Waters."

The most popular of nocturnal sports indulged in by the mischievous students was marauding, the seizure of everything edible in the neighborhood, notably fruit, fowls, melons, potatoes, roasting ears, tomatoes, honey, and the like; and such parties usually "wound up with setting the village to rights": removing gates, building hastily improvised fences across the highways, installing objects, animate and inanimate, upon the roofs of Steward's, Person, or Gerrard halls, ringing the college bell in the lone watches of the night, and even attaching the bell rope to the neck of "Old Cuddie," President Swain's white mule, or to the horns of some luckless cow, laboriously pushed and pulled up to the belfry of Old South. Regular foot races were not the "order of the day"; but were not infrequent nocturnal sports, when roving students, up to all manner of devilment, were hotly pursued by the fleet President Caldwell and by numerous agile professors. During the 1820's (1826) and succeeding years, there was a much-frequented race-track about a mile from the Campus and a few hundred yards west of the present site of the railroad station at Carrboro; and occasionally students who attended the forbidden sport in some convenient disguise were disciplined by the Faculty for this offense. It has even been rumored that, in those rough and ready days, students were by no means averse to attending cockfights.[6]

Owing to the proximity of various streams of water, to the north, east and south of the village, aquatic sports for both summer and winter were generally engaged in by the students. Bowlin's, Purefoy's, and Closs' creeks, the Valley, Barbee's, later called Cave's, Suter's, and Mallett's ponds, and "Scott's Hole" among others, were joyously frequented by lovers of

6. *Ibid.*, I, 277, 314. Much drinking, betting and gambling went on at this race track. Mrs. Spencer recalls that one of her mother's favorite drives, in the "heavy old barouche," with her brother Charles on the box, was "around the race track." Chamberlain, pp. 19-20. As early as December, 1802, the Trustees ordered that no student should hold horse races or cockfights, or bet on them. *T. M.*, 1801-1810, pp. 33-40.

ALEXANDER JACKSON DAVIS

First engaged in 1843 to enlarge Old East and Old West, this brilliant
architect made many lasting contributions to the beauty of the Campus.
Perhaps his most notable architectural achievement on the University
Campus was Smith Hall (now the Playmakers Theatre). After a water
color, by an unknown artist, in the Avery Library, Columbia University.

SMITH HALL

Built in 1851 and originally serving as library and ballroom, it later housed the law school and is now the Playmakers Theatre. In the classic design of a Greek temple, it was the creation of the famous architect, Alexander Jackson Davis.

swimming and diving. During the nineteenth century, ice skating was the chief winter sport of the students; and even as late as the nineties, the surfaces of ponds and creeks were occasionally frozen over hard, furnishing good skating for a week or two at a time. These periods of severe frigidity, known as "cold snaps," have occurred at less frequent intervals during the present era; and ice skating can no longer be rated here as a winter sport. It was a custom of the Faculty to give holidays when the streams were frozen over; and at such periods a large proportion of the Faculty, student body, and Chapel Hillians would turn out *en masse* and spend the better part of the day skating on Bowlin's Creek, on Purefoy's Creek all the way from Purefoy's Mill down to the Mason Farm, and on the various ponds in or near the village, Hedrick's, Mallett's, Suter's, and the Valley Pond. "The only certain holiday was the 22nd of February, with a 'skating holiday' if there happened to be a sufficiently cold spell. There was a good pond on (what is now) President Winston's land in front of his (present) residence, which in 1844 I saw covered with gentlemen skating, some 'cutting didos,' as fancy skating was called, others racing, others pulling chairs and sleds, on which were seated ladies all the prettier because the cool morning air brought roses to their cheeks."[7] In the ante-bellum days sleighing with improvised sleds is recorded as a sport occasionally indulged in.[8]

Despite this catalogue of outdoor sports in the early days, the chief activities of the students were indoor sports: games of cards, draughts, and chess; the drinking of large quantities of hard liquor, illicitly manufactured and generally of an inferior and deleterious character; and engaging in prolonged, fervent, and for the most part, pointless vocal jamborees, today termed "bull sessions"—"bull" being a concise term for loud bellowings simulating a crude form of dialectic.

In the early days, drill, drill, drill, of a rather mechanical sort, in mathematics and the classics, was the *mot d'ordre* of President and Faculty. The amount of studying done was, it is suspected,

7. K. P. Battle, "The University Fifty Years Ago," *U. N. C. M.*, XIII (1894), 289-318; also, for ice on Tenney's mill pond in 1852, see Chamberlain, p. 58.
8. Chamberlain, p. 35.

surprisingly small. The students appear to have spent most of their time eating, drinking, card-playing, reading, and sleeping. One of the rules of a North Carolina military academy in 1802 reads as follows: "All kinds of gaming to be prohibited except such athletic exercises as tend to invigorate the constitution and for obvious reasons the game of chess; but even these to be admitted as pastime and not with a view of gain." Discussing the subject of sport before the Literary Societies, June 5, 1844, James B. Shepard said: "My only object is to caution against those excesses which debilitate the body and thus enfeeble and deprave the intellect, and to encourage whatsoever may tend to strengthen and expand the mental powers." With rueful humor, a student confesses in 1855: "Instead of spending the hours devoted to learning in the requisite manner, we waste them in idle jargon and Bacchanalian rites." Another would-be student laments that he can accomplish little or nothing in his studies because he, like everyone else, is expected to take a hand in a card game almost every other night.

It is believed that the first agitation for a physical education program arose as the result of a succession of deaths of lamented fellow-students. Columns of the *North Carolina University Magazine*, which first appeared in 1844, were filled with these lugubrious reminders of susceptibility to disease and rising student mortality. In this very year a campaign advocating a physical education program was inaugurated in the *Magazine;* but so predominant was the stress laid by the Faculty upon the obligations to regular and sustained study that this campaign was based, not on general sanitary and hygienic grounds but in the interest of greater scholastic proficiency. The object of the proposed program, as specifically stated by one writer in the *Magazine*, was "to keep the person healthy to gain greater literary achievements." Improvement in the general health of the students within the next few years tended to swing opinion even more strongly than ever in favor of scholastic achievement; and we even find a writer in the *Magazine* of 1852 stoutly affirming: "He who devotes the time assigned for study to field sports and gaming . . . is guilty of a breach of the plainest dictates of common sense."

As the *Magazine* grew in value and importance, and exchanged with other college magazines, the students soon learned of highly valued physical education programs carried on and field sports encouraged and practiced at other institutions. Impressed with the far more general participation in sports by English public school boys than by the students at Chapel Hill, a reviewer of *Tom Brown's School Days at Rugby*, writing in the college magazine somewhat enviously comments: "They exhibit feats of bodily strength and activity and take an amount of outdoor exercise that shame our indolence. Will this not account in part, for their superior intellectual training?"[9] A powerful and well-reasoned plea for mass physical training, signed "Observer," appeared in the *Magazine* in 1853; and deserves to rank as memorable in the history of athletics here. In advocating the establishment of a "school of active athletic exercise" in which all can participate, the writer points out: "Many of the Northern institutions of learning have such a department, and the students are as carefully and as faithfully drilled in manly, healthful exercise as they are in Latin, Greek and mathematics. An instructor is chosen to fill this place, and he is as punctual to meet the students *en masse* as the others are to meet their several classes." After indicating the virtues of Chapel Hill and the fine qualities of the University, the writer nevertheless admits: "Still there is something wanting—a school of athletic exercise—in a word, a gymnasium." He proceeds with a lucid and cogent argument for athletic exercise, concluding:

My suggestion is as follows: That the Trustees of the University have a suitable house built for this purpose, employ an instructor who is well skilled in all the feats performed in like departments in the institutions of the North, set apart three hours in each day for the duty of exercising, and make its performance as essential and as imperative as any other college duties. Then the young men who are at our University, and who are diligent, might hope to be able with their good educations and good constitutions to become useful members of society and bright ornaments of their country.[10]

This vigorous plea found enthusiastic response from some

9. *U. N. C. M.*, VIII (1858), 92-93.
10. "Ought the Trustees to Establish a Gymnasium?", *U. N. C. M.*, II (1853), 236-38.

member of the editorial board of the *Magazine* two years later. He based his arguments upon two sound premises: the folly, futility, and pointlessness of the disorderly activities of the students, which constituted the chief "athletic exercises" taken by them; and the threat to health through neglecting the exercises afforded by a gymnasium and supplied by outdoor sports, in favor of a life exclusively sedentary. "The erection of a gymnasium would, we think," he plausibly argues, "have a decidedly moral effect upon College. Having something else to amuse [them] the young men would hardly then as now 'make night hideous' with whooping, horn-blowing and bell-ringing.... They spring from an exuberance of youthful spirit which must have something upon which to vent itself. . . . Something is needed which will stimulate the students to take wholesome exercises—those which will bring into play every muscle and sinew of the body, and we know of nothing which will do this more effectually than a good gymnasium. Such a one as would answer our purpose would cost but a trifle compared to the incalculable advantages which would be derived from it."[11]

At this very time, there was accommodation in the existing dormitories for not one half of the students, namely 144, leaving 180 who must rent rooms in the village at prices ranging from $10 to $25 per annum.[12] The Trustees were preparing, without sufficient funds immediately available or positively in sight, to erect two new large dormitories, the New East and the New West; and the hope of the students for the erection of a gymnasium appeared little short of chimerical. No sooner were these dormitories completed than the gales of war began blowing down in steadily increasing volume from the North; and plans for a gymnasium were abandoned in exchange for martial fields of physical activity. While four military companies of students were drilling in March, 1861, upon the Campus which at that time had indeed become a *Campus Martius,* an editorial on "The Military" in the *Magazine* contains these pertinent comments: "We think that during a four years stay at this institution a tolerably fair knowledge of military science could be had with-

11. "Editorial Table," *U. N. C. M.,* IV (1855), 378-80.
12. *Ibid.,* pp. 333-34.

out any interference with the regular studies of College. It would certainly induce young men to take exercise which it is known the majority never do in the absence of a gymnasium which unfortunately we have not got, upon which to develop the physical man."[13]

About Chapel Hill there still lurks the romantic tradition of duels, fought for love or honor or both. This fantasy is fostered by the apocryphal tale of Peter Dromgoole, and the stone upon the summit of Point Prospect bearing the gory marks which "attest" the tragic end of one of the duellists.[14] Professor James Phillips, who was somewhat casual in dress and brusque in speech, was believed by the students to be a reformed pirate; and a certain plausibility was lent to this wholly unfounded legend by his skill with the foils and single stick. Even Dr. Mitchell, who at times was the target for the animosity of lawless students, was charged by them with carrying a sword-cane for self-protection. Student duels were not unknown at the University of Virginia, from whence the great mathematician, J. J. Sylvester, is said to have been expelled for fighting a duel with a student. At Chapel Hill, duelling was never a "major athletic sport," a mistaken notion promoted by the two romantic North Carolina novels of ante-bellum days which treat of student life at the University: Edwin W. Fuller's *Sea-Gift* (1873) and John W. Moore's *The Heirs of St. Kilda* (1880). There was a great parade of fire-arms, much shooting in hilariously inebriated mood, and a few instances of affairs in which a student was either wounded or killed. But no duel, conducted with dignity in accordance with the *code duello*, was ever fought at Chapel Hill. Indeed, the distorted ideas of "honor" which alone kept duelling alive

13. *Ibid.*, X (1861), 441-42. On the subject of universal enlistment, the editor further observes: "The eagerness with which they [the students] enlisted into the ranks and their strict punctuality in attendance upon every 'drill' speak well for the animus of our 'Southern Chivalry,' a name so gloriously won on every battle-field wherever the emblem of American liberty flaunted in the breeze, and which their gallant sons will proudly and defiantly sustain or perish on the field of glory willing victims in a holy cause."

14. For the legend of Peter Dromgoole, consult a well-documented article by Bruce Cotten, "Peter Dromgoole: In which Much Light is thrown on an Interesting Tradition," *U. N. C. M.*, XLIV (1924), 5-9.

were for the most part treated by students and Faculty alike with derision; and at the Commencement of 1827, a skit on the subject by the witty Professor William Hooper, entitled "Improvements in Modern Duelling," was produced with marked success by five students.

In the ante-bellum era, fencing with button foils, single stick, which is not unlike bayonet practice still employed by the United States armies, and boxing without gloves were all taught—in particular by Captain O. A. Buck in the forties. James Johnston Pettigrew, who afterwards assiduously studied the art of warfare and personally led the greater part of the Confederate troops in the sublime charge of Longstreet's corps at Gettysburg on July 3, 1863, excelled in these martial sports.

In the spring of 1861, virtually all the students of the University were drilled, successively, by Mr. Lilley, afterwards a brigadier general in the Confederate Service, by Professor William J. Martin, and by a son of a professor at the University, Lieutenant Frederick Fetter. In 1864 plans were entertained for giving instruction in military science, after consultation with Colonel William J. Martin, then in a hospital suffering from severe wounds; but these plans were never carried into effect.[15]

Had the students as a body been as eager for a gymnasium as they were for a ballroom (Smith Hall), which they vigorously petitioned for in 1848 and secured in 1851, to the dismay of many of the narrower religious sectaries in North Carolina, they might well have seen their wishes gratified in the ante-bellum era. They presented no petition for a gymnasium to the Trustees, who were as little interested in athletics and gymnastics as were President and Faculty; and, indeed, no gymnasium was erected in Chapel Hill until thirty-four years later and then, amusingly enough, primarily to provide a ballroom off the Campus, to escape the storm of denominational criticism of balls held on the Campus under the aegis of the University.

15. Battle, I, 590, 724, 736-37. Lieutenant Fetter assumed his duties as drillmaster, employing the rules of military tactics developed in *Upham's Manual*, on March 18, 1862. Compare Chapter 18.

PART III
TESTAMENT TO BEAUTY

12

THE INAUGURATION OF CAMPUS DE-VELOPMENT; ROCK WALLS BUILT AND LANDSCAPE ARCHITEC-TURE PLANNED

FROM THE ESTABLISHMENT of the University in 1795 down to the death of President Caldwell in 1835, President, Faculty, and Trustees constantly and seriously were concerned with the raising and the expenditure of funds and the erection and repair of buildings. A quite secondary consideration was protection of the magnificent trees and of the forests generally from depredation, and the clearing of the Grove of underbrush and trash. It is difficult to realize and to visualize, today, that the open spaces, partially timbered, south and southeast of the Main Building and the fields west of the Raleigh Road now occupied by the Arboretum, were used as pasture grounds for cows, horses, and mules. After the University went into operation, Caldwell and later Swain followed the somewhat monastic policy of keeping the Campus and dormitories, so far as possible, immune from outside influence and communication, and of immuring the students within a quadrangle of buildings and a restricted area of ground.

The eastern boundary of the wooded portion of the Campus was a rail fence, running along the west side of the present Arboretum, with a hedgerow growing alongside. There was no access by highway to the Raleigh Road from the Campus; and there were only two paths to the east: one from Steward's Hall (near present Carr Building) across the swampy land (southern portion of the Arboretum), following the line of the present "President's Walk"; and the other from the Old Chapel (Person Hall), past the "old poplar," to the home of President Caldwell (just east of the present President's house). By carriage, there was no access to the college from the west, save along a short section from the Pittsboro Road following the line of the present

Cameron Avenue, earlier called College Street. To the north-ward ran several unsurfaced and undrained paths through the Grove, from the Old East and the Old Chapel to the Main (Franklin) Street.

During the first four decades and more of the University's history, the development of the village was almost unbelievably slow. When David L. Swain came to the University in January, 1836, to assume the duties of the presidency,

Chapel Hill . . . had but one store; one practising physician whose saddle-bags held all the physic of the neighborhood; no schools; no churches; no pastor; no lawyer. He lived to see (in 1869) eight or ten flourishing stores; four handsome churches besides the Chapel, each supporting its own pastor; two drug stores; half a dozen schools; all the learned professions amply and ably represented; and a popula-tion of some 1000 inhabitants, industrious and thriving. In the half dozen years [1855-1861] immediately preceding the war, handsome residences had sprung up all over the town, new streets were opened, and a very general impulse given to its business.[1]

President Swain was greatly interested in the development and prosperity of the village; and, good citizen that he was, fre-quently remarked that as Chapel Hill was coexistent with the University the two must sink or swim together. He soon noted that building activities were slowly developing along the main street, and that churches, schools and stores tended to cluster around a central nucleus, the home of Major Pleasant Hender-son, which was later occupied by Dr. J. B. Moore. The Grand Avenue extended a considerable distance north of the main street; and frequent applications were made to the University authori-ties for the purchase of land in that quarter. A decision was thus forced upon the Trustees; and they endorsed the policy, advo-cated by Swain, of gradually selling off University lands to north and west only; and of developing the University exclu-sively to east and south.[2]

Soon after his arrival in Chapel Hill, Swain appointed a New

1. S. P. I., June 8, 1869.
2. The western boundary of University land ran about N 21° W, and was located some 50 yards east of the east side of present Columbia Street. Consult the Charles Phillips map (1852), archives, University of North Carolina.

England man, experienced builder and master mechanic, Thomas Waitt, to the post of superintendent of University buildings. He was originally engaged to supervise the repair of the buildings. By putting the conservation and repair of buildings in the hands of one man, Swain was enabled to assign the post of bursar, with oversight of the Grove, ornamental grounds, and lands of the University as part of his duties, to someone else. Since 1827 Dr. Mitchell had been serving as superintendent of buildings and grounds, as well as professor of chemistry, mineralogy, and geology; moreover, he devoted much of his time to the financial aspects of the University, as skilled accountant; took over the direction of the University Library; and busied himself in many other activities. Like Bacon, Mitchell yearned to take all knowledge for his province; and it is still a moot question whether the alleged "chair" he occupied at the University was a sofa, a davenport, or a settee. During his career at the University and in Chapel Hill, he served, at one time or another, as mathematician, physicist, botanist, chemist, mineralogist, geologist, surveyor, engineer, road-builder, agriculturist, professor, preacher, acting-president, bursar, justice of the peace, superintendent of buildings and grounds, town commissioner, and magistrate of police. President Swain made the wisest possible choice in 1837 in the selection of Mitchell as bursar, with broad powers over Campus and grounds. This energetic, devoted Admirable Crichton was possessed of a soul which, as Battle expressed it, "thirsted for all work, as well as all knowledge."

A shrewd and practical man with a keen sense of orderliness, Swain happily conceived the idea of utilizing the enormous number of rocks of granitic gneiss, many of them of huge size, lying both on and below the surface of the ground, in building walls around the Campus, to replace the unsightly rail fences then in use. There was a multitude of rocks identified by geologists as of volcanic origin in Chapel Hill and vicinity. When the large lot purchased by a certain professor was cleared, the number of large granite rocks and boulders unearthed was amazing. They were forthwith used for building walls enclosing the yard and for two huge chimneys. When the professor's wife jocularly inquired of one of the Negro laborers if he were encountering many rocks in his digging, he leaned wearily on his pickaxe and replied: "Every time I throw in my pick, M'am, if I don't hit a rock, I hit a gold dollar."

President Swain, who wished to wed beauty with utility, entertained some doubt as to the stability of walls built of rocks of every conceivable shape and size; but the Connecticut-born Mitchell, who hailed from a state where "stun fences" were a feature of the landscape and outcropping stones much used in building, reassured him, even volunteering to furnish an object-lesson for his inspection. Clad in rough togs, the dignified scientist with his own hands laid a rod's length of rock wall, which was not only a model of picturesqueness, but bore the delusive aspect of stability. Swain was delighted with the result; and in 1838 Mitchell entered upon the arduous task of superintending the building of a rock wall entirely around the Campus.[3] With slave labor to draw upon, the expense was inconsiderable as compared with the cost of such a project today. In emergencies, when the University's laborers and mules were jaded, Mitchell substituted his own; and, as bursar, he allowed himself just compensation for their work.

This enterprise was carried on intermittently for six years; and, even then, not all of the Campus was included within the rock-wall enclosure. In October, 1843, President Swain was authorized by the Trustees to make settlement with Dr. Mitchell for improvements to the Campus, and the official record of December 19, 1844, shows that the sum of $500 was ordered to be paid to Dr. Elisha Mitchell for the "stone wall erected by him around the campus and college grounds."[4] The minutes for the latter date continue: "Ordered further that as an additional compensation for said work," a deed be given Dr. Mitchell for a "small strip of ground near his ice house." After Dr. Mitchell's death, a conveyance was made to his heirs of a very large strip, two acres in extent, on the south side of College Street (present Cameron Avenue), opposite the original president's house, the University reserving the option for its repurchase should Mit-

3. These "stone fences," so designated by Mitchell in his account book, are universally called "rock walls" by Chapel Hillians.
4. E. C. T. M., October 16, 1843, p. 112. T. M., 1841-1868, pp. 48-49. Cf. also Battle, I, 444; Chamberlain, p. 41.

chell's heirs ever desire to sell. The property was eventually sold to an individual by the Mitchell heirs, no money being available at the time in the University treasury for its repurchase.[5]

Another sound reason, aside from economic and esthetic considerations, for building durable walls around the Campus was to obviate the nuisance of wandering cattle, hogs, and sheep, which were allowed by law to roam at large. Rail fences, which were continually falling or being knocked down, proved ineffective barriers. The erection of the rock walls, as a sort of military circumvallation of a *Campus Martius*, proved to be a contribution of the first importance to the life of the college and the community. These rough, grey walls conferred distinctiveness, picturesqueness, and beauty upon this forest-girt "Sweet Auburn of the plain." Individual property owners, impressed by the artistic "touch" and decorative note imparted to the college grounds by these stone enclosures, began to replace their own picket, rail, or paling fences with rock walls, with the result that today few residential plots in or around Chapel Hill, whether spacious estate or mere pocket-handkerchief lot, are regarded as complete without rock-wall enclosures and often massive stone pillars as gateways.

For the first half-century and more, these walls were built exclusively of rocks, dexterously piled one upon another, without adhesive, whether plaster or cement. In the course of time many of these walls collapsed, as the result of meteorological bombardment in the form of rain, sleet, and snow. Half a century ago, the rock walls in the rear (south) of the Campus were in a dilapidated condition, having declined in many places to half their original height. Periodically and piecemeal, such loosely constructed walls had to be rebuilt at no little trouble and expense. During the present century the practice has grown up of building rock walls with an inner core of cement, the outer tiers of rock being laid to indicate loosely placed stone, instead of the regularity of mathematically laid brick. So numerous were the demands for the new type of rock wall, at once stable and pic-

5. Battle, I, 683-84. In later years this entire area, through purchase and gift, became the property of the University.

turesque, that the laying of such walls became a lucrative profession in Chapel Hill. In many yards, these rock walls are
covered with climbing roses and trailing vines, creating at once
a note of beauty and an air of permanence and antiquity. For its
ivy-clad or ampelopsis-covered college buildings, classic shades,
its noble oaks and poplars, graceful elms and sugar maples, flowering shrubs, giant rose bushes, Arboretum, rock walls for which
it is unique in North Carolina, and its beautiful environs, Chapel
Hill and the University Campus constitute one of the loveliest
and most charming spots in the United States.

During the first twenty years of his life in Chapel Hill, Dr.
Mitchell fixed himself in the minds of his colleagues and of the
people of North Carolina generally as a scientist of multilateral
mind and encyclopedic knowledge. During the years from 1818
to 1825, he devoted much of his attention to botany, and became
an indefatigable student of the flora of Chapel Hill and environs.
His attention focussed upon various species of trees indigenous
to the region, notably oaks. In a memoir published after Dr.
Mitchell's death on June 27, 1857, Dr. James Phillips stressed his
delighted preoccupation in the pursuit of the natural sciences.
"Even while a Professor of Mathematics he had frequently indulged his taste for botany by pedestrian excursions through the
country around Chapel Hill. After he took upon himself instruction in chemistry, mineralogy, and geology he extended and
multiplied these excursions, so that when he died he was known
in almost every part of North Carolina, and he left no one behind
him better acquainted with its mountains, valleys, and plains, its
birds, beasts, bugs, fishes, and shells, its trees, flowers, vines, and
mosses, its rocks, stones, sands, clays and marls."[6] Once he began,
in 1838-1839, to accumulate rocks for the erection of a wall
around the Campus, President Swain awoke to the realization
that Mitchell, with his knowledge of botany, plant life, and soils,
was an ideal choice for the long-neglected post of amateur landscape architect.

It was probably after consultation with Mitchell, conspicuous
for thoroughness and efficiency, that Swain, a stickler for orderly

6. James Phillips, *A Memoir of the Rev. Elisha Mitchell, D.D.* (Chapel
Hill: J. M. Henderson, 1858), p. 8.

arrangement and pleasing appearance, recommended to the Trustees the appropriation of a sum which may be counted as large for that day of small things, for the purpose of developing and beautifying the Campus. Mitchell, as bursar and supervisor of the Campus and University grounds, was to have the matter in charge. But Swain personally interested himself in the matter for the next quarter of a century, and accomplished wonders in the improvement and beautification of the grounds, and in the introduction of the study of soils, agriculture, and the subject of scientific crop production now known as agronomy.

On October 1, 1839, the Board of Trustees, on the recommendation of President Swain, appropriated the sum of $3,000 for improving the buildings and Campus to be expended under the direction of the Faculty.[7] It is indicative of the general interest of the professors in the improvement of both buildings and grounds that these matters were placed under the direction of the Faculty, and not left exclusively in the hands of Dr. Mitchell and President Swain. This resolution, taken with the action commissioning Mitchell to build a rock wall around the Campus, marks the first important step looking toward constructive beautification of the grounds and consistent landscape gardening. An ordinance that the "late residence of Dr. Caldwell is hereby set apart and appropriated as the future residence of the President," was also passed by the Trustees.

The work of improvement of the buildings, provided for under the ordinance, was not long in getting under way. In correspondence with Charles Manly, Secretary of the Board, Swain was soon discussing the type of lime preferred for coating the buildings. At this time, David Paton, who had come to this country in 1833, was in Raleigh, putting the finishing touches upon the State Capitol, a masterpiece of architectural beauty and dignity.[8] In reply to President Swain, who had applied to him as an authority on the subject, Paton wrote on March 2, 1840: "Annexed and inclosed I send observations and Estimates about the fronts of College Buildings," together with directions for the best method of washing the fronts of the buildings with

7. *E. C. T. M.*, 1835-1873, p. 81.
8. See Chapter 9.

plaster. A few days later, doubtless referring to Paton's formulas and directions, Swain wrote reassuringly to General.Daniel L. Barringer: "The University continues to advance. The system of instruction is more perfect, and the discipline much better maintained than I have ever known it. We are besides improving the Campus, making important additions to the apparatus, and are about to change the dull aspect of the college edifices by covering them with a preparation, made of equal quantities of Roman Cement, and common mustard lime, with the addition of one-tenth sulphuric acid, to the quantity of water with which they are mixed." By midsummer, Swain was hopefully notifying Barringer that the Executive Committee of the Trustees was determined to erect additional dormitories by the beginning of the next session.[9]

The Commencement of 1841, which began on June 3, revealed to visitors that marked improvements had been made externally in both buildings and grounds. A transient reporter praised the tinted wash for the fronts (outer walls) of the college buildings. A considerable portion of the handsome and impressive rock wall around the Campus was already in place. The Campus, as well as the buildings, presented a neat and orderly appearance, in consequence of the grubbing up of unsightly stumps and the removal of the water-boughs of the trees. Owing to unsatisfactory types of roofing formerly used for the college buildings and the warning afforded by the two fires which started on the roofs of the old State Capitol, the second resulting in its complete destruction, June 19, 1831,[10] President Swain made extended inquiries regarding the most approved materials. In response to his request for information, Mr. Samuel F. Patterson, Trustee, applied to Henry Leavitt Ellsworth, United States Commissioner of Patents, and also to Robert Mills, architect of the Washington Monument, then residing in Washington. Mr. Ellsworth called attention to "recent discoveries in the application of Iron for covering roofs"; and recommended that the

9. Swain Papers, Southern Historical Collection. David Paton to D. L. Swain, March 2, 1840; D. L. Swain to Daniel L. Barringer, March 6, 1840; Charles Manly to D. L. Swain, April 20, 1840; D. L. Swain to D. L. Barringer, July 22, 1840. Cf. also Ashe, "David Paton," *loc. cit.*
    10. *Raleigh Register*, June 21, 1831.

GENERAL BENJAMIN SMITH, FIRST BENEFACTOR
OF THE UNIVERSITY

His generous gift of 20,000 acres of land in Tennessee was announced by
Davie at the first meeting of the Board of Trustees, December 18, 1789.
Smith Hall, now the Playmakers Theatre, was named for him. From
original drawing by St. Memin.

VIEW OF THE CAMPUS, *circa* 1860

From left to right, New East, Old East, South Building (center), Old West, New West. Smith and Gerrard halls are pictured in the inserts at left and right, respectively. The lithograph was made while New East and New West were being erected.

OLD LAW OFFICE

Office of Samuel Field Phillips, sometime Solicitor General of the United States. He conducted his classes in this building during the period (1854-1859) when he acted as assistant professor of law at the University. The building is still standing on the southwest corner of the late Mrs. A. A. Kluttz's lot on East Franklin Street.

New York engineer, Ithiel Town, who "stood at the head of the profession in his line, in the United States," be consulted. Mr. Mills supplied reasonably full suggestions, which were deemed by Mr. Patterson adequate for the University's "present purpose."[11]

During the following year President Swain continued to voice the strongly expressed desire, felt by Trustees, Faculty, and himself, for the employment of a University official, highly skilled in landscape gardening. At the meeting of the Executive Committee of the Trustees, October 16, 1843, President Swain was authorized to make a settlement with Dr. Mitchell "for the appropriation made by the Trustees for the improvement of the Campus." The following constructive steps, particularly that looking toward the engagement of a landscape architect, were taken at this same meeting, slightly more than a century ago:

Resolved that Govr. Swain be and he is hereby instructed to open a correspondence with Robt. Donaldson, Esq. of New York in relation to the best mode of procuring plans for the Society Halls at Chapel Hill, and for obtaining the services of an individual skilled in laying out pleasure grounds, landscape gardening, etc.; and the prices at which these plans can be had and the services had.

Resolved that Govr. Swain be and he is hereby authorized and requested to ascertain from Hant and Polly of Wilmington the cost of repairing the tin roof of the South Building and of re-covering the Old Chapel with tin, and to make contracts for the same upon the best terms he can.[12]

President Swain had familiarized himself with the original plans and desires of the Trustees for the establishment of a botanical garden in the southeastern portions of the University grounds, and the allocation of a large area for agricultural purposes, a project which today we should call a "model farm."

11. Swain Papers, Southern Historical Collection. S. F. Patterson to D. L. Swain, Raleigh, January 11, 1842.

12. *E. C. T. M.*, 1835-1873, pp. 112-13. See Chapter 13, regarding the Society Halls. Robert Donaldson, born in Fayetteville, North Carolina in 1800, was graduated from the University of North Carolina in 1818. He took a lively interest in the progress and development of his Alma Mater and left a considerable sum to it when he died. His will was invalid, however, and the University received nothing. *T. M.*, 1835-1873, pp. 145-46. October 17, 1872. Consult Donaldson. *et al.* v. American Tract Society: 1 Thompson & Cook 15 (New York Supreme Court Reports).

The time seemed ripe for investigating the best means by which these constructive and well-conceived plans might be carried into effect. President Swain's letter to Robert Donaldson is historic, in the best sense of the term, as establishing a great precedent and affording an example worthy of emulation.

Raleigh 28th Nov. 1843

My Dear Sir

Your favor in relation to Society Halls, improvement of College grounds, &c &c was rec'd ten days since—(after informal consultation with some of Trustees) I feel myself authorized to invite Mr. Davis to visit the University with a view to the execution of working drawings, specifications &c &c on the terms indicated in your letter, the sum ($100) required for travelling expenses, can either be remitted to you, or paid to him, on his arrival here by Chas. Manly Esq as you may direct—Our winter vacation will terminate on the 6th of January, about which time (say the 10th) I should be glad to see Mr. Davis—No meeting of the Trustees can be had at an earlier day, & if his convenience will admit I have reasons for desiring that his visit may not be postponed to a later date.

I fear that our resources will not justify an immediate appropriation for the establishment of a Botanical garden and pattern farm— I am not without hopes however of being able to obtain such aid from the next General Assembly as will justify our attempting it on a proper scale—In the meanwhile we will have enough to do in erecting the Halls & in improving the grounds and on the latter subject I would be very glad to have a communication and a very full one from you—Will not Mr. Davis be competent to advise and direct on this hand?

As to "fencing acct" as you term it, would not the cedar which is easily obtained answer our purpose as well or better than anything else? Our village is improving—The Episcopalians have erected the wall (brick) of a very neat church planned by Mr. Walton of Philadelphia—The Presbyterians & Methodists have subscription papers in circulation for similar undertakings—Judge Battle and other respectable families are settling among us, and at present, I think there is no difficulty in pronouncing it the most moral & best governed village in the state—The act of the last General Assembly prohibiting the sale of ardent spirits, wines, or malt liquor by a measure within two miles of the University or to a student anywhere for the purpose of being used within two miles of C. Hill has produced a very decided improvement without as well as within the College precincts.[13]

13. Swain Papers, Southern Historical Collection. The erroneous reference to "Mr. Walton of Philadelphia" is to Thomas Ustick Walter

When A. J. Davis, eminent architect, appeared before the Executive Committee of the Trustees on February 19, 1844, among many other matters presented by him for consideration were the plans he had drawn up for "laying out and improving the Campus and College grounds."[14] During the next decade and more, he remained in communication with President Swain and the Board of Trustees; and it is of record that he submitted to the Trustees at least nine reports on architectural plans and designs for landscape gardening. A large drawing, preserved in the Metropolitan Museum of Art, New York City, gives a fine perspective view of the Campus and University buildings; and also a detailed plan of treatment of lawn, tree-plantation, shrubbery, and walks. A "Botanic Garden" occupies precisely the area covered by the present Arboretum and also a similar rectangle south of "Chatham Street," present Cameron Avenue. This feature was in conformity with the original design of the University's founders.[15] Of especial interest is the suggested treatment of the area south of Chatham Street, with an elliptical walkway having two offshoots entering that street, east of Smith and west of Gerrard halls, respectively; and a straight walkway running southward at right angles to South Building and bisecting the above-mentioned elliptical walkway. This charmingly decorative design, by one of the most gifted architectural draftsmen of his day, piques the observer's curiosity concerning other landscape gardeners' and landscape architects' designs for this Campus, considered and perhaps drafted by him. Plans for the improvement and adornment of the Campus preoccupied President Swain during the immediately succeeding years; but large-

---

(September 4, 1804—October 30, 1887). Walter sent, not an original design, but one from a book by Bishop John Henry Hopkins, *Essay on Gothic Architecture* (Burlington, Vermont, 1836), Nos. 29, 30, 31 on Plates XI, XII. Consult *Dictionary of American Biography* (New York, Scribner, 1936), XIX, 397-98, for a sketch of Walter.

14. *E. C. T. M.*, 1837-1861, pp. 116 ff. For A. J. Davis, see Roger Hale Newton, *Town & Davis, Architects, Pioneers in American Revivalist Architecture, 1812-1870* (New York, Columbia University Press, 1942); Hamlin, *Greek Revival Architecture in America;* Richard H. Pratt, "Alexander Jackson Davis," *House and Garden*, LII (1927), 122-23, 154, 156. The portrait in the last mentioned article is of Ithiel Town, and not of Alexander Jackson Davis as labeled.

15. Consult Chapters 6 and 15.

scale plans for Campus beautification had to wait until 1847 for the acquisition of professional landscape architects and gardeners.[16]

During this year of 1844, a general emotion of reverential gratitude prompted the Faculty to propose the establishment of a sort of "Fame's Acre" on the University Campus for the interment of the remains of eminent men associated with the University's history.[17] The exciting cause of this movement was the death, on January 23rd of that year, of William Gaston, greatly beloved and admired citizen, and for forty-two years an active, wise, and constructive-minded Trustee. On January 27, 1844, the Faculty, after passing fitting resolutions in memory of Judge Gaston, requested permission of the Board of Trustees to lay off a burial ground in plain view of the buildings; and also requested of the relatives of Judge Gaston, whose remains were then temporarily resting in Raleigh, permission for their interment in the proposed cemetery here. The Faculty, in making this request of Judge Gaston's relatives, gave assurances that efforts would be made to remove to this same spot the remains of other men prominent in local and national history "with the high and noble object of keeping before the youths of the institution such ever present remembrances of the great as may incite them to a vigorous prosecution of their studies and assiduous cultivation of their hearts." It is highly doubtful whether the establishment on our Campus of an open-air, quasi Westminster Abbey of the University of North Carolina would have effected the high purposes so eloquently voiced in the memorial to the Trustees drafted by Professors Charles Force Deems and William Mercer Green.[18] The Trustees acted wisely in allowing the petition to lapse without action on their part.

16. In the University of North Carolina Library, Carolina Room, are photostats of designs and records of Alexander Jackson Davis, preserved in the Metropolitan Museum of Art, New York City.

17. A century later the General Alumni Association appointed a committee to investigate the proposal to remove the remains of William Richardson Davie from the family burial ground in the Waxhaw Cemetery to the Campus here; but nothing has been accomplished.

18. Battle, I, 492-93.

13

A FAMOUS ARCHITECT TAKES COMMAND; SMITH HALL: AN ARCHITECTURAL MASTERPIECE

A N EVENT of the first importance, in the history of the architectural and landscape development of the University Campus, including buildings and grounds, was the engagement in 1843 of the famous architect, Alexander Jackson Davis of New York, to enlarge the Old East and Old West buildings. Immediately following a period (1829-1843) of highly successful partnership with Ithiel Town under the firm name of Town and Davis, this brilliant craftsman and prolific designer gave of his best talents, intermittently, for a decade to the creation of harmonized style in the principal buildings on the Campus here. Included in the duties of supervising architect was the preparation of comprehensive plans for the Campus, including landscape gardening and the laying out of areas of ground for open-air occasions, picnics, and occasional celebrations of the sort described by the French as *fêtes champêtres*. The planting of decorative trees and massed shrubs, the proper construction and surfacing of roads and paths through the Campus, and the lining of the principal walks with ornamental flowers, in particular roses of brilliant hues and luxuriantly flowering shrubs, were subjects for the supervising architect's attention. This important innovation in University policy is attributable to President Swain.

The era of 1843-1861 marks the real beginning of an appreciation of nature and a sense of beauty, in respect to Campus development. Attentive consideration was given to harmony and fitness, in connection with both individual design and securing pleasing effects in the general mass of college buildings. The basic structural plan of building extension, one axis bisecting the Grand Avenue, the other at right angles thereto, was fortunately preserved; and while Davis followed in general the simple design of unadorned colonial architecture exhibited in

Old East, Old West, and South, he introduced certain embellishments in the enlargement of the two former buildings. Following the cue of Neo-Grecian and pseudo-Classic style, for which the example had been set in the portico with Ionic columns, added to the barnlike structure of Gerrard Hall with its bare faces and exiguous eaves, Davis placed upon the Campus its most beautiful building, Smith Hall (now the Playmaker's Theatre), a structure of impeccable proportions, the perfect portico with classic Corinthian pillars showing a delightful variation from the Hellenic norm in the capitals of wheat and corn plants, with foliage of grace and beauty, symbolic of the native American landscape. A felicitous treatment of the north faces of both Old East and Old West, which originally were forbiddingly arid in quality, was given by the recessive entablatures, the vertical frames presenting a columnar effect of impressive dignity, conspicuously Egyptian in character. This striking treatment has been deliberately reflected in the design of the new village Post Office Building facing south toward the Campus.[1]

Historically, the engagement of the architect Davis has an interesting origin. The two Literary Societies, really debating clubs, which were housed in cramped quarters in the South Building, chafed at the inadequate facilities both for the stated meetings and the habitual use of the libraries. As early as 1834 the Philanthropic Society offered $1,000 as a contribution towards a new library room, forty feet square with six windows and three fireplaces; but shortage of University funds forbade the acceptance by the Trustees at that time of this handsome offer. Three years later the Society petitioned for a new hall, as did the Dialectic Society the following year. According to the plan outlined, both Societies were to be housed in a new building estimated to cost $5,000; and they offered to contribute liberally toward the construction of such a building. The committee of the Trustees, to whom the petition was referred, recommended that, after the payment of the debt to the banks and as soon as the funds of the University would permit, the Trus-

---

1. The present Chapel Hill Post Office was first occupied on July 4, 1938. For the plan to harmonize the Post Office with architecture of the University, consult *Chapel Hill Weekly*, July 10, 1936.

tees join with the Societies in the erection of a fireproof hall of the same dimensions and external plans, for each Society, or one building of suitable proportions, for the two of them, the University to pay at least two-thirds of the cost.

The reasons for executing such a plan were patent and pressing. The valuable libraries of the Societies, totaling some 7,000 volumes, were subjected to constant fire hazards, being housed in the shingle-covered South Building wherein during the winter season over twenty-five wood fires were constantly alight. There was inequality in the size of the Society Halls, the space in the Philanthropic being smaller than that in the Dialectic. Furthermore the vacated halls would provide needed dormitory rooms; and either four or eight additional dormitory rooms would also be supplied, depending upon whether one or two new buildings should be erected. Dormitory accommodations on the Campus existed for only 130 of a student body of 170. Because of the delay due to pending litigation in effecting sales of the University's Tennessee lands, six years were to pass before the Trustees' resolution was implemented.[2]

The matter was again agitated by the Societies in December, 1841, and a year later the Board of Trustees directed the Secretary to submit to the General Assembly a memorial urging the erection of the buildings.[3] Robert Donaldson in 1843 wisely advised the selection, as structural and landscape architect, of Alexander Jackson Davis, already well and favorably known to the University authorities for designing the portico of Gerrard Hall. The Trustees approved the appointment and during the closing days of January and the first week in February, 1844, Davis held conferences with Governor Morehead and President Swain, in Raleigh, Chapel Hill, and Greensboro, regarding renovation, remodeling, and additions to the University buildings. The following is an excerpt from Davis' own records:

1844
Jan. 23
Trip south to Chapel Hill, N. C. to plan additions to the University of N. C. Ar. at Raleigh Jan. 30. Met Gov. J. M. Morehead. Ar. at

2. Battle, I, 511-12.
3. *T. M.*, 1841-1860, pp. 27, 36.

Chap. Hill night 31. Met Gov. and Pres. Swain while at Gov. David L. Swain's, examined buildings and grounds about College and made plans for extending the Dormitories northwardly, also considered of modes of improving South building and Chapel.[4]

Davis in person presented his plans and specifications before the Executive Committee of the Trustees. These plans provided for the enlargement of Old East and Old West, which were to be extended toward the north, one-half their former length. The Society Halls were to be located in the second storey of the extension in each case, and the libraries, divided into alcoves, in the third. The architect's charges were surprisingly low, namely one hundred dollars, plus expenses of his trips to and from New York, and an additional hundred dollars on the completion of the work. The plans were approved by the Executive Committee.[5]

The way was cleared for action when the Trustees, on December 13, 1844, rejected all former bids and proposals in favor of those of Davis; and appointed President Swain and Judge William H. Battle a committee to contract for and supervise the enlargement and remodeling of the Old East and Old West buildings. The Committee acted promptly, reporting to the Board ten days later that they had executed a contract for the additions with Isaac J. Collier and Kendall B. Waitt, the contract price being $9,360 and the work to be completed by 1848.[6] On the completion of the remodeled buildings, the Societies moved into their new homes, with appropriate ceremonies.

In 1846 in accordance with the decision of the Trustees, the allocation of the space in the three main buildings had been

4. Photostats of records, plans and specification, University of North Carolina Library, from the original A. J. Davis Papers, Metropolitan Museum of Art, New York.

5. E. C. T. M., 1835-1873, p. 116. Photostats from Davis Papers, University of North Carolina Library.

6. T. M., 1841-1868, pp. 51, 52. Kendall B. Waitt, for a considerable period college carpenter, furniture maker, and undertaker, was the son of Thomas Waitt, for many years superintendent of grounds and buildings here. Cf. supra. In 1923 Old West was thoroughly renovated, giving 46 rooms, 16,400 square feet of floor space, and 170,000 cubic feet at a cost of $45,900. In 1924 Old East, identical in size with Old West, was also thoroughly renovated, at a cost of $82,000. For both, the architects were Atwood and Nash, the contracting firm, T. C. Thompson and Brothers.

settled by lot, the Old East and the eastern half of South going to the Philanthropic Society, and a similar western division for the Dialectic Society. The president of the Philanthropic Society, Matt W. Ransom, afterwards famous as a Confederate brigadier general and United States Senator, who was the winner in the lottery, chose the eastern division for his Society. From this circumstance arose the custom which has prevailed for a century, that students from the west join the "Di" and those from the east join the "Phi." [7]

It does not seem to be generally known that in the ordinance passed on June 3, 1846, providing for the allocation by lot of space to the Societies, the Trustees declared that "thereafter the entire Edifices now known as the East and West buildings shall be regarded as the Halls of the Societies and each shall bear the appellations [sic] of the Society to which it may be allotted." [8] This decision was not popular with students and Faculty; and the official renaming failed through disuse. Established traditions and tender associations with cherished old names, although these indicated only points of the compass, forbade these changes.

The next building to be erected upon the Campus has a curious origin and a long and chequered career, marked by kaleidoscopic changes. Steward's Hall, which had been rented by the University for some twenty-odd years past and conducted as a private boardinghouse, was ordered by the Trustees on June 5, 1846, to be removed and rebuilt as an addition to President Swain's Negro houses. [9] The students, who for almost half a century had characteristically execrated Steward's Hall as the dispensary of insufficient food and unappetizing fare, nevertheless prized it highly as the scene of their supreme delight and most jealously guarded privilege, the Commencement ball. A wail at once went up from the disgruntled students who promptly petitioned the Trustees that an appropriate structure housing a spacious ballroom be built; and the petition was

---

7. When invited to join the Philanthropic Society in 1851 the popular Zebulon Baird Vance from the western county of Buncombe playfully replied: "Fie, Fie! I'd rather Die."

8. *T. M.*, 1841-1868, p. 66.

9. *Ibid.*, p. 81. However, see Chapter 5.

referred to the Executive Committee.[10] With a shrewdness worthy of accomplished diplomats, the two Societies petitioned that the proceeds from the sale of Steward's Hall be used for the construction of a hall for the annual meeting of the Alumni Association, which had been established May 31, 1843, *and* for the holding of balls at Commencement! [11] The Trustees themselves offered an additional reason for the new building: a more spacious hall for Commencement exercises. On January 31, 1849, the Executive Committee resolved to erect upon the Campus a building "to be used as a ball room, Alumni and Trustee meeting place, and as place to hold Commencement Exercises."[12] They further provided that the building should be of brick, one storey high, located near the other college buildings. The expeditious handling of the business of the enlargement and remodeling of Old East and Old West by the Swain-Battle committee, and the general appreciation of the architectural skill of A. J. Davis, led to the reappointment of all three for the new building.

William Mercer Green, professor of *belles-lettres* and rector of the recently completed Episcopal Church, the Chapel of the Cross, had established a brickyard, in order to supply the brick for that church at a minimum cost. His proposals to the Trustees to supply bricks for the new University building were accepted; and the Building Committee made a contract with him for 125,000 bricks at the rate of $5 per thousand. Apparently 80,000 more bricks than were included in the original estimate were supplied by Green who was paid the sum of $1,025. An amusing incident is told of the refined professor and pious rector turned brickmaker. Throughout the protracted period of building the Episcopal Church, Green was a liberal donor, lent the parish a thousand dollars, and generously contributed gratis the labors of several slaves and a pair of mules. "A considerable addition to the building fund he planned to contribute by the donation of a kiln of brick prepared for firing on his land and at his expense. His reverence for the Lord's Day, however, was

10. *T. M.*, 1841-1868, pp. 81, 90.
11. *Ibid.*, p. 90; Battle, I, 617.
12. *T. M.*, 1835-1873, p. 149; 1841-1868, p. 106.

fatal to his generous intentions. He caused the fires to be extinguished Saturday night at twelve o'clock and the kiln became a mass of crumbling half-baked bricks. The loss was estimated at two hundred and fifty dollars. His parishioners, less reverential than he, differed with the Rector and freely quoted the Scripture passage relating to the ass falling into a pit on the Sabbath and being justifiably rescued."[13] The energetic Green, it is only fair to say, eventually supplied the requisite number of bricks, succeeded after six years in seeing the Chapel of the Cross completed, and satisfactorily fulfilled his contract for the brick with which the new University building was constructed.

President Swain and Judge Battle were authorized to choose a site for the building, which was to accommodate the University library and belfry, in addition to the uses already designated. The documentary evidence makes it abundantly clear that careful study and analysis of the various problems involved, affecting both buildings and grounds, were made by the architect in consultation with Swain, Battle, and the Trustees. Preliminary drawings were made by Davis in the autumn of 1849, and on November 3 sent by Mr. Andrew Mickle, sometime Bursar of the University, to President Swain. Davis contemplated a visit to North Carolina the following spring for a full discussion of the plans with Governor Morehead, President Swain, and Judge Battle. According to excellent authority, "he restudied several of them, and built a new library building in an effort to weld the whole group into an impressive and monumental scheme."[14] The following letter to President Swain conveys a suggestion of the meticulous study made by Davis of the many architectural problems involved.

N. Y. Monday, March 4, '50

My dear Sir:

I have been so overwhelmed with business that I could not tell when I might visit Chapel Hill, and therefore contented myself by writing to Gov. Morehead begging to put off the visit to Raleigh until April or thereabout, trusting that you would learn of him as

13. K. P. Battle, "Historical Notes," archives, Chapel of the Cross.
14. Hamlin, *Greek Revival Architecture in America*, pp. 211-12.

to the probable time of my visit. I have had but this one day to devote to your new building, since seeing Mr. Mickle, and to morrow
he is to leave.

I have prepared this day the drawings I now send and they seem
to me to be all you will want to enable you to go on with the mason's
work, and in the mean time, (or perhaps time enough when I visit
the south) I can explain and make out such other details, as the carpenter may require. It seems to me that it will be doing your town a
wrong, to copy any building that you may have already in it; besides
the *church* is *too grave* and simple to express the purpose of an assembly room, I have therefore made a front, *still similar* to the
church but lighter in the details with a corinthian column, and richer
cornice (from an example at Athens). The height is the same in
both, but the cornice does not project so much in the latter,—and
there might be four columns instead of two, and not *more* than 4 ft.
or 4 ft. 7 inches apart. This would leave a free space for passage and
you may judge if the front would be more elegant, or express the
"Library and Assembly Room." This room is small enough already;
so is the portico; and therefore if you would enlarge the front ante-
rooms beyond 7 ft. of width—add as much more to the length of the
building as you please or if 4 columns be decided, *fill the corner* by
extending the 7 ft. room into it as shewn by the flap—returning to
the two columns, but adding *antae* in the place of the two outer
columns.

I keep a sketch of the plan, and as you may decide upon the leading parts write me if you require other details, or explanations. *The
floor of* [*the*] *great room* will require a wall in the cellar under the
middle of same for support. The ceiling I make nearly flat, shewing
the principal trusses of roof running across *furred* to and plastered,
the part between is in two inclined planes thus: A. B.

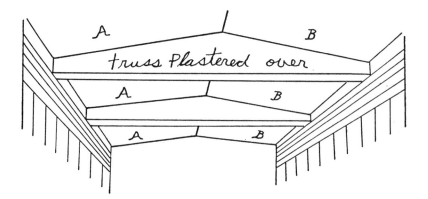

This is the cheapest mode of breaking up the flat surface of ceiling, and would be more in *pure Greek* style than the arch. I think we must give up the arch on account of expense, and want of height in side walk, and so of the sky light, which will not be wanted either for light or ventilation.

Yours respectfully & truly

A. J. Davis[15]

It must be pointed out in explanation of the reference to "the church" in the above letter, that at the request of Mr. Robert Donaldson of New York, acting on behalf of Professor Charles Phillips, Davis in the first half of 1847 submitted plans for the Presbyterian Church at Chapel Hill. The design was marked by simplicity and austerity, the portico being of pure Tuscan character.

In May, 1850, Davis spent five days in Chapel Hill in consultation with President Swain and Judge Battle; and upon his return to his office in New York, drew up a revised set of nine drawings, embodying the changes which were the outcome of the conferences. At the same time Davis was working on designs and specifications for the State Asylum for the Insane in Raleigh, which is essentially the design originally proposed for the University's first three buildings.[16] The covering letter to President Swain follows:

N. Y. May 31, 1850

Gov. Swaine [*sic*],
Dear Sir:

I hasten to send you the design for your Alumni Hall. I was obliged to redraw the whole, but the result has been to improve the plan, so as to make it such as would be creditable to any University, as a specimen of Classical taste, its general character, and proportions, what-ever defects there may be in the details, or execution.

I shall send a specification, and some other drawings with the roll or port folio (to Raleigh) on the Lunatic Asylum, in a few days, as I now go about to prepare the same without delay. Please say to any member of the lunatic committee that I shall send early next week,

15. Swain Papers, Southern Historical Collection.
16. For Davis' design for the State Asylum for the Insane, Raleigh, North Carolina, see Hamlin, *Greek Revival Architecture in America*, Plate LVI, between pages 216 and 217.

by post, a plan of the foundations of the center building, which the workmen will first want to dig and lay stone by.

In the mean time I remain
Yours respectfully and truly
Alex J. Davis

The two capitals to the columns of
your Hall I wish to have carved *here*
with foliage of *Maise, wheat and tobacco;*
and the shaft should be reeded, with or
without a base as I shall determine
here after.[17]

In accordance with the basic Campus plan, with its two mutually perpendicular axes of symmetry, the proposed assembly hall was designed to correspond, in position but not in design, to Gerrard Hall;[18] to be located with its north wall 120 feet south of Old East, to contain a basement and a floor level, and to be 122 feet long by 35 feet wide. It was later decided, after the Trustees had seen Davis' plans and specifications and his architectural drawings of "the Library and Alumni Hall," to shorten the main hall to 90 feet, presumably in order to conform more nearly with the length of Gerrard Hall, its western opposite. Davis' final plans were approved by the Building Committee at Chapel Hill on November 15, 1850.[19]

Instead of following the unsatisfactory treatment of Gerrard Hall, a brick barn of barren severity, with an Ionic column

17. Swain Papers, Southern Historical Collection.

18. As early as 1835, the Trustees had decided upon the erection of a memorial to the University's first president, to be named Caldwell Hall and to contain a laboratory, library, and lecture hall. It was to be located east of South Building, symmetrically placed along the east-west axis of the Campus, to correspond with Gerrard Hall, at or near the site of the Playmakers' Theatre (former Smith Hall). Because of dissatisfaction with the business management of Thomas Waitt, superintendent of building construction and repairs, the plan was temporarily shelved; and definitely abandoned after 1847 when funds were raised for a second memorial to Caldwell, a marble shaft erected in the center of the North Quadrangle. The building, designed to house the Medical School, and erected in 1912, was given the name of Caldwell Hall. See two-page printed appeal for support of the University, Raleigh, April 15, 1847, signed by E. B. Dudley, Chairman; T. D. Benehan, D. Cameron, C. L. Hinton, Charles Manly, Romulus M. Saunders, Executive Committee. *U.N.C.I. 1791-1867,* p. 261.

19. *T. M.,* 1841-1868, p. 110; *E. C. T. M.,* 1835-1873, pp. 157, 158.

portico tacked on to the south side as an obvious afterthought, Davis submitted the classic design of a Greek temple, with an eastern portico as an organic part of the structure. In the original drawing by him, the capitals are of the classic Corinthian type, namely acanthus leaves. Responsive to the wave of aggressive Americanism then sweeping the country, which expressed itself in the desire to replace ancient designs and classic motives with innovations of native inspiration, Davis planned to replace the acanthus leaves with stalks of tobacco, wheat and corn, and ears of the latter. In the final design tobacco was omitted, perhaps to avoid over-decoration. These four beautiful capitals executed by Crane and Smith after Davis' designs, and not merely the two inner ones as originally planned, imparted a pleasing American "note" to a Grecian structure of classical inspiration erected at the height of the Greek Revival period in the United States. They have been much admired by architects, as well as by the uninitiated observer, and praised as a more skillful treatment than a similar experiment by Benjamin H. Latrobe almost forty years earlier.[20] The assembly hall, which was built principally of brick, was at Davis' suggestion stuccoed in stone grey, with its pleasing simulation of granite.

The progress of events, in connection with the designing and erection of the "assembly hall," is best followed from Davis' own record.

1850 [Design of portico]		[Design of Side Elevation]
	[Scales]	
[Design of floor Plan]		
		Assembly Hall
		University of N. C.
		Chapel Hill

1849
Nov. 3 Sent by Mr. Mickle set of first drawings   30.00
        At Chapel Hill from 10 to 15th May   25.00
        and revised set of drawings, as above sketch

20. Hamlin, *Greek Revival Architecture in America*, p. 212; Van Wyck Brooks, *The World of Washington Irving* (Philadelphia, 1944), pp. 272-73; "Notes and Letters on the Erection of the Capitol at Washington," *Appleton's Booklovers Magazine*, VI (1905), 345-55; Talbot F. Hamlin, "Benjamin Henry Latrobe: The Man and the Architect," *Maryland Historical Magazine*, XXXVII (1942), 339-60.

1850   On return to N. Y. Sent off 31st May roll of drawings: redrawn

1. Basement   5. Front elevation
2. Principal   7. End, July 5
3. Gallery floor   6. Flank north   50.00
4. [Blank]   8. Long section
10. Window   9. Transverse section

Nov. 7. At Raleigh, the Gov. & Committee requested A. J. D. to visit Chapel Hill and
enlarge plan. Accordingly he passed
several days with Gov. Swaine [*sic*]. conferred with the contractor, Capt .Berry,
and enlarged the plan to 122 ft. with a portico of 4 columns detached. Contract for
whole work $6250.00 deduct $625 for 125,-
000 brick furnished.

paid
$110.00
25.00

July 7 Obtaining 4 corn capitals, pulley blocks, paint   10.00 Paid
   Working drawings for Interior cornices   10.00 Jan. 4
                        Chim. piece   5.00 1853
Capitals, with wheat and corn of Crane &   by check
   Smith, were 37 inch deep   C. M.
         Col. 30 base, . . . 26 drain neck
In sending goods to Chap. Hill direct to
"Gov. Swaine [*sic*], C. H. Care of De. Rossett & Brown
1852 April 26 Purchased two chandeliers at 100 each to hold
   48 or 50 candles each.

The main hall, as actually built, was 84 feet long and 20 feet
high, with five large windows on each side. Happily, the idea
of a belfry, quite unsuited to the building as designed, was abandoned. The contractor for the building was Captain John Berry,
a prominent citizen of Orange County, who was State senator in
1848, 1850, 1852, 1864 and 1866, and representative in 1862.
The exact cost of the building, $10,303.63, was regarded as
moderate, both in view of the beauty of the structure and the
available interior space in proportion to the size. For some years
the building was known as and universally called "The Ball
Room." Captain Berry did considerable work for the Univer-

MEMORIAL HALL

Completed in 1931, this imposing building replaced the old Memorial
Hall built in 1885 on the same spot.

ALUMNI BUILDING

Completed in 1901, this building of gray pressed brick was erected to fill
the need for a building containing public offices, lecture-rooms, and
laboratories.

sity, being paid for his services as contractor during the period 1836-1863, the sum of $4,762.05.

A student contributor to the college magazine, of April 25, 1853, ironically refers to the rivalry between the two names: ballroom and library:

The new University Library is a credit to the State. Why will any body call it a "ball-room?" In these latter days, I judge it no feather in her cap that North Carolina should be supposed willing to spend $12,000 on a *ball-room*. When that splendid hall is properly tenanted, there will be grave and honorable company frowning from the shelves, and indignant denial of their living in a "ball-room," though I entertain no doubt but that like a good many other indulgent sages, they will allow the young folks a frolic once a year on their premises.[21]

A contemporary description of the building is found in an article in the college magazine, over the signature "La Mar":

The library building is quite an ornament to the College grounds, but by no means ostentatious or unsuitably elegant for this retired seat of learning. . . . It measures 130 feet long by 36 feet wide, and it is provided with shelves for 12,000 volumes. Our Ball Managers have insisted on furnishing the room with two imposing chandeliers. These added to its height give it an appearance at once beautiful and impressive. The basement has been converted to a reading room, which is much relished by those who *pride* themselves on their reading powers and acquaintance with the world's every day affairs.[22]

21. *U. N. C. M.*, II (1853), 253-54.
22. *Ibid.*, III (1854), 63. Evidently these are the two chandeliers, to hold 48 or 50 lights, purchased by A. J. Davis at a cost of $100 each, on April 26, 1852. See *supra*. In 1854 a laboratory was fitted up in the basement of Smith Hall, for the use of the department dealing with application of chemistry to agriculture and the arts.

14

THE ANTE-BELLUM UNIVERSITY EVOLV-ING; NEW EAST AND NEW WEST; WILLIAM PERCIVAL

PRESIDENT DAVID LOWRIE SWAIN is conspicuous as the University's first notable student of North Carolina history. He was an avid and indefatigable collector of letters, manuscripts, and documents indispensable to the writing of an authoritative and comprehensive history of the State. Three years before his election as president of the University, he co-operated with Joseph Seawell Jones in establishing the North Carolina Historical Society which was incorporated in 1832. When this paper organization proved to be still-born, not a single meeting ever being held, Swain organized the Historical Society of the University of North Carolina, which was founded in 1844.[1] He collected and collated many historical documents; and arranged for publication a number of historical essays which often were written by brilliant students of the type of his nephew, Leonidas F. Siler, class of 1852, and signed by Swain. He founded the *North Carolina University Magazine* in 1844, chiefly as a medium for the publication of essays and sketches by himself and others dealing with notable personalities and conspicuous events in North Carolina history. It is not an exaggeration to state that he produced probably the best college historical journal in the United States of his day.

Despite, or perhaps because of, his intense preoccupation with North Carolina history and the collecting of documentary materials, Swain exhibited an almost inexplicable indifference to science, the general problems of scholarship, and the building up of a great university library. He made no effort to restore the astronomical observatory after Caldwell's death and expressed satisfaction over the building's destruction. The Trus-

1. Consult the first report of the Society, a printed four-page pamphlet, issued in 1845. Swain was the first president of the Society. Swain Papers, Southern Historical Collection.

tees shared Swain's view, which did not differ greatly from Davie's, that the youth of the South should be taught here to become "ornaments of society" through the discipline of general culture, pillars of society through well-formed habits and suitably moulded characters, and leaders of society on the spacious stage of public and political life.

Each of the Literary Societies had its own library, commensurate in size and quality with that of the University. Despite the efforts of the more scholarly members of the Faculty, the students, save in the preparation of their innumerable orations, speeches, debates, and literary essays, which had to be carefully memorized and publicly delivered, took an airy, casual attitude toward books and reading; and when recourse to authoritative printed sources was required, frequented the libraries of their own Society Halls, rather than the University Library. For twenty years of Swain's administration, according to the distinguished lawyer and Trustee, Bartholomew Figures Moore, not a single book was purchased for the library. It was said of Swain, facetiously yet veraciously, that he always kept the University library in the attic, where the books were inaccessible and sure to be destroyed in the event of fire.

Swain realized, after almost two decades of total neglect of the library, that it would never do for the people of North Carolina to suspect that a large sum of the State's money had been expended for the erection of a "ball-room," to be used only once a year for Commencement dances. The building must become a library in fact as well as in name. The books, some 3,600, were transferred from the dusty and neglected shelves of President Swain's lecture-room in the South Building to their new "retreat." The student satirist "La Mar," concealed behind the mask of anonymity, through the Campus organ of opinion reflects the supercilious if not actually scornful student attitude towards this meagre collection of *res scriptae:*

The University library has been lately removed to a very appropriate building. The books are so few in number that it would not do to put them all together for crowded into one corner they would entirely escape observation. Scattered as they are, a few on each shelf, it is much feared by some that they must soon lose each other's acquaintance; while their beggarly appearance would make *vanity* in the best of them exceedingly ill-timed.[2]

General Benjamin Smith, Governor of North Carolina in 1810, one of the first and most generous benefactors of the University, had been promised by the Trustees that a building would be named for him. Accordingly, on May 31, 1854, the Trustees, on motion of President Swain, ordered that the building recently erected be named "Smith Hall."[3.]

At this time and for many years thereafter the pitifully slight and almost negligible collection of books was arranged haphazardly on shelves around the walls of the "Ball-Room." It is true that a reading room was provided in the basement; but it was open only one hour a week. In 1886 the Society libraries were moved into Smith Hall. By 1889, the year of the University's centennial celebration, the library had been turned into a modest sort of museum, with portraits, busts, paintings, old prints, maps, globes,—and even a few rare books!—on display. The shelves around the walls were well-filled; and double open bookcases were arranged, with casual irregularity, about the ballroom floor.[4]

When David Lowrie Swain was elected to the University presidency in 1835, the scholarly Professor William Hooper, who rightly believed that high academic standards and cultural interests should be paramount, caustically commented: "The people of North Carolina have given Governor Swain all the offices they have to bestow and now have sent him to the University to be educated." Nevertheless, it is indubitable that, save for a temporary arrest in progress during a period of grave financial depression, the University during Swain's administration advanced steadily, both in numbers and in popularity, down to the opening of the Civil War. The student attendance grew appreciably immediately following Swain's election as president: 89 in 1836, 142 in 1837, 169 in 1839. During the years 1835 to 1847, the average attendance was somewhat larger than that

2. *U. N. C. M.*, III (1854), 33.

3. *T. M.*, 1841-1868, pp. 163, 179. This building bore the name of "Smith Hall" for seventy years.

4. See illustration of the library interior, *Centennial Catalogue*, 1789-1889, facing page 36.

during the best years of Caldwell's administration. The anticipated growth in proportion to population increase and improvement in transportation facilities, however, was not at first realized, largely because of the severe depression in the prices of
agricultural products. During the decade 1848-1858, the discovery of gold in California, the wide extension of cotton culture throughout the South, the increase in slaves, and the completion of railroads ushered in an era of prosperity which was
clearly reflected in an almost trebled student attendance. Many
North Carolinians had purchased plantations in the deep South,
and a regular hegira from North Carolina into that fertile region
took place. These transplanted families sent their sons back
to Chapel Hill to acquire a liberal education. The rapid rise in
student attendance at the University is attested by the following
figures: 1849-1850, 191; 1850-1851, 230; 1851-1852, 251; 1852-
1853, 270; 1853-1854, 281; 1854-1855, 324; 1855-1856, 380;
1856-1857, 437; 1857-1858, 461.[5]

The college buildings were soon crowded to overflowing; and
the citizens of Chapel Hill who had money to invest built small
two-room cottages, called "offices," in corners of their yards or
on vacant lots, all over town.[6] The Societies, which had so joyously celebrated the occupancy of their "new" halls in Old
East and Old West in 1848, six years later found them totally
inadequate to accommodate the large influx of new members.
Boldly taking the initiative, as they had so often done thitherto,
the Societies on June 2, 1854, presented a joint memorial to the
Trustees urgently requesting the erection of an additional college
building and new Society Halls and library rooms.[7] No action
was taken at this time owing to lack of adequate funds; but the
situation clamoring insistently for action, President Swain called
a joint meeting of the Faculty and the Executive Committee of
the Trustees at Chapel Hill during Commencement in June,
1855, to consider, among other immediate needs, the enlarge-

5. University Catalogues, 1849-1858. The 1857-1858 figure of 461 is
erroneous, the corrected figure being 456.
6. Battle, I, 593; II, 40. The building of these cottages temporarily
relieved the congestion as to housing the students. In 1856, as A. J.
Davis' records show (see *infra*), the Trustees considered building cottage dormitories.
7. *T. M.*, 1841-1860, p. 162.

ment of Gerrard Hall and the erection of new dormitories. These needs were formally recognized as urgent; and A. J. Davis, who had so greatly contributed toward the University's improvement in appearance, was requested to visit Chapel Hill and submit plans for consideration.[8]

No action was taken in the matter until a year later (June 3, 1856), when the Trustees appointed William A. Graham, David L. Swain and William H. Battle a committee to consider the whole question of building, with power to employ an architect.[9]

On the invitation of the committee, A. J. Davis spent a week (July 24–31, 1856) in North Carolina, making a study of certain buildings, with reference to enlarging them, increasing the number of seats in the study halls, and possibly building cottage dormitories. During the next two months, Davis executed several designs for proposed alterations and additions, including enlarging Gerrard Hall by westward extension, building a transverse section of the gallery, and utilizing the third storey of the South Building for recitation rooms.[10] On June 3, 1857, the

8. Battle, I, 652.
9. *Ibid.*, I, 660.
10. The office records of A. J. Davis, covering this period, are given below in full:

1856

July 24 to 31	Visited University of N. C., Chapel Hill for purpose of examining buildings with view to additions. viz.		
	1 Enlarged Society Halls	1 Add to No. of benches	
	2 Recitation rooms	2 Convert Old South 3rd story	
	3 Enlarged Chapel	3 Extend present Chap.	
	4 Dormitory accom.	4 Build cottage dormitories	
	Expenses to Chapel Hill	30.00	
	Seven days at C. H. and on road	70.00	
Sept. 4	Sent plan for increasing seats in Society Halls	10.00	
Sept. 13	Elevation of Old South, Chap. hill with new cornice 2 3	10.00	No. 4
16	Section, transverse, and Section longitudinal	15.00	2.3
Sept. 17 15°	Plan for altering Old South 3rd story in recit.	10.00	No. 1
Sept. 18	Chapel. 1. plan for extending. 35 feet west		
19	2. Gallery, with section transverse	20.00	
20	3. Section east and west	10.00	
Sent Sept.	4. Elevation. West. South. East	110.00	

20
15°

Trustees authorized the Building Committee to "proceed forthwith to devise a scheme of college extension and improvement on the scale not to exceed thirty thousand dollars."[11] The matter finally came to a head at the meeting of January 4, 1858, when the Trustees, acting upon Graham's verbal report, instructed the Building Committee to take immediate steps to make all necessary contracts and to proceed without delay to the erection of the buildings.[12]

In view of the great artistic talents of A. J. Davis and of his notable architectural contributions to the Campus, it is a source of regret that the contract for the new buildings was awarded to a competitor. William Percival, a retired English army officer, who contracted to do the work at a cost not to exceed $40,000,[13] thus advertised himself: "With an educational training for his profession and a practical experience for more than 16 years on public and private works in Europe, Canada and the United States, he hopes to give satisfaction. . . . WILL furnish designs for Churches, Public Buildings, Stores, Town and Country residences and alterations of old buildings, Specifications and Superintendents. He will also attend to the laying off grounds and supply maps of the same. . . . N. B.—A large variety of original designs for Churches, Villas, &c., can be seen at his Office."[14]

William Percival was one of the firm of Percival & Grant, Architects and Civil Engineers, with offices in Goddin's Hall, Richmond, Virginia. Having received contracts to superintend

---

Sent Sept. 24. Plans and Elevations for two designs
Dorm 15.00 $200.00
1858 Feb. 1. Received from Gov. Chas. Manly, Raleigh,
January 28, 58 Paid
Cashier's Check on Merch. Bank, N. Y. for $200.00
See photostats, Davis Papers, Carolina Room, U. of N. C. Library.
11. *T. M.*, 1841-1868, p. 208.
12. *Ibid.*, p. 218. On June 5, 1858, the Trustees, lacking sufficient means to finance the building program, ordered the Treasurer to apply to the State Treasurer "for payment of the sum of $6,000 heretofore lent to the State by this board." *Ibid.*, pp. 218-19.
13. *Ibid.*, p. 225. William Percival, whose plans for the two new buildings had been submitted to the Board of Trustees on June 2, 1858, appeared personally before that body on June 21, 1858.
14. *North Carolina Standard*, February 3, 1858.

the erection in North Carolina of important buildings for which they supplied the designs, the firm in January, 1858, opened a branch office in Raleigh, located on the second floor of Smith's Brick Building, Fayetteville Street. The buildings mentioned were the New East and New West buildings on the University Campus, listed as the "Chapel Hill University Improvements," and the Baptist Church in Raleigh.

In engineering, a subject in which he might have been expected to show competence as a result of his military training, Percival registered a dismal failure with the new-fangled system of heating which he installed in the new structures. It was doubtless the glittering promise of this system of heating by water pipes, to supplant the form of heating the rooms with open fireplaces, which led to his selection in place of Davis. The Trustees did not have long to wait to rue the day of Percival's selection. "Furnaces were placed in the basement of each building and the hot water system adopted. The plan proved a failure, the rooms near the furnaces being too warm and those at a distance being too cold. After much expense the system was disused, not because the principle was faulty, but because there was a defect in the work."[15]

The buildings, with Thomas H. Coates as contractor, were completed and ready for occupancy in September, 1861, and the cost, which included the erection of a cupola and belfry on South Building, far exceeded anticipations: $54,798.62.[16] New West, as completed, was 114 feet by 40 feet, and three storeys high; and New East 116 by 40, four storeys high. The former contained 14, the latter, 22 dormitory rooms, each 16 by 18 feet. In the former were the debating hall and library of the Dialectic Society, in the latter, the debating hall and library of the Philanthropic Society, each room being 36 by 54 feet. These quarters were described at that time as probably superior to those of any

15. Battle, I, 660.
16. This is the figure which is given by Battle (Vol. I, p. 827) itemized by years. The figure given by Link (*op. cit.*, p. 53), $45,703.72, is clearly erroneous. The plans for the enlargement of Gerrard Hall, so far as the records show, were not carried out. Partial payments toward the buildings, amounting to $18,000, were made to the contractor, Thomas H. Coates, in 1859. *T. M.*, 1841-1868, p. 265; Battle, I, 724.

other similar societies in the country.[17] The buildings, stuccoed with cement, had two entrances on each side (north and south). The buildings are distinctive in having small glassed-in observatories on top, resembling the captain's "lookout" on the hurricane deck of a ship. Percival wisely followed the basic ground plan of the Campus in placing the two buildings symmetrically with respect to the major axis bisecting the Grand Avenue.[18] The discrepancy in height between the two buildings, as to which the records are silent, is perhaps explained by the unequal levels of the sites, the New East Building on a lower ground level being appreciably higher than New West.

In 1925, New West was remodeled, with 35 rooms and floor space of 12,800 square feet, at a cost of $80,391. In 1926 New East was remodeled, with 34 rooms and floor space of 16,750 square feet, at a cost of $102,228. In both cases, the architects were Atwood and Nash, the contracting firm, T. C. Thompson and Brothers.

The Literary Societies, which had already established a reputation as "Peripatetic Schools," were now at last accommodated in spacious halls. A backward glance to a time only eleven years earlier will show that increase of attendance had rendered the beautiful old Society Halls, upon which had been lavished so much effort and expense, quite inadequate. Truly the lot of the Literary Societies was not an entirely happy one; for they had drawn heavily upon their treasuries to contribute toward the furnishing of their debating halls and libraries in Old East and West.[19] President Swain, Governor Graham, A. J. Davis, Robert Donaldson, and James Johnston Pettigrew had especially

17. Battle, "History of the Buildings of the University of North Carolina," in Wheeler, pp. 344-57.
During the present century the growth in student attendance and vast increase in number and variety of extra-curricular activities, as well as the decline of interest in debating, declamation, and oratory in a more realistic age, eventually led to the abandonment of these spacious and elegant halls for more compact and restricted quarters on the Campus. The Dialectic Society Hall is on the third floor of New West, the Philanthropic Society on the fourth floor of New East.
18. See Chapter 1.
19. Battle, I, 511-14. The Societies eventually were released from their offer to pay one third of the cost of the extension of the buildings.

interested themselves in the adequate furnishing and equipping of the Society Halls. Writing to Governor Graham in September, 1847, President Swain said:

The best mode of arranging the shelves in the Libraries is a matter of interest. Mr. Davis and Mr. Donaldson have furnished plans, and Mr. Pettigrew, now of the National Observatory, who is familiar with their plans, the capacity of the Halls and the views of the young men, has examined the Library room at Washington and submitted his view in a letter which I enclose.[20]

Swain sagaciously suggested that a cabinet-maker, and not a carpenter, was required to construct the shelves and alcoves in the Society Halls' libraries. The construction of the shelves and finer woodwork in these libraries was entrusted, in November, 1847, to a gifted cabinet-maker, Thomas Day of Milton, North Carolina, a free Negro, who had come here from the West Indies. Day was well-known as a cabinet-maker in his day.[21] The most conspicuous features of the two libraries were the handsome shelves executed by Day, and the beautifully sculptured marble mantels.[22]

20. University of North Carolina Papers, Southern Historical Collection.

21. Consult *The State* (Raleigh), February 15, 1941; *Greensboro Daily News*, April 13, 1941. See also University Account Book.

22. Swain Papers, Southern Historical Collection. Charles Manly to David L. Swain, February 25, 1848: "Item, your Draft on me in favor of the Marble Mantels & shelves for Library Rooms shall be duly honored."

15

THE BOTANIC GARDEN AND PATTERN FARM; LANDSCAPE GARDENERS AND THEIR WORK

THE ARTISTIC DAVIS, whose versatility as architect, esthetic delicacy in draftsmanship, and catholicity of taste were all conspicuous, responded sympathetically to President Swain's hopes and projects for Campus improvement. In a letter from New York, April 17, 1844, already cited, Davis reassured Swain: "At my leisure I intend to add a plan for your botanic garden."[1] Somewhat earlier, it will be recalled, Swain, aware of Robert Donaldson's deep concern in these matters, suggested to Charles Manly "the propriety of exhibiting Mr. Davis' drawings to him, and urging if his convenience will admit of it, a visit to the University."[2] During the succeeding year, Davis, Donaldson, and Swain kept in close touch with one another by correspondence; and by summer, 1845, steps were being taken towards locating and employing a highly trained landscape architect who was likewise skilled as agriculturist and horticulturist. In a letter to Swain at the summer's close, Davis acknowledged Swain's communication of August 8, containing an enclosure to Donaldson; and recommended as a gardener a "talented young man of education and an active spirit," a Mr. Eliot, "satisfactorily located" in Ohio, who had studied with Mr. Downing at Fishkill, New York, opposite Newburgh. Young Eliot was described as one "fond of his art, and I think destined to take a high rank as a landscape Gardener." From Davis' letter, it is clear that Swain was in search of a man who was well informed on soils and climate, and could perform useful service, along the line of "extension work," as a lecturer on agriculture.[3]

1. University of North Carolina Papers, Southern Historical Collection.
2. *Ibid.* Swain to Manly, Chapel Hill, February 24, 1844.
3. *Ibid.* A. J. Davis to D. L. Swain, New York, August 25, 1845. Andrew Jackson Downing, eminent horticulturist, mentioned above, dedicated his book, *Cottage Residences* (New York: Wiley & Putnam, 1844) to "Robert Donaldson, Esq. of Blithewood on the Hudson, *arbiter elegantiarum.*"

Donaldson's reply to Swain's enclosure in the letter to Davis, throws a flood of light on Swain's plans and presents Donaldson's views regarding the vital need in North Carolina for a scientific study of agriculture.

September 30, 1845

My dear Sir,

Your letter of the 8th of Augt did not reach me 'till very recently—It will not be difficult, I think, to procure such a Gardener as you wish—and as the season is nearly over I shall not take any steps in the matter until I see you—I expect to visit No Carolina next month & will probably pass through Chapel Hill on my way to Pittsborough—about the 20th Octr. when we may converse freely on the subjects of your letter—In the meantime I cannot help expressing my surprise that there should be any hesitation among the Trustees of the University of *North Carolina* in giving the preference to the Professorship of *Agriculture* rather than to one of the *Military* sciences—Improved modes of Husbandry & Tillage & a change in the *staple Products* of No Carolina can alone arrest the declension of the state, and it is very obvious to me that the principles & practices of Agriculture must be taught by means of Lectures & the experiments of a model Farm to *educated* young men & by them disseminated. N. Carolina is & always will be an *agricultural* one and the more its Agriculture is improved the better—As for soldiers—your Chevaux de Frize of a coast will keep off invaders— and could not the Proffessor of mathematics teach civil engineering & Drawing?—but I forbear.

Yours very truly,
Robert Donaldson

N. B.
   My Post Office is
      Red Hook
         Dutchess County
            N. Y.[4]

During the next two months, Donaldson revolved the problem in his mind, requested members of Thorburn's Seed Store in New York City to "be on the lookout" for a "Gardener," and also wrote to his brother James, suggesting that he engage a gardener, tentatively, for the post at Chapel Hill, and to communicate with Swain. The results of Donaldson's reflections, which are highly constructive and modern in conception, are

4. University of North Carolina Papers, Southern Historical Collection.

embodied in a letter to Swain early in December following, of which the major portion is quoted below:

As a preliminary movement, to the "Botanic Garden & model Farm"—would it not be as well to get up an Agricultural Society at Chapel Hill?—to be composed of the Villagers—who have farms—or neighbouring Planters & the members of the Faculty and *Students* who may feel inclined to unite for the purpose—Let some of the Acres of the old Steward's Hall field be used to try experiments in manures, tillage, seeds &c under the direction of the Gardener & appoint some day in the season—when the most remarkable fruits, vegetables & animals shall be exhibited in the village & a suitable address made—

President Polk will, I've no doubt send from the Patent Office in Washington the most valuable seeds which are annually distributed there—

Thus an additional source of pleasant interest will be made to the other attractions of your village—If James Taylor could be connected with the College he would in a short time be very useful in that & similar things—[5]

Nothing could have been more progressive than Donaldson's proposal of the establishment of an Agricultural Society at Chapel Hill, and under its auspices the conduct of a "pattern farm," suggested by Swain, which might be a stimulating example and model to large-scale agriculturists and to small farmers throughout North Carolina and elsewhere.[6]

It proved to be by no means easy to secure a suitably cultivated person to perform all the functions and duties of a theoretical and practical agriculturist and also of a skilled landscape gardener, at the modest salary offered by the Trustees. Swain, who was practical by nature but academically unenlight-

5. Swain Papers, Southern Historical Collection. Robert Donaldson to D. L. Swain, Red Hook, December 6, 1845.

6. In 1820 a State Agricultural Society had been established in North Carolina; and Mr. George W. Jeffreys of Person County, the corresponding secretary, was active and energetic in promoting important communications from leading Southern agriculturists which were published in the *American Farmer*, issued in Baltimore. Defunct for a time, the Society was subsequently revived under more favorable auspices and with wider support in 1852, and became an important factor in the development and improvement of agriculture in North Carolina, especially under the leadership of Chief Justice Thomas Ruffin, Robert A. Hamilton, Frederick Hill, and J. W. Norwood.

ened, outlined a vast program of University lectures to be delivered by the incumbent, presumably a member of the Faculty, in addition to his onerous duties of Campus improvement, forest conservation, and landscape architecture. The most promising letter came from S. Chandler Ball, who was a candidate for the position. After agreeing to the condition of delivering lectures on Agriculture and Geology, Ball continues:

In regard to compensation—the improvement of the college grounds and gardens will not only be laborious, but connected with a course of lectures will, if the duties are faithfully performed, occupy all my time—I shall therefore expect the compensation to be adequate to the comfortable support of my family. . . . In consideration of the labor required, the qualifications necessary to perform it profitably to the institution together with the offers I have received from other schools, I am induced to name the sum of one thousand dollars as the salary I ought to receive—For this amount I would make a permanent engagement with a view of becoming a citizen of your place, and devote all my time to the improvement of the college grounds, and the instruction of a class in the theory and practice of Agriculture.[7]

Ball's reasonable requirement of a salary of $1,000 a year caused the rejection of his offer, since the Trustees, who were uninformed on such matters, apparently expected to secure the services of a paragon of knowledge and energy and a workman of versatility and skill, for less than half that amount. It may well be that the University authorities could afford no more than $400 per year.

Throughout the year 1847, Swain with the active assistance of A. J. Davis and the two Donaldson brothers prosecuted inquiries for a landscape gardener. Through the aid of a Mr. Ripley, and Alexander Smith, seedsman, of 388 Broadway, Davis conferred early in March with two new applicants: James Barry, sent to him by Smith, and John Loader, an Englishman, who presented his application through Ripley. Davis' continued letter to Swain, reproduced in the main below, supplies the requisite historical data regarding the first landscape gardener ever employed as a University official.

7. University of North Carolina Papers, Southern Historical Collection. S. Chandler Ball to D. L. Swain, Hoosick Falls, Rensselaer County, New York, August 13, 1846.

. . . . At 10 this morning [March 9], a Mr. James Barry called from Smith.—Barry required in addition to the $400—a *house*, kitchen, sitting room and one bedroom, *fuel*, and *vegetables* with milk—I was writing his terms out, when Mr. Ripley came in with an application from an "English Gardener," who will call upon me to-morrow, and who will accept of the $400 without other provision. As this last applicant is so ready, and is quite as able (so represented by Mr. Ripley) as Barry, perhaps, I have almost determined to send him on at once, so that you will *suffer* no more delay, and if you find him the right sort of man, you will cheerfully add his road expenses to the $400, but this will lie at your option—

Wednesday, 6 P. M.—Since writing the above I have seen Mr. John Loader, with Ripley, and have agreed with him, the said Loader, that he shall set out for Chapel Hill on Monday or Tuesday next, 15 or 16th March, and that you will pay him twenty dollars when he arrives at Chapel Hill for road expenses, the same *not* to be subtracted from his salary of $400 per year—The engagement to continue for one year from the time of his leaving New York, and longer if you should agree together. Mr. Loader has letters from England having been employed at Sion House in the botanic Garden of his Grace, the Duke of Northumberland, and Mr. Ripley speaks well of him; in his opinion as fitting for your purposes as either Cavanagh or McLaughlin—Trusting that we shall not be deceived *again*, as in the case of McLaughlin, I remain

Yours &c
Alex. J. Davis.[8]

It will be recalled that, in the interim, Davis had been busy in preparing plans and designs for paths and plantings for the Campus, to be laid off by the landscape gardener to be engaged. Regarding one sketch already sent to Swain, he attaches the following explanation in a postscript to the letter quoted above:

P. S. Please observe that the road or path turnings and crooks in the sketch I send by Mr. Donaldson are not *capriciously* made, but *designed*, so as to present *sunny* and *shady* places for trees that flourish best in sun or shade. This however I leave for you and the gardener to discuss on the grounds, before adopting the plan.

The records indicate that Loader was engaged for the academic

8. *Ibid.* A. J. Davis to D. L. Swain, New York, March 9, 1847. On the ground that the salary was inadequate, Mr. McLaughlin declined the post of landscape gardener at the University of North Carolina. P. G. McLaughlin to David L. Swain, Fitchville, Connecticut, April 27, 1847. Swain MSS., Department of Archives and History, Raleigh.

year, 1848-1849, beginning in the month of June; and that the total amount appropriated for Campus improvement and adornment for the year, which included Loader's salary of $400 per year, was $1,000. Colored gardeners and workmen, the use of teams for hauling, the conduct of a nursery, and the purchase of ornamental flowers and shrubs used up the remainder of the fund. Loader's work as landscape architect for the first year proved satisfactory, as Dr. Mitchell's letter to Secretary Manly, reproduced in full below, indicates:

University of N. Car Febry 3[d] 1849

Gov. Swain interchanged a few words with you on the subject of improving the grounds & campus about the University and the employment of Mr. Loder [Loader] another year—There was no opportunity for the action of the Committee at that time but it was supposed that it would be safe and prudent for us to go ahead and trust to having our proceedings sanctioned by the Committee—It was voted at the close of the last session by the Faculty that they would recommend the employment of Mr. Loder [Loader] another six months.

Mr. Loder [Loader] was busy a good deal last year in getting ready in a nursery plants and shrubs to be transferred to the grounds —He has hitherto been engaged a good deal this year in making the transfer—was wanted in fact to render the expenditure of last year available—If he is employed tis almost a matter of necessity to furnish him with such assistants as shall make his superior skill of use beyond his mere manual labor—

Whilst he is employed therefore—whether for half a year or a whole one we think it best that the rate of expenditure should be about the same as last year or a thousand dollars per year—

Further—as the engagements of gardeners are generally entered into at the beginning of the year it seems that it will be hardly fair to dismiss Mr. Loder [Loader] and throw him out of business in June—We rather imagine that you will be inclined to retain him till next January [1850], giving him timely warning now that his services may not be required after that time.

In the whole business we are not prepared to recommend anything with any very intemperate zeal—If an appropriation is made a part of the money should be placed at our disposal for application as it may be wanted.[9]

9. *Ibid.* Elisha Mitchell to Charles Manly, February 3, 1849. *E. C. T. M.,* 1835-1873, pp. 147-48. February 6, 1849. "The application of Dr. E. Mitchell on behalf of the Building Committee at Chapel Hill for a

THE CAMPUS, 1907

Note old Memorial Hall, second building to right of South Building.
This picture is a reproduction of the photogravure in sepia, published
by W. T. Littig and Co., New York.

MAIN STREET OF CHAPEL HILL, LOOKING WEST

At the left is the old University Inn, located almost on the present site of Graham Memorial. Walter Pickard, proprietor of the University Inn, can be seen at right crossing the street. From a photograph taken about 1892.

OLD UNIVERSITY INN AND ANNEX

This rambling, mustard-colored structure was managed by Mr. Walter Pickard and generally known as Pickard's Hotel. From a photograph taken in 1897.

It is inferred from the evidence at hand that Mr. John Loader was retained as landscape gardener for the University until the end of the calendar year 1851.

The appropriation of $1,000 annually for the improvement of Campus and grounds, inaugurated in 1848, marked the beginning of a thorough-going, efficient handling of the perennial esthetic and practical problems involved. On December 15, 1851, the Trustees authorized the Faculty to hire a gardener to take charge of the college grounds at a salary not exceeding $500 annually; and resolved that this appropriation be continued from year to year, as a regular part of the University budget.[10] The immediate occasion of the resolution, it is surmised, was the departure of John Loader, and the engagement of a successor. This was a burly Englishman of powerful frame, Thomas Paxton, who had the highest recommendations as a landscape gardener. Incidentally, he was reputed to be a relative of the Duke of Devonshire's famous gardener, Sir Joseph Paxton, who was knighted by Prince Albert at the first Crystal Palace Exhibition in 1851. Both Loader and Paxton trained Negroes, of different ages, to become skilled gardeners, especially in handling flowers, shrubs and cuttings and scions of various sorts. In 1853, at the age of twelve, for example, Wilson Caldwell, who had long been the companion or "body servant" of President Swain's son, Richard, entered the service of the University and became in time an expert gardener under Paxton's direction.

Early woodcuts, lithographs, and water colors of the antebellum Campus, ranging from 1846 to 1860, are not wholly successful in presenting a convincing impression of the sylvan scene. The earliest drawing, 1846, made from the east, reveals a circular row of tall trees ringing South Building on the southeast, shrubbery along College Street east of South Building, and a grove to the west of Gerrard Hall. The drawing made from the neighborhood of the Davie Poplar (*circa* 1852) portrays a

---

continuation of the appropriation for improving the campus & for the Grounds was laid before the Committee and thereupon Resolved that the sum of One Thousand Dollars be & the same is hereby appropriated for said purpose to be expended under the direction of the said Building Committee."

10. *T. M.*, 1841-1868, p. 134.

Campus largely in the natural state, with irregular paths criss-crossing the original quadrangle enclosed by South, Old East, and Old West. A drawing, by William Momberger, made at a point slightly east of Person Hall (*circa* 1855), reveals a row of trees beside the walks, on the inner side of the original quadrangle, running north and south along Old East and Old West. A drawing (*circa* 1856) made from about the same spot as the 1846 drawing, exhibits the recently completed Smith Hall, encircled by a quadrant of tall trees. A beautiful water color (*circa* 1856), executed by the famous architect, A. J. Davis, a gifted draftsman, and made from the approximate site of the present Confederate monument, exhibits a Campus unadorned, with grass growing in patches and a nucleus of trees within the Grand Avenue reduced to a minimum (far below the real number), in order to give an unobstructed view of the buildings. A view of almost the entire North Quadrangle, taken from the approximate site of the present Confederate monument is obtained in a beautiful colored lithograph (*circa* 1860), showing a Campus of smooth lawn dotted with ornamental trees expressing the imaginative ingenuity of the artist rather than the magnificent, umbrageous oaks then *in situ*. Scattered about in pleasing irregularity are small trees and shrubs which, judging by the conventional representation of the giant oaks, do not present a true image of the scene. Drawings of Gerrard and Smith halls, obscured by other buildings, are shown in insert, at right and left, bottom. A lithograph, of undetermined date, shows a carriage and two horses (probably an artist's gloss) on the path from Old East to the old Chapel of the Cross. Seen in their chronological succession these illustrations convey a faithful picture of the progress of University building.

Fortunately, the recollections and records of both residents and visitors, and in particular of newspaper correspondents suffice to conjure up fascinating visions of a glamorous scene, scarcely suggested by the engravings, lithographs, and woodcuts. The North Quadrangle, including the Grand Avenue, a gentle decline stretching as far to the east as the west line of the present Arboretum, was the theater for the display of the art of the horticulturist and the landscape architect. By the middle of the last century little save normal clearing and the laying out of a few simple pathways seems to have been effected in the South Quadrangle. This area has been developed only within comparatively recent years. There was, however, a botanical garden, probably with a greenhouse, located, as originally planned, at the rear of the Campus. Here Loader and after him Paxton are believed to have cultivated the decorative plants, flowering shrubs, and luxuriantly blossoming roses and other bushes which were later transplanted to the "ornamental grounds" north and east of the South Building.

The Campus in the fifties and sixties, so far as concerns natural growth of trees, was much as it is today, save that the giant oaks and poplars, and the graceful elms, were more numerous and, in the case of the larger trees, more massive and with denser overarching branches than at the present time. So numerous were these ancient monarchs of the forest in the fifties that Paxton had to sacrifice many of them in order to give play for the younger growth. Between the Ball Room (Smith Hall) and College Street (Cameron Avenue), which then terminated at the site of present Carr Building, was a thick hedge of immense rose bushes covered, in the late spring and summer, with an incredible number of white blossoms. The two broad walks, very simply surfaced with light gravel, running northward from Old East and Old West buildings to Franklin Street, were lined on each side with bushes and shrubs: red, pink, and white rose bushes, alternating at short intervals with flowering shrubs of various types.[11] Scattered about over the Campus, in particular along present Senior Walk and the pathway diagonally crossing the Campus area east of present Alumni Building, were well grown bushes of then universally called *Pyrus japonica*, brilliant floral fires flaming excitingly against the darker background of verdure and foliage.

Along present Senior Walk, the landscape gardeners—Loader

11. These rose bushes, looking not a little the worse for wear, may be seen in a view of the Campus published in *U. N. C. M.*, XIII (1894), facing p. 273. They made attractive borders for the graveled walks, especially when the red roses were in full flower. These bushes were removed in 1895-1896, during the administration of President Winston.

and Paxton, whether one or both, one cannot say—planted handsome "mock" oranges which, until very recent years, fruited abundantly. Osage oranges and holly trees were planted thickly along the walk passing in front of present Graham Memorial as far south as present Senior Walk as well as for some distance along that walk. Around this same corner these walks were bordered with beautiful rose bushes and flowering shrubs. This dense decorative hedge played a·double role as ornament and screen, happily concealing from view, for the pedestrians along these walks, the unsightly backyard and stables of the hotel. Unturfed embankments five feet high, covered with sand, were built around the Old East and Old West buildings; and it is surmised that this was the work of Loader or Paxton.[12]

President Swain followed President Caldwell in the policy of isolating the college dormitories from the outside world. He went much farther than Caldwell in this respect, eliminating the section of the Raleigh Road which ran across the Campus, and leaving access to the college buildings by vehicular traffic only at the west via College Street. This was a plain road until the fifties, when the college gardeners, with an ample force of colored laborers, the whole directed by Dr. Mitchell, hardsurfaced it somewhat after the modern manner. They also made the graveled walks which survive to the present day.[13]

One of the peculiar folkways of the time and place, a sort of exaggerated assertion of American liberty and democracy, was the popular aversion from fencing in horses, mules, donkeys, cows, sheep, and hogs. They roamed the streets so freely as to delay vehicles in the road and to drive women and children from the sidewalk. There is reason to believe that in disgust over the constant and serious damage thus done to lawns, shrubs, bushes, and plants, the fruit of his handiwork, the long-suffering English gardener, Thomas Paxton, resigned his post with the University in 1858. In that year, looking toward the employment of a successor to Paxton, the Trustees ordered that the

12. Battle, I, 578, 583-84. These terraces survived until the late eighties. The Literary Societies imposed fines upon any member who sat upon, or walked over these terraces. Love, p. 3.

13. K. P. Battle, "The University Fifty Years Ago," *U. N. C. M.*, XIII (1894), 289-318; Battle, I, 524-25, 614. In describing the reopening of the University in 1875, Mrs. Spencer praises the "noble gravel walks."

bursar of the University employ a competent white man to superintend the Campus and enclosed grounds; to preserve and cultivate the shrubbery and plants; to keep up the fences; to prevent trespasses by wandering cattle and other such nuisances; and to do all other work about the buildings and grounds as the bursar might direct.[14] In belated if veiled justification of Paxton's resignation, the Trustees on June 6 of the same year indignantly and mournfully resolved: "That the Board of Trustees have seen with much regret the beautiful grounds of the Campus become the common pasture ground for the cows and hogs of the village. [And further] Resolved that the Bursar be directed to take the most effectual measures for expelling all stock from said grounds and keeping them away."[15]

It was certainly not dislike of either the village of Chapel Hill or the University of North Carolina which impelled Thomas Paxton to give up his position. On resigning he set up in business in Chapel Hill as a professional "Florist." In a printed folder, preserved in the University archives and labeled "For the Fall of 1860, and the Spring of 1861," notice is given as follows: "Particular attention paid to laying out Gardens, planting Orchards, Vineyards, &c. Asparagus beds Strawberry beds, &c., made on the lowest terms. . . . Persons visiting Chapel Hill are solicited to call and see the Nursery." Paxton further comments: "The taste for rural improvement is rapidly advancing in this country, and as many people plant trees or flowers who are unacquainted with the proper mode of doing so, I would advise all that can to employ some skillful person to lay out and plant their gardens for them. They would realize the benefit from so doing and it would be less expense." It requires no Sherlock Holmes to detect in the "skillful person" described by the writer none other than the famous English landscape gardener, horticulturist, and florist: Thomas Paxton.[16]

14. *T. M.*, 1841-1868, p. 134.
15. *Ibid.*, p. 273.
16. It is of interest, historically, to record that in this folder Paxton lists 39 varieties of "hybrid Perpetual Roses," 12 of "Bourbon Roses," 5 of "China Roses," 13 of "Tea Scented Roses," 36 of Verbenas, 4 of "grape Vines"; and other miscellaneous plants. Prices for cuttings range from 10 to 25 cents each. Attention is called to "flower seeds"; and the reader, in particular the college student during the season of balls, dances and routs, is laconically notified: "Bouquets made to order."

16

THE APOGEE OF CAMPUS CARE; PRESIDENT BUCHANAN'S VISIT

THE HIGHEST POINT in the development of the Campus, from the standpoint of forest conservation and horticultural care, prior to the Civil War was reached shortly before the opening of that struggle. President Swain's disappointing experiences for the better part of a decade in the search for a combination landscape gardener and college lecturer on agriculture convinced him of the futility of the attempt with the meager funds placed at his disposal by the Trustees. The initial cost of a trained gardener ranged from $400 to $500 annually. The many additional items: assistant (Negro) gardeners, teams for hauling, purchase of bushes, plants, shrubs, and trees, the care of grass and trees, the repair of fences and rock walls, the tasks of planting, cultivation, and transplanting, greenhouse, etc.—used up the balance of the sum of $1,000 appropriated annually.

In a list of the various amounts spent on the University buildings and grounds for the period 1836-1863, compiled by Charles Manly, Treasurer, the cost of "stone fences" is set at $2,000; and of "campus improvements and keeping in repair," the figure, a rough estimate, is set at $10,000.[1] In the University records, it is worthy of mention, the last three items expended on Campus care prior to the University's closure in 1871 are listed as follows: 1860, Campus, $500; 1861, Campus, $500; 1862, Campus, $448.88.[2] The expenditures on Campus care fell off to about 50 per cent or less, beginning with 1860; but as the annual appropriation for the period 1848-1858 had averaged close to $1,000, Manly's rough estimate of $10,000 for the twenty-six year period, 1836-1863, is obviously too low. The impressive sum of $15,000 for that period, not including the cost of the rock walls, which were built around the University dwelling houses as well as

1. Battle, I, 779.
2. University Account Book, 1857-1880, pp. 24, 26, 28.

around the Campus, is estimated as a fairly close approximation to the amount actually disbursed. This will always stand as a monument to the wisdom, fine taste, and esthetic sense of President Swain; and to him and to Dr. Elisha Mitchell, who originated some of the creative ideas and as the President's trained lieutenant executed them, will always be due the gratitude of the University's alumni, friends, and lovers.

Before proceeding to a description of the University and the Campus prior to the outbreak of fratricidal strife, the final success of President Swain's prolonged efforts to establish a lectureship in agriculture, geology, and associated topics deserve to be recorded here. In pursuance of a resolution of the Board of Trustees adopted in 1852, a School for the Application of Science to the Arts was established as a phase of University instruction. The courses were designed to prepare students to become engineers, artisans, chemists, farmers, miners, and physicians. Two professorships were established: civil engineering, and chemistry as applied to agriculture and the arts. In the latter department were delivered lectures in the chemistry of agriculture, and in analytical chemistry, which embraced the analysis of soils, manures, and mineral waters, the assaying of ores and minerals, and the testing of drugs and medicines. Benjamin Sherwood Hedrick, of Salisbury, N. C., first honor graduate of the class of 1851, a gifted mathematician, and a student of Chemistry at Harvard, was placed at the head of this department.[3] Although Swain did not carry out Robert Donaldson's suggestion of establishing an Agricultural Society at Chapel Hill nor a lectureship in agronomy at the University, he laid the foundation for the pursuit of engineering knowledge and the scientific study of agriculture in North Carolina where it was then so sorely needed. He thereby set the example for the establishment, some four decades later, of the North Carolina College of Agriculture and Mechanic Arts which in 1932 became one of the co-ordinated institutions of the Consolidated University of North Carolina.

The brightest picture of the University of North Carolina offered during the ante-bellum period was presented at the Commencement exercises of 1859. For a moment in American his-

3. Battle, I, 642-44.

tory, this Campus was clearly caught in the national spotlight. The Campus was at the apogee of its beauty and picturesqueness. The "continuity" of this film, a succession of moving and talking pictures, warrants projection upon the screen of fancy for our scrutiny and admiration.

In 1859, the war clouds were lowering; and men of good will, in many quarters, were bending their efforts towards reconciliation of the sections and a tightening of the bonds, then rapidly loosening, which for seventy years had held the states in a Federal Union. The Secretary of the Interior at this time was Jacob Thompson, formerly of Caswell County, North Carolina, and a graduate of the University of the class of 1831. President Swain, an old-line Whig in politics and a confirmed Unionist, through Thompson's kind offices extended a cordial invitation to James Buchanan of Pennsylvania, President of the United States, to attend the Commencement exercises of 1859. In extending this invitation, President Swain was doubtless actuated by the desire of focussing national attention upon the University which, under his administration, had grown to be one of the leading universities in the United States in numbers, dignity, and prosperity, linked with the earnest hope of mitigating the moral, political, and economic animosities which appeared to threaten the dissolution of the Union.

In 1845 the degree of Doctor of Laws had been conferred *in absentia* by the University upon James Knox Polk, a graduate of the class of 1818; and two years later, as President of the United States he had attended the Commencement exercises. The Trustees voted the same degree for President Buchanan. Such visits to the University Commencements, at the brief interval of twelve years, were regarded as highly auspicious auguries. In commenting on these visits by two chief magistrates of the Republic, the venerable Dr. William Hooper, in his memorable address, "Fifty Years Since," delivered before the alumni on June 7, 1859, wittily, if not scientifically, observed: "I am proud to find, from two astronomical observations, that Chapel Hill lies right in the orbit of Jupiter and his satellites, and that the period of his revolution is twelve years." President Buchanan, who was delighted with the Commencement exercises, remarked, in a speech from the platform of Gerrard Hall, concerning Hooper's reminiscences: "I think I have never heard in my life more genuine humor and wit than that presented today by the gentleman who delivered the address, and who was formerly a professor here."

President Buchanan, Secretary Thompson, Governor Ellis, and a company of gentlemen were met at the boundary of the village on the Durham Road at 1:00 p. m., Wednesday, June 1, 1859, by a large gathering of Faculty members, students, members of the Board of Trustees, citizens, and visitors, headed by two students, marshals for the day, Thomas Whitnall Davis of Louisburg, North Carolina, and Charles Bruce, Jr., of Halifax County, Virginia. On alighting from his carriage, President Buchanan was greeted by Professor John Thomas Wheat and escorted to the home of President Swain. On the velvet carpet of the front lawn, beneath the shade of magnificent oaks, the chief magistrate of the nation was graciously received by the President of the University; and warmly greeted in an appropriate address of welcome.

The President of the United States, in great good humor and inspired with a strong feeling of patriotic devotion to the Union, replied. The concluding paragraph follows:

I would advise these young men to devote themselves to the preservation of the principles of the Constitution, for without these blessings our liberties are gone. Let this Constitution be torn to atoms; let the members of this Union separate; let thirty Republics rise up against each other, and it would be the most fatal day for the liberties of the human race that ever dawned upon any land. Let this experiment fail, and every friend of liberty will deplore the sad event. I belong to a generation now passing rapidly away. My lamp of life cannot continue to burn much longer. I hope I may survive to the end of my Presidential term. But emphatically do I believe that mankind, as well as the people of the United States, are interested in the preservation of this Union, that I hope I may be gathered to my fathers before I witness its dissolution. . . .

The crowd then enthusiastically called for a speech by Jacob Thompson, who responded feelingly in reminiscent mood. Significant was his appreciation of President Caldwell, whom he recalled as indefatigable in bringing to the public mind in North

Carolina the importance and feasibility of running a central railroad from the seaboard to the mountains. "It was argued by him with singular force and clearness," said Thompson, "that great and lasting good could be derived by the State from the establishment of such a road. But how was it considered in his day and generation? He was considered a dreamer of dreams. The people had compassion for the good old man. They thought that, like Festus of old, 'too much learning had made him mad.' And now, today, I have been enabled to come here by the very track which the old man traced out upon the map." The crowd greeted with "great cheering," according to the written report of one who was present, this tribute to the great Caldwell, practical visionary and prophetic dreamer.[4]

The warm reception given to President Buchanan at the University of North Carolina was significant as an indication of the strongly conservative trend of thought in the "Old North State." Buchanan invoked the spirit of unity in the name of the patriotism of the Revolutionary fathers. "His passage through the Old North State," says the correspondent of the *New York Herald*, "is marked by all the characteristics of a grand ovation and a display of heartfelt enthusiasm such as rarely attends the visit of any statesman hero to the south." Five governors of North Carolina greeted President Buchanan at Chapel Hill: the incumbent, Governor Ellis, and four ex-governors, Graham, Bragg, Morehead, and Swain.

The reception and open-air dinner on the beautiful lawn of the president's mansion were notable. The tables beneath the shade of the mighty oaks were arranged in the form of a right-angled triangle, the hypotenuse of which, a broken line, was

4. Battle did not reproduce the speeches, erroneously stating that they were not reported. They appeared in two South Carolina newspapers, the Columbia *Banner*, and the *South Carolinian*, June 8, 1859. The latter report appeared also in the *National Intelligencer*, June 8, 1859, with credit to the correspondent of the *South Carolinian*. The complete and official texts of the speeches were printed in an exhaustive account of the Commencement exercises, in two parts, *U. N. C. M.*, IX (1859), 59-63, 105-20. The text of President Buchanan's speech, in a corrupt and in places ungrammatical form reproduced from the *National Intelligencer*, is found in Philip Auchampaugh, "A Forgotten Journey of an Antebellum President," *Tyler's Quarterly Historical and Genealogical Magazine*, XII (1935), 42-48.

loaded with fruits, confectioneries, and Southern delicacies of every description. Buchanan, with hair of silvery whiteness surmounting a high, massive forehead, was pleasant and affable to all comers; and Swain, dignified and intensely serious, fully measured up to the responsibilities of the occasion. Says one of the local correspondents:

The two Presidents as they stood facing each other halfway between the house and the gate, formed a striking picture. There was the man of theory and the man of practice—the maker of educated men and the user of educated men—the fitter of youth for rewards and the bestower of rewards: the one drawing lessons of wisdom and courtesy from the past, the other endorsing those lessons from his experience of the present—both earnestly looking to the youth of their country as the strength and hope thereof.[5]

The successive scenes through which President Buchanan passed during the course of the Commencement exercises were rendered further memorable in being staged upon a sylvan theater surrounded by dense forests. To a correspondent from South Carolina, the spot appeared to be "one of the best selected sites for an institution of learning that can be found in the whole country. On each side of the walks are large and beautiful rose bushes, interspersed with garden roses and flowers of great beauty." Commenting editorially in *The Constitution* of Washington, D. C., George W. Bowman remarked: "The situation and surroundings of Chapel Hill are such as are most suitable to a hallowed retreat of learning and religion, and are fitted to awaken and cultivate that taste for the beauty and grandeur of Nature which is the earliest to be developed and the last to be parted with by minds of the highest order and sensibility."

The people of North Carolina appreciated to the fullest extent the labors of Swain and Mitchell, of Paxton and Loader, in adding the services of Art to the further adornment of Nature. A correspondent of one of North Carolina's leading newspapers, which fully covered the events of this Commencement, pertinently commented:

Chapel Hill, as a location for a college, cannot be surpassed in

5. *The Fayetteville Observer*, June 6, 1859. The Joseph Caldwell house had been designated by the Trustees in 1839 as the president's mansion.

fitness. It is a most beautiful location, and from its elevated position and the rolling character of the adjacent country must of necessity be healthful. What can be done by art to assist nature in beautifying the place has been done with no niggardly hand. In the midst of a neatly ornamental Campus tower up the spacious college buildings, which are being extended east and west by two other buildings fully as large as the largest of those already built. The village is in perfect keeping with the college and grounds, and is remote enough from all public routes of travel to be at once accessible, and peaceful and quiet.[6]

Fitting conclusion of this description of the University Campus and village at the apogee of their loveliness is the record by a perceptive observer, one of the student editors of the college magazine, in the year following President Buchanan's visit and preceding the fateful year which heralded the wreckage of this vision of an "earthly paradise":

The College Campus is now arrayed in all the charms of Nature assisted by the fostering hand of Art, and the soft, balmy air is perfumed by the almost eternal flowers that bloom in vernal beauty along the walks that lead from the Buildings to the Village. If it be true that the noblest traits of character and intellectual progress and development are the effects of such natural scenery—if it be true that it is owing to such scenes as these that a Wallace and a Tell were reared, and if "the untrammelled element of liberty, the safeguard of religion and virtue" be there nourished to bloom and bless the world—then, surely, it is fortunate for students here that such gay, smiling landscapes are spread out before them, with forests, hills and valleys extending in majestic grandeur and the freshness of perpetual morning far away to the distant limits of the horizon. . . .[7]

6. *The Raleigh Standard*, June 8, 1859.
7. *U. N. C. M.*, IX (1860), 571-72.

17

THE FIRST INFIRMARY:
"THE RETREAT"

THE DECADE preceding the opening of the Civil War marked the University's most conspicuous period of prosperity and greatest increase in numbers in its history. The construction of the beautifully proportioned Library and Ball Room combined and of the New East and New West buildings, containing the spacious and dignified Society Halls, esthetically rounded out a building plan based on axial symmetry and harmonious design.[1] When President Swain took office in 1835, there were only 89 students in attendance. In February, 1858, according to the *American Almanac*, the University of North Carolina had the largest enrollment of any college or university in the United States, with the single exception of Yale.[2] The enrollment for the academic year 1858-1859 was 456, of whom 278 were from North Carolina and 178 from other states. "The site is admirably located, the college grounds are beautifully adorned, and the walks are pleasant and agreeable. . . . The committee are proud to say that the University has scarcely a superior, and very few equals in the United States."[3] The University was widely popular, its economic condition sound. The outlook for the future, which at many times in the past had been dark and forbidding, was at last bright and full of promise.

It was not to be. Dimly prevised, uneasily sensed, was Will H. Thompson's later query:

> But who shall break the guards that wait
> Before the awful face of fate?

Mighty forces, conflicting interests, political, sociological, economic and religious, were irresistibly converging toward a fore-

1. Consult the lithograph of the Campus, *circa* 1860, reproduced in this book. The original is in colors.
2. *U. N. C. M.*, VII (1858), 291-92. For interesting comparisons regarding attendance, cf. Battle, I, 644-45.
3. Report of the Visiting Committee, presented by Judge W. H. Battle, June 4, 1859.

ordained collision. The opening gun fired at Fort Sumter heralded the rapid decline of the University's fortunes, eventuating in brief, temporary cessation in 1869 and enforced closure, for lack of students, in 1871.

There is an intimation, at once symbolic and prophetic, in the arresting circumstance that the last building of the ante-bellum University was a hospital. That the University was not devastated with fire, considering the numerous and almost constant fire hazards, is as inexplicable a miracle as that the Campus was not periodically swept, as by a besom of destruction, with disease waves epidemic in character and deadly in effect. Providence seems to have temporarily suspended the mathematical law of probability. Sanitation and hygiene were unpractised, and seemed to be unknown. The metal cups, attached to chains, which hung outside each student's room, excited the embarrassing curiosity of visitors, strollers and trippers; and the South Campus was a *terra inhibita* to all visitors. Failure of the authorities to safeguard life, health, and property, in such matters as sewage disposal, toilet facilities, protection against fire, health, and life-hazards, and to provide college physician, nurses, and infirmary, represents a state of mind of curious callousness and almost childlike innocence unthinkable to the contemporary scientist and guardian of health.

The climate was extraordinarily salubrious. The students, removed from the hazardous conditions, temptations to inebriety, and other vices of urban life, were conspicuously healthy. Apparently there was no typhoid; and other diseases, especially of a malignant or deadly character, seldom originated in Chapel Hill. Lady Luck seemed to preside over the destinies of an institution filled with careless, irresponsible, and often lawless youths, devoid of organized athletics, health supervision, sanitary inspection, official medical care, and sanctuary for the ailing and diseased.

In the fifties, especially after 1853, when the attendance began to skyrocket, the facilities for the accommodation of the students provided by the University proved entirely inadequate. Two spacious dormitories, the New East and the New West, were contracted for; but they were not ready for occupancy until the decade 1850-1860 was drawing to a close. Miss Nancy Segur Hilliard, whose parents had come to Chapel Hill from Alabama in 1817, had for many years since the early thirties, maintained the Eagle Hotel with extraordinary popularity and success. According to Mrs. Spencer, she was best known for "maintaining in good style for many years its [Chapel Hill's] boarding house, numbering from 100 to 150 daily boarders, besides the transient company of a large hotel. . . . It used to be objected to her (except by her boarders) that she kept rather too good a table for her college boys." In 1852 she gave up the management of the hotel, which was purchased for $10,000 by Col. Hugh B. Guthrie; and built a home of her own close by, a "neat white residence known as the 'Crystal Palace' where she continued to receive a limited number of boarders."[4] At the Eagle Hotel, for years, board was usually $8 per month; but eventually it rose to $9 and finally to the top price of $10. By 1856, after the large influx of students, prices rose from $50 a session to $55 and even $60 at some boardinghouses.

The need for extra space, which constantly became more pressing, induced many citizens to rent part of their dwellings; and as mentioned in a former chapter, various small houses of two and three rooms were built in town yards and on various isolated lots. Quaint names, not so attractive as "Crystal Palace," were given to these little shacks and shanties by the riotously imaginative students: Bat Hall, Pandemonium, The Poor-House, Possum Quarter, Craigsville, Pickard's, the Retreat, and the Sniddows (a curious anagram on the Widow Snipes). After the havoc wrought by the war, the economic decline of the village, and the closing of the University, many of these structures fell into dilapidation and ruin, and others were removed to remote spots and sold for Negro habitations.

The administrative and legislative inhibitions against the blandishments of intoxication and the allurements of theatricals and

4. Obituary (MS.) in Mrs. C. P. Spencer's scrap-book, Southern Historical Collection. *U. N. C. M.*, V (1856), 94. This was the home later occupied by Mr. and Mrs. Algernon Sydney Barbee, where the late Major William Cain resided for years. It still stands, on the south side of Franklin Street, opposite the Institute of Government. In 1946 the Barbee property was purchased by the University.

the like, with their atmosphere of dissipation and immorality, were not completely operative;[5] and not infrequently bands of students would visit nearby towns in pursuit of intemperate indulgence and forbidden pleasure. On the whole, however, because of the isolation of the University and the discomforts of travel, these sumptuary and other laws went far toward maintaining moral standards and the general health and welfare of the students.

During the first half of the decade, 1850-1860, the average student attendance was 269, during the second half, 427. Since 1835, when Swain became president, the student attendance had increased more than 400 per cent. When the attendance was small, the proportion of the ailing and the ill constituted a small number of individuals during the course of a year; but when this number was multiplied by five, the number became formidable. Conditions in regard to medical service, nursing, and hospitalization were primitive and distressing. An indisposed student usually remained in his room, trusting to the tender mercies of his roommate or friends. If seriously ill, he might be removed to the hotel, to receive there the ministrations of mother, sister, or other relative; or remain in the dormitory, to be attended by relative or nurse tenanting a nearby room. Prior to the building of the branch railway line to Chapel Hill in 1882, the bodies of students who died in Chapel Hill were buried in the village cemetery with appropriate ceremonies; and elaborate memorial resolutions were invariably passed and placed on permanent record by the Literary Societies which usually had these mortuary and funerary rites in charge. The need for an infirmary or student hospital was pressing and dire.

In 1850 John Thomas Wheat, born in Washington City, November 15, 1801, a distinguished Episcopal minister and a resident of Nashville, Tennessee, was elected professor of logic and rhetoric in the University, as successor to the Rev. William

5. Beginning in 1825, the Trustees inaugurated a series of by-laws forbidding the purchase of spirituous liquors, the exhibition of theatrical, sleight of hand or equestrian performances, etc., without written permission given seven days beforehand by the president or some member of the Faculty; electioneering treats, public billiard tables, or other public tables for playing games of chance or skill. Battle, I, 301, 435, 645-46.

VIEW OF FRANKLIN STREET, LOOKING WEST

The old Central Hotel is at extreme left. Originally known as Roberson's Hotel, this ten-room structure was located opposite the present
Post Office, on the site of Battle-Vance-Pettigrew. From a photograph
taken about 1898.

THE CAROLINA INN

Built by John Sprunt Hill in 1924 and presented to the University in 1935, it furnishes superior accommodations for alumni, visitors, and distinguished guests of the University. It is of Southern colonial design, and the long porch facing Cameron Avenue was inspired by the porch of Mount Vernon.

Mercer Green, recently elected Bishop of Mississippi. The wife of Dr. Wheat, born Selina Blair Patten, was a very maternal and benignant woman; and as she became familiar with medical and sanitary conditions at Chapel Hill, she pursued the bold course of a Florence Nightingale. She devoted herself to the saintly task of nursing ill students, and induced other women of the congregation of the Chapel of the Cross, wives of members of the Faculty, and women of the village generally to follow the same humanitarian course. Recognizing the danger from the prevailing lack of hospital facilities and the necessity for the permanent amelioration of such conditions, Mrs. Wheat strongly urged upon the Faculty and Trustees the establishment of a home for the sick; and offered a corner of her own yard for the site of such a building, in order to be near the patients at all times.

These eloquent representations to both Faculty and Trustees eventually produced the desired effect. On June 3, 1857, on motion of Charles Manly, Secretary, the Board of Trustees resolved

That it is expedient to erect on the lot now occupied by Professor Wheat a home of suitable dimensions and materials for an Infirmary or Hospital for the accommodation of sick students. That a committee consisting of Gov. Swain and Judge Battle be appointed to cause said building to be erected and supplied with suitable furniture for a sick room; and that without delay the said committee make a contract with a builder, superintend its faithful execution and that they draw upon the Treasurer for such sums as may be necessary to enable them to fulfill this order.[6]

The committee had been most favorably impressed with the former work of Alexander Jackson Davis; and although this building was to be only a two-room, one-storey cottage, they selected him as architect. On June 2, 1858, the Board of Trustees requested the Executive Committee to make provision for supplying the small hospital and nursing home with suitable nurses and attendants. Building continued, and on December 1, 1858, the Building Committee formally reported: "The resolution of the Board directing the erection of a suitable building, to be used as occasion may require, as an asylum and retreat for

6. *T. M.*, 1847-1869, p. 208.

sick students, has been complied with; and a handsome cottage containing two rooms and supplied with necessary furniture has been built and paid for."[7] The cost of the building, which included the architect's fee, was surprisingly small, $2,259.11. This building, which stood in the southwest corner of the lot on which Spencer Hall now stands, was universally called "The Retreat"; and was not supplanted by a second University infirmary until thirty-six years had elapsed.[8]

7. *T.M.*, 1841-1868, pp. 227, 235, 779.

8. From the period of the opening of "The Retreat" until some years after the re-opening of the University in 1875, sick students were under the supervision of Dr. William Peter Mallett. Dr. Mallett, who was greatly beloved, died October 16, 1889. He continued his practice until the day preceding his death. The building was abandoned finally as a hospital, and used as an office by Dr. Eben Alexander, who came to the University in 1886. A sort of improvised hospital was established in rooms on the second floor of the New East Building. Mr. Robert S. MacRae was then the nurse in charge; and although not scientifically trained, he personally labored most generously and humanely to aid in the care of ailing students. These rooms were in use for this purpose for some time after Dr. Richard H. Whitehead came here in 1890 as the first Dean of the University Medical School. When the second Infirmary was erected in 1895, largely if not wholly through the generosity of Mr. Harry S. Lake of New York City, it was in charge of Doctors R. H. Whitehead and C. S. Mangum. When the third Infirmary was erected in 1907, the student patients were cared for by Doctors C. S. Mangum, I. H. Manning, and William de B. MacNider, each for three months of the nine-months academic year. Dr. E. A. Abernethy cared for the Summer School students except during World War I. When Dr. Abernethy returned from France he was elected University Physician, and had sole charge of the Infirmary. During the S. A. T. C. period of World War I and the influenza epidemic of 1917, Dr. MacNider took over the care of the students at President Edward K. Graham's request; and he was assisted by Dr. William Coppridge of Durham. Miss Ferril Choate was head nurse during this period. Following Dr. Abernethy's death on March 21, 1933, Dr. Foy Roberson of Durham was given charge of the Infirmary and retained that post until the election as University Physician of Dr. W. Reece Berryhill in September, 1933.

The above information regarding the staffs of the several infirmaries was furnished by Dr. W. de B. MacNider. For additional data regarding the second, third, and fourth infirmaries, see *infra*.

PART IV
THE FLAME AND THE PHOENIX

18

THE VALLEY OF THE SHADOW:
1861-1865

THE DISTURBED CONDITION of the times and anticipation of the imminence of war caused a spectacular and rapid decline in the University's numbers and fortunes. On the afternoon of Commencement Day, June 2, 1859, Judge W. H. Battle, speaking on behalf of the Committee of Examiners, reported the University to be in a most prosperous condition, with 456 students. The autumn 1860 session, however, opened with only 376 students, and by the end of the academic year this number had decreased to about 75. The autumn session of 1863 opened with 63 students; and the following year, 1864-1865, the student body totaled about 50. Despite contrary counsels and disheartening diminution in numbers, Governor Swain was adamant in his determination to keep the University open.

With great ardor, the Southern youth rushed to the front to enlist; and during the late spring of 1861 students were leaving Chapel Hill at the rate of eight or ten a day. All the students, "from the smallest Freshman to the gravest Senior," became members of the four military companies established on the Campus. Writing to his brother from Chapel Hill, March 2, 1861, Archibald Erskine Henderson, a student, relates: "The Military excitement is still increasing, most of the companies have uniforms, some red, others blue flannel and some speckled jackets. They have muskets borrowed from the village company." The student companies were as follows: A, Captain Michie, 16; B, Captain Nuckols, 16; C, Major Lilley, 56; D, Captain Garrett, 20. Arms for the student companies were not supplied by the State; and muskets for drill were lent the students by the Orange Light Infantry of almost 80 men, commanded by Captain Richard J. Ashe. This company left Chapel Hill for the front on April 27, 1861; and another local company left the following September. Eventually four companies went into service from Chapel Hill and vicinity. Drilling, in which all students participated, was conducted according to *Upham's Manual;* and was continued intermittently until 1865.[1] Early in the struggle, President Davis said that he didn't want "the seed-corn to be ground up." In 1863, after conscription had been resorted to and only 63 students were left at the University, President Swain, at the instance of the Trustees, wrote a long letter to President Davis, urging the relaxation of the conscript law regarding the members of the two higher classes in the University. This exemption was granted in 1863; but when the request was repeated the following year, so pressing had become the need for recruits for the armies of the South that the request was peremptorily denied by Secretary of War Seddon.

Another grave problem confronting University authorities was the preservation of University property. On March 2, 1862, the Executive Committee of the Board of Trustees appointed an officer to teach military tactics and to protect the buildings. While the former, for certain reasons, was not fully carried out, the latter injunction, for the duration of the war, was executed as well as conditions permitted.

On April 9, 1865, President Swain, whose father was a native of Massachusetts, and ex-Governor William A. Graham, both old-line Whigs and Unionists at heart, were appointed by Governor Vance as commissioners of peace to treat with the Union commander, General William T. Sherman, for the surrender of Raleigh and the protection of the State capital and the University. Major John Devereux, Quartermaster of the State, was designated as the officer to conduct the train and to carry the flag of truce; and, at his own request, Dr. Edward Warren, Surgeon General of North Carolina, was permitted to accompany the commissioners.[2] In response to Swain's declara-

1. Battle, I, 724, 736-37. For copy of letter of A. E. Henderson, the author is indebted to George F. Scheer, Chapel Hill. Consult *U.N.C.M.,* March, 1861, pp. 441-42. The editor queries: "Can any other place of its size in the State beat Chapel Hill for soldiers?" See also A. C. Howell, "A History of the Chapel Hill Baptist Church, 1854-1924" (Chapel Hill, 1945), p. 16.

2. Spencer, X and XI, *passim.* "While walking to the rear," says Dr. Warren in describing the "capture" of the commissioners, "we encountered a number of [Union] regiments whose soldiers amused themselves in rude jests at our expense, making the venerable ex-governors their especial butts and targets as they were dressed in long-tailed coats

tion that the "war was over," Sherman gave his personal assurance that the destruction of property should cease as soon as terms were signed.[3] At the original conference of the commissioners with the Union Commander, Sherman, who had been Superintendent of the State Military Academy of Louisiana before the war, assured Swain, "as one college president to another," that the University of North Carolina, the buildings and property, would be safeguarded.

The Confederate cavalry entered Chapel Hill on Friday, April 14; and General Wheeler established his headquarters in a house, since destroyed, on the north side of Franklin Street opposite the Chapel of the Cross. Closely pursued by Union cavalry, General Wheeler at first contemplated defending the place; and his troopers dug rifle-pits on the southern slope of Point Prospect, the remains of which are still visible.[4] Reports of the overwhelming superiority in numbers of Kilpatrick's pursuing cavalry, however, soon convinced Wheeler of the hopelessness of the attempt to defend the position; and at noon on Sunday, April 16, he called in his pickets and at 2 P. M. galloped away in retreat, at the head of his jaded, grey-clad horsemen.

About eight o'clock on the following morning the thirty-year-old Union general, Smith B. Atkins, grave and handsome, rode

---

and tall beaver hats, *ante-bellum* relics, which they had especially donned for the occasion. But with measured tread and the dignity of Roman senators, the commissioners walked along indignant to the last degree, but stately, silent and apparently as indifferent to their tormentors as to the rails upon the surrounding fences or to the weeds of the surrounding fields. Indecorous as were these assaults, and philosophically as they were borne, there was something so essentially ludicrous in the whole performance that despite the time and circumstances I could not help being amused or succeed in repressing an occasional outburst of laughter." Edward Warren, *A Doctor's Experiences in Three Continents* (Baltimore, 1885), pp. 337-38.

3. On April 13, 1865, President Swain personally met at the State House in Raleigh the Federal officer charged with the hoisting of the Stars and Stripes over the dome; and informed that officer of Sherman's promise that the capital of the State, with its libraries, museum, public records, and charitable institutions should not be damaged, "provided no hostile act is committed" against the Union army. That same afternoon, accompanied by ex-Governor Graham, President Swain personally delivered the keys of the Capitol to General Sherman.

4. Chamberlain, p. 85.

in at the head of 4,000 cavalry. Without delay, General Atkins took effectual steps to execute Sherman's orders. "Guards were placed at every home immediately, and with a promptness that was needful," says an eye-witness. ". . . The village guards, belonging to the 9th Michigan Cavalry, deserve special mention as being a decent set, who, while they were here, behaved with civility and propriety."[5] In the suburbs of Chapel Hill and the surrounding country, however, where the vigilance of the officers was relaxed, Sherman's "bummers," during this period when confusion reigned and peace negotiations were still in progress, pillaged freely and without restraint, although doing no violence to those whom they robbed.

The 4,000 Michigan cavalry under General Atkins encamped in and around Chapel Hill for more than two weeks, April 17 to May 3, inclusive.[6] Some of the officers were quartered in the University buildings; and their mounts, whether hitched or left to graze, doubtless did no little damage to the lawn and trees of the Campus. General Sherman is reported to have quizzically remarked that his cavalry officers' mounts were the best educated horses in the Union army, as they spent all their time, during their stay in Chapel Hill, in the University Library. Indeed, cavalry horses were stabled in several of the University buildings. Referring to the South Building, Battle says: "It has lately sheltered cavalry of the conquering Union army in the great civil war." Mrs. Spencer is authority for the assertion that Federal cavalry stabled their horses in the Library. An old inhabitant reported to a committee of the Trustees in 1874 that he had seen "horses looking out of the windows of Old West building"; and in the committee's report specific mention is made of the passage, running east and west, in the South Building being defiled by the "ordure of cattle and horses."[7]

Classes were discontinued during the Federal occupation, as

5. Spencer, pp. 171-72.
6. *Ibid.*, pp. 256-61. The greater proportion of the troops were encamped in the sloping fields north of town, from the Tenney plantation westward for about a mile.
7. Letter from Augustus W. Long, class of 1884, Brevard, N. C., April 25, 1945, to the writer; Wheeler, p. 351; Charles Phillips, *op. cit.*, p. 7; letter from Mrs. Lucy Phillips Russell, daughter of Charles Phillips, Rockingham, N. C., November 7, 1945, to the writer; report of the com-

the few students not residents of Chapel Hill had returned to their homes before the arrival of the Federal cavalry. On the departure of General Atkins with his command on May 3, 1865, he detailed a guard of 35 "blue coats" of the 10th Ohio Regiment, under Lieutenant Bradley, to protect University property; and these soldiers attended the Commencement exercises, May 31 and June 1, 1865. At these exercises, of the fifteen members of the Senior class only four were present. It is believed, surmised Battle, that the University of North Carolina was the "only institution of rank, for males or females, [in the Southern States] which held Commencement exercises in the terrible year of 1865." This University was one of the two colleges in the South to remain in operation throughout the Civil War.

The voluntary action of President Swain and ex-Governor Graham in securing appointment as peace commissioners eventually wrought great damage to the University. On hearing of their activities in negotiating with Sherman for satisfactory peace terms and the saving of the State capital and the University from destruction, President Davis was so outraged that he ordered their arrest—an order which was not executed.[8] A Confederate general, standing on the sidewalk of Franklin Street in Chapel Hill, as his division of infantry marched through the town on April 14, vigorously denounced Swain and Graham as traitors, and declared that they ought to be hanged.[9]

An extraordinary incident, an intersectional romance of the type which has furnished the theme of countless novels and dramas since 1865, set the final seal upon President Swain's downfall. When the handsome young Union brigadier, General Atkins, called upon President Swain at Chapel Hill on April 19, he was introduced to the President's lovely daughter, Eleanor; and they were stricken with love at first sight. The parents were greatly perturbed; and the entire community, including soldiers

mittee, to examine the condition of University buildings, consisting of Walter L. Steele, Paul C. Cameron, and William L. Saunders, April 9, 1874: *T. M.*, 1868-1882, pp. 185-92.

8. J. G. deR. Hamilton, *Correspondence of Jonathan Worth* (Raleigh, 1909), I, 381. Letter to J. J. Jackson, Company's Shops (later Burlington), April 21, 1865.

9. Spencer, p. 166.

of both armies, was highly incensed. General Atkins presented his lady-love with a magnificent riding horse; and General Sherman likewise presented President Swain with a fine, but skittish, driving horse, at the same time placing a vehicle at his disposal. The acceptance of these animals, doubtless correctly believed to have been spoils of the conquerors "swept from southern stables," was generally regarded as tactless and unwise, and brought down a storm of condemnation upon the recipients.

The wedding, which took place in Chapel Hill, August 23, 1865, constituted a sensation, a more than nine days' wonder. The following extract from the contemporary diary of a member of the class of 1865, who describes the village as "alive with excitement" over the wedding, is illuminating:

This alliance has shocked the feelings of all true Southerners; and it is not surprising that the lovely couple should have been shown so little attention by the citizens of C. Hill and the students of the Univ. The college bell was tolled by the students while the ceremony was being performed. Such a rude and unlooked for interruption must have grated harshly on the bride and groom. The tolling of the bell was kept up for three mortal hours. And the performances were concluded by hanging Gov. Swain and Gen. Atkins in effigy. Students never know when to stop; but I hardly know whether to admire or blame this frantic outburst of indignation. Who can sympathize with or even pity a young lady who willingly throws herself into the arms of a Yankee general, while his sword is yet reeking with the blood of its victims, her own relations or at least her own countrymen?[10]

Almost overnight the University appears to have lost its old friends and gained a host of powerful enemies. It became the target of violent attacks from both sides; and these charges, instead of canceling each other out, only increased the University's unpopularity. The University was denounced by old-line Whigs as the stronghold of "unreconstructed rebels" to whom the idea of the restoration of the Union was abhorrent. The author of the anonymous letters, known as the "Delphi" papers, congratulated the public of North Carolina on the downfall of

10. Original diary in the possession of the writer. The diarist was not present in Chapel Hill on the day of the wedding, arriving two days later.

its University as the destruction of a "pestilential hotbed of slavocracy."

On the other hand, President Swain was regarded with distrust by the "irreconcilables" because of the honors and attentions paid him by Federals and Republicans of the highest position, such as General Sherman and President Johnson. Moreover horrid rumor was on the wing; and "it was told from mouth to mouth and believed all over North Carolina that Ellie Swain went to Illinois loaded with finery and jewels stolen from the women of states farther south and given to her by her husband." Throughout the entire South, indeed, the wedding was regarded as a disgrace to North Carolina.

Matters went from bad to worse. Prominent members of the University were forthright and tactless in their violent denunciations of W. W. Holden, influential editor and politician, who as early as the beginning of 1864 headed the "Peace Party," which was organized to bring North Carolina back into the Union while the war was still in progress. On June 4, 1867, when President Swain delivered the address at the erection of the monument to Jacob Johnson in the Raleigh cemetery, an occasion attended by Jacob Johnson's son, President Andrew Johnson, Holden, then governor, was not invited to sit on the rostrum with the distinguished guests. Whether by oversight or design, no invitation to the 1867 Commencement was sent to Governor Holden. Greatly incensed, the Governor did not accompany the presidential party to Chapel Hill. In retaliation for these slights, which may have been either calculated or unintentional, Holden in the spring of 1868 sent a guard of Negro soldiers to Chapel Hill ostensibly to take possession of the University Campus and buildings; and here they remained for many months, to the great disgust and indignation of the inhabitants.[11]

11. Speaking of the astronomical observatory Dr. James Lee Love says: "All records of observations have been lost; whether during reconstruction days when the University was closed for some years and some of the dormitories turned into stables by Negro troops, or before, no one knows." "The First College Observatory in the United States," *The Sidereal Messenger*, pp. 417-20. During the outbreak of Ku Klux Klan activities in Chatham County, a squad of militia was sent there by Governor Holden in mid-summer, 1870. Under the command of Dr.

Throughout these parlous and troubled times, President Swain remained hopeful for the rehabilitation of the University and the restoration of national good will. There were not a few who shared Swain's hopes for a speedily re-united country; and one devoted personal friend wrote him these heartening words of faith and good cheer: "Live ten years longer, Governor, and you will be the most popular man in North Carolina."

Fate, however, dramatically intervened to forestall this optimistic prophecy. There is a tincture of tragic irony, suggestive of an Aeschylean drama, in the singular fortuity that the wild and skittish horse presented to Swain by Sherman, was, both subjectively and objectively, the cause of President Swain's undoing. Three times the horse was stolen from the Swain stables; and thrice the resolute owner pursued the culprit and recovered the stolen animal. On August 11, 1868, accompanied by Professor Fetter, President Swain drove his "famous Sherman horse" into the country; and on their return journey, the unruly horse bolted and turned over the buggy, throwing both occupants to the ground. Although no bones were broken, President Swain gradually declined in health and died peacefully on August 27. Swain had been displaced as president of the University by Governor Holden and the "Reconstruction" Board of Trustees, July 23, 1868; and he found himself a victim of mental and moral concussion, a fate he found unthinkable. "I have heard many of the friends of Governor Swain," said the distinguished lawyer, Weldon N. Edwards, "state that he became melancholy and began to droop away on the termination of his duties as president of the University, and they believed a broken heart was as much the real cause of his death as the fall from his carriage. He felt the last link was broken that united his heart and hopes to all earthly objects." The decease of David Lowrie Swain sounded the death-knell of the ante-bellum University of North Carolina.

Emery, Adjutant, they came to Chapel Hill, July 27, 1870, and camped in the grove south of the college. Chamberlain, p. 189.

19

"RECONSTRUCTION," DISSOLUTION, AND RE-OPENING; MEMORIAL HALL, OLD AND NEW

WITH THE inauguration of the plans for the University's "reconstruction," and for a social and racial upset, strongly advocated by Dr. Fisk P. Brewer and seriously entertained by President Solomon Pool, the college and village entered upon a period of rapid decline and deterioration. Came the irruption of the "Goths and Vandals," the breakdown of property safeguards, the pillage of libraries, the rape of the Society Halls, the indiscriminate felling of trees, the injuries to the Campus, the occupation and defilement of the college buildings. Speaking of the new régime, Vance says:

The reformation wherewith they reformed it, bore a strong family likeness to that with which Attila and his Scythian progressionists civilized Italy. . . . This noble property of the State is fast sinking into ruin. Many of the grand old trees have been laid low for firewood. Doors are off hinges and broken down, windows without blinds or glass, carpets torn up and carried off, the halls [Society Halls] are measurably stripped of their furniture, pictures and adornings; and almost everything portable is either injured, destroyed, or stolen. And, worst of all, the libraries—comprising about twenty thousand volumes belonging to the University and the two societies [Dialectic and Philanthropic]—have in great measure shared the same fate. How many volumes have been pillaged and carried away it is impossible to tell—happily books are not a popular object of larceny—but the damage to those remaining is distressing. An air of melancholy, of *ruin*, pervades everything where once there was so much active and intelligent life, where so much of North Carolina's moral and intellectual greatness were found and fitted for her advancement; where were centred so much of her hope and her pride. Truly, in the words of an ardent and cultivated daughter of the State, who lately gazed upon the painful spectacle: "On these walls written Ichabod—for the glory is departed."[1]

1. *Sketches of North Carolina*, by Zebulon B. Vance, together with an *Elegiac Ode and Other Poems*, by James Barron Hope (Norfolk, Va., 1875), pp. 57-58.

During the war the forests surrounding the Campus were seriously depleted by the indigent professors who were allowed by the Trustees to cut firewood from the University lands. Mrs. Swain and Mrs. Spencer lamented the felling for firewood by Professor Patrick of the oaks in the President's yard: "great trees which had sheltered the good and the great who made Chapel Hill what it was." This same vandalistic professor looted the Phi Society Hall, carrying off velvet rug, carpet, and handsome chairs in order to entertain the Trustees at the President's house in all the rich splendor of pilfered furniture. Says "Billy Barlow" in Thomas M. Argo's "colyum" in the Raleigh *Sentinel*, a squib "inspired" by Mrs. Spencer:

I hev hearn thet the Perfessers made a raid on the Fie Cersiety Hall & tuk the cheers & cyarpits. Perfesser McIver who is a Die said he didn't care a red cent what the Trustees sot on. Split bottom cheers was good enough fer him. Ef Trustees didn't like em, they might set on the floor, en so the Die hall was not bummed so bad as the Fie. One new student is come [June, 1869] to jine the spellin' class.[2]

The doors of the Society Halls were burst open, the panels kicked in, and the valuable historical manuscripts and records, as well as the books, were scattered indiscriminately all over the building. "The Society Libraries," wrote Mrs. Spencer, on December 28, 1870, "have been sadly pillaged since Holden's negro troops first arrived and took charge, while the militia last summer broke in the Phi and Di libraries and helped themselves."[3] Within the next two years, matters went from bad to worse; and the college buildings were callously used for Negro debauches. Says Mrs. Spencer:

Gangs of negroes spend the nights in the Old South Building, rioting, shouting, drinking. You have no idea of the degradation. The Halls and Libraries are broken into at all times, and I am told that the Phi Library, which is especially in Mr. Pool's hands, has its books scattered all over the building. It makes me heartsick to write about it.

I stand at my window late in the night, sometimes looking that way, expecting to see it all on fire.[4]

2. Chamberlain, pp. 167, 168.
3. *Ibid.*, p. 195. Letter to Mr. Abram Venable, Granville County.
4. C. P. Spencer to Mrs. D. L. Swain, Dec. 31, 1872. *Ibid.*, p. 215.

Where the Federal cavalry were encamped in April-May, 1865, no trace of vegetation was left: "Not a blade of grass, nor leaf of any kind is to be found there. The ground is stamped as smooth as a floor."[5] George Dixon, an English Quaker, was appointed professor of agriculture; and among other things, did grave damage to the grove south of the South Building, where he was authorized to establish a model farm. Mrs. Spencer's lamentations (February 27, 1870) went up to high Heaven as most of the great trees came crashing down; and she vehemently declared that Dixon's appointment had never been ratified by or even brought before the Board.[6]

The Bursar, Professor David S. Patrick, reported to the Trustees in 1869, that at the time of the suspension of University exercises, January 3, 1869, a communistic spirit prevailed; and much theft and damage was done as the result of the popular opinion that "the university property belonged to the people." It was not surprising, infers the self-righteous Bursar, "that some laboring under this pleasing impression should have been guilty of theft. Books were taken from the libraries and all working utensils used about the college Campus were stolen. Some have returned property with the request that 'no questions should be asked' while others still retain property under the impression that 'something may yet turn up.' "[7] Evidently something *did* "turn up" for this Chapel Hill "Mr. Micawber." This was the same Patrick who raided the Phi Society Hall, as described above. A guard was put over the University property in 1869; but it was soon withdrawn, whereupon depredations proceeded unchecked. After the University was closed, the professors' houses belonging to the University were raided, floors torn up, furniture carried away, and fences torn down, the whole being used for firewood. The University property, as early as March,

5. *Ibid.*, p. 88.
6. *Ibid.*, p. 186. Soon afterwards Dixon obtained leave to revisit his native land, and never returned to Chapel Hill. The damage, however, was already done. Mrs. Spencer uses the spelling "Dickson."
7. Report of Professor David S. Patrick, Bursar, March 6, 1869. *T. M.*, 1868-1882, pp. 90-92. The solicitous Bursar reported that $20 had been spent for repairs on the college buildings, and $33.31 on repairs of his own house!

1869, was found to be in "very bad condition"; and the sum of $1,000 had to be appropriated (June 17, 1869) for necessary building repairs. Fine and costly apparatus, mathematical and astronomical instruments, were "badly injured and totally unfit for use."[8] In reports of November, 1871, and November, 1872, Robert W. Lassiter, Secretary and Treasurer, stated that there had been no material damage to the University buildings; but that the re-opening was desirable, because of the gradual deterioration and decline of the University's property since there was "no watchful eye and constant hand to guard it from injury and decay. The immediate supervision of the property of the university at Chapel Hill including grounds, buildings, halls, furniture, libraries, apparatus, etc., has been given to Messrs. Pool, Mason and McIver, the last named having a house and lot free of rent in consideration of his services for taking care of the property."[9] According to Mrs. Spencer, the guardianship of the University buildings by Pool and Mason was a mere farce.[10]

With the ratification of the new constitution of North Carolina in March, 1868, a clean sweep at the University, of president and Faculty, and the inauguration of the new régime were foreshadowed. In a public statement early in 1868, Mr. Solomon

8. *Ibid.*, pp. 90-92, 119, 262. In a poetical satire of the time, obviously by Mrs. Spencer, occur the following lines:

> Why don't they come to college
> And get a little knowledge?
> While all the Sciences,
> Means and appliances
> Are lying around loose
> To rust out for want of use.
> No misplaced economy
> Need deter one from Astronomy.

See Battle, II, 28-29, for the full text of this poetical satire.

9. *T. M.*, 1868-1882, pp. 135, 150. Reports of November 21, 1871 and November 19, 1872.

10. Chamberlain, p. 215. Writing to Mrs. Swain, December 31, 1872, Mrs. Spencer mournfully remarks: "I think I do Mr. Pool no injustice in saying that he would much prefer to see every building belonging to the University burned down, to having his place taken from him. He and Mason are superintendents of the University property. They will not do anything toward protecting the buildings. I think they invite their destruction."

GRAHAM MEMORIAL

This building, completed in 1931, was erected as a memorial to President
Edward Kidder Graham, who had dreamed of a student center on the
University Campus.

MOREHEAD-PATTERSON BELL TOWER
Dedicated on November 26, 1931, the tower, located on the Raleigh
highway, is 167 feet high and its twelve bells have a total weight of
14,350 pounds.

Pool had expressed the view that the University "should be thoroughly loyalized. Better close it than have it a nursery of treason to foster and perpetuate the feelings of disloyalty. Let the present Board of Trustees be superseded by a loyal Board and the University will be a blessing instead of a curse."[11] Governor W. W. Holden, a man of the people, was determined to take the management of the University out of the hands of the aristocrats, who controlled the Board of Trustees and thereby made of it virtually, though not by statute, a self-perpetuating body, representative of the old order, and place it under the control of the reconstructionists who championed the cause of the common people. From the standpoint of the Republicans there were cogent reasons, political and social, for educational "reconstruction" of this sort; but the passions engendered by the war and the deep loyalty of the Southern people to the old order in the end doomed the drastic new experiment to irretrievable failure.

The acceptance of the resignation of President Swain and Faculty by the newly constituted Board of Trustees, July 24, 1868, was the first step toward University "reconstruction." The election of the Rev. Solomon Pool to the presidency and of an entirely new Faculty, by the Executive Committee of the Board of Trustees, January 2, 1869, set in train the new order of things at Chapel Hill. The University was re-opened on March 3, 1869. President Pool, native of Elizabeth City and second honor graduate of the class of 1853, who for five years (1861-1866) had held the post of adjunct professor of mathematics, was a man of resolution and ability; but his administration proved to be a lamentable failure, largely due to want of support engendered by lack of confidence in the ideologies and capacities of the new administration.

During the Reconstruction period, fears of social and racial overturn were widespread, and by no means groundless. Alarm over the race issue was created by the election to the Faculty, as professor of Greek language and literature, of Fisk Parsons

11. Letter of January 23, 1868. This statement appeared in connection with his draft of a proposed article in the Constitution on Public Education.

Brewer, a graduate of Yale, 1852, a man of scholarly attainments and distinguished family, who for some time had been teaching a school for Negroes in Raleigh.[12] There he had entertained Negroes at his home; and had boarded with a Negro for a brief period after reaching Chapel Hill.[13] Following the meeting of the Trustees, November 19-20, 1868, it was widely reported throughout the State and generally credited that Messrs. Rodman, Ashley, and J. F. Taylor had introduced a resolution providing for the admission of Negroes to the University.[14] Actually, at this meeting, Judge Albion W. Tourgée, ablest of the "carpetbag" judges, moved, and the motion was carried, that the General Assembly be requested to amend the University's charter so as to provide equal facilities for whites and blacks; and also to establish normal and preparatory schools for children of both races. Mr. Victor C. Barringer moved that a school be established near Raleigh for the instruction of Negroes; and Tourgée proposed the amendment, which was adopted, that this school should be a branch of the University. The President *ex officio* of the Board, Governor Tod R. Caldwell, moved that not less than 100 acres be acquired for the school for Negroes. Although these measures were passed, they were never put into effect; nor were Negroes taught in the University during Pool's administration. On November 20, 1868, the Trustees passed a resolution regarding admission to the University, stating in part: ". . . and with the further understanding that pupils of color will not be admitted to that institution, provision having

12. Professor Brewer served efficiently as University librarian during his stay here. He was a brother of David J. Brewer, an Associate Justice of the United States Supreme Court, appointed by President Benjamin Harrison. His sister came to Chapel Hill in 1869 to teach a school for Negroes. Consult an excellent sketch (typescript) of Fisk P. Brewer, by his son W. F. Brewer, University of North Carolina Library.

13. Battle, II, 10; *Memories of an Old-Time Tar Heel*, pp. 218-19.

14. *Raleigh Sentinel*, November 23, 1868. The *Raleigh Standard* circulated the report that there were Negro students and one Negro professor at the University. This erroneous belief has survived, from that day to this. In 1875, describing the University under Pool's administration, Z. B. Vance says: "The institution was thrown open to all colors." *Sketches of North Carolina* . . . (Norfolk, 1875), p. 50. In his autobiography, the late Judge R. W. Winston states that in 1868 the University was "thrown open to blacks and whites alike." *It's a Far Cry* (New York, 1937), p. 75.

been made, by previous resolution for the erection of a separate institution for the benefit and instruction of pupils of color."[15]

The University under Pool survived for less than two years, almost half the total number of students attending being in the Preparatory Department.[16] So disgruntled was Pool by the slim attendance that in March, 1869, in response to the advice of John Wesley Carr, leading merchant of Chapel Hill, that he resign the presidency, he defiantly replied: "I would not resign for $50,000. If no whites will come here, I will have negro students."[17] At the Commencement exercises, June 8-9, 1870, Governor Holden in a carefully prepared speech asserted that the professors must support the Union, and that the whites must be educated at Chapel Hill, the colored elsewhere, but both in one University, since education knows no color or condition.[18] Professor Brewer expressed the hope of being present in Chapel Hill when the doors of the institution should be thrown open to Negroes.[19]

At last, recognizing the futility of prolonging the activities of a college which, as Professor F. M. Hubbard remarked, had "sunk to the level of an old-field school," Mr. James A. Graham moved, at the meeting of the Board of Trustees, November 20, 1870, that the salaries of all the Faculty be discontinued from December 1, 1870; but a subsequent motion by James B. Mason, setting the date for discontinuance of salaries at February 1, 1871, prevailed. The fifth session was opened on January 14, 1871, with an "average attendance" of four students. Exercises were postponed until January 29, when only two students remained.[20] William Joseph Peele relates that, on entering the re-

15. *T. M.*, 1868-1881, pp. 43-44.
16. During the first year the attendance was 35, with 25 in the Preparatory Department; and during the second year, the attendance was 53, of whom 20 were preparatory pupils. J. G. deR. Hamilton, *Reconstruction in North Carolina* (New York, 1914), p. 626. This second Preparatory Department (consult Chapter IV for first Preparatory Department) was rendered necessary by the large number of boys who were too poorly prepared to enter the University classes.
17. Chamberlain, p. 163; Hamilton, *Reconstruction in North Carolina*, p. 627.
18. Battle, II, 35.
19. Chamberlain, pp. 195-96, 200-1.
20. Battle, II, 41; Mrs. C. P. Spencer's scrapbook, Southern Historical Collection.

opened University in 1875, he read, chalked up on a blackboard in one of the old recitation rooms, the ribald inscription:

FEBRUARY 1, 1871

This old University has busted and gone to hell to-day[21]

After the Democratic party regained control of the State in 1870, more than three years elapsed before the passage by the legislature of an amendment to the Constitution of 1868, giving to the General Assembly the power of electing the Trustees. Following the election of the Trustees, January 28, 1874, under the new law, the Board met in Raleigh in February, 1874, and provided for an inquiry into and report as to the actual extent, nature, and general state of preservation of the property of the University, and the amount of money required to repair the buildings.[22] The investigating committee, consisting of Walter L. Steele, chairman, Paul C. Cameron, and William L. Saunders, presented to the Trustees on April 9, 1874, an exhaustive and meticulous report on the condition of the University. The damage was extensive, in part due to vandalism, but mainly the result of deterioration owing to neglect and lack of use. The rough estimate of repairs, made by Mr. Utley, the college carpenter, was $2,050; but the committee estimated that the cost would be double that amount. The final cost of restoration, which included the purchase of gas works and piping, together with chemical and natural philosophical apparatus, exceeded the rough estimate of the investigating committee by $8,826.85. The committee "empowered Mr. Andrew Mickle, a resident of Chapel Hill and gentleman of intelligence and character, to take charge of the buildings and grounds of the University." Mr. Mickle took possession of the buildings on February 4, 1875, the keys having been delivered to him by Kemp P. Battle, Secretary and Treasurer of the Board of Trustees.[23] There is but one "high light" in the report of the investigating committee: "The old Dialectic Hall on the third floor [South Building], is remarkably well preserved, especially in the overhead plastering where the gilded name of the Society and its motto, look as fresh and bright as

21. Battle, II, 584.

22. *T. M.*, 1868-1882, pp. 177-78.

23. For the report of the investigating committee, see *ibid.*, pp. 185-93. See also *ibid.*, pp. 203-4, 208; and Battle, II, 58.

they did more than forty years ago." The restoration of the University Campus and buildings was effected through the indefatigable efforts of Paul C. Cameron, aided by his son, Bennehan; and the new University arose, if not like the Phoenix from the ashes, certainly like the butterfly from the battered chrysalis, of the old.

The re-opening of 1875 was accomplished only through the devoted labors of alumni, friends, and supporters of the University, among whom William A. Graham, Zebulon B. Vance, and Kemp P. Battle were conspicuous. The movement for the revival of the University, said President Winston, "was conceived, inaugurated and executed by the Hon. Kemp P. Battle. . . . The institution was without friends, and heavy debts hung over it. Its revival seemed almost impossible. . . . Nothing daunted by these evils and inspired by a life-time love of the University Mr. Battle set vigorously to work and canvassed the State for funds. No other man would have undertaken the task, and certainly no other would have accomplished it. He appealed to the *alumni* and to patriotic men, not *alumni*, through the press, by letter and by personal interview. The result was $20,000 and the revival of the University."[24]

On February 11, 1867, President Swain procured from the General Assembly the transfer to the University of the State's right to the Agricultural and Mechanical College Land Scrip.[25] On August 22, 1867, the University Trustees sold the 270,000 acres allotted them under the Morrill Act; and subsequently invested the proceeds, $125,000, in special tax and other State bonds. On March 20, 1875, after the most strenuous efforts, the friends of the University secured the passage of the historic act requiring the State of North Carolina to pay to the University $7,500: six per cent interest annually on the $125,000, representing the Land Scrip Fund, then in the State Treasury. The passage of this act was the decisive factor in enabling the University to reopen.[26]

24. George T. Winston, "Benefactions by the Alumni: I. The Revival of the University in 1875," *Alumni Quarterly*, I (January, 1895), 48-49.

25. The Morrill Act, July 2, 1862.

26. Battle, I, 756-57; II, 16, 64-69. The Land Scrip was taken from the University by the legislature in 1887. *Ibid.*, II, 217.

The self-constituted press-agent for the "Cause" of restoration was Mrs. Spencer. She conducted a veritable campaign of education in the newspapers, by means of both signed and unsigned articles; and carried on an extended private correspondence with the University's friends, in behalf of regaining possession of the institution. Her appeal was well-reasoned and profoundly emotional, a veritable *cri de coeur;* and therewith she poignantly touched the hearts of thousands of her readers. Hers was assuredly one of the noblest endeavors in the history of higher education in the United States. Her delight over the Democratic victory in 1874 was unbounded; and she was notified by wire of the passage by the Assembly, March 20, 1875, of the bill for the financial reorganization and support of the University. There was dramatic fitness in the circumstance that this was Mrs. Spencer's birthday. Accompanied by friends and pupils, she repaired to the attic in South Building, and herself exultantly rang out the glad tidings of a brave new day to come.[27] In commenting on such an historic event, it is appropriate to recall the observation of Governor Vance who, when someone declared that Mrs. Spencer was the smartest woman in North Carolina, wittily added: "And the smartest man, too."[28]

The growth of the re-opened University was leisurely but steady. The completion in 1882 of the spur track of 10 2/3 miles, from University Station to present Carrboro, guaranteed greatly increased attendance at the University's Commencements. Direct rail communication with the "outside world" accentuated the need for the erection of a building for public exercises much more spacious than Gerrard Hall, the enlargement of which had long been contemplated. The Trustees ultimately decided, at the suggestion of Governor Thomas J. Jarvis, to build a new hall, as a memorial to President Swain, and to appeal to the alumni to join them in contributions for this purpose. Samuel Sloan, an architect of Philadelphia, was designated by Governor Jarvis to draw up plans for a building to seat 4,000 persons.[29] The plan was a foreshortened hexagon like a fat coffin, 154 by

27. *Ibid.,* II, 69; Chamberlain, p. 222.
28. Chamberlain, p. 102.
29. *Cyclopaedia of American Biography,* new and enlarged edition (New York, The Press Association compilers, Inc., 1915). V, 550.

128 feet. The brick walls, 52 feet high, were supported by massive wooden buttresses; and the floor was on an inclined plane, sloping downward from the front door to the rostrum at the south end. A roof of slate surmounted the series of great wooden arches. So far beyond the conjectural estimate of the architect did the costs run that, for lack of funds, work was discontinued in November, 1883. President Battle and Professor Winston, appointed by the Trustees to push the campaign for the raising of funds, proposed a promising plan, which was adopted: to charge $125 each for memorial tablets to deceased officers and students of the University, to be placed on the walls of the building. By February, 1884, the Building Committee reported the expenditure of $24,701.04, of which Paul C. Cameron had lent almost $6,000. The amount realized from the sale of tablets was about $10,000.[30] By November, 1884, all available money was exhausted; and $6,000 was borrowed by the Trustees from the Citizens Bank of Raleigh, on the individual credit of the Building Committee. A sum to complete the building in its last phase was borrowed by Paul Cameron at his own risk. The over-all cost of the building was about $45,000.

On June 3, 1885, this building was dedicated with appropriate ceremonies. It was named Memorial Hall, not for Swain as originally contemplated; and part of the inscription upon the Swain tablet is elucidative:

> The Trustees and Alumni have erected this Hall in grateful recognition of the services of David Lowry Swain, for thirty-three years President of the University; in proud and loving remembrance of her heroic sons who fell in the service of the Confederate States; and as a Memorial to all others connected with the University, who, by honorable lives, in civil or military service, deserve commemoration here.[31]

Samuel Sloan, the architect, fell a victim of exposure to the summer sun; and the structure was completed under the direction of the assistant architect, A. G. Bauer, with the co-operation of the builder, J. P. Daugherty, and the chief mason, John Rich-

30. *T. M.*, 1883-1891, pp. 31-33, 42, 61-62, 78, 103, 125-26, 127, 128. See also John Manning, "Benefactions by the Alumni. II," *Alumni Quarterly*, I (January, 1895), 49-53.
31. *T. M.*, 1883-1891, p. 103.

ards.[32] Although President Battle optimistically promised that Memorial Hall would be a "model to the students of architecture in the institution" and the Visiting Committee enthusiastically hailed it as "one of the most imposing auditoriums in America," the structure actually resembled a huge antediluvian monster of the turtle variety, a resemblance strengthened by the slate roof. Indeed, it was an architectural monstrosity; and the acoustic properties, with cacophonous echoes caused by the clash of conflicting sound waves, were execrable. Furthermore, the President and Trustees were indubitably "bilked" by Sloan who imperturbably pushed the price up, up, up, like a mighty auctioneer: $20,000, $25,000, $30,000, $35,000, $40,000, $45,000— go, going, gone![33]

By the time of the Centennial Celebration, Commencement of 1889, Chapel Hill and the University Campus had regained much of their former beauty and charm. A correspondent of a New York newspaper furnished the following description:

Chapel Hill is a quiet and beautiful village on a branch line of the Richmond and Danville Railroad (properly North Carolina Railroad) and twelve miles from the famous tobacco town of Durham. The village with its broad streets, picturesque walls, large yards, gigantic grape-vines, noble elms, old fashioned houses, and the University Campus with its buildings of imposing proportions, widespreading oaks and acres of grass, is remarkably attractive, especially in autumn and spring. What with porches, yards and College Campus, the town scarcely needs a park, yet in "Battle Park" it has one which by its natural beauties might well excite the envy of the wealthy. Lovers and children are fond of wandering along the paths cut out through the forest. Clear springs, rustic seats and shady nooks wear appropriate names and almost every tree might a tale of love unfold if it could only tell of the names carved on its sides.

In 1896, after the old gymnasium had been fitted up as a commons, Memorial Hall began to be used as a gymnasium (see Chapter 24). As early as 1900 repairs were found to be neces-

32. A singular and almost symbolic fatality seemed to pursue the builders of this weird mausoleum. As narrated, Sloan died from a sunstroke, and later on, both Bauer and Richards committed suicide.

33. *Ibid.*, pp. 103, 142. For an amusing description of the first Memorial Hall, consult Don McKee, "Spooky Architectural Monstrosity," *The Carolina Magazine*, LXIV (May, 1935), 17-20. Shortly before the com-

sary on the immense arches, the enclosed ends of which had in some places become subject to dry rot.

In 1925, Atwood & Nash were instructed by the Trustees to make plans for a new Memorial Hall. Examination by experts in 1929, among these being the architects' firm of Atwood & Nash, revealed the original structure to be unsafe; and its use was discontinued. On January 28, 1930, John Sprunt Hill for the Building Committee recommended the erection of a modern fireproof building of greater dignity, to replace the old Memorial Hall. Toward this new structure a sum up to $150,000 was made available from the State Emergency Fund. In his last report, President Chase recommended the demolition of the old building, concluding with these words, which proved decisive: "What we ought to visualize, it seems to me, is a shrine of University history, a visible symbol of what it has meant to the state and the nation. We should, I think, feel about it as the medieval builder felt about his cathedral, which was a visible symbol of his religious faith. For him nothing was too beautiful, too rich, or too enduring for incorporation within his plans." The new Memorial Hall, Atwood & Nash, architects, was completed in midsummer, 1931, at a cost of approximately $182,000. The benches, from the original building, then placed in the hall on account of lack of funds, have never been replaced by comfortable individual seats.[34]

---

pletion of Memorial Hall, Paul C. Cameron presented to the University a large number of maple trees, which were planted on College Avenue between the east and west gates of the Campus. These glorious trees, a symphony in red and yellow, have furnished conspicuous embellishment to the Campus during the past sixty-odd years. Only a few remain, but fortunately without diminution of foliage and brilliant coloration. It was in appreciation of this gift, as well as of many other acts of service and generosity in connection with the re-opening of the University and the building of Memorial Hall that College Avenue was renamed Cameron Avenue. A committee of the Trustees dubbed Memorial Hall "Cameron's monument."

34. *T. M.*, 1898-1904, p. 167; 1924-1930, pp. 333, 413, 437, 443, 450-51, 456; 1931-1938, pp. 4, 6, 26-27.

PART V
FROM THE CHRYSALIS

20

PROGRESS THROUGH PHILANTHROPY:

1819-1907

ONE OF THE most amazing and impressive features of University history has been its extraordinary vitality, the persistence of the life-spark. For the University's first eighty years, the total amount of money appropriated by the State for its maintenance and support was $17,000! Tuition, escheats, and lands donated to the University enabled the institution to survive. Down to 1830 the sales of land had yielded about $71,000, with about 106,000 acres, estimated in value at upwards of a quarter of a million dollars, unsold; and the actual cost of the University buildings had been $95,537.41. With such a disheartening exhibition of lack of specific financial support, the progress of the University was little short of phenomenal. Shortly before the University's half-century mark was reached, Judge Williamson, distinguished historian and Governor of Maine, penned this glowing, yet well-considered estimate of the school's progress and accomplishments:

Such is the University of North Carolina which has been a seat of science and literature nearly half a century. In the rise and progress of this institution posterity may perceive what is due to men of letters and public spirit. Through their efforts and bounty in the legislature and in the community, 736 young gentlemen, three-fourths of whom were probably North Carolinians, have received a classical education, and as many more have been refreshed by the waters of the same public fountain. If a due proportion of the graduates has not gone into the learned professions, and if comparatively few are burning lights at the altars of religion, they have added fresh wreaths to the rising glory of literature. Not only have legislators, supreme courts of judicature and other places of official trust been ornamented by them and benefitted by their services; numbers have vied for the palm in the halls of national government. They have trimmed the lamps their fathers lighted; and given strength and vigor to the enterprize their predecessors so perseveringly espoused. . . .

What State, in like circumstances, has in fact done more in behalf of learning, since the Revolution, than North Carolina? . . . They [the Trustees] are residents in different parts of the State, 65 in number, and would in general adorn any community. Were northern men of letters more conversant with them, their literary institutions and teachers; had they more personal acquaintance and familiar intercourse with each other, and were there more reciprocity felt in the same exalted cause, would not the effect give to members of the American family more fraternal mutuality of sentiment and feeling?[1]

In the history of the University's development, and indeed survival, two grave incidents of financial crisis cannot be left unmentioned. The first concerns escheats and western lands, the second the investment of University funds. The satisfactory solution of the first problem assured the University's survival; unwise investment in the latter case was a contributing factor in the University's decline and discontinuance.

The treaty with the Chickasaw tribe of Indians negotiated by Isaac Shelby and Andrew Jackson, Commissioners for the United States, and successfully concluded October 19, 1818, resulted in the flow of a great tide of emigration from North Carolina to the West. Within a short time, these Tennessee lands greatly appreciated in value. Some two and a half million acres of the "Chickasaw Purchase," as it was called, were contained in grants, formerly made or awaiting confirmation. Archibald D. Murphey prophesied that the University of North Carolina would be made rich by this treaty. Large areas were included within the Chickasaw Purchase which had been allotted to officers and soldiers of North Carolina. Those which remained unclaimed passed by way of escheat (law of 1789) to the University.

In January, 1819, the University Trustees appointed John Haywood, State Treasurer, Colonel William Polk, Judge Henry Potter, Chief Justice Thomas Ruffin, and Judge Archibald D. Murphey, a committee charged with the care of lands belonging to the University. Judge Murphey and General Joseph H. Bryan were designated to secure the land interests of the institution in Tennessee. They associated with themselves, as advisers, Senator John H. Eaton, University alumnus, and Colonel Thomas Henderson, owner and editor of the Raleigh *Star*. At Murfreesborough, Tennessee, in August, 1821, negotiations were opened,

1. Williamson, *op. cit.*

Murphey speaking for two days before the Tennessee legislature. On August 5, 1821, Polk made a contract with Henderson, who was a realtor of approved skill. The terms of this contract were as follows: Henderson was first to procure evidence as to all persons formerly serving the Continental line of the State who had died without heirs capable of inheriting land; second, to lay the evidence before the Governor, Public Treasurer, and Comptroller, the Board of Adjudication appointed by the North Carolina Assembly in 1819; and third, if these claims were passed and warrants issued to the Trustees, to present them before the Board of Adjudication in Tennessee, consisting of the Governor, Secretary of State, and Register of the Land Office. Polk's contract with Henderson, who shared commissions with Samuel Dickens and John C. McLemore, prominent Tennessee realtors, was liberal, setting the compensation at one-half of the warrants. Within two months, Henderson, who had been busy accumulating the requisite data during the preceding year or two, presented his report. The division was duly made and warrants calling for 147,853 acres went to the University. The legislature of Tennessee confirmed Polk's contract with Henderson. The acquisition of these claims assured the University's continuance and prosperity; and the fees likewise enriched the commissioners and their associates.[2]

In striking contrast to the legally successful and highly profitable settlement of the problem of the University's lands stands the ruinous investment of the University's reserve funds just before the opening of the Civil War. Down to 1840 the sales of University lands had netted upwards of $200,000; and considerable increments to this fund had come in prior to 1861. Down to the opening of the war, considerably more than $100,-000 had come to the University through escheats.[3] When the charter of the Bank of the State of North Carolina, in which the University had 1,000 shares of stock, valued at $100,000, expired, the University re-invested this sum in 1,000 shares of the new Bank of North Carolina. Although funds for this were not available, the legislature authorized the Trustees to subscribe for

2. Murphey, I, 248-49, 254, 256, 260-63, 267.
3. Battle, I, 461-62, 577.

another 1,000 shares. President Swain, generally shrewd in financial matters, supported the plan, as did Governor Ellis; and the subscription was confidently made. No one at that day was endowed with prophetic vision to foresee the war within two years. The great and disastrous blunder was not in subscribing for the second 1,000 shares of stock, but in not disposing of it, at whatever sacrifice, when war clearly threatened and was almost surely imminent. The end of the war saw the 2,000 shares worthless, and the University saddled with a ruinous debt, the liquidation of which retarded the University's growth for many years.[4]

Various efforts were made to raise funds to pay off the bank debt. The bank agreed to compromise the debt for $25,000 in gold or $35,700 in paper currency; and on this basis a mortgage was taken, April 30, 1867, on all the property of the University. Proposals to lease or rent University property came to nought, as did the effort to have the mortgage declared invalid. In the suit brought by Charles Dewey, assignee in bankruptcy, to have the property of the University sold under the mortgage, the Federal Circuit Court at the June term, 1874, unanimously decided that the bank debt was valid, but that neither the judgment creditor nor the Trustees themselves had power to alienate "such property as constituted the life of the University," as distinct from the endowment for its support. Following a thorough investigation by the commission appointed by the Court and a committee of three appointed by the Board, the Court reserved to the University the Campus and 600 acres of land, all houses, libraries, and property appurtenant. The land sold to pay the debt was some 250 acres, which included the famous tract of about 70 acres extending to and comprising about one-half of Point Prospect, and many thousands of acres in western North Carolina. The Campus, which had originally contained 98¾ acres, was defined by the Trustees as extending from the west line of K. P. Battle's fence to the east line of the original President's House, and of the same extent north and south.[5]

4. *Ibid.*, I, 706-7. The Trustees were deterred from selling the bank stock owned by the University by the fear that such a step, indicating doubt as to the ultimate success of the Confederacy, would injure the University by alienating popular sympathy.

5. *Ibid.*, I, 756; II, 8-9, 13-14, 17, 26, 57-60, 171, 193, 266.

THE FIRST GYMNASIUM

Built in 1885, this building served as ballroom and gymnasium until, in 1896, additions were made and it was converted into a Commons Hall. Mrs. Frederick Baker's gift of $3,000, "in token of appreciation of the benefits received by her son [Henry S. Lake, by her first marriage] in this institution," made this conversion possible. Photograph about 1895.

THE OLD ATHLETIC FIELD

This field was located at the south side of Smith Hall, now the Playmakers Theatre. From a photograph taken about 1893.

BASEBALL GAME ON THE OLD ATHLETIC FIELD

The pitcher is standing at about the center of the present site of Bynum Hall. The spectators' stand, which held approximately 150 people, was located about 30 yards southwest of present Carr Building.

FOOTBALL GAME ON OLD ATHLETIC FIELD

The field, which was large enough for two football games to be played simultaneously, ran south to the present site of Murphey Hall, and included the sites of Bynum Hall, Steele Dormitory, Manning Hall, the parking lot, and part of Carr Building. This picture shows a portion of the 3,000 spectators at the football game between Carolina and VMI, October 1, 1910.

It was most fortunate for the University that its revival, although undertaken with limited funds and inaugurated with a small student body, was signalized by a great outburst of optimism and enthusiasm. The next half century witnessed a considerable number of important gifts through personal generosity and foundational philanthropy, which greatly accelerated the pace of the University's restoration and rehabilitation.

In 1891 the welcome gift of Mary Ann Smith, a resident of Raleigh and the daughter and heiress of Richard Smith, prominent merchant, was announced. In her will, made in 1861, she had bequeathed half of her estate to the University for the endowment of "such a chair as shall teach both the science of Chemistry and its application to the useful arts." When the benefactress died in 1891, the University received $37,000. The following year, at a cost of $2,644.19 from the anticipated income from the Smith Fund, a west wing, to provide additional laboratory space for the use of the Department of Chemistry, was added to Person Hall.[6]

In 1900, upon the recommendation of President Venable that more dormitory space be provided on the Campus, the Executive Committee of the Trustees instructed the treasurer to collect out of the Mary Ann Smith Fund a sum not to exceed $18,000 for the erection of a dormitory on the Campus, to be named for Mary Ann Smith. The building, completed the following year, provided room for 65 students and cost only $16,000.[7] By a resolution of the committee, the building was to be leased for 99 years to the Treasurer of the University as the Trustee for the Mary Ann Smith Fund, the Trustee to receive as rental 6 per cent yearly on the cost.[8] The building appears erratically placed with respect to the basic ground plan of the Campus; and the construction must have been inexpert, the materials below standard. Only ten years later the Visiting Committee found the building in poor condition. For a considerable time,

6. *T. M.*, 1891-1898, pp. 169, 182.
7. The architect was Frank P. Milburn; the builders, Zachary & Zachary.
8. *T. M.*, 1898-1904, p. 207.

many rooms in this dormitory had remained unoccupied, entailing a substantial loss to the University. Adequate repairs, at a cost of $1,500, put the building in excellent condition in 1912.[9] Again, in 1927, it was exhaustively renovated, at a cost of $31,500, virtually double the cost of the original structure.

In 1894 President George T. Winston had pointed out to the Trustees that every room in the college buildings had been occupied in 1893-1894; and that many students, for lack of dormitory space, were compelled to take lodgings in the village at higher rentals. Five years later the Trustees resolved to erect another dormitory building. The proceeds from the sale of a block of Blackwell Durham Tobacco Company stock which belonged to the Chair of History Fund, was supplemented in the sum of $3,328 by Julian S. Carr of Durham, the total amounting to $10,000. Mr. Carr made an additional gift of $5,000 after the Trustees called upon the Finance Committee to consider the propriety of utilizing the $10,000 in the erection of a dormitory to be known as the Julian S. Carr Building. It was decided to borrow from the Chair of History Fund $15,000 which was to be loaned to the University at 6 per cent interest and invested in the new dormitory. In anticipation of the completion of the building, which was being constructed by Zachary and Zachary, President Edwin A. Alderman on February 16, 1900 reported to the Trustees: "It is an imposing building of gray brick and stone and will be a splendid ornament to the Campus, a service to the students and a worthy memorial to its founder."[10] With appropriate ceremonies, on Commencement Day, June 8, 1900, the Carr Building was formally presented to the University in an eloquent address by Colonel W. H. S. Burgwyn, graduate of the class of 1868. After lauding Carr for his generosity, he pointed out that this was the largest individual gift in concrete form as yet made to the University. In accepting for the University, Mr. Richard H. Battle, Secretary and Treasurer of the Board of Trustees, stated that the Carr Building provided ac-

9. *T. M.,* 1904-1916, pp. 319, 355.
10. *T. M.,* 1891-1898, pp. 285, 390-91; 1898-1904, pp. 34, 88, 128, 211. The architects were Pearson & Ashe of Raleigh. The original cost of the building was $18,000.

commodations for eighty-four students. At the time of its completion, this was the most modern of the Campus dormitories, being divided into suites, consisting of two rooms each, one for study and the other for sleeping, with adequate toilet facilities and steam heating. Unfortunately, it was but little appreciated by the occupants who gave it very rough treatment; and only ten years later it was found to be in such a deplorable state as to be described by the Visiting Committee as "uninhabitable in its present condition." Repairs at a cost of $4,081.21, including painting, plastering, and reflooring were made in 1911. This deterioration was not wholly due to rough treatment at the hands of the students; for the Visiting Committee in its report was outspoken: "The trouble is due in part to poor & faulty construction, showing that the lowest bidder is not the cheapest man, after all, & that too much care cannot be taken in selecting those who do the construction work upon the buildings." The Carr Building was located just south of Cameron Avenue, not far from the original site of Steward's Hall; and faced to the west.[11] This dormitory, from the date of erection, has proved exceptionally expensive, the total costs of four renovations, $4,081.21 in 1911, $16,292 in 1923, $17,677 in 1928, and $17,341 in 1931, being more than three times the original cost. The total cost of the building to 1931 was $73,391.21.

For the first century of the University's existence, the primary purpose of the Trustees in creating a material plant was to provide accommodations for sleeping and eating, with classrooms and laboratories scattered more or less indiscriminately throughout the dormitories. The one exception to this was Person Hall which, since its relinquishment as a chapel in 1837, had been used exclusively for instruction. The beginning of a second century of University life stressed the long-felt want and immediately pressing need for a building to contain public offices, lecture-rooms, and laboratories. The decision to erect such a building was made at a meeting of the Alumni Association at its Commencement dinner, June 3, 1891; and seven years later, June

11. *T. M.*, 1898-1904, p. 447; 1904-1916, pp. 280-81, 319. For the ceremonies of presentation and acceptance, consult *Carr Building Presented* (Philadelphia, 1900).

1, 1898, the cornerstone was laid, by the Free and Accepted Order of Masons, with appropriate ceremonies. General Julian S. Carr on behalf of the alumni presented the building to the Trustees; and it was accepted for the University by the Hon. Francis D. Winston.[12] Subscriptions mounted up slowly; and President Venable, at the request of the Trustees, June 15, 1899, canvassed the country for additional funds. The raising of $9,000 in this way he afterwards described as "the hardest task which has fallen to me as President." The total cost of the building, which was completed by the close of the year 1901, was $39,500, a sum in great part contributed by the alumni, but eked out by considerable loans from banks and the Chair of History Fund. The contract was awarded to the architectural firm of Zachary and Zachary. The building, named the Alumni Building and located on the east side of the North Quadrangle with an imposing portico facing Person Hall, was constructed of gray pressed brick. The narrow spacing of the massive columns created considerable criticism; but President Venable, who described the building as the "chief ornament of the campus," averred that his responsibility in the matter of architecture was not esthetic and was fulfilled with the letting of the contract. In 1904 $5,000 was expended in fitting up the basement, consisting of five rooms, for the Department of Physics. In 1939 the building was remodeled at a cost of $92,065, the architects being Atwood and Weeks, the contractors, the Muirhead Construction Company.[13]

12. In the cornerstone were deposited the University charter, list of donors of the site, sketches of Presidents Caldwell, Swain, Battle, and Winston, and of Vance; Dr. Hooper's "Fifty Years Since"; Golden Jubilee Number of *University Magazine*, 1894; Mrs. Spencer's "University Ode" and "Song of the Old Alumni"; Inauguration of Memorial Hall; list of the Confederate dead of the University; Sketches of Benefactors and their Gifts; the Inauguration of Alumni Hall, with list of subscribers in 1895. Many of the documents were of striking value. Also were enclosed copies of *The Tar Heel, University Magazine, News and Observer*, and *Charlotte Observer* of June, 1898. Battle, II, 552.

13. *T. M.*, 1891-1898, pp. 389, 492-93, 636, 637; 1898-1904, pp. 46-47, 88, 122, 128, 132, 204, 208, 213, 292, 307, 313, 463. For details concerning the raising of funds, consult Link, pp. 116-22.

Three buildings upon the Campus, which arose from financial sources not provided by legislative enactment, deserve commemoration.[14] Smith Hall, which had never proved satisfactory as a library, being built primarily to serve as a ballroom, was by 1895 found to be unsuited for the arrangement of the 40,000 volumes so as to make them readily accessible for use. Moreover, the unitary structure of the building obviated necessary enlargement in order to provide for a rapidly expanding collection of books. Andrew Carnegie, the philanthropist, during this period was engaging in a magnificent campaign of donation for the establishment of libraries throughout the United States. Through the efforts of President Venable, a gift of $50,000, eventually enlarged to $55,000, was offered by Mr. Carnegie on March 21, 1905, conditional upon the providing of a similar amount for the library's upkeep and future expansion. The required sum was contributed by alumni and friends who set up a number of endowments for this purpose; and on June 1, 1907, the cornerstone was laid under the auspices of the Grand Lodge of Masons of North Carolina. The building, with architects Milburn and Heister, cost approximately $59,000, and was located south of the Methodist Church and northwesterly from Person Hall.[15] An imposing, two-storey structure built of gray pressed brick, the Library had a capacity for holding upwards of 200,000 volumes; but so rapidly did the collections of books and pamphlets grow that in less than two decades it was forced to yield place to a new library of much magnified proportions. The Carnegie Library was then turned over to the Department of Music; and in fulfilment of the conditions of a gift of $70,000 by the John Sprunt Hill family of Durham, an organ costing $30,000 was purchased and an auditorium addition, with a seating capacity of 800, was built at a cost of $40,000. According to the announcement of President Chase, January 29, 1930, the building was to be known as the Hill Music Hall. Among the terms of the gift were the stipulations that the auditorium was to be reserved for musical events and that some sort of musical

14. The third building, Bynum Gymnasium, will be considered in Chapter 24.
15. *University of North Carolina Record*, No. 54 (1907), 5-6.

program, open to the public, should be rendered weekly. As usual with restrictive stipulations, these have not been rigorously observed; and the auditorium is often used for University occasions other than musical.[16]

Significant of the equal concern for the intellectual and spiritual welfare and development of the students, on the part of administration, alumni, and friends of the University, is the circumstance that both the Carnegie Library and the Y. M. C. A. building were dedicated at the 1907 Commencement. The first organization in North Carolina for the spiritual improvement of young men was formed in Wilmington prior to October, 1857; and this was soon followed by organizations in Charlotte (1857), Raleigh (1859), Salisbury (1859), and Washington, N. C. (1859). The Young Men's Christian Association at Chapel Hill was organized in May, 1860.[17] The Civil War interrupted the activities of the Association, which was not reorganized until September 17, 1876. Soon afterwards the Y was allotted two rooms in South Building, first floor; and it has regularly functioned from that date to the present. Public meetings of the Y were held in Gerrard Hall until the erection of the Y. M. C. A. building, with its excellent auditorium, in 1907.[18] By 1894 the beneficial effect of the Association upon student life accentuated the need for a building for its multifarious activities, secular and religious. With the sanction of the Visiting Committee of the Trustees, which recommended the erection of a building for the Y. M. C. A. as soon as the condition of the University's finances should permit, a campaign to raise funds was inaugurated in 1895. The fund sought was $20,000; but by 1903 only $8,000 had been raised. Confident of ultimate success in raising the necessary funds, President Francis P. Venable on February 24, 1904, announced that building would begin immediately. The

16. *T. M.*, 1924-1930, pp. 73, 210-11, 435, 457.

17. The first announcement of the organization of the Y. M. C. A. here appeared in *U. N. C. M.*, IX (1860), 574. There were twelve officers, with James Kelly president, Archibald McFadyen recording secretary, and A. Hill Patterson corresponding secretary. See also announcement card, *ibid.*, p. 646.

18. This auditorium is now occupied by the University Book Exchange.

building, begun in 1904 at a cost of $15,000, was dedicated on June 2, 1907. The architect was Frank P. Milburn.[19]

The Y. M. C. A. building has been called the "hub" of student activities on the Campus. The present director has listed seventeen services constantly rendered, which include the housing of the Campus Book and Supply Store, universally termed the "Book Ex." The last mentioned originated in a modest form in 1892; and after various transmutations and migrations was moved into its present home in the summer of 1921. As described in the Buildings Department records, the Y. M. C. A. contains 15 rooms, 9,000 square feet of floor space, and 163,500 cubic feet.

19. The presentation address was made by Professor J. W. Gore, who had been active in the work of the Association; and the speech of acceptance was delivered by Dr. Richard H. Lewis of Raleigh. The Rev. Clayton S. Cooper of New York delivered an address on the function and significance of the Y. M. C. A.

21

PROGRESS THROUGH PHILANTHROPY:

1913-1939

UNIVERSITY DEVELOPMENT seldom proceeds uniformly, with an even flow of funds and orderly progress in all directions. Such an institution, for its development, is responsive both to outer pressure of thought-movements and the inner pressure of growing needs. Historic in the advance of the State and the South was the great awakening to the need for the education of all the people and for the facilities required in training teachers, engineered by Governor Charles Brantley Aycock, class of 1880, during the years 1901 to 1912.[1] His efforts to advance education in the public schools, which focused national attention upon North Carolina, were not slow in producing repercussions accentuating the University's great opportunity in the field of teacher-training. Responsive to the implications of this pervasive educational awakening, the Visiting Committee recommended to the Trustees the establishment of a college for teachers at the University, voicing the conviction that such an important and progressive step would increase student attendance by at least two hundred and greatly elevate the standing of teachers in this State.

In a letter of February 7, 1867, to a group of gentlemen designated as trustees, George Peabody, philanthropist, announced a first gift of $1,000,000, the income of which, he said, "should be used by you in your discretion for the promotion and encouragement of intellectual, moral or industrial education among the young of the more destitute portions of the Southern and Southwestern states of our Union; my purpose being that the benefits shall be distributed among the entire population without other distinction than their needs and the opportunities of usefulness to them."[2] Two years later Peabody added another

1. Aycock died April 4, 1912.
2. One of the original trustees was Governor William A. Graham of North Carolina.

$1,000,000 to the Peabody Fund; but a still later gift of nearly $1,500,000, invested in Mississippi and Florida bonds, proved unproductive, as these states repudiated the bonds. The grand total of expenditures, 1868-1914, was $3,650,556.[3] The hope was entertained in North Carolina that aid might be obtained from this source, for the erection of a building, estimated to cost from $40,000 to $50,000, for housing a school of education. After performing services of great educational value over a long period of years, the Peabody Fund was in process of final distribution; and President F. P. Venable, through persistent and indefatigable efforts to secure an allocation of funds, was enabled to report, on May 29, 1911, that the sum of $40,000 had been donated from the Fund for the establishment of a School of Education, with the stipulation that the University devote $10,000 annually for its support. The two-storey building of white brick, containing 42 rooms and a floor space of 19,600 square feet, was erected to the west of the then Commons upon a lot of 4.3 acres acquired from Mrs. Julia C. Graves at a cost of $10,000. This building, for which the architects were Milburn and Heister of Washington, D. C., was begun in 1912 and dedicated on May 2, 1913.[4] It was renovated in 1930 at a cost of $50,000; architects, Atwood and Nash; contracting firm, T. C. Thompson and Brothers.

The dream long entertained by Edward Kidder Graham for the erection of a student center upon the Campus began to give promise of realization only after his death, October 26, 1918. The brilliant young President, who was inaugurated April 21, 1915, desired a center of social activity, recreation, and relaxation combined, with offices for student activities and a spacious lounge where one might "loaf and invite his soul." On December 16, 1918, the joint committee from the Trustees and the

3. J. L. M. Curry, *A Brief Sketch of George Peabody (1795-1869) and a History of the Peabody Education Board through Thirty Years* (Cambridge, Harvard University Press, 1898); Charles W. Dabney, *Universal Education in the South*, 2 vols. (Chapel Hill, University of North Carolina Press, 1936), *passim*.

4. *T. M.*, 1904-1916, pp. 233, 258-59, 317, 408. For sketch of George Peabody, consult *Dictionary of American Biography*, XIV (1934), 336-38. See also Dabney, *Universal Education in the South*.

Faculty on memorials to Edward Kidder Graham, met in Raleigh; and Dr. Louis R. Wilson later reported to the Trustees the decision to publish a memorial volume of President Graham's papers and to erect a students' union to be known as the Graham Memorial.[5] The original aim of the committee was to raise upwards of $150,000, with a minimum set at $100,000. From two campaigns, carried on over more than five years, the total of the promised subscriptions was upwards of $275,000. Up to January 10, 1924, $101,899.04 had been received. The total expenditures to that date amounted to $36,566.39, leaving a balance of $65,342.65. The building was originally designed to contain a central unit, with north and south wings; and by January 27, 1927 the exterior of the central unit, located on the west side of the lot formerly occupied by the old University Inn, was completed. As only $155,351 of the sum of $292,783 subscribed had been paid in by the late spring of 1928, a third campaign was inaugurated by the Graham Memorial Committee. The completion of the building was made possible in April, 1931, through the gift, by a donor who desired to remain anonymous, of $80,-000.[6] The total cost of the building, including $4,000 for furniture, was $257,341. In presenting the Graham Memorial, Dr. Wilson used these words concerning Graham: "As librarian, teacher, dean, and president, he strove for the development of student responsibility in Campus government—a development to which he was convinced an adequate student union would

5. The committee consisted of Victor S. Bryant, chairman, Leslie Weil, George Stephens, William M. Dey, Vernon Howell, C. T. Woollen, Clem G. Wright, and Louis R. Wilson, secretary. After Bryant's death Dey succeeded him as chairman and President Chase was added to the committee. Subsequently added were Judge Jeter C. Pritchard, Dr. W. S. Rankin, and Mr. W. A. Erwin, citizens chosen to represent the state at large. A. M. Coates was executive secretary in charge of fund-raising, 1919-1920. *Education and Citizenship, and Other Papers*, by Edward Kidder Graham, edited by Dr. Louis R. Wilson, was published in 1919 (G. P. Putnam's Sons, New York); and some 2,150 copies were distributed.

6. The name of this warm admirer of E. K. Graham and devoted friend of the University is an open secret: L. Ames Brown, A.B., 1910; A.M., 1911. But for this timely gift, the completion of the Graham Memorial would doubtless have been long delayed. A large proportion of the pledges to erect this building were never redeemed.

greatly contribute. And at the very heart of such a building, with appropriate verandas, dining rooms, and activities offices, he wished for a beautifully furnished lounge in which students, alumni, members of the faculty, and visitors could meet simply and informally in an atmosphere of friendliness and understanding."[7] The Graham Memorial is a three-storey building, including the basement; has 32 rooms and a floor space of 21,800 square feet. The plans for the building were designed by the firm of Atwood and Nash; and the contracting firm was T. C. Thompson and Brothers. The main lounge, centered on the ground floor, with oak-paneled walls, has been described as the most beautiful room in the United States south of Washington.

During the first century and a quarter, the University never had a hostelry, in size, appearance, and dignity, consonant with the architecture of the college buildings and the beautiful natural setting. Chapel Hill's first tavern or inn, located near the site of the present Baptist church, and kept by William and Elizabeth Nunn for upwards of half a century, was a badly constructed, unprepossessing wooden building. Without architectural distinction was the Eagle Hotel, a large wooden structure, more boardinghouse than hostelry, located almost on the site of Graham Memorial, long maintained by Miss Nancy Segur Hilliard, later, as the Union Hotel, by Major Hugh B. Guthrie, and still later, as the Chapel Hill Hotel, by Mr. Walter Pickard. The University Inn, universally known as Pickard's Hotel, situated where the Eagle Hotel once stood, resembled a large wooden beach cottage, rendered hideous by mustard-colored paint; and the long, low wooden extension to the southward, known as the University Inn Annex, was devoid of any semblance of charm. The second Pickard's Hotel, at the front of the yard of the present Institute of Government, was indistinguishable in appearance from a conventional, wooden private residence. The Central Hotel, a large, box-like wooden structure opposite the Post Office, was redeemed by its verandas facing Franklin Street. A somewhat similar wooden structure was Patterson's Hotel,

7. *T. M.*, 1917-1924, pp. 195, 207, 356, 368, 394; 1924-1930, pp. 25, 305, 331, 356-57; 1931-1938, p. 26. Cf. also *Graham Memorial, the Student Union* (1933).

located just south of the Baptist church on Columbia Street.[8] The spacious lot and fine oaks imparted charm and attractiveness to the wooden boardinghouse, originally the Richard J. Ashe home, on the site of the present Carolina Inn, maintained by Mrs. Julia Graves, widow of the brilliant professor of mathematics.

A genuine boon then, in the nature of definite advance toward better living conditions, comfort, and even elegance, was the plan, engineered by John Sprunt Hill in behalf of a group of alumni, which he presented to the Trustees on November 2, 1922. A non-stock corporation, known as the Carolina Club Inn, Inc., was to be formed; and Mr. Hill offered to donate an acre and a half of land (the lot occupied by the home of Mrs. Julia C. Graves) as site and the sum of $10,000 in addition. Mr. Hill was to have the right to nominate ten life members of the club; and the corporation was to endeavor to obtain subscriptions to the amount of $100,000 from alumni and friends of the University. Upon the property, consisting of the lot extending 210 feet on Cameron Avenue and 500 feet on the new Pittsboro Road, and the building to be erected was to be placed a mortgage of $50,000, this sum to be used toward defraying the costs of the building. Unable to secure the requisite funds through the plan outlined, the generous philanthropist, John Sprunt Hill, built at his own expense the Carolina Inn, approximating in cost the sum of $200,000. The building, containing 52 rooms, dining room, ballroom, and cafeteria, is architecturally beautiful and in the Southern colonial style. The design of the long porch on the Cameron Avenue side was obviously inspired by the porch of Mount Vernon facing the Potomac River. Designed by Arthur C. Nash, this gracious hostelry exhibits a high sense of esthetic values and harmonious adaptation to environment. The contractor was H. L. Smith of Durham. The Carolina Inn was ready for use by the alumni in December, 1924.

8. The Central Hotel, originally known as Roberson's Hotel, was a renovated and enlarged structure of ten rooms, made on the foundation of the private home long occupied by Mr. Jones Watson. Patterson's Hotel, conducted for a number of years by Mr. Bunn Patterson, was likewise constructed, on an enlarged scale, from the private home of Squire P. A. McDade.

After maintaining the hostelry for ten and a half years, Mr. Hill, on June 5, 1935, presented the entire Carolina Inn property to the University. In his letter to Governor J. C. B. Ehringhaus, June 5, 1935, Mr. Hill, after describing the Carolina Inn property, the gift of Mr. and Mrs. Hill and their three children, continued:

It is our desire that this property be held in trust by the Trustees of the University of North Carolina, and the income therefrom used: First: For the maintenance and upkeep of above mentioned property. Second: For the maintenance and support of the University Library, and especially for the support of that collection of books and papers known as the "North Caroliniana," a part of the University Library heretofore partially endowed by us.[9]

As a contribution toward gracious living and the suitable housing of alumni, visitors, and distinguished guests of the University, the Carolina Inn is the most noteworthy and universally appreciated gift, in the form of a building, ever made to the University.[10] In 1939, at a cost of $263,000, extensive additions were made, the architectural firm being Atwood and Weeks, the contractors, Muirhead Construction Company and V. P. Loftis.

Another gift, designed to enhance the beauty of the Campus and to add a touch of musical harmony as an appropriate accompaniment of University life, was originally conceived by John Motley Morehead, class of 1891, in the form of chimes to be placed in the South Building. Owing to the universal sentiment attaching to the name "South," connected with the origin of the University, the proposal of the prospective donor that the name of the building be changed to Morehead Hall, as a condition of the gift, was not favorably received by the Trustees; and the offer was declined. Another offer, the construction of a bell tower on South Building, was then made by Mr. Morehead who explained that he had been unaware of the sentiment attaching to the name, South Building, which was no longer

9. *T. M.*, 1931-1938, p. 173b.
10. *T. M.*, 1917-1924, pp. 415-16. For a detailed description of the Carolina Inn, consult *Alumni Review*, XIII (1924-1925), 69-70. For further details, *ibid.*, X (1921-1922), 261, and XI (1922-1923), 183.

geographically correct. The erection of a tower upon South Building did not recommend itself to the Trustees, and the second proposal was no more successful than the first. Eventually a happy solution for Mr. Morehead's generous intentions was found in the offer, jointly by Morehead and Rufus Lenoir Patterson, class of 1893, of a memorial bell tower. This offer, made on March 10, 1930, was eagerly accepted by the Trustees. The bell tower, the plans for which were drawn by McKim, Mead, and White, was erected on the main axis of the Campus, just south of the Raleigh Road. The tower, 167 feet in height, is built of red brick, the trim being of Indiana limestone; and the ceiling of the arcade is of Guastavine tile. The twelve bells in the tower, ranging in weight from 300 to 3,500 pounds, aggregate 14,350 pounds. They were cast by the Meneely Bell Company of Troy, New York. The tower, the cost of which was $100,000, was dedicated on November 26, 1931. The construction was supervised by Atwood and Nash of Durham, the work being done by T. C. Thompson and Brothers. An imposing inscription at the tower's base attests its purpose: "to perpetuate the memory of those members of the Morehead and Patterson families who have from the foundation of the University been associated with its activities as trustees, teachers, or students."[11]

One of the most striking establishments on the Campus, at once unique, distinctive, and representative of the genius of a democratic state, is the Institute of Government. It presents in operation the marriage of academic instruction with the practical conduct of government: precinct, town, county, district, state, and federal. Its primary function is to bridge the gap between classroom and courthouse, between textbook instruction and the law as actually administered. The creator and only begetter of this law laboratory, where teacher and pupil constantly inter-

11. T. M., 1924-1930, p. 26; 1931-1938, pp. 5, 26. See also Morehead-Patterson Memorial Tower (1931). The location, on the north-south axis bisecting Grand Avenue, while apparently satisfactory as seen on the ground plans, results in creating singular illusions to the naked eye. Viewed from the portico of the South Building, the tower appears to rise from the dome of the Library; from other positions, the tower's apparent dislocation with reference to that dome, creates the impression of architectual distortion.

change roles, is Professor Albert Coates of the University School of Law. By acquainting the citizen with processes of government, by carrying on an unremitting campaign of education, through numerous publications, handbooks, guides, and a magazine, *Popular Government* (first issue, January 1, 1931), the Institute serves the State and its people in countless ways: in the courthouse, on the highway, in government bureaus and legislative halls, and through frequent conferences of various types of officials engaged in the administration and enforcement of the laws. The people of North Carolina once (1765-1771) went to war over the maladministration of the law concerning taxation. Had the Institute of Government existed two centuries ago, no War of the Regulation could have taken place.

The story of the conception and birth (1928-1932) of the Institute of Government, which has been stirringly told by Professor Coates, is a drama in the real sense: aspiration, struggle, defeat, recovery, advance, conquest, success.[12] Again and again, plans went awry, failure loomed, financial ruin despite the severest sacrifices of Mr. and Mrs. Coates appeared imminent. The real beginning of the Institute dates from September, 1932, when six hundred officials, citizens, teachers and students attended sessions of the Institute in Chapel Hill. For seven years Coates carried a mental picture of the Institute, like a pocket theatre, around with him for display. Eventually a handsome brick building, in colonial Georgian style, was erected on Franklin Street opposite the A. S. Barbee lot; and the formal opening took place on November 29, 1939. It is the first institution of the kind established in the United States. In commending the work of the Institute for the valuable public service it was rendering, the late President Franklin D. Roosevelt said: "I hope that states having no comparable agency will recognize and follow North Carolina's leadership."

The architect of the building was Raymond Weeks of Durham, the contractor, H. F. Mitchell of Burlington, North Caro-

12. Albert Coates, *The Story of the Institute of Government*, National University Extension Association, Studies, No. 2 (July 1, 1944). Cf. also J. P. McEvoy, "Don't Shoot Your Sheriff: Teach Him!," *Reader's Digest*, October, 1943; Warren Olivier, "The Ugly Duckling at Chapel Hill," *Saturday Evening Post*, February 24, 1945.

lina. The building is 72 by 36 feet in base, with 9,800 square feet of floor space, and contains 104,976 cubic feet. The cost of the building was approximately $100,000. It houses a governmental laboratory, library, classrooms, offices, and, for the use of staff and visiting scholars and officials, sleeping accommodations in the basement and on the third floor. By an act of the Trustees, the Institute of Government became an integral part of the University in January, 1942.[13]

13. On January 20, 1942, the Executive Committee of the Board of Trustees approved an agreement between the University and Professor Albert Coates "covering the comprisal of the Institute of Government as a Public Service Department of the University." On January 27, 1942, the agreement previously approved by the Executive Committee was "ratified, approved and confirmed" by the Board of Trustees. The Institute of Government was then included by the State legislature as a separate division of the University of North Carolina in the State Budget in 1943.

WILLIAM CHAMBERS COKER

Kenan Research Professor Emeritus of Botany, he founded the University Arboretum in 1903 and has been its Director ever since. The Coker Arboretum, named in his honor, is one of the loveliest small naturalistic gardens in the United States.

KEMP PLUMMER BATTLE

For fifty-one years Trustee of the University; President, 1876-1891;
Professor of History, 1891-1907. As a recreation from his University
duties, he spent an hour or so daily in the Chapel Hill woods, clearing
paths and building bridges and wooden seats to make the beauties of the
woods easily accessible to students and Faculty. Many of his favorite
haunts still bear the names he gave them: Trysting Poplar, Anemone
Spring, Fairy Vale, Lion Rock, Vale of Ione, Dogwood Dingle, and
Wood-Thrush Home. The woods east and southeast of the village were
named Battle Park in his honor.

22

NEW RECORDS IN LEGISLATIVE APPROPRIATION AND SUPPORT

I N THE OPENING YEAR of the twentieth century, Francis
Preston Venable was elected president of the University,
in succession to Edwin Anderson Alderman, who had ac-
cepted the presidency of the Tulane University of Louisiana.
President Venable, a distinguished chemist, was confronted with
a monumental task: that of convincing the people of North
Carolina, and their representatives in the legislature, that the
State must maintain its rapidly growing and grievously neglected
University or suffer serious˙ consequences. President Venable
succeeded one of the most gifted platform speakers in the United
States; and Thomas Dunstan, the colored "Professor of Tonsorial
Art," as he unobtrusively termed himself, is reported to have
said: "Dr. Venable is a very noble, Christian gentleman. He'd
make a fine president of the Y. M. C. A. or Presiding Elder of
the Presbyterian Church. But he ain't no orator, naw sir. He
can't norate, he can't dilate, he can't prevaricate like Marse
Ed." He could, however, with the skill and accuracy of the scientist, present appalling facts in a convincing way. By sheer
persistence, resolution, and compelling earnestness, he shattered
the lethargy of the public and woke up the State with his stern
presentation of stark actualities. During his administration the
State voted the money for the first building ever erected on the
Campus out of a direct appropriation, in the entire 110 years
of the University's history. It is significant that this was a building to house the department which Dr. Venable had so long
and eminently headed.

The development of the Chemistry Department for upwards
of three quarters of a century and its unbreakable habit of
quickly outgrowing any quarters assigned it, furnish a narrative
of absorbing interest. While that story cannot be told here in
any detail, a mere sketch will evidence this department's vitality

in the history of Campus and buildings. Assigned by the Trustees on August 14, 1876, to Person Hall, then consisting merely of the east wing of the present building, the Chemistry Department soon found the quarters sadly cramped; and four years later secured the use of the basement of Smith Hall as a laboratory. By the end of 1886 a necessary addition to Person Hall, 70 by 30 feet, had been completed; and this new chemical laboratory was described by President Battle as "well arranged for all the needs of General, Industrial, and Agricultural Chemistry, including rooms for qualitative and quantitative analysis by students, and private laboratory rooms for the professors."[1] Six years later, the department's continued expansion compelled the erection of another, the west, wing of Person Hall at a cost of $2,645.[2] By 1903 the laboratory, built to accommodate 100 students, presented a state of dangerous congestion in the attempt to take care of 367 students. President Venable's appeal to the legislature in 1905 for $50,000 to build a new chemical laboratory proved successful; and on February 6, 1906, he reported that the new building, to house "three times as many students as could now be provided for" by Person Hall, would be completed in March. Although described by Venable as a "handsome structure," it was architecturally inharmonious with other college buildings and its style was deplored as an "unhappy combination of early Pullman and late North German Lloyd."[3]

1. *T. M.*, 1883-1891, pp. 186, 269. The addition was built by W. H. Linthicum of Durham, at an estimated cost of $2,350, the bricks being furnished him at Chapel Hill at a cost of $5 per thousand.

2. *T. M.*, 1891-1898, pp. 169, 182. This addition was made possible out of a fund of $13,000, left by Miss Mary Ann Smith, for the support of a Chair of Agricultural Chemistry.

3. Because of legislative priorities for a total of $5,000 to cover cost of refitting quarters for the departments of Biology and Medicine, the Chemistry Building cost only $45,000. It had a capacity of 488,000 cubic feet. In 1925 when the Chemistry Department occupied new quarters in Venable Hall, the Department of Pharmacy, which had been housed in Person Hall, followed in Chemistry's footsteps and occupied the chemistry building, giving it the name Howell Hall after Edward Vernon Howell, first Dean of the School of Pharmacy. Howell Hall, which was reconditioned in 1925 at a cost of $55,215, has 30 rooms and a floor space of 21,000 square feet. The architect was Frank P. Milburn; the builder, N. Underwood. The tablet on the building bears the date 1904. See "The School of Medicine and Pharmacy," *University of North Carolina Record*, No. 89, February, 1911.

As we have already seen in an earlier chapter, the University miraculously succeeded in doing without an infirmary for the first 63 years of its existence. The small two-room cottage, designed by the architect A. J. Davis, and known as "The Retreat," then served the needs of the University for thirty-six years. The general health of the students and Faculty was so unexceptionable that, apparently, no real need for an infirmary was ever felt or expressed. In February, 1894, the Dean of the Medical School, R. H. Whitehead, modestly suggested that a small infirmary for sick students was clearly needed, in order to halt the undesirable and oftentimes dangerous practice of sending to their homes students threatened with serious illness.[4] In response to this recommendation a simple frame cottage of three rooms, costing $1,443.63, was erected in 1895, being completed about May 1. Few students were sick and the infirmary was so little used that it soon became the practice to house Trustees there on their visits to the University, especially during Commencement. The Visiting Committee, reporting on May 31, 1898, engagingly records: "We found the Infirmary so neat and clean and comfortable that we preferred it as a sleeping place, to the hotel—during our visits."[5]

By 1907 the number of students had reached a total of 785, registering a steady increase during the preceding fifteen years. In response to the urgent need for an infirmary worthy of the University and equipped with modern facilities, such a building was erected and opened in 1907. The architects were Frank P. Milburn & Company, and the builder, N. Underwood. The cost was $18,000, with equipment at an additional cost of $3,000.

4. The death from typhoid fever of William Preston Bynum, Jr., in the summer of 1893, which was probably due to this unwise practice, evoked strong criticism; and was directly provocative of the agitation for the building of an infirmary.

5. A popular joke among students was to the effect that the large number of empty bottles carted off from the infirmary after each of these visits, mentioned above, indicated either grave illness or exceptionally good health and high spirits on the part of the visiting Trustees. When the third infirmary, recently abandoned as such, was erected in 1907, the small wooden building of the second infirmary was purchased by the late Dr. Eric A. Abernethy; and with extensive additions is now the home of his widow on Columbia Street. The second infirmary stood near the site of the auditorium of present Hill Music Hall.

The second infirmary had accommodation for only about twenty patients; but the third infirmary contained 64 rooms with 14,275 square feet of floor space.[6] The latter was located near the northeast corner of the intersection of Cameron Avenue and Columbia Street, and west of Swain Hall.

In 1907 a spacious president's house, long greatly needed, was erected. It stands on the highest point of a large lot, at the southeast corner of the intersection of Franklin and Raleigh streets, covering almost three-fourths of the area between Raleigh Street and Battle Lane. This is the same lot on which stood, somewhat east of the present building, the second president's house, burned on Christmas Day, 1886. The present president's house, conventional in pseudo-Classic design but redeemed by wide porches, was erected at an original cost of $15,000; and remodeled in 1929 at a cost of $6,985.

Once the tradition, which had prevailed in practice since its establishment, that the University must be self-supporting and self-evolving, was shattered, appropriations for the erection of buildings began to flow in a small and sporadic trickle; and successive legislatures provided for permanent improvements: $50,000 in 1907 and $200,000 in 1911. Accordingly "Davie Hall," a belated recognition in the naming of a building for the University's founder, was erected to house the departments of Biology and Botany. This building was completed by the end of 1908. Davie Hall, of gray pressed brick, 126 by 145 feet, was constructed at a cost of $35,535, the architects being Frank P. Milburn and Company and the contractor, N. Underwood of Durham. The choice of the location, east of New East Building and north of Cameron Avenue, indicated the desire on the part of the Trustees to execute the original plan of the founders and to continue building along the Cameron Avenue axis.[7]

6. *T. M.*, 1891-1898, pp. 233, 363, 391, 473; 1898-1904, p. 13; Battle, II, 672. In 1924 an extension was built at a cost of $23,300; architectural firm, Atwood and Nash; contracting firm, T. C. Thompson and Brothers. In 1938 a wing was added at a cost of $30,000; architectural firm, Atwood and Weeks; contractor, V. P. Loftis.

7. Davie Hall, which contains 472,000 cubic feet, was renovated, by T. C. Thompson and Brothers, in 1925 at a cost of $55,215. The present structure has 38 rooms and floor space of 21,025 square feet. The architectural firm was Atwood and Nash.

The period following the legislative grant of $200,000 for buildings in 1911 to the end of President Venable's administration registered steady progress in the University's physical expansion. The medical building, which had been strongly urged by Dean I. H. Manning during the preceding five years, was given priority, begun in June, 1911, and completed some ten months later. It was dedicated with impressive ceremonies on May 8, 1912, addresses being delivered by Dr. Edgar Fahs Smith, Provost of the University of Pennsylvania, Dr. Richard H. Whitehead, former Dean of the Medical School, and Dr. A. A. Kent, class of 1879, President of the North Carolina Medical Society. The cost of the building, verging upon the classical Renaissance style and placed opposite Davie Hall on the south side of Cameron Avenue, was $50,000, including equipment. The architects were Milburn, Heister and Company and the contractor, I. G. Lawrence and Son. The building was designed to provide laboratories for histology, bacteriology, pharmacology, physiology, and anatomy, together with lecture-rooms and a library. It was named, singularly enough, Caldwell Hall for the first president of the University, although Joseph Caldwell was neither physician nor surgeon, but a mathematician and engineer.[8]

In May, 1912, building began on a great dormitory in three sections, these being named respectively for Kemp Plummer Battle, Zebulon Baird Vance, and James Johnston Pettigrew, all famous in the history of University and State. The selection of the site, on the west side of the main west walk, was of first importance, necessitating the purchase of a fine property adjacent to the Campus on the west and fronting on Franklin Street. Actually the University purchased the Pickard's Hotel property, the Central Hotel property, and the lot whereon stood the Phi Delta Theta fraternity lodge, all abutting on the Campus on

8. Caldwell Hall released for other uses 6 rooms for lecture purposes in Person Hall and 10 rooms for dormitories in New West; and housed temporarily the School of Pharmacy. The building has been extensively remodeled, renovated, repaired, and reconditioned, in 1932, 1934-1935, 1939, and 1942, at a total cost of some $25,000. For the extensive renovation in 1939, at a cost of $10,775, the contracting firm was T. W. Poe and Son, the architectural firm, Atwood and Weeks. The building has 25,300 square feet of floor space. *T. M.,* 1904-1916, pp. 340, 344, 384.

east and west.[9] The intention of the Trustees was to erect two sectional dormitories facing each other and looking inward upon the Campus. The plan was later abandoned when the Pickard's Hotel property was selected as the site of the Graham Memorial. Each section of Battle-Vance-Pettigrew, 60 feet long, 40 feet wide, and three storeys high, was originally designed to contain 24 rooms. The style is collegiate Gothic, popular at that period for dormitories; and the architects, Milburn, Heister and Company, were instructed to model them as nearly as possible after dormitories at the University of Pennsylvania. The three buildings were completed by the end of 1912.

In 1896 Mrs. Frederick Baker of New York donated $3,000 to make additions to the gymnasium and convert it into a Commons. This building wherein meetings of the Alumni Association and Commencement balls also were held, provided board, at the extraordinarily low price of $8 per month, to only 200 students. Following repeated recommendations from 1907 on by President Venable for the erection of a new Commons Hall of double the former capacity, the Executive Committee on February 12, 1913, ordered a new dining hall to be built and paid for out of the $50,000 appropriation for 1914. The new dining hall, built of light brown pressed brick and located on the lot whereon had stood for almost a century and a quarter the first "President's House," was erected in 1913. The architect was Milburn, Heister and Company; the contractor, W. B. Barrow. The hall could accommodate 460 students and was designed for future expansion. The cost of this large one-storey building, containing 414,000 cubic feet and provided with the most modern equipment, was $46,654.93. It was named for the third President of the Univer-

9. The prices paid for the Central Hotel property and the Phi Delta Theta lot were $10,000 and $5,321.41, respectively. The Pickard's Hotel property consisting of two acres, was acquired by the University from Professor H. H. Williams in 1906 at a cost of $19,700. As actually built, Battle-Vance-Pettigrew contains only 46 rooms, 22,000 square feet of floor space and 385,000 cubic feet. The contracting firm was I. G. Lawrence and Son, the cost, $51,757. The University dormitories, as reported by President Venable in 1909, could accommodate only about 320 students; and the town was taxed to the utmost to provide lodgings for the remainder. Cf. T. M., 1904-1916, pp. 206, 232, 258, 328, 338-39, 364, 394; Battle, II, 657.

sity, David Lowrie Swain; and suffered the unhappy, but inevitable, fate of receiving at the hands of the students the uncom-
plimentary cognomen of "Swine Hall."[10]

During the brief administration of President Edward Kidder
Graham, who took office in September, 1914, a new approach
was made to the problem of obtaining adequate State aid to meet
the University's constantly increasing needs. In 1869 Mrs.
Spencer bitterly complained of the niggardliness of the State
which, to that date, had directly appropriated to the University's
growth and maintenance the pitifully small total of $17,000 in
74 years![11] In his report to the Trustees, January 26, 1915, President Graham pointed out that, to that date, the State had contributed by direct appropriation only $341,500 to the University,
the property of which had recently been carefully estimated at
more than one million dollars in value.[12] Again, in 1916, he
called attention to the comparatively small amount the State had
directly contributed to the University's building program. Of
the 29 buildings on the Campus, 22—approximately 75%—had
been contributed by private gift and subscription.

In the midst of a war, when grave national and international
issues were at stake, to request any very large sum for University support was hazardous and at best uncertain. Graham was
a man of great dignity, moral force, and genuine eloquence.
Rejecting all counsels of despair, he carefully estimated the University's needs and boldly pleaded for the calculated amount,
half a million dollars for permanent improvements, and an adequate increase in maintenance funds. For the first time in the
University's history, the legislature of North Carolina granted
a president's request in full. On June 15, 1917, the Visiting Committee reported the glad tidings that the legislature had granted
the Board's full request for $500,000, to be used during the next
six years. Graham brought about a striking innovation in Uni-

10. *T. M.*, 1904-1916, pp. 126, 206, 364, 395, 487, 497. In 1924 Swain
Hall was enlarged and remodeled at a cost of $27,700; architectural firm,
Atwood and Nash; contracting firm, T. C. Thompson and Brothers. In
1936 it was reconditioned at a cost of $10,000.

11. S. P. I., July 6, 1869.

12. Cf. report of Charles T. Woollen, Proctor, June 2, 1914, giving in
itemized form the valuation of University property at $1,008,400. *T. M.*,
1904-1916, pp. 464-65.

versity approach and State policy in appropriation. This new mode of handling the problem of State appropriation was to have a revolutionary effect upon the administration of Graham's successor.

The untimely death of President Graham occurred on October 26, 1918, during the deadly influenza epidemic. The curious consequence was that no buildings, except the Power Plant, paid for out of the memorable $500,000 appropriation, were completed during Graham's administration.[13] The first expenditure from that appropriation was for a physics, mathematics, and engineering building. The Department of Mathematics was a genuine Peripatetic School, teachers and students wandering over the Campus from building to building to obtain classrooms with blackboards. The congestion in the case of the Physics Department, crammed into the bowels of the earth, the basement of Alumni Building, was appalling. After several years of struggle under these hardships, relief finally came in the autumn of 1919. The new building was named "Phillips Hall" in honor of James Phillips, Professor of Mathematics and Natural Philosophy, 1826-1867; Charles Phillips, Professor of Engineering, 1845-1860, and of Mathematics, 1861-1868, 1875-1879; and William Battle Phillips, Professor of Agricultural Chemistry and Mining, 1885-1888. The style for the building was designated in the contract as English Collegiate, in red tapestry brick with limestone trimming; but the general effect was that of an industrial plant, suggesting automobiles or sewing machines. Two storeys high, with a basement, the building, completed in 1920, was fortified with an interior structure of steel and reinforced concrete. The architect was C. C. Hook of Charlotte; and the contracts were awarded: to I. G. Lawrence for building; to L. F. Waldron of Rock Hill, S. C., for heating. The ultimate cost, including equipment, was $138,590—the building costs exceeding the contractor's estimate by some $10,000. Two wings were subsequently added: one in 1925 at a cost of $53,098, the other in 1927 at a cost of $58,771. The architectural firm for these additions was Atwood and Nash, the contractor, T. C. Thomp-

13. Details concerning the Power Plant will be given in Chapter 28.

son. The building, which has undergone a constant succession of interior changes during the past 25 years, has 98 rooms and 65,900 square feet of floor space; and contains 888,730 cubic feet.[14]

14. *T. M.*, 1904-1916, pp. 233, 364, 460, 487, 489; 1917-1924, pp. 35, 43, 59, 88-89, 112, 156, 220, 239. It may be mentioned that satisfactory adjustment was finally made with the building contractor who confessed to an error in drawing up the contract, making his bid $10,000 less than he intended. For table showing all expenditures under the $500,000 improvement fund, consult Link, p. 189.

23

NEW DIRECTIONS IN UNIVERSITY PLANNING; COMMITTEE ON GROUNDS AND BUILDINGS ESTABLISHED

THE DECADE, approximately from 1913 to 1923, signalizes the inauguration, during three successive administrations, of the most constructive steps ever taken concerning the Campus and the physical improvement and enlargement of the University. These were, in order: the creation of the Committee on Grounds and Buildings, the study of Campus development by a great landscape architect called in consultation, the appointment of a University consulting architect, the introduction of the zoning concept and policy, and the unparalleled popular uprising which brought about the $6,000,000 building program for University development and expansion.

On September 6, 1913, at the first Faculty meeting presided over by Acting-President Edward K. Graham, a vital step was taken in the establishment of a "Committeee on Grounds and Buildings," for preserving the natural beauty of the Campus, safeguarding University lands available for college building sites, and maintaining adequate standards for architectural propriety in harmony with the physical University in being. The original members of the Committee on Grounds and Buildings were Professors William Chambers Coker (chairman), George Howe, and Collier Cobb.

During the absence of Professor Cobb, when the Committee on Grounds and Buildings numbered only three members, Dr. John M. Booker was placed on the committee. While the matter had often been under discussion by the committee, Dr. Booker actively pressed the matter of securing a consulting architect for the University, which was approved in principle by President Graham; but nothing was done in this direction until the appointment, under President Chase's administration, of McKim,

Mead, and White as consulting architects.[1] Somewhat later, Dr. Booker took the lead in urging the employment of the zoning principle, the grouping of structures according to function, for future Campus building; and his two articles with maps of the Campus, showing location of present and proposed buildings and outlining three possible zoning plans, stimulated interest in zoning which has since become a guiding principle in plans for Campus building.[2]

The Committee on Grounds and Buildings, although composed exclusively of members of the Faculty, is unique in that it is not elected by the Faculty but is appointed by and responsible only to the president. It is actually an indispensable cog in the machinery of University administration. Since its establishment this committee, serving in an advisory and recommendatory capacity, has concerned itself with the development of the grounds, the location, function, capacity, and architectural style of all structures erected on the Campus and outlying territory, the care and conservation of our forest lands, and the designation of all areas for athletic and recreational purposes. Included within its jurisdiction is the location of all roads and walks. During the past thirty-four years, the committee has been uninterruptedly engaged in long-term planning in regard to use of University property for the institution's future orderly and harmonious expansion.

An important step was taken by President Edward K. Graham early in his brief but creatively fertile administration. Dr. John Nolen, sometime graduate student at Harvard and Munich, famous city planner and landscape architect, was engaged in mapping out the suburban area, known as Myers Park, of President Graham's birthplace, Charlotte. The late George G. Stephens, class of 1896, banker and realtor closely concerned in a financial way with Myers Park, was deeply impressed with Nolen's engineering ability and esthetic sense; and it was through his instrumentality that Nolen was invited by President Graham to visit Chapel Hill and study, in conjunction with the Com-

1. Consult Chapter 26.
2. J. M. Booker, "The 'Back Part' of the Campus," *Alumni Review*, X (1922), 191, 198-99; "Zoning the Campus," *loc. cit.*, pp. 218, 226.

mittee on Grounds and Buildings, the immediately pressing problems of Campus development.[3] Nolen, it will be recalled, had an unrivaled reputation, throughout the entire Southeast, as a master-planner of golf-courses, of which Pinehurst affords the most conspicuous example in North Carolina. Nolen visited Chapel Hill on a number of occasions, during 1917 to 1919, conferred with the Committee on Grounds and Buildings, and critically analysed various plans and projects for future Campus treatment. While he never submitted any master-plan or general design for Campus treatment and landscaping, he advocated the immediate use of the beautiful and virgin grove south of the South Building for large-scale development as park area and as ideal sites for University buildings. A study, with accompanying plan of development, was also made and submitted to the committee by Hobart B. Upjohn, architect of the Presbyterian and Episcopal churches of Chapel Hill.

During this same period, Colonel J. Bryan Grimes, a member of the Executive Committee of the Trustees, brought prominently into the foreground a plan he had long advocated for developing the 550 acres of woodland adjoining the 48-acre Campus. After studying plans of the leading American universities, he sent out an able letter embodying his ideas to the Trustees and many of the alumni. Among other things, he said: "Instead of pressing and crowding towards the village street, it [the University] should handsomely expand toward the south, as the original plans contemplated. It would be greatly to the interest of the University to have a large park laid off on the south side of the Campus." After describing in detail his ideas of developing this area, he continued: "A competent, broad-minded and sympathetic landscape architect could lay off college and park grounds unequalled anywhere in the country. The avenues, parks, squares, circles and vistas would bear names of men associated with University life and history. . . . With the new era that has dawned for the University, now is the time for this development."[4]

3. Letter of George G. Stephens from 50 Walnut Street, Asheville, N. C., May 31, 1945, to the author.

4. *News and Observer*, April 5, 1919; *Alumni Review*, VII (1919), 189, 194-95.

The outcome of the studies of the Committee on Grounds and Buildings, in consultation with John Nolen, and of the aggressive campaign of Colonel Grimes, was the recommendation by President Chase, adopted by the Executive Committee of the Board of Trustees, April 4, 1919, of the appointment of a committee of five Trustees to investigate the feasibility of developing the grove in the South Campus into a park for building purposes.[5] On June 17, 1919, President Chase reported to the Trustees that the Faculty Committee on Grounds and Buildings, in co-operation with John Nolen, landscape architect, had been at work for two years on a plan for the future development of the Campus.[6]

Many of the most desirable locations on the Campus north of Cameron Avenue had already been utilized; and it was feared that the temptation to use other sites in this area might well result in crowding, thereby impairing the beauty of wide sweeps of lawn and lovely park expanses. This was a feeling which had become well nigh universal among perceptive Faculty members and observant alumni and Trustees. It was recalled that Alexander Jackson Davis, three-quarters of a century earlier, had presented designs for the treatment, horticulturally, of the South Campus; and the tetrastyle Ionic portico on the south side of Gerrard Hall had eloquently testified, until its removal in 1900-1901, that in the period 1835-1845, it was the plan of Dr. Mitchell to build a wide avenue, the main highway from Raleigh, south of Gerrard Hall and to have the main entrance to the Campus at its southern extension. In 1793, two years before the University's opening, the plan for the Campus included "ornamental grounds," to north and east of the University center, and a botanical garden, doubtless with associated buildings such as greenhouses and structures under glass for horticulture, in the southeastern portion of the Campus, probably the sunken area now occupied by Mangum, Ruffin, Manly, and Grimes dormitories.[7]

5. *T. M.*, 1917-1924, p. 129. The committee consisted of J. Bryan Grimes, George G. Stephens, James A. Gray, John Sprunt Hill, and Haywood Parker.

6. *Ibid.*, p. 156.

7. At the meeting of the Executive Committee of the Trustees, April

Meanwhile an extraordinary development, amounting to a crisis in the history of the evolution of higher education in North Carolina, had supervened. Largely in consequence of the first World War, which ended on November 11, 1918, a greatly increased enrollment in the high schools was rapidly shifting the burden of accommodation to the colleges and the State University. In the autumn of 1920 there were 26,000 students in the four-year high schools, with heavy increases expected; and the colleges and University were inundated. The dearth of dormitories, classrooms, and dining-room facilities at the University was appalling; and drastic action was imperatively necessary, both to relieve immediate congestion and to provide expansion over a considerable period of time to meet the constantly increasing enrollment. Dormitories built to house 469 were housing 738, under highly uncomfortable and unsanitary conditions, with four students in rooms designed for two. Dining halls designed for 450 were actually feeding 725. Excepting lecture space in scientific and professional buildings, there were only 19 classrooms on the entire Campus available for general teaching.

Matters were coming to a crisis at Chapel Hill. The feeling was general that drastic action was required. Ever since the establishment of the *Alumni Review* in 1912, that publication under the direction of its editor, Dr. Louis R. Wilson, had been stressing in editorials and articles the necessary steps for effecting the transition from college to university. Deeply impressed by an editorial in a leading North Carolina daily[8] deploring the niggardly policy of the State and the "conspicuous failure of North Carolina leadership," Dr. Wilson on September 26 drafted and handed to President Chase a vigorous memorandum advocating the inauguration of a campaign, pointing toward the legislature, for meeting the educational crisis in a liberal and

---

4, 1919, the view was expressed that further "pressing and crowding" of University building toward the village street [Franklin] was inadvisable; and it was recommended that the Campus should be opened up and continued to the south of South Building, "as the original plans contemplated." Cf. *Alumni Review*, VIII (1919), 189.

8. "The Thing We Lack," *Greensboro Daily News*, September 23, 1920.

statesmanlike manner. Acting upon this and other representations from Faculty members and students, President Chase called
a meeting in his office on the afternoon of September 26, at which
were present Business Manager Woollen; Librarian Wilson;
Professors Bernard and Graham; Lenoir Chambers, Director of
the News Bureau; Francis Bradshaw, Dean of Students; and
Ralph Rankin, Secretary of the Alumni Association and Assistant Director of Extension. The situation was thoroughly
canvassed; and the prospects for securing legislative support
proved to be discouraging. At the instance of Graham, who had
faith that the key to the situation lay in the alumni, it was decided to summon to Chapel Hill by wire a carefully selected
group of some 125 alumni; and this decision was ratified by
President Chase. On Wilson's motion, Chase, Wilson, and
Woollen withdrew from the meeting—"as we might be over-
cautious," and the drafting and sending of the telegrams, signed
by President Chase, were left to the remaining members of
the committee.

The remarkable meeting held at Chapel Hill on October 2,
as the result of this call, is historic. This meeting to take counsel
regarding the University's plight, which took place in the students' boardinghouse known as "The Coop," was attended by
43 alumni from all parts of the State, on fire to "go down the
line for Alma Mater." Present, in addition to President Chase
and Business Manager Woollen, were a few members of the
Faculty and University officials entirely aware of the gravity
of the situation: Bernard, chairman of the meeting, Graham,
Wilson, Patterson, Knight, Henderson, Chambers, Bradshaw,
and Rankin. This gathering was described at the time as the
"most earnest, most enthusiastic, most seriously-minded, and
determined" as well as the largest group of alumni ever to as-
semble, outside of stated occasions, on general University business. "Nothing short of a revolution in higher education," declared President Chase, "will handle the situation in North
Carolina." Professor Frank Graham, a leader in promoting and
bringing about the conference, and who directed the field campaign after it was launched, asserted with burning, crusading
spirit: "We will not tamely submit to the issue: more buildings
or less boys. If it is a question of exemption of property or

redemption of youth, North Carolina will vote for her youth. . . .
Suffer the youth of North Carolina to come unto the colleges
and forbid them not, for of such is the kingdom of to-morrow."
Vigorous and cogent resolutions, six in number, unanimously
passed by this body, outlined plans for "organizing the State"
and fully acquainting the people of North Carolina with the
actuality and gravity of the educational crisis—both at the
University and at other institutions of higher learning in the
commonwealth, whether state-supported or institutionally and
privately endowed and maintained.

Ten days later, on University Day, President Chase, in a brief
talk concluding the ceremonies honoring the University's
founder, William Richardson Davie, ended on a climactic
challenge:

History has witnessed that Davie was right. He was right because
his ground was the firm ground of principle, not the shifting sand
of expediency. And today, when the University of his vision is overwhelmed by its very success, crowded beyond its capacity, no longer
capable of opening its doors to all youth of the State who are knock-
ing for admittance, on fire with a passion for service that must of
necessity be repressed and restrained—what, think you, would be
Davie's response to such a challenge? Can you doubt his reply? Can
you doubt the reply of any man who, like him really believes that
it is the duty of the State to educate its youth? This University of
the State, this University that is the realization of what Davie hoped
and dreamed, asks but that she be set free to do adequately her task.
If higher education is really worth while, if the University of North
Carolina is worth while, the issue must be squarely met, as Davie
would have met it. It must be met in the spirit that sets above every
other consideration the fulfilment of a just and righteous principle.[9]

The editor, Tyre C. Taylor, class of 1921, effectively used
The Carolina Magazine as a powerful organ of information and
opinion in this campaign of popular illumination, which began
as a feeble taper and ended as a mighty conflagration. The slow-
burning fuse was touched off in the November issue:

At this present moment—a crucial one in the history of the institution—the University of North Carolina is beset by grave dangers: the lack of space, of means, of equipment, of adequate facilities.
I have confidence that the people of the state will respond to the

9. "University Day," *Alumni Review,* IX (1920), 49-51.

VIEW OF THE COKER ARBORETUM

The five-acre tract of land now occupied by the Arboretum was once only a swampy pasture. Today it contains approximately 400 kinds of ornamental plants, grouped in such a way as to illustrate their use in design and planting.

PRESIDENT'S WALK, LOOKING WEST FROM
RALEIGH STREET
A gravel path through the University Arboretum.

urgent call of higher education, once they become fully aware of the gravity of the situation. Not higher education alone, but democracy itself, is at stake. For after all, was not Pasteur right when he defined democracy as that form of civilization which enables every individual to put forth his utmost effort? No democratic state can remain permanently great which curtails the normal development of the human spirit and sets bounds to the progress of investigation. Material wealth is desirable; prosperity is gratifying; mere utility has its place in education. But the highest function of the University, which the state must conserve and foster, is greater than all of these. It is nothing less than productive genius, the spirit of pure research, the creative force of civilization itself.[10]

The Alumni Review carried on the front cover of the December issue a strong statement from the student body of the University, addressed "To the People of North Carolina" and ending with these words: "In mass meeting assembled [Chapel Hill, N. C., November 5, 1920], 1000 strong, we send this message of hope to the people of North Carolina with confident faith that the people, armed with the facts, will rise up to meet a big problem in a big way."

A direct outcome of the gathering of the faithful at "The Coop" was a notable meeting of University alumni at Greensboro on October 11. At another enthusiastic meeting of citizens of the State, held on November 12 at the North Carolina College for Women, under the leadership of the late Alfred M. Scales, nine people subscribed $500 each, to carry on the campaign. Soon University alumni meetings, addressed by eloquent spell-binders, including President Chase and Professors Graham, Wilson, Bernard, Noble, Patterson, Henderson, and others, were being held throughout the State. Parent-Teacher Associations, Chambers of Commerce, Rotary and Kiwanis Clubs, Scottish Rite Masons, Junior Order of United American Mechanics, and many others soon followed. Connor's three powerful articles on the educational crisis appeared shortly after Christmas in all the leading dailies;[11] and impressive advertisements in prominent

10. "A Thought for the Hour," *The New Carolina Magazine,* LI (1920), 8-9.
11. R. D. W. Connor, "North Carolina's Crisis in Higher Education: I. The Crisis; II. The Remedy; III. Our Ability to Meet It," Raleigh *News and Observer,* December 26, 27, 28, 1920.

journals, drafted by Sam Dickson, the journalist of the *Greensboro Daily News* staff, and underwritten by the Scales committee, carried their message to the remotest corners of the State and produced resounding repercussions. A special issue of *The New Carolina Magazine* (January, 1921), which was placed in the hands of every member of the legislature, carried a smashing story by John H. Kerr, class of 1921, chairman of the Student Committee, of the great popular uprising, with liberal quotations from the press and revealing illustrations of the disgraceful congestion and unsanitary crowding in the University dormitories. This special issue used a front-page box-story which epitomized the essentials of the situation:

The supreme problem in North Carolina today is to reconcile two mutually contradictory facts: the splendid circumstance that North Carolina in agricultural resources is fourth from the top in the United States; and the humiliating circumstance that North Carolina in illiteracy is fourth from the bottom in the United States. How shall we bridge over this hideous gap, this yawning crevasse, between industrial progress and intellectual reaction, between our financial wealth and our educational poverty, between our agricultural glory and our cultural shame?

Three great dangers confront and threaten the welfare and progress of the commonwealth. First, as the result of grossly inadequate housing facilities at this University, there looms ominous the perpetual menace to the health of the youth of North Carolina. Second, as the result of lack of means to supply dormitory space and full teaching force, the army of our youth coming up hopefully from the high schools will be confronted at the gates with the legend: "Abandon hope. Ye cannot enter here." Third, as the result of thwarted educational programs and stinted provisions for study, investigation, and research, the higher levels and reaches of thought will not be attained by our scholars, and the civilization of our commonwealth will suffer harmful arrest and impediment. . . .

Neither timidity in discussing the question nor evasion of the potent fact that large financial responsibilities must be incurred by the State, will suffice in the present hour of crisis. . . . The crisis is acute, immediate, and appalling. The remedy is obvious, imperative, and obligatory.

At the very hour of birth of the University of North Carolina, William Richardson Davie declared that the object of the University was "to form *citizens* capable of comprehending, improving, and defending the principles of government; *citizens* who, from the highest possible impulse, a just sense of their own and the general happiness, would be induced to practice the duties of social morality." No democratic State can become or remain permanently great which denies to its youth the right and privilege of higher education for constructive leadership and the practice of enfranchising duties of social morality and good citizenship.

Throughout the entire period of the campaign, November, 1920 to April, 1921, the *Alumni Review* presented the case for education in a broad and comprehensive way, printing fundamental documents in their entirety, notably the University's program, needs, and legislative requests.

As early as June 15, 1920, the Visiting Committee of the Trustees, setting forth the urgent necessity of the financial steps proposed, the inadequacy of available funds and the almost inevitable tendency to slump after the all-out prosecution of a depleting world war, nevertheless forthrightly faced up to the issue: "To take the affirmative in good faith and with a full understanding of the great and pressing needs and opportunities ahead means nothing less than half a million annually for maintenance and five millions for building purposes." The Trustees as a body could not bring themselves to the point of sustaining so drastic and ambitious a proposal; and, after deleting the paragraph outlining the University's requirements, went on record as favoring a request to the General Assembly of 1921 for the necessary funds, unspecified lest the figures appear too sensational, in order to meet the University's needs in the matters of both maintenance and permanent improvements.[12] Nine months later in a detailed story, Frank Graham, the spark plug and "fiery particle" of the movement, vividly described the stirring events which constituted the several chapters in a great popular movement and vocalization of sentiment and opinion.[13] Organizers of victory in the legislature were Governor Cameron Morrison, ex-Governor Bickett, Secretary of State W. N. Everett, R. A. Doughton, and Walter Murphy; and the able field general, directing operations on the ground, was President Chase who for

12. *T. M.*, 1917-1924, pp. 221-28.
13. F. P. Graham, "An Epic in Democracy and Progress," *Alumni Review*, IX (1921), 229-34. At that time Graham was Associate Professor of History.

several months maintained headquarters in Raleigh. At a special session of the Trustees, December 30, 1920, President Chase and the Trustees' Legislative Committee were instructed to present the full building program to the proper committees of the General Assembly, urging for that purpose an appropriation of $5,585,000.[14] Both impressed and perturbed by the state-wide campaign of appeal, protest, and indignation, the legislature rose to meet the crisis and courageously embarked upon a large-scale program and policy of enlarging all of the State's educational and charitable institutions by floating a $20,000,000 bond issue. The request of the Trustees, as presented by its Legislative Committee, was granted, in an historic action of supreme importance to the University and the State; and the sum of $1,490,000 was made available for expenditure, covering the years 1921 and 1922.[15]

14. *T. M.*, 1917-1924, p. 272.
15. *Public Laws of North Carolina*, 1921, Chapter 165.

24

COLLEGE ATHLETICS AFTER THE
RE-OPENING: 1875-1905

ITH THE RE-OPENING of the University in 1875 a new
era in collegiate athletics at Chapel Hill was inaugurated. A general interest in sports, outdoor and
indoor, for their own sake, naturally grew up among the students. The energetic and restless youths began to realize the need
for "chest exercise" which "Observer" had stressed twenty-two
years earlier. There was little desire for, or even thought of,
intercollegiate contests. Students exercised in their own rooms
with dumbbells and Indian clubs; went singly and in small groups
on long walks, along the main street of the village from Couchtown to Carrboro, to the summit of Mount Bolus, to the mill on
the creek along the old Hillsboro Road, to Purefoy's Mill and
the Mason Farm, and, above all, to Point Prospect, where a
remarkable view to the eastward over the bed of the old Triassic
sea rewarded the pedestrian. In the year following the re-opening
of the University, an athletic association, with Julian M. Baker,
class of 1877, as president, was organized through student initiative. An outdoor gymnasium, located about halfway between
Gerrard Hall and the south stone wall of the Campus enclosure
of the day, was set up, with trapeze, horizontal bars, and swing-
ing rings. The athletic field, roughly cleared at the same time for
baseball and football, lay south and east of the old Library.[1]
Shinny was played along the driveway, earlier known as College
Street, running west from the South Building. "These contests
were full of continuous movement and excitement," writes a
graduate of the class of 1881. "We had no training in athletics
of any kind. We played our games just for the exercise and the
sport they gave us, and nearly every student played in one kind

1. As late as 1854 and doubtless later, a small number of large trees
stood on this area. Compare view of the University in 1854 from athletic
field, *U. N. C. M.*, XIII (1894), facing page 301. Cf. also earliest published view of the University of North Carolina, *The Illustrated Hand
Book, a New Guide for Travelers through the United States of America*
(New York, 1846).

or other of them. We regarded all games merely as recreations, wholly extraneous to the real purpose of college life. Perhaps a greater number [proportion] were benefited by outdoor games then, when every one shared in them, than since school and college athletics have become such an important factor in college life."[2]

Indoctrinated as is the Carolina man of today with the concept of elaborately trained teams, efficient and costly coaches some of whom receive salaries higher than those received by any Faculty member, superb stadiums, beautifully turfed playing fields, colorful throngs running up to between 30,000 and 43,000 at the thrilling intercollegiate football matches, and all the numerous and expensive adjuncts for the playing of many kinds of sport, he can scarcely imagine a state of affairs when there was no University Athletic Association, no direction and supervision of field sports and track athletics, no concern whatever by the administrative authorities in mass recreational activities of athletic character. The explanation is clearly supplied by a graduate of the class of 1882: "It is no reflection on the University that no recreational facilities were provided. It was no time to think about recreation. Existence was the important thing at that time. The University had not been re-opened long, the student body was a mere handful, less than two hundred, and legislative appropriations were meagre, and existence was too precarious to think about recreation. There was no demand on the part of the students for recreation [under administrative aegis], for the reason that they had come to the University at a time of severe economic stress and reconstruction. They were there for the serious purpose of getting an education. They were there to work, rather than to play. I cannot recall one who came to the University during that period to have a good time. They came there to work, because that was an economic necessity. For the University to have recreational facilities might have been resented as superfluous pampering by the rugged individualists of that self-reliant individualistic period."[3]

2. Memoir of Walter E. Phillips, written in 1941, and supplied by Mr. A. W. McAlister.

3. Letter of A. W. McAlister, Greensboro, N. C., to R. J. M. Hobbs, January 4, 1945.

The first important public contribution to popular interest in athletics was the Field Day, put on by the Athletic Association, then eight years old, in the spring of 1884. Dr. S. B. Turrentine, '84, describes these field events as consisting of athletic stunts and contests, such as the five-mile race, the hundred-yard dash, the greased pig race, and many others designed for exercise and recreation for the participants, and amusement for the spectators. Field Day was staged on the old athletic field south and east of the old Library. These events, which would have enraptured R. A. Fetzer as the historic inauguration of field sports and track athletics in the University, have been briefly described by a member of the class of 1885: "In the spring of 1884, a few daring spirits, like John F. Schenck of Lawndale, N. C., actually planned and executed the first field games, I believe, ever played at Chapel Hill—such as jumping, running, and possibly wrestling. I cannot recall any of the actual contests, except the vivid picture I have of my classmate William G. Randall, as he plodded, alone, the only entry, around the track in the five-mile race. He finished, but I doubt if he had practiced for it or 'trained' in any way beyond jogging around some of the Chapel Hill streets. No trainer or coach was engaged; but natural talents and gifts were employed; with grit and will of superior quality." [4]

Mass interest in baseball had already been displayed on the Campus in the early post-bellum period. In 1867 Alexander Graham, father of President Frank P. Graham, was elected captain of the baseball team, which included Augustus W. Graham and Joseph C. Webb. The University team played several games with each of two organized, independent clubs of Raleigh, the Crescents and the Stars, winning three contests over the former, and two over the latter. [5] During the latter years of the Civil War, baseball had frequently been played, under official supervision, by the Federal prisoners in the Confederate prison at Salisbury, North Carolina. [6]

4. Love, pp. 11-12.

5. For accounts of these games, see *Daily Sentinel*, Raleigh, September 9, 10, and 16, 1867; Raleigh *Register*, September 16 and 25, 1867. For these data the writer is indebted to Miss Carrie L. Broughton, North Carolina State Library, Raleigh.

6. A colored lithograph, exhibiting one of these games in progress, is preserved in the New York Public Library.

After the University's re-opening in 1875, baseball was not long in getting under way. It had become popular by the spring of 1878, when football also was finding some devotees.[7] Shinny, however, continued to hold supremacy until the late 1880's, when it yielded place to the fascinations of baseball and football, and the allurements of the new gymnasium. A baseball team was organized and competed with several non-collegiate teams elsewhere. It was not the rough-and-tumble game of today, but a highly aristocratic game played by Southern gentlemen, as indicated by the distinctive dress, which can scarcely be termed uniform: white shirts, palm beach trousers, and tennis shoes. The first intercollegiate athletic contest in which a University team participated was with Bingham Military School in the spring of 1884, the latter winning by the close score of 12 to 11.[8] Class teams, in both baseball and football, were organized in the early eighties; and intramural contests, arousing great excitement among the students, were staged throughout the entire decade. There was even a hotly contested football game between the two Literary Societies on Thanksgiving Day, 1887.[9]

The growing preoccupation with various sports, athletic exercises, and both intramural and extramural contests, on the part of a student body seldom numbering more than 200, became a phenomenon which could not elude the attention of Faculty and Trustees, especially since in the course of a few years, this vital interest in sports was accompanied by a marked decline in student disorder and violence. In his report to the Trustees in January, 1882, President Battle, who recognized the value and

7. The first mention of football in any University publication is found in *U. N. C. M.*, I (1878), 65. After referring to baseball's rising prominence, the writer observed: "A few weeks ago football engrossed the attention of the students but 'kicking a bag of wind' is no longer indulged in."

8. Barrier, p. 20. "It was one of the closest contests we have ever seen on our grounds. All applause was refrained from during the game. After the contest was over, our boys gave a 'huzzah for the Binghamites.' This was gracefully returned by 'three cheers for the University nine.'" Venable suggests that this was the first game at which a University yell was given. F. P. Venable, "Athletics at the University," *U. N. C. M.*, XIII (1894), 25. Dr. Battle is in error in stating that the University team was "beaten ignominiously." Battle, II, 513.

9. Barrier, p. 20.

popularity of the open-air gymnasium and the resultant excellent health of the students, urged the erection of a gymnasium building: "A gymnasium is greatly needed, one could be built for $2,000 probably with a room as large as the Library room. The students on the long rainy days have no means of healthy exercise. It is the duty of the University to provide for the physical as well as mental health if indeed one can be had without the other."[10] The Trustees agreed to equip a gymnasium if the alumni would build one; and President Battle reported to the Trustees, February 1, 1883, that "efforts are being made by our alumni to secure funds to erect a gymnasium," which he regarded as "essential to the comfort of a large body of students." He adverted to the matter again in 1884, regretfully acknowledging that the active canvass in behalf of Memorial Hall had brought the efforts to raise funds for a gymnasium to a standstill.

Meanwhile a curious situation, involving many complexities, had arisen. A crusade against dancing at the University, as promotive of various evils, was inaugurated among certain groups in several religious denominations; and President Battle shared the view of some representative Trustees that Smith Hall, a library filled with alcoves, should not be used as a dance hall. The Trustees made this drastic decision in 1884, to take effect after the Commencement of that year. As there was no other hall in Chapel Hill large enough to accommodate the Commencement balls, the outlook for future dances was dark. With great ingenuity, President Battle solved the problem by organizing a corporation to erect a building, in Chapel Hill but off the Campus, as both a gymnasium and ballroom. The funds were raised by Dr. Richard H. Lewis of Raleigh, and the plans were drawn up by Samuel Sloan, the architect of old Memorial Hall. The wooden frame building, 118 by 45 feet, with a pitch to the eaves of 20 feet, was erected on a lot, opposite the old president's house, which was purchased by the Gymnasium Association from Professor Ralph H. Graves.[11] On either side of the front

10. *T. M.*, 1868-1882, p. 519.

11. For full details of this chapter in the history of Campus development and recreational activities, terpsichorean and athletic, consult the following sources: *T. M.*, 1868-1882, pp. 358, 590; 1883-1891, pp. 62-65, 142, 153, 179; Battle, II, 263, 312-15, 796-97; *Alumni Quarterly*, Vol. I,

entry was a room 18 x 18 feet, the main hall having the dimensions 100 x 45 feet. Upon the walls the happy students emblazoned the legend: "We welcome the daughters of North Carolina to our own hall, on our own floor, where the critics of our pleasure have no rights nor power to deny us." Dr. F. P. Venable was in charge of the gymnasium for six years. In 1891 he succeeded Professor H. H. Williams as the Faculty member of the University Athletic Advisory Committee.

On the opening of the autumn, 1885, session of the University, the magnet for the students was the new gymnasium. As the hall was crowded every evening, it was even feared by the Faculty that the boys were using it to the detriment of their studies. By 1888 football of the Association type was booming; and during the autumn the Sophomore Class "put out a team that, in a game lasting three hours for three afternoons, finally defeated a team picked from the rest of the college." The University's first intercollegiate football contest was played with Wake Forest on October 18 of that year, in Raleigh during State Fair week, Wake Forest winning 6 to 4. Shortly afterwards a football association, with the late Lacy LeGrand Little, class of 1889, as president and Stephen C. Bragaw as captain, was organized with 87 members.

The development of interest in mass athletics was evidenced in the autumn of 1889 when the Y. M. C. A., at the suggestion

---

No. 1 (1894-1895), 25-31; No. 2, 56-57. The gymnasium was just off the Campus, 80 yards west of Memorial Hall. Although utterly plain in construction and with an unattractive exterior, it was pleasing on the interior, the walls and ceiling being finished in paneled woodwork. The walls were painted in the University colors, white and blue; and handsome seals of the Literary Societies, 5 feet in diameter and painted by the artist W. G. Randall, '86, filled two large circles in the panels at the southern end of the hall. The floor of 2-inch edge grain plank of best heart pine, sawed across the grain, was of superlative excellence for dancing. The cost of the building was $3,500. On August 8, 1885, the Executive Committee of the Trustees leased the building from the Gymnasium Association for three years, at an annual rental of $300, with the privilege of renewal. They ordered further, that in order to pay the rent and provide for the expenses of the gymnasium, each student should pay a gymnasium fee of $2. Eleven years later, after the gymnasium was converted into a commons hall, Memorial Hall was used as a gymnasium until the erection of Bynum Gymnasium in 1905.

of Dr. John R. Mott, Y. M. C. A. and religious leader, requested the Faculty to turn over the direction of college athletics to the Y. M. C. A. The request was granted and Lacy L. Little, who had taken a course in athletic training at Springfield, Massachusetts, under Dr. Luther Gulick, was chosen director of athletics and captain of the football team. A "race course," now called a running track, was constructed, which supplemented the existing facilities; and Little gave regular classes to the students, as well as playing guard on the football team. After this, records Little, "intercollegiate contests became the order of the day."[12]

Tennis was introduced in 1884 by Dr. F. P. Venable, who built an excellent court in Battle Grove south of the president's house. In the autumn of 1884, the University Lawn Tennis Association was organized, with James C. Roberts as president. A number of tennis courts were laid out south of Gerrard Hall by 1889; and these courts were so well surfaced that they were regularly used throughout the winter season. In the nineties and perhaps earlier, there was a tennis court in the yard of Mrs. Sallie Anderson (John Wesley Carr place) but the popularity of the court was presumably more directly attributable to the fascinating and flirtatious daughter, Mary Anderson, a reigning belle, than to the unquestioned merits as athletic sport of the game of tennis. Other popular courts on the Campus were two northeast of the Mary Ann Smith Building, one northwest of Memorial Hall, and one near the present site of Alumni Building. By 1894 there were fifteen courts upon the Campus; and within the next few years there were a number of excellent courts about the village, particularly: the superb and expensive court of Harry Lake, built on the lot of Professor J. K. Ball (present R. B. Lawson home), his guardian; and the court of

12. Rev. Lacy L. Little, Greensboro, N. C., to R. J. M. Hobbs, n. d., 1945. In this Athletic Association, each student paid one dollar for the first term and one dollar and a half for the second. Mr. Little was a missionary in China for many years; and his athletic training once stood him in good stead there, on a rapid retreat he was compelled to make during the Boxer Rebellion. The running track, according to Mr. Little, "was located behind the old Gymnasium which was on the right of the road running from west to east through the Campus. It was an oval track almost 800 feet long."

Professor Karl P. Harrington, in the yard of the old Cave, later known as the Guthrie, place.[13]

As we have seen, gymnastics and racing (running) under the direction of Lacy L. Little began in 1889. Considerable impetus was given to racing with the gift, nine years later, by Henry S. Lake, of a 100-yard straightaway cinder track, and a sixth of a mile oval cinder track.[14] Four years later, at New Orleans, this University's first track team, in competition with teams from Vanderbilt, Texas, and Tulane, won the Southern championship. Intercollegiate competition in field sports and track athletics was thus happily inaugurated.

In promotion of field sports, the athletic authorities laid out through the Campus a one-mile running track, which was also patronized by cyclists in the bicycle-craze era. This track, which was not much more than a trail, began at the old gymnasium, ran back of Memorial Hall eastward, crossed the South Quadrangle north of the present Library site, passed near the present (north) entrance of Emerson Field, swung northward along the east wall of the Campus, then turned westward across the swampy area of the present Arboretum, ran parallel to Franklin Street westward to the North Quadrangle, and then, turning gradually southward, ended at the point of departure.

13. In 1907, 6 courts were in use on the class field, present upper quadrangle. In 1908, under the supervision of Dr. R. B. Lawson, four new courts were built south of Bynum Gymnasium; and at about the same time Charles T. Woollen built a battery of tennis courts east of the Raleigh Road and north of present Alexander Building. Of the legislative appropriation of $1,490,000 expended up to November, 1922, $3,353.34 was expended on tennis courts. When John F. Kenfield, tennis trainer, came to Chapel Hill in 1928, 6 clay courts were in use, and 6 more of the same material were built that summer. In 1934, funds from the W. P. A. and E. R. A. were used to renovate the University tennis courts. In 1937 there were 44 tennis courts on the Campus. At present there are 60 courts, of which some are specially surfaced; 12 are clay, 24 asphalt, 2 concrete, and 6 Teniko (quick drying).

14. The 100-yard track began in front of the old Delta Kappa Epsilon fraternity house (now Public Health headquarters) and ran east of the row of fraternity houses toward Cameron Avenue. It was part of the 880 foot track, which was an oval encircling the site of Mary Ann Smith Building and at one point running quite close to the New West Building. In 1897 a whole day was devoted to field sports, under the direction of H. E. Mechling, Director of Athletics: 100-yard dash, 220-yard dash, pole vault, hammer throw, and 440-yard run.

It is worth mentioning, in connection with sports, that Henry Bridgers, class of 1895, tennis star, introduced here the game of golf in the early nineties, laying off a 3-hole course, one of the holes, for there were no "greens" as we now employ the term, being located in the Battle Grove, site of present women's dormitories. According to Louis Graves, football and tennis star, the course was marked by bottom- and top-less tin cans, with a white flag-topped stick rising from these ready-to-use cylinders. In the introduction of golf here, Bridgers was abetted by his friend, the genial sporting-goods salesman, Noyes Long, who had a shop first in the old Roberson's Hotel, opposite the Post Office, and later in the building which housed the Phi Delta Theta fraternity, located in the northwest corner of the intersection of Senior Walk, westward extension, and the path from Franklin Street to the Old West Building. Bridgers was an expert with the shot-gun, both at the traps and in the field. Later on, trap-shooting was cultivated by the Chapel Hill Gun Club, and also by the Country Club, then located on Mr. R. L. Strowd's land.

From the very beginning, eastward and southeastward the course of athletics took its way. Just prior to the University's re-opening, the Trustees on May 4, 1875, ordered that the eastern part of the Campus (south of Cameron Avenue) be reserved for athletic purposes and for a parade ground.[15] When in 1890 the Trustees as the result of controversies and disorders arising from the first intercollegiate football contests, barred all such contests, interest in sports, even in track athletics, rapidly plummeted towards zero, and the playing field was allowed to grow up in tough sedge grass and weeds. Enthusiasm for intercollegiate sports skyrocketed in 1891 when the ban was lifted, chiefly through the influence, among Faculty members, of H. H. Williams, F. P. Venable, and Eben Alexander.[16]

15. *T. M.,* 1868-1882, pp. 215-21.

16. A vigorous and manly petition, presented by George W. Graham, '91, Alexander Stronach, '89, and Samuel M. Blount, '90, gave the Faculty a happy excuse for withdrawing the ban, which was universally unpopular among the students. The expedient adopted, which has proved highly successful in the gradual evolution of athletics throughout more than half a century, was the placing of the regulation of athletics in the hands of an advisory committee consisting of one Faculty member, one graduate student, and one undergraduate. Professor Williams, the first

The students now went industriously to work and again cleared off the old athletic field for both baseball and football.[17] This field remained unenclosed until the spring of 1893 when a new field was laid off with a different orientation of football and baseball grounds, a ten-foot plank fence enclosing the entire area, and a spectators' stand seating about 150 people.[18] As with the first athletic field, the football ground ran east and west, parallel to the southern wall of the Library. The pitcher's box was located at about the center of the site of Bynum Gymnasium; and the pitcher threw to the catcher in a northeasterly direction. The spectators' stand was located about 30 yards southwest of present Carr Building. There were no bleachers and no barrier fences to hold back the spectators. In 1894, the excitement over football became so intense that the enthusiastic students began the disagreeable custom of crowding upon the playing field during practice. "A team cannot play," protested the *Tar Heel*, "when there is a great crowd to be rushed through every time a run is made round the ends." As the season progressed, this practice so retarded the training of the team that, beginning in late October, everyone save the members of the varsity and scrub teams was excluded from the playing field. There was an entrance gate at the southwest corner of the Library, and a players' entrance at the northeast corner of the enclosure. All teams were photographed, seated on the steps, or against the background of the beautiful portico, of the old Library. A grassy bank along the south side of the Library was "reserved" for Negro spectators; but beginning with 1893 many colored boys, without protest, took Annie Oakley tickets for seats in the branches of the tall trees just outside the park and overlooking the high board fence. The field ran south to the present site of Murphey Hall, and included the sites of Bynum Hall, Steele

---

Faculty member elected to the Advisory Committee, took an active interest in sports during the decade of the nineties; and was often heard to claim that he was the creator of a true athletic spirit here.

17. An excellent photograph of this unenclosed field, taken about 1892, is reproduced in Battle, I, facing page 616.

18. George G. Stephens, 50 Walnut Street, Asheville, N. C. to the author, July 6, 1945. Stephens knocked the first home run over this fence, in a game against a make-up team from Durham in the spring of 1893.

Dormitory, Manning Hall, parking lot, and part of Carr Building. The field was large enough for two football games to be played simultaneously.[19]

For more than a century, athletics at the University, under administrative direction and maintenance, had awaited appreciation and endorsement at the hands of some liberal and humane philanthropist. The demand for a new gymnasium became so pressing and the need so obvious that, contrary to the wishes of many who considered its use for indoor athletics a desecration, Memorial Hall became the gymnasium in 1895. This building contained 2,400 seats, with room for almost one hundred more on the rostrum; and it was effectively argued that the University could ill afford to use so large and costly a structure only one day in the year. Indirectly the efforts to improve the acoustic properties of the building, which were notoriously poor, led to its use as a gymnasium. At the instance of President Winston, huge drapes of muslin, which bellied far out from the walls, were hung but with indifferent success. In the further hope of remedying the acoustic defects, the floor, which sloped sharply downward toward the platform, was elevated to a horizontal position. This was made possible through the donation of $500 by the Rev. James F. Wing. It was this horizontal floor, of extensive area, which made Memorial Hall usable as a gymnasium for a decade until the erection of the Bynum Gymnasium in 1905. Memorial Hall was ill suited for a gymnasium, not only spiritually, but physically; for this curious, turtle-like structure afforded no dressing rooms, no heat, and no baths! Despite these handicaps, the building permitted the athletically inclined among the students to work off much "steam" which, if dammed up, would doubtless have broken out sporadically in destructive forms of explosive ebullition.[20]

It was with relief and satisfaction, amounting to delight, that

19. Consult *University of North Carolina Record*, IV (1898), 6, which contains the prediction that the new field, then in preparation, will be ready for use in 1899. See also President Venable's Report to the Trustees, February, 1902, dealing with activities of the three preceding years, which mentions the laying off of the "new athletic field with stand," in Battle, II, 607.

20. Battle, II, 328-29.

the entire University, students, Faculty, and Trustees, welcomed the joyous news, announced by President Venable to the Trustees, February 4, 1904, that Judge William Preston Bynum of Charlotte had donated the requisite funds for the erection of a modern gymnasium, complete in all details, as a memorial to his grandson and namesake, William Preston Bynum, Jr., of the class of 1895, a member of the University football team who had died of typhoid fever, universally lamented, at the close of his Sophomore year. At the meeting of the Alumni Association at Commencement, May 29, 1905, the building was formally presented by President Venable; and accepted by Dr. Richard H. Lewis on behalf of the Trustees.[21] In his address President Venable gave no account of the life and career of the donor, William Preston Bynum; and this omission was occasioned by the request, it appears, of that modest and retiring gentleman.

William Preston Bynum, born in Stokes County, North Carolina, was a graduate of Davidson College, 1843, read law under Chief Justice Richmond M. Pearson, and prior to his elevation to the State supreme bench in 1875, was for eleven years solicitor. During the Civil War, he served as lieutenant colonel in the Second Regiment of State troops, and was promoted to colonel by Governor Vance. His judicial opinions, found in volumes 70 to 79 of North Carolina Reports, rank with the best; and his opinion in the case of Belo v. Commissioners won him national distinction. A marble bust of this distinguished jurist by Lorado Taft stands atop one of the newel posts at the foot of the stairway of the (old) Supreme Court Building in Raleigh.

The imposing building of gray pressed brick with round brick columns was erected at a cost of $25,000. The architect was F. P. Milburn. In addition to a spacious gymnasium floor, stocked with apparatus for exercise, the building contained a large swimming pool, locker rooms, shower baths and rooms for boxing and fencing, Swedish movements, anthropometric tests, and trophies. It was a great boon, amply adequate for the student body of that day.[22] The building facing north overlooks a quad-

21. *T. M.*, 1898-1904, p. 483; 1904-1916, p. 20. Cf. Battle, II, 644-46.
22. Bynum Gymnasium has since been displaced by Woollen Gymnasium, Women's Gymnasium, the various pools, and other buildings,

SOUTH BUILDING SHOWING PORTICO

In 1926-1927 South Building was renovated and reconstructed. At that time a massive portico, designed by McKim, Mead, and White, was added on the south side, greatly increasing the beauty of the building.

THE UNIVERSITY LIBRARY

The Library, completed in 1929, was designed by Arthur C. Nash, with finishing touches added by William Mitchell Kendall. It is 219 feet in length, and has a depth at the center of 140 feet. It provides space for **450,000 volumes.**

rangle upon which front Carr Building and the Playmaker's Theater. Bynum Hall has 19,050 square feet of floor space; and has been twice renovated: in 1928 at a cost of $4,350; in 1939 at a cost of $46,550, architects, Atwood and Weeks; contractor, V. P. Loftis.

---

with their vastly magnified and extended facilities for athletics. Bynum Gymnasium, now known as Bynum Hall, at present houses the offices of the University Press, University News Bureau, Department of Journalism, and other services.

25

A NATURALISTIC GARDEN;
THE FORESTS;* THE WORK
OF DR. COKER

I. THE ARBORETUM

THE ARBORETUM at the University of North Carolina, technically the Coker Arboretum, occupies a five-acre tract of land, rectangular in shape, adjoining the University Campus on the northeast, where once there was only a swampy pasture. The first part to be laid out and planted was the northern section in 1903-1904 by W. C. Coker, who has had charge of the Arboretum since its beginning and is the Director. From year to year the developed area was extended southward to its present limits on Cameron Avenue. On account of the swampy nature of the ground it was necessary to do much sub-tile draining, but even with this improvement the soil is still unfitted for the growth of many kinds of trees and shrubs that otherwise would be included. This fact and the small acreage have made it impossible to collect in the Arboretum more than a small proportion of the very numerous trees and shrubs native to North Carolina, and it would be better not to consider this development an arboretum in a technical sense but rather a garden or ornamental grounds, making use of a part of the Campus that is poorly fitted for building purposes. However, so far as possible, it has been the object of the Director to get together in the Arboretum as great a variety of our native woody plants as possible, and it is hoped that before long it can be extended across the Raleigh Road to include that part of the present woman's campus lying between McIver Dormitory and Cameron Avenue, where better soil may finally allow the successful cultivation of species unfitted for the present location.

In the Arboretum on its southern border is an area of about

*The first two sections of this chapter were contributed by William Chambers Coker, Kenan Research Professor Emeritus.

half an acre which was first used as a drug garden but now mainly for the cultivation of some of our rarer native shrubs, and with one end occupied by a greenhouse given by the General Education Board in 1942. Extending between this area and Cameron Avenue is a pergola covered by wisteria (three species), yellow jessamine, and Lady Banksia roses. This pergola was a gift from Mrs. William E. Shipp in memory of her father and uncle, Fabius H. and Charles M. Busbee.

James Sprunt, John Sprunt Hill, Dr. Wade H. Atkinson, and others have made substantial contributions at one time or another to advance the development of the Arboretum.

There are now in the Arboretum about four hundred kinds of ornamental plants, grouped in such a way as to illustrate their use in design and planting. A number of these are rare native shrubs and trees. It will not be possible here to mention more than a few of these that might be of interest to the casual visitor. In the northern section there is the handsome Walter's pine, so called by us because the famous Thomas Walter named it in 1788. He called it *Pinus glabra*. It is in our opinion one of the most beautiful of all pines, but it is almost never seen in cultivation. It grows in low swampy areas from near Charleston southward along the coast. Another native rarity is the Magnolia called *Magnolia cordata* by Michaux, brought by us from Newberry County, South Carolina. We now consider it a variety of the more northern *M. acuminata*. Probably the most beautiful tree in the Arboretum when in bloom is the Marshall's thorn, a red haw not rare in the woods around Chapel Hill but almost unknown in gardens. We have of course other red haws in the Arboretum but none is so spectacular as this. A fine display comes in mid-to-late March when the river plums (*Prunus americana*) and the redbuds are in bloom. They usually come at the same time and their contrasting colors make one of the finest shows of the year. Both of these trees, as well as the dogwood, vary greatly in their flowers, the redbud in color, the river plum in density of clusters, and the dogwood in size and color. Some are far superior to others, and it is to the disparagement of our nurseries that the better sorts have not been selected and made available. The dogwood comes a little later than the other two and its abundance in both the town and the woods makes its season the most glorious of all. The double-flowered dogwood, found in this county and propagated by the late J. Van Lindley, is now available and is one of the most striking and valuable of recent acquisitions. Two plants of this form may be seen in front of Memorial Hall.

Among the Viburnums, also called haws, there are two species reaching the size of small trees and native to Chapel Hill that are highly ornamental in flower. One of them, the blue haw, with its very large cymes reaching a width of four to six inches, is one of the handsomest of our native flora, but for some reason has been neglected by horticulturists. The other, the black haw, is also a fine ornamental but is likewise rarely used. One of the rarest shrubs in North Carolina is a species of spice bush (*Benzoin melissaefolium*). The specimen in the Arboretum was brought from the only clump we know of in the state, found on the margin of an eastern bay by one of our students. The well-known spice bush (*Benzoin aestivale*), not unusual in rich woods near streams at Chapel Hill, has been planted near it. Another genus of fine native ornamental shrubs is Styrax. There are three species in the Carolinas, one of them found in Chapel Hill uplands, the other two farther south in coastal plain swamps or barrens. Two of these have been brought in and are growing exceptionally well. Also represented are three handsome shrubby buckeyes, native to the southeastern states, *Aesculus parviflora* (white), *A. pavia* (red), and *A. sylvatica* (yellow to dull red). The first is native to southern Georgia, the second to our coastal sections, and the third is common in our Chapel Hill woods. Among other ornamental or rare native shrubs and trees here planted are: *Azalea atlantica*, *A. arborescens*, *A. canescens*, *Glabraria geniculata*, *Gordonia lasianthus*, *Halesia carolina*, *Neviusia alabamensis*, *Hydrangea quercifolia*, *H. americana*, *Clethra acuminata*, *C. alnifolia*, *C. pubescens*, and *Nyssa Ogeche* (Ogeche lime).

An exotic shrub in the Arboretum that is perhaps of most interest to the public is the compact evergreen (*Thea sinensis*) from which tea is made. It is related to the Camellias and its small white flowers have the same structure and are particularly noticed because of their appearing in cold weather, in late fall and early winter. Others are the handsome broad-leaved shrubs or small trees, *Osmanthus fragrans*, *O. Fortunei*, *Michelia fuscata*, *Photinia serrulata*, *P. glabra*, and the Japanese evergreen oak, *Quercus glabra*. Flourishing also are two small Chinese trees, one the Jujube, an odd-looking angular tree with an edible, plum-like fruit, the other the Chinese Pistach (*Pistachio chinensis*). The latter, which is considered subtropical in its range, has proved to be perfectly hardy here. A tree planted in the Arboretum about twenty-five years ago is at least twenty feet high and with a spread as great. In the fall its delicately compound foliage is brilliantly ornamental.

Of the ground covers we have used, the most successful are trailing Euonymus, the small periwinkle, both blue and white-flowered forms, the oriental Ophiopogon (*O. Japonicus*), and two species of ivy, the ordinary English and the Algerian, the latter with very large leaves and more robust habit.

One of the most successful bulbs we have tested in the Arboretum is the spider lily (*Lycoris radiata*). The flowers are brilliant red, appearing in September just before the leaves. The rich green leaves come up as the flowers are withering and as they pass unhurt through the winter and spring they make a fine winter border for paths and flower beds. The plant is almost unbelievably hardy and independent, increasing rapidly in almost any soil, either in sun or in shade, and so far has been entirely free of any noticeable disease. Extensive beds and borders of it give us our most brilliant display of the whole year.

In an area of about one and a half acres back of Peabody Building are a nursery and another greenhouse, the latter a gift of Mr. George Watts Hill of Durham. In this nursery and greenhouse are grown, mostly from cuttings and seedlings, a large number of species of ornamental shrubs and trees, both exotic and native, that are used in planting the constantly expanding grounds of the University. Here are found a number of kinds that, for lack of space, have not yet been placed in the Arboretum. Among the natives are American olive, myrtle-leaved holly, Carolina hemlock, swamp juniper (*Chamaecyparis thyoides*), cross-vine, and the mountain Fothergilla.

There should be mentioned here our collection of living shrubs and woody vines native to the southeastern states that we have been developing since 1936 on a plot of several acres on the Mason Farm about two miles from Chapel Hill. This may properly be considered as an extension of the Arboretum. It contains many species which have never before been brought together in the living condition for study and comparison. This collection is too large to be enumerated here and contains a number of species rarely or never seen in cultivation and a few that may be found to be new.

Shrubs that are most used in Chapel Hill and have proved themselves for many years to be most hardy, permanent and free from disease are: bridal wreath Spiraea *(S. prunifolia)*, Van Houtte Spiraea *(S. Van Houttei)*, Forsythia (several species), Japanese quince (*Cydonia japonica* of the trade—*Chaenomeles lagenaria*) in red, white and apple-blossom color forms, cut-leaf Persian lilac (*Syringa persica laciniata*), sweet breath of spring *(Lonicera fragrantissima)*, Abelia *(A. grandiflora,* evergreen here), winter jessamine *(Jasminum nudiflorum)*, and several species of privet, the best of which are the Quihoui privet *(Ligustrum Quihoui)*, the smaller Japanese privet *(L. japonicum)* and the larger *(L. lucidum)*, all evergreen or nearly so. Another shrub which should be mentioned as generally valuable is Nandina, but this requires care in pruning to be really satisfactory. *Pyracantha yunnanensis* is a vigorous spreading plant with small brilliant red berries, recently introduced and a great improvement on *P. coccinea Lalandii.* Another much less known shrub that we find very valuable is snow-wreath (*Neviusia alabamensis*). This is a relative of the Spiraeas which is found wild only in a limited area in central Alabama. It has a graceful habit, increasing by runners, and will live and flourish indefinitely either in sun or in shade. It is most useful in rather deep shade, as in such situations most shrubs dwindle away and disappear. In the fall its leaves turn a pretty golden color and remain unwithered until the hard frosts of winter. A favorite of ours is the single-flowered or wild form (not the snowball) of the oriental shrub *Viburnum tomentosum,* a large gracefully spreading plant that is covered with large flat cymes, the ray flowers white, the berries first red then turning black. There is a large clump of it in the northeastern angle of Davie Hall.

We are adding below some native and exotic plants growing on the grounds of the Director of the Arboretum that are available for study by our students of botany, but have not yet been planted on the Campus. Among the natives are yellow honeysuckle, white-flowered redbud, four species of Rhododendron, *R. carolinianum, catawbiense, maximum*, and *minus*, and *Viburnum obovatum*. The exotics include *Camellia japonica, C. sasanqua, Cedrus atlantica*, Bhotan pine, *Cornus Kousa, Cleyera japonica, Meratia praecox, Feijoa Sellowiana, Ilex latifolia, Viburnum Carlesi, Eryobotria japonica*, and about thirty other species.

Often planted in Chapel Hill lawns but now quite rare in the woods because of its abuse for Christmas decorations for over a hundred years, we would like to mention the Christmas holly (*Ilex opaca*). In the private grounds just mentioned there is a row of nineteen of these hollies brought in from the woods about thirty-five years ago when they were too small for their sex to be determined. They are now about thirty to forty feet high and have proved to be ten females and nine males. In addition to the sex difference, these trees are a striking demonstration of the great variation that our native plants exhibit. This is shown both in habit of growth and in density and color of leaves. As mentioned above for plums, dogwoods, and redbuds, there is a great opportunity here for the production by selection and propagation of valuable improved forms of our holly, as has been done for related species in other countries.

It will be of interest, we think, to note here our experience in Chapel Hill through a good many years in regard to resistance to cold of some of our ornamental plants generally considered of questionable hardiness at this latitude. Of such species that have passed unhurt or almost so through the coldest weather we have had for thirteen years, a temperature of 3° on Jan. 28, 1940 (average for the month, 21.9°), we list the following. These plants are at present growing in the Arboretum or its propagating grounds or on the home grounds of the Director.

Native

Pinus glabra	Ilex vomitoria
Pinus palustris	Illicium parviflorum
Sabal glabra	Magnolia glauca
Smilax lanceolata	Magnolia grandiflora
Smilax Laurifolia	Osmanthus americanus
Smilax Walteri	Persea palustris
Aesculus pavia	Quercus pumila
Gelsemium sempervirens	Quercus virginiana
(native to Chapel Hill)	Vaccinium arboreum
Ilex Amelanchier	(native to Chapel Hill)
Ilex myrtifolia	Viburnum obovatum

Exotic

Aucuba japonica and var.	Osmanthus aquifolium
Albizzia julibrissin	Osmanthus Fortunei
Camellia japonica	Pistachio Chinensis
Camellia sasanqua	Thea sinensis
Cleyera japonica	Zizyphus Jujube
Meratia praecox	

Injured but not killed by this extreme cold were:

Feijoa sellowiana	Pittosporum Tobira
Gardenia florida	Rosa Banksia
Laurocerasus caroliniana	Rosa bracteata
Michelia (Magnolia) fuscata	Rosa laevigata
Osmanthus fragrans	Viburnum tinus

II. THE FORESTS

Of all the universities in America, so far as we can learn, the University of North Carolina is unique in its setting. To see nature in its almost primeval richness there is no need here for all-day excursions on trains and busses in order that students of botany, geology, and zoology may find the material their subjects demand. Situated on the terminal of a rolling plateau, the Chapel Hill area falls rather abruptly to a wide, gently undulating country stretching as far as the eye can see toward the coastal plain. The University is bounded both on the east and south by woods that have not been disturbed for at least 150 years. These include Battle Park and Gimghoul woods, about 45 acres in extent, and to the south other similar woodlands of about 200 acres, together with many acres of privately owned but undisturbed forests. About two miles farther southeast the University owns a large area known as the Mason Farm, consisting of 800 acres. The larger part of this is cultivated land, now used in cooperation with the United States Soil Conservation Service; the remainder is forest. To the west two miles beyond Carrboro is the University Lake, with a surrounding watershed area, owned by the University, and consisting of 720 acres, a part of which is forest. To the north is the tract of over a thousand acres on which the airport is located. Most of the woods above mentioned cover the rocky slopes, ridges and draws that lead down to the less hilly land between here and the coastal plain.

The Chapel Hill promontory and the slopes bounding it have never been submerged and are a part of the oldest area in North America. Its forests have never been covered by water nor scoured away by glaciers, and its slow evolution has been undisturbed by such catastrophes. We find here a type of vegetation closely corresponding in families and even genera with a similar extension from the north downward in eastern Asia.

As Chapel Hill is on the eastern edge of this elevated plateau, with its warm slopes facing south and southeast and cool bluffs facing north, we find here a surprising meeting of both mountain and coastal flora. On the bluff south of Morgan's Creek, which runs in part through University land, are extensive thickets of a variety of *Rhododendron catawbiense*, one of the most strikingly beautiful coverings of our high bald mountains to the west. Growing with these are *Hydrangea arborescens* and *Fothergilla major*, the last mentioned rare even in the mountains. Here too is one extensive colony of wintergreen, abundant in the mountains but so far known from no other place in Orange County. On another bluff near these are the mountain laurel (Kalmia) and, strangest of all, a considerable colony of ginseng, which is not recorded for a hundred or more miles west of us. On the other hand, on the north bank of Morgan's Creek on bluffs facing south one finds such typical plants of the coast and sandhills as yellow jessamine and sparkleberry. Here also is a station for the very rare parasitic shrub Nestronia. On the outcropping rocks of this bank is also found the little club-moss, *Selaginella rupestris*, a characteristic plant of the mountains. On the Mason Farm near the stream is found the rare vine *Smilax hispida*, the farthest eastern station except one now known for this more northern and western plant.

On the University Lake property are found the rare and fragrant shrubs *Rhus aromatica* and *Calycanthus floridus*, and to the west of this property in a cool damp ravine near extensive beds of Christmas fern, far out of its supposed range, is found the Indian cucumber-root (*Medeola virginiana*).

Among other handsome flowering shrubs found not rarely in our woods are the broad-leaved Styrax and six species of Viburnum, one of the latter (*V. rafinesquianum*) being locally abundant here but rarely seen in other sections of the State. Both species of pawpaw found in the Carolinas occur here, the common large species in low grounds along streams, the other, the dwarf pawpaw, a much rarer species, in the drier woods.

The trees of our woods, undisturbed for so many years, are as varied in kind and impressive in size as are to be found in any similar area in the State. This is not a region of pines in climax forests, but on University property, probably cultivated two hundred years ago, are some very large individuals of the loblolly pine (*Pinus Taeda*) and of the short-leaf (*P. echinata*). In the south woods below Kenan Stadium stood a splendid loblolly called by our Dr. Battle the "Queen of Pines," and on the northern edge of Chapel Hill on a slope facing north once stood the largest pine in Orange County, a short-leaf called "Lone Pine," visible from the hills at Hillsboro fifteen miles away. It was killed by lightning about thirty years ago, and the stump rings showed it to be over two hundred years old.

The historic old Davie Poplar near the center of the North Campus is almost certainly two hundred years old, probably more. On our Campus, probably here before the first building was erected, are some immense white oaks, the one by Alumni Building being one of the largest in the State. We have fifteen species of oaks in our woods. Among these is the pin oak, popularly planted as a street tree but known wild in the State only from swamps a few miles east of Chapel Hill.

Of the hickories we have seven species, as many, we think, as any other location in America. They are the white heart, scaly-bark, southern shell-bark, small-fruited hickory, pignut, pale hickory, and bitternut.

Near our springs and at the foot of hillsides in rich woods we have fine beech trees and in the same situations the umbrella magnolia is common. In our rich rocky woods the dogwood and redbud make a notable display and the beautiful fringe-tree is not rare.

One of the handsomest berried trees in our eastern American flora is frequent in our woods. It is the deciduous holly, whose brilliant scarlet berries, unobscured by leaves, make a striking feature of our winter landscape.

The primitive seclusion of our woods, grown more withdrawn during the automobile and movie era which has educated our young people to avoid walking, is reflected in the presence of the wild turkey, which until recent years has nested on University property and even now is breeding just across Morgan's Creek from the Mason Farm. The pileated woodpecker still makes its home on University property and a few years ago came up into Battle Park a few hundred yards from the Campus and oc-casionally even into the Arboretum itself. Every year quail build their nests within the limits of the town. Almost every night in winter the mellow hoots and wild screams of the barred owl can be heard in the village and until recently a pair nested in Davie Poplar on the Campus. Also recently a bald eagle has been seen a few miles from Chapel Hill. Up to the present the number of species of birds recorded from Chapel Hill, including residents and transients, is 195.

One of the distinctions of Chapel Hill and its woods is the abundance of chipmunks. We are said to be on the eastern limit of the chipmunk's range, but they seem to be more common here than even in the center of their distribution. They may be found all over the village in the rock walls which are a feature of Chapel Hill.

All of the University lands above mentioned, together with

the Country Club golf links and adjoining lands of W. C. Coker and W. L. Hunt, amounting in all to approximately 3,500 acres, are now united as a wild life refuge for animals and plants.

I cannot close this short story of our forests without some reference to Dr. Kemp Plummer Battle, long president of this University, who for all those years loved our woods and almost daily spent a recreational hour or so in them with his hatchet or saw, clearing paths and making bridges and seats and introducing his friends and students to his favorite spots.

As Joe Jones has said (*The Daily Tar Heel*, Feb. 1, 1931): "The wooden seats he made are falling to decay, many of the paths he cleared with his hatchet are dim, but some of the glens and dells still bear the names he gave them: Trysting Poplar, Woodthrush Home, Vale of Ione, Anemone Spring, Flirtation Knoll, Glen Lee, Dogwood Dingle. For many of us the memory of Kemp Plummer Battle is as much a part of these hills as the oaks and pines, but it is well that the Gimghouls have graven his name in bronze at the summit of Piney Prospect. Somehow, in a few simple words, they have ensnared in the dull metal some of that poignant charm which broods forever over the woods which surround the old university town of Chapel Hill."

III. THE WORK OF DR. COKER*

During the last decade of the nineteenth century the low, swampy field where the Coker Arboretum is now located was covered in season with a fabric of brilliant red on a green-grey base of vegetation. This marshy pasture, unfit for building purposes, had been sown with crimson clover and grasses under the direction of Joseph Austin Holmes, Professor of Geology and State Geologist. Both he and Joshua Walker Gore, head of the Physics Department, attempted to drain the area; but their efforts proved unsuccessful. In the hope of at least enriching the soil, it was resown each year for a decade with crimson clover and grasses. The only use to which this apparently irreclaimable

---

*This section, by the author of the present work, is appended in acknowledgment of a service of incomparable value to the University rendered by W. C. Coker.

marsh had hitherto been put was to serve as a pasture for "Old Cuddie," President Swain's white mule, and for some of the professors' cows, horses, and mules.

One day in 1902, as Dr. William Chambers Coker, recently come to Chapel Hill to take charge of the Botany Department, and President Venable were walking along the extension of Senior Walk, the President suggested to Dr. Coker that he take over this five-acre bog and try to make something more sightly and useful out of it as a garden or arboretum. President Venable recalled that, in the original plans for Campus development and adornment, the southeastern area was designed for horticulture as part of a scheme for "ornamental grounds" and a "botanic garden."

This suggestion was received with enthusiasm and although those were the days of small things, Coker's dream began slowly to take concrete form. Available funds were small to the vanishing point; but Coker had one Negro helper, and his unquenchable hope was worth an army of laborers. By sub-tiling, the area was gradually drained and reclaimed for planting and cultivation. Tentative horticultural and botanical studies of this region had been made by Dr. Elisha Mitchell, a more than amateur botanist; and his notebooks show, for example, that he had found twelve varieties of oak within a mile's radius of Chapel Hill. Extended botanical observations were also recorded in the published scientific writings of the eminent botanist and mycologist, Dr. Moses Ashley Curtis, of Hillsboro, only twelve miles distant, containing studies of new and rare plants, and in particular the "woody plants" of North Carolina.[1] Professors Coker and Totten have discovered one hundred and sixty-four species of trees, shrubs, and woody plants in the vicinity of Chapel Hill.

As the land, for all the drainage and sub-tiling, remained low and moist, it was impossible to transform the area into a true arboretum, hospitable to all arboreal growth. Much of the area was turned into lawn; and as a harborage for a very wide variety

1. *The Woody Plants of North Carolina*, published by the Geological and Natural History Survey of North Carolina in 1860. Also, *Botany; Containing a Catalogue of the Indigenous and Naturalized Plants of the State*, by the same author and publisher, 1867.

of plant growths, the cultivable portion was transformed into a true "naturalistic garden." Indeed, with hundreds of species of plants and trees artistically arranged for beauty and display, this is one of the most exquisite and harmonious small naturalistic gardens in the United States. This lovely spot, a haven of quiet like some "garden close" of the Middle Ages, is a sanctuary also for feathered and furry life—unfrightened birds which build their nests near the ground, and rabbits, squirrels, and chipmunks almost casual in their friendliness and easy familiarity.

With an abiding sense of beauty and a disciplined passion for natural adornment, Dr. Coker has taken the Campus and indeed the entire Chapel Hill area for his province. As Chairman of the Committee on Grounds and Buildings for many years, he has been enabled to exercise a constructive and creative influence toward further beautification, through horticultural means and landscape architecture, of grounds and growths of rare natural beauty. Each new area, opened to Campus extension is treated with reverence for its qualities of natural beauty, and that beauty is suitably enhanced by artificial means. As each new building arises, Dr. Coker takes it under his wing; and some of the angularities and garish freshness of brick, mortar, stone, and plaster are soon graciously softened and shaded by great rose bushes, flowering shrubs, and luxuriant plants of lush foliage. The outlay for Campus decoration for many years has run considerably in excess of appropriated funds, and it is an open secret that the purse strings of the "onlie begetter" of the Arboretum and the apostle and creator of Campus conservation, development, and beautification have been kept extraordinarily loose.

Present denizens of the Campus, alumni of the University, citizens of North Carolina, and future generations owe, and will increasingly owe and feel, a deep and abiding sense of gratitude to four great nature lovers and constructive artists who have left here, for all to see, their testaments to beauty: Elisha Mitchell, David Lowrie Swain, Kemp Plummer Battle, and William Chambers Coker.

26

A MODERN UNIVERSITY PLANNED:
1920-1926; MCKIM, MEAD, AND
WHITE

THE PLANS now worked out for the building of the modern University, with an adequate graduate school and with professional schools of law, medicine, and pharmacy paralleling in importance and distinction the departments of long established reputation, reveal a broad grasp of essentials and genuine vision regarding the University's future. In all these plans, President Chase, the Committee on Grounds and Buildings, and the Trustees cooperated efficiently and harmoniously. Feeling a deep responsibility to generations to come in this rare opportunity, as he expressed it, to "make of our Campus a thing of beauty and dignity, as well as of utility," President Chase analyzed the undertaking as a three-fold problem. Confronted with the features of long-term planning, he discerned that, for a master-plan, two key factors would enable the University to carry out building operations more effectively and economically than would the former unsatisfactory method, unavoidable through limitation of funds, of erecting one building at a time, in an isolated sort of way and without a master-plan of control. The first natural corollary of a master-plan was an overhead organization, governed by a suitably safeguarded contract, to have complete charge of all building operations. The total group-project, and not the single building, became the objective for long-term planning. A spur railroad track, terminating on the southwest Campus, assured a uniform supply of building materials for use in erecting one structure after another as the need might arise. Moreover, the permanent character of the University, the beauty of the setting and environment, and a certain austere dignity in the simple colonial style of the early buildings, a deviation from which in the post-bellum period produced mistaken and unhappy consequences, dictated the engagement of a consulting firm of architects of high reputation for esthetic taste and harmony of mass design.

The original act granting $1,490,000 to be used in building operations at the University for 1921 and 1922 provided that the State Building Commission have complete control and direction of all the buildings constructed. Under the act, as later amended, the positions of State Building Commission and State Architect were abolished; and in consequence their duties would devolve upon the Trustees of the various state-supported institutions. Meantime President Chase appointed Professor W. C. Coker, Chairman of the Committee on Grounds and Buildings, and Mr. Charles T. Woollen, Proctor, to make a survey of the architectural firms of the country and to recommend that one best suited for the designing and oversight of the buildings in contemplation. The plan included, as its core, the erection of four dormitories, to house approximately five hundred students, three classroom buildings, and the reconditioning of Memorial Hall, which suffered from perturbing acoustical defects, for use as auditorium for chapel and other exercises.

At their meeting on December 30, 1920, the Trustees ratified the recommendation, by their Building Committee, of Thomas C. Atwood as chief supervisor of the building program. Mr. Atwood, recognized as one of the ablest supervising engineers in the ·country, had been associated with the construction of great engineering works, water, sewage, pumping stations, reservoirs, in New York, Boston, and Pittsburgh; of shipyards, drydocks, and marine railways for the Emergency Fleet Corporation; had built the monster stadium, the Yale Bowl, and was favorably known in North Carolina as the chief engineer of the Durham Hosiery Mills. At this same meeting, the Trustees ratified the recommendation by W. C. Coker and C. T. Woollen of McKim, Mead, and White of New York as consulting architects. The members of this firm individually and cooperatively have left an ineradicable impress of noble influence upon American architecture for the past half century; and perhaps their most distinctive contribution has been the revival of the style of Italian Renaissance architecture. This Italianate style is percepti-

MANNING HALL QUADRANGLE

At left, Saunders, built in 1922 and designed for History and Social Science. In center is Manning Hall, built in 1923, which houses the law school. Murphey, built in 1922-24 for Languages, is at right.

VIEW OF WOMEN'S DORMITORY QUADRANGLE

At left, Alderman; at right, Kenan. McIver Dormitory, not pictured, faces Alderman. These dormitories were erected during 1937-39.

THE FOREST THEATRE

The first performance given in this lovely natural amphitheatre in Battle Park was Shakespeare's *Taming of the Shrew,* presented in 1919. The theatre was remodeled in 1940, at a cost of $20,000, the funds being supplied by the Works Projects Administration. The picture shows the theatre after the extensive improvements had been made. The late Professor Frederick H. Koch, founder of the Carolina Playmakers, can be seen at left.

ble in the designs for the buildings they planned for this University.[1]

Following the prolonged discussions and final recommendation of the Committee on Grounds and Buildings, in which Mr. John Nolen, skilled landscape architect, participated, as described in Chapter XXIII, the Committee on the Development of University Property unanimously recommended that the space south of the South Building should be laid out in a quadrangle, now known as the "South Quadrangle," similar to that of the "North Quadrangle."[2] Two additional dormitories were accentuated as the most pressing necessity; but as only $137,450 was available, the Trustees decided on August 20, 1920, to build only one dormitory. So towering were prices and wages at the time that this amount had to be supplemented by $16,881.63 in order to complete the building. This imposing structure, historic as the first building to front on the newly laid out South Quadrangle, was named in honor of Walter Leak Steele, class of 1844. Steele Dormitory, facing west, was placed just south of the old Smith Hall; and built of red pressed brick, with attractive doorways and Venetian suggestions, was to that date much the handsomest and best equipped dormitory ever erected upon the Campus. This was the last University building erected under the auspices of the State Building Commission and under the direction of the State architect. For Steele Dormitory, completed in 1921, the architect was J. A. Salter, and the contracting firm Salmon, Shipp, and Poe. The building contains 48 rooms and 14,000 square feet of floor space, and encloses 241,000 cubic feet. The over-all cost, including furniture, was $156,600.

Some interesting and amusing reminiscences of President Chase follow:

"The Grounds and Buildings Committee had been working for a long time on a plan for the development of the campus

1. "Charles Follen McKim," *Dictionary of American Biography*, XII (1933), 99-102; "William Rutherford Mead," *ibid.*, 473; "Stanford White," *ibid.*, XX (1936), 116-18.

2. Compare Chapters 30 and 31 on Campus architecture. The North and South quadrangles have been named by the Board of Trustees McCorkle Place and Polk Place, respectively.

and in consultation with Mr. Nolen and others, including I believe, Mr. Hobart[3] the architect, had made several tentative layouts. In the meantime the war had come to a close and there were funds available for the building of a good sized dormitory, the position of which would, in a sense, be the key to the whole future planning for the southern part of the campus. The committee was extremely anxious to have this worked out right both in terms of position and in terms of the architecture of the building itself which would set the type for the whole new area.

"At the same time the State Legislature set up a Building Commission made up of laymen who were given the perfectly impossible task of supervising all building done at all State institutions in North Carolina. They were able to secure only the part-time services of an architect, which rendered the problem doubly acute. A great deal seemed to us to be at stake and we were convinced that the whole problem should be gotten at the earliest possible moment into the hands of an architectural firm of recognized eminence. Therefore, after looking around with the authorization of whatever committee of the trustees was then responsible, we retained the services of McKim, Mead, and White, making it clear to the State Building Commission that we were doing so not to supplant but to supplement the services which they could render. McKim, Mead, and White gave us the services of one of their partners, Mr. Kendall, who died only recently at an advanced age. He came down for a preliminary conference, the Committee on Grounds and Buildings showed him its tentative plans and at that time he made a suggestion as to the position and layout of the then still-to-be-developed campus which they at once seized on as something for which they had been looking for years. From that time on the Building Committee of the Trustees kept him on and he was frequently in attendance at their meetings and his suggestions we always felt were highly profitable. I don't think we ever departed from a single important recommendation that he made during the years that he was with us, certainly for over a decade, and I don't know how much longer after I left.

"The subsequent history of the State Building Commission

3. Evidently a mistake for Hobart Brown Upjohn of New York City.

is interesting. We were going ahead continuously with our plans, more funds had become available for the first installment of the large building program, and Mr. Hill of Durham, who was Chairman of the University Building Committee for the Trustees, was very active, and in one way or another there came to be some feeling in political circles that we were just a bit too independent of the Building Commission in what we were doing. Consequently when the Legislature met there was an investigation and a number of us including myself had to testify as to what it was all about. I remember among the political manoeuvres at the time it was brought out that Kendall was a partner of the notorious Stanford White. However, when the investigation was over the verdict was that the Building Commission had done a good job and that it should be dismissed. So I suppose everybody was happy. At any rate we had no further difficulties and the campus plan profited thereby. I shudder to think what might have happened if it hadn't had competent architectural direction at that critical stage.

"That, in brief outline, is about what happened as I recall it. What remains to be set down simply has to do with the fine, harmonious cooperation of the faculty committee and the Trustees' Building Committee over the years. The faculty committee always had representation on the Trustees' Committee. My recollection is that Dr. Coker and Dr. MacNider were the members who sat with the Trustees' Committee. The meetings were frequent and frequently argumentative. But we were all very proud of the fact that a decision was never taken until it was unanimous and we got to the point where we really enjoyed calling each other names. The meetings were on the whole, I think, just about the most enjoyable series of discussions I ever attended."[4]

In confirmation of the keynote of the state-wide campaign for University expansion, living space, the Trustees decided to erect four new dormitories; and to place them along the long sides of, and facing inward upon, a quadrangle, located opposite the

4. Letter from Harry Woodburn Chase to the author, from New York University, Office of the Chancellor, Washington Square, New York 3, N. Y., May 29, 1945.

Arboretum south of Cameron Avenue and west of the Raleigh Road, at the eastern extension of the old athletic field. This represented the first step in the systematic Campus planning directed by McKim, Mead, and White. Eastward and southward the course of future Campus utilization for dormitories was expected to take its way. October 12, 1921, was set as the date for the laying of the cornerstone of the first of these four dormitories; and all four were completed by the opening of the autumn session, 1922. These four-storey dormitories, simple in design, were completed in the order mentioned; and were named for Bryan Grimes; Willie Person Mangum and Rev. Adolphus Williamson Mangum; Matthias E. Manly and Charles Manly; and Thomas Ruffin and Thomas Ruffin, Jr.[5] The architectural firm for all four was Atwood and Nash, the contracting firm, T. C. Thompson and Brothers. The approximate cost of each dormitory was $100,000; and each has 69 rooms and 21,000 square feet of floor space. The capacity of these dormitories is as follows: Grimes, 253,000 cubic feet; Mangum, 275,800; Manly, 275,800; Ruffin, 253,000.

Building on a large scale was congenial to President Chase, as having about it "something of the romance of pioneering." While the erection of the four dormitories was proceeding, the architects of McKim, Mead, and White began to direct the execution of a zoning project according to their preconceived plan of Campus development. This was a new minor quadrangle opening into the great South Quadrangle on its eastern side. There were three lecture halls, which were also designed to contain the offices of specific departments and schools. Two of these, built lengthwise east and west, faced inward upon the quadrangle; and on the east side, filling out the third side of the quadrangle and facing west, was the third. These buildings are, in order: Saunders Hall, named for William Laurence Saunders, class of 1854; Murphey Hall, named for Archibald DeBow Murphey, class of 1799; and Manning Hall, named for John Manning, class of 1850, former Dean of the Law School. Saunders Hall was designed for History and Social Science, Murphey Hall for Languages, and Manning Hall for the School of

5. *T. M.*, 1917-1924, pp. 402-3.

Law, including the law library. The first two buildings, of three storeys each and quite simple in design, were built of regular building brick. Manning Hall, only two storeys high but with a spacious basement, is more ornate, having an imposing portico with concrete columns two storeys high and a square white wooden tower on top, surmounted by a rather diminutive gilded cupola, dwarfed by the massive pillars. Improvements upon the grounds, which included reseeding the lawns, laying out and gravelling new paths, and the planting of decorative trees and shrubbery resulted in the creation of a charming court and enhancement of the natural beauty of the setting. With McKim, Mead, and White as consulting architects, the building architects for all three were T. C. Atwood and H. P. Alan Montgomery; and T. C. Thompson and Brothers contractors. Saunders, built in 1922 at a cost of $154,000, has 62 rooms and 25,000 square feet of floor space, and contains 511,020 cubic feet. Manning, built in 1923 at a cost of $163,000, has 25 rooms and 16,000 square feet of floor space, and contains 399,480 cubic feet. Murphey, built 1922-1924 at a cost of $170,000 has 48 rooms and 26,500 square feet of floor space, and contains 538,900 cubic feet.

On University Day, 1923, Dr. Wade H. Atkinson, class of 1888, delivered an address at Chapel Hill, sponsoring a movement by the Alumni Association of Washington, D. C., of which he was president, to make the University Campus the "most beautiful spot in the South." For some twenty years Dr. W. C. Coker, head of the Department of Botany, had been actively and solicitously engaged in this very project, in the laying out and development of the Arboretum, named in his honor, and in the beautification of the Campus. Funds supplied by the Washington, D. C., Alumni Association were expended in the printing and wide distribution to alumni of a pamphlet entitled "Campus Beautiful." A considerable sum was raised to carry out the major objectives, the principal contributors being Dr. W. C. Coker, James Sprunt, and John Sprunt Hill, each of whom gave $1,000. The announced objectives were: a new park system, new roads through woodlands, extension of the Arboretum eastward into Battle's Grove, and the planting of Japanese cherry trees.[6] This movement appropriately came shortly after the firm of McKim, Mead, and White had been engaged as consulting architects for the University; and President Chase heartily approved active alumni interest in carrying out plans upon which Dr. Coker had long been engaged. This step marks the beginning of the development of the women's dormitory area east of Raleigh Street, which is still in progress. The University should engage a full-time landscape architect, associated with the Art Department, to carry on uninterruptedly the development and beautification of the Campus upon which Dr. Coker has lavished so much care and devotion.

Each forward step in the expansion program was of necessity paced to fit the legislative appropriation for the corresponding biennium. Although President Chase's program for the years 1923 and 1924 was estimated to cost $2,312,380, the legislature appropriated only slightly more than two-thirds of that amount, viz., $1,668,000 to provide for a great new chemistry building, several men's dormitories, a women's building, a permanent water supply, and other necessary additions and improvements.[7] In his report to the Trustees, January 30, 1924, President Chase pointed out that anticipated increases in student enrollment had been realized; that the number of high school graduates for the spring of 1924 was expected to reach the staggering figure of 8,000, as contrasted with 1,500 in 1921; and that the 1921 estimate of $5,500,000 for expansion was conservative. Impressive was the increase in the University's student enrollment: from 1,200 in 1920 to 2,529 in 1924.[8]

In anticipation of steady increases in enrollment, a revolutionary but salutary decision was made: to erect dormitories off the Campus proper but within the original bounds of University property. Off-Campus extension was possible in only two directions: east and south. With the need for half a dozen new dormitories impending for the coming decade or two, clearly indicated sites were in Battle Park along and east of the Raleigh Road. During 1924 three new dormitories were built in Battle Park, to

6. *Campus Beautiful* (Washington, D. C., Anderson Printery, 1923); "Campus Beautiful Plan Explained," *Alumni Review*, XII (1923), 111.
7. *T. M.*, 1917-1924, pp. 422, 447.
8. *T. M.*, 1924-1930, pp. 22-23.

the southeast of the East Gate of the Campus, forming one long side and half of another long side of a new quadrangle. The dormitory nearest the East Gate was named for Charles Brantley Aycock, class of 1880; the one east of Aycock for John Washington Graham, class of 1857; and the one corresponding to Aycock on the south side of the quadrangle for Richard Henry Lewis, University student, 1866-1868.[9] The building architects for these three dormitories were Atwood and Nash, the contractors, T. C. Thompson and Brothers. Aycock Dormitory, built in 1924 at a cost of $100,000, has 60 rooms and 17,600 square feet of floor space, and contains 301,425 cubic feet; Graham Dormitory, built in 1924 at a cost of $100,000, is a duplicate of Aycock in size and structure; and Lewis Dormitory, built in 1924 at a cost of $100,000, differs from the two former only in containing 275,385 cubic feet. During 1924 were also built the first women's building, and the huge new chemistry building. A superb site for the women's building was chosen, the lot at the southwest corner of the intersection of Franklin Street and Raleigh Road, where formerly had stood the house, just east of the new Chapel of the Cross, originally erected by Thomas H. Taylor, merchant and Superintendent of University property and finances. This building was named Spencer Hall after Mrs. Cornelia Phillips Spencer, devoted champion and celebrant of the University.[10] The building architects were Atwood and Nash, the contractors, T. C. Thompson and Brothers. The building, constructed of red brick, beautiful in design and handsomely appointed, was erected at a cost of $121,000. It has 63 rooms and 19,000 square feet of floor space, and contains 261,-000 cubic feet. During this same year was erected the new chemistry building, Venable Hall (named for Francis Preston Venable) estimated to cost, with physical equipment, $400,000, to accommodate adequately the large influx of new students. De-

9. *Ibid.*, p. 50. These names for the dormitories were recommended by John Sprunt Hill, chairman of the Building Committee, on June 11, 1928.

10. It was at the instance of the class of 1888, in a resolution passed during a reunion at Chapel Hill, June 4, 1927, that the Building Committee named the women's building Spencer Hall for the "first woman to receive the degree of Doctor of Laws from a southern institution." *Ibid.*, p. 334.

signed to house the entire department with its numerous laboratories, this building embodied the latest principles of design for structures of this character. The building architects were Atwood and Nash, the contractors, T. C. Thompson and Brothers. This two-storey building, with basement for laboratories, has 69 rooms and 65,100 square feet of floor space, and contains 1,004,900 cubic feet; and is located in the depression some fifty yards west of the Library.

During the years 1925 and 1926 a total of $800,000 was estimated as the requisite sum for permanent improvement. Major items were: wings added to Phillips and Davie halls, extensive renovation and repairs of older buildings, and the reconstruction of Smith Hall into the Playmakers' Theatre. In 1922, Robert K. Smith of New York City, a native of Caswell County, North Carolina but not an alumnus of the University, bequeathed the sum of $50,000 to the institution in appreciation of its services to higher education. Half of the bequest was used to establish the Smith Endowment for Graduate Research. The Trustees in 1924 gave Smith Hall to the Carolina Playmakers and appropriated funds from the Robert K. Smith bequest for remodeling it. Since the sum appropriated was not sufficient, the following amounts were used from the grant of $13,000 to the Playmakers from the Carnegie Foundation: to complete the Playmakers Theater, $4,721.93; for additional construction and the purchase of equipment, supplies, and materials, $1,201.15. The theater was dedicated November 23, 1925.[11]

A notable and impressive contribution to the beauty of the Campus was the addition of a massive portico at the south of South Building, as part of the renovation of that structure in 1926-1927. This work of renovation and reconstruction was completed by January, 1927, at a cost of $153,354.42. In 1929 a new stone wall and steps, south of South Building, were erected.[12]

11. The cost of transforming Smith Hall into the Playmakers Theater and securing essential equipment was $30,923.08. Consult President's Reports, 1922, pp. 5-6; 1925, p. 132; 1926, p. 188.

12. *T. M.*, 1924-1930, pp. 331-32, 366-67. The architects for the renovation of South Building were Atwood and Nash, the contracting firm, T. C. Thompson and Brothers.

As the new biennium approached, President Chase on June 24, 1926, presented to the Executive Committee of the Trustees an itemized estimate totaling $2,383,715 for permanent improvements. Perhaps sensing that the estimate was too high, as containing too many projects to be carried out in too brief a period, the President on November 22, 1926, recommended that a lump sum be requested of the legislature. Of the original request of 1920 for $5,585,000 over a six-year period, somewhat less than $4,000,000 had actually been received. On January 18, 1927, Judge Francis D. Winston proposed to the Trustees, who adopted the proposal, that the legislature be petitioned to appropriate the unpaid balance, in the sum of $1,645,000, due on the amount of $5,585,000 under the original agreement of 1921. The amount actually granted, however, was only $1,220,000.[13] Another wing was added to Phillips Hall; a dormitory to complete the Aycock, Graham, Lewis quadrangle in Battle Park was erected; a basement floor was added to Peabody Building; costly renovations were made, a respectable sum was expended on improvement of the grounds; a new classroom building, Bingham, the fourth and lowest in the huge steps of masonry on the east side of the South Quadrangle, of which the first three were Steele, Saunders, and Murphey, was erected; and a magnificent new library, the crowning glory of the Chase administration, was placed in a dominating position, facing north and forming the south side of the South Quadrangle.

The dormitory mentioned above, which was erected in 1928, was Everett, named for W. N. Everett of the class of 1886.[14] It was a replica of Lewis Dormitory already described, of the same dimensions and cost, with the same architects and contractors. The classroom building, which was completed in 1929 at a cost of $160,000, and designed to house the Economics Department and the School of Commerce, was named Bingham Hall after Major Robert Bingham, of the class of 1857. It has 52 rooms and 22,-100 square feet of floor space, and contains 444,360 cubic feet. The building architects were Atwood and Nash; the designer,

13. *Ibid.*, pp. 292-93, 294, 295, 310-11, 317.
14. Omitted by Battle from the class of 1886. Battle, II, 721, 808. In a sketch of Mr. Everett, it is explicitly stated that he was a member of the class of 1886. *Yackety Yack*, 1921, p. 22.

H. P. Alan Montgomery; the contractors, T. C. Thompson and Brothers.

At the center of President Chase's thinking about University development, during the course of his administration, was the vivid consciousness of the supreme need for a great library. However pressing were the demands for new buildings to house schools, departments, classrooms, and students, he was never unaware that structures and equipment alone do not constitute a great university. Obviously no modern university, as he expressed it, "can carry on its complex and specialized tasks without adequate material provision for its needs in such things." But these things are merely instruments, symbols, of the intellectual drive, the pedagogical effort, the vast study, the intensive research, which constitute the pulsing life-currents of the true university. In his report for 1924, therefore, President Chase made abundantly clear that a new library, to enable the University's scholars to avail themselves of the rich storehouses of past knowledge and the unhalting advance of modern scholarship, was indispensable. In 1907, when the Carnegie Library was erected, the University's enrollment was only 764, and the library contained only 45,822 volumes. In the light of contemporary conditions, "university" was an ambitious, not to say exaggerated, term to describe the size and facilities of what was actually little more than a small, however excellent, college. The number of volumes in the library's collections had increased three-fold in less than two decades; and almost every foot of stack space was occupied. With anticipated like or even greater increase in the library's collections, proceeding *pari passu* with rapid increase in student attendance, a library of large dimensions and with the most modern equipment was needed to meet the conditions attendant upon the imminent development of a college into a university.[15]

Study of the Carnegie Library clearly demonstrated that it was not capable of magnification, because the scale was too small; and the intricate, interlocking communications of a library required for a modern university could not be supplied by additions of wings or mere spatial expansion. A wholly new plan,

15. *T. M.*, 1924-1930, p. 73.

on a vastly larger scale, was the only solution. On September 24, 1924, and again on June 24, 1926, President Chase pressed for steadily enlarging programs, with a new library, estimated to cost $816,715, placed at the head of the list by common consent of Trustees and Faculty. In response to President Chase's representations, in his report to the Board of Trustees on January 25, 1927, the legislature made a grant of respectable proportions which, however, fell short by $425,000 of the amount requested. In consequence, the University, in a special hearing, recommended the sum of $625,000 for the construction of the central unit of a new library, on a plan designed to provide for future integral expansion on a proportionate scale and in harmony with the central structure. This recommendation, presented by President Chase on April 12, 1927, was adopted by the Trustees.

The new Library, completed in 1929, was dedicated on October 19 of that year. This palatial structure, providing space for 450,000 volumes and adequate for a staff, general and special students, and a floor (third) for a school of library administration, was pronounced by President Chase, so far as solutions in such matters may be so described, a "permanent solution for the housing of this important aspect of our University life."[16] The architectural firm was Atwood and Nash; the contractor, T. C. Thompson and Brothers.

This impressive structure, with contents of 1,333,860 cubic feet, is 219 feet in length and has a depth at the center of 140 feet. The main entrance leads to a spacious *foyer*, with marble and terrazzo floor, Travertine walls, and ornamental ceiling. To right and left of the *foyer* are the large General College and Reserve Reading Rooms; and at the east side, approached through a 12-foot cross corridor, are offices for the librarian and his administrative staff. At the west side are the Commerce Reading Room and the Order Department. A double staircase to the second floor leads to the main delivery room, which separates the reading rooms from the stack area with its seven levels. The spacious reading rooms lie symmetrically to east and west of the central rotunda which houses the Reference Depart-

16. *Ibid.*, p. 455. Consult Chapters 30 and 31 on Campus architecture.

ment. The remainder of the second floor is taken up by the Cataloguing and Periodical departments and stair halls. Except for a few seminar rooms, the third floor is entirely devoted to the School of Library Science, with its study and classrooms, offices, and special school library. In the basement are accommodations for many services, notably the Southern Historical Collection, North Caroliniana, Library Extension Department, Bull's Head Book Shop, Rural Social Economics Reading Room, seminar rooms and offices, staff room, and service quarters for the receiving and shipping of books, janitor's workroom, vaults and storage rooms. The constructive mind in planning the Library was the Librarian, Dr. Louis R. Wilson, an official of exceptional efficiency and high organizing ability, with comprehensive views concerning the functions and capacities of a great library.[17]

17. "The Report of the Librarian," 1924-1925 and 1925-1926; *The University Library* (Chapel Hill, University of North Carolina, 1929); *The Dedication of the Library Building, October 19th, 1929* (Chapel Hill, University Library, 1930). The Dedication was an event which brought the Southern Conference on Education and the Southeastern Library Association meetings to Chapel Hill to participate in a symposium relating to libraries. Gifts of money and materials for library purposes were announced at the dedication, in the amount of $145,000, $100,000 being received for the establishment of the School of Library Science.

PART VI
BUILDING A NATIONAL UNIVERSITY

27

PUBLIC WORKS PROJECTS AND
THE NEW DEAL[1]

FOR THE PERIOD 1905-1935 the student attendance at the University increased at the average rate of about 800 students each decade. Despite the impressive and spectacular appropriation by the State of upwards of $6,000,000 during the twenties, President Frank Porter Graham, on taking office in June, 1930, was confronted with the formidable task of securing provision for many urgent needs created by the extraordinary yet continuing expansion in attendance. Electrical facilities, physical education, athletic fields, dormitories, buildings for art, natural science, medicine, and a dining hall were pressing needs which must be adequately fulfilled in the near future. A new and fascinating chapter, dramatic and impressive in accomplishment, was to be written. This proved to be a building program, involving the expenditure, on permanent development and improvement, of the sum of $3,500,000 during the decade of the thirties.

The vast program of public works, initiated to provide in part for unemployment problems and deflation confronting President Franklin Delano Roosevelt at the outset of his first administration, supplied a new deal of the financial deck of cards, for the Nation and happily too for the State and the University of North Carolina. The ill wind of financial depression at least blew some good toward the Old North State. In 1932 was effected the consolidation of the University at Chapel Hill, State College at Raleigh, and the Woman's College at Greensboro into the Greater University of North Carolina. With wisdom and vision, President Graham, University officials, and the Trustees united in the determination to endeavor to secure, through the Public Works Administration of the Federal gov-

1. Developments in the field of services and athletics are omitted here, being considered elsewhere in chapters dealing specifically with these subjects.

ernment, funds of large proportions to provide for the requisite expansion of the University.[2]

Under the act passed by the legislature of North Carolina, Public Laws of 1935, chapter 479, state institutions were enabled to participate in the program of the Federal Emergency Administration of Public Works. On September 5, 1935, pursuant to a favorable decision of the Attorney General, Governor Clyde R. Hoey and the Council of State endorsed the program, already approved and adopted by the Board of Trustees at its June, 1935, meeting, for the erection of two new University buildings with the aid of PWA funds. These were a Physical Education Building and a Graduate Women's Dormitory, the total cost $629,100 to be divided in the ratio 9 to 11: the government donating $283,000 and the University providing $346,100. Already, on October 14, 1933, the Executive Committee of the Trustees had adopted a program totaling $700,-000, providing for, among other items, a Fine Arts Building. The outcome of this last item was the renovation of Person Hall, to be known as Person Hall Art Gallery.

The Civil Works Administration, in conjunction with FERA and WPA, granted the sum of $10,000 for the remodeling of Person Hall. Mrs. Katherine Pendleton Arrington, of Warrenton, North Carolina, active supporter and generous patron of various art projects in North Carolina, made a handsome contribution as a memorial to her brother, Milo M. Pendleton of the class of 1902. Other contributors were Mrs. Rufus L. Patterson, William D. Carmichael, Frank L. Fuller, and Mrs. B. H. Griffin; and, with a supplementary sum from the University, the total came to approximately $25,000.[3] The remodeled Person Hall became not only an art gallery but also the home of the Art Department. The east wing was designed as an *atelier*, the central bar of the T serves as the main art gallery, and the west wing holds a smaller gallery, the art library, and offices for the staff. Plans were made by Otto R. Eggers, of the archi-

2. It is outside the scope of this work to deal with programs and accomplishments of expansion at the Raleigh and Greensboro branches of the University of North Carolina.

3. Office files of P. L. Burch, Superintendent of Buildings, University of North Carolina.

SECOND INFIRMARY

rected in 1895, it replaced "The
etreat." It stood near the south-
est corner of the present Hill
Music Hall.

THE OLD WATER TOWER

This 80-foot standpipe was near
the present site of Swain Hall. From
a photograph taken about 1900.

SECOND DISSECTING HALL

Erected about 1900, it stood on the present site of Venable Hall.

CADETS MARCHING DOWN CAMERON AVENUE

tectural firm of John Russell Pope, and by Walter L. Clark, president of the Grand Central Art Galleries. "This little hall," said President Graham at the rededication of the building on January 15, 1937, "has a story which it could tell of a University's decision in slender times to make an investment in art, with no assurances of a roof for many months to keep out the rain which beat upon its inner walls. Faith and failure, aspiration and frustration, but always dreams and struggle, have been in this little pile since the first bricks of the red clay of Orange County were laid for Person Hall in the last decade of the eighteenth century. Today it stands, roof and all, with most of the original bricks and all the original simple lines, the work of many hands, the blending of three centuries, and the final result of the coöperation of Uncle Sam's CWA and North Carolina's K. P. A. [Katherine Pendleton Arrington], the beautiful home of the Department of Art, the youngest of all our departments in the next oldest of all our buildings."[4]

The need for women's dormitories grew steadily more pressing throughout the thirties. By 1935, five years after the completion of Spencer Hall which accommodated only 74, the number of women students had increased to 300. During a period of three years, 1937-1939, three handsome dormitories for women were planned and erected, facing an open court on the old Raleigh Road south of the president's house and east of the Arboretum. The first of these structures, named Alderman in honor of Edwin Anderson Alderman, under whose presidency co-education was introduced here, was of modified Georgian architecture, red brick being used as the building material with limestone trim and slate roof. It is three storeys high with a large open portico facing southward upon the inner court. The architectural firm was Atwood and Weeks, with A. C. Nash as consulting architect. The contractors were: George W. Kane, building; Rowe-Coward, Inc., plumbing; and Carolina Heating and Engineering Company, heating. The building has 68 rooms and 25,250 square feet of floor space, and

---

4. For additional data concerning Person Hall, consult Gladys Hall Coates, "The Story of Person Hall," *Bulletin of Person Hall Art Gallery*, Vol. III, No. 2 (April, 1943). See also *T. M.*, 1931-1938, pp. 112, 216-17.

contains 385,000 cubic feet. It was erected at a cost of $123,-166.70, which included the cost of furnishings.

The second of these women's dormitories was begun in 1938 and completed in 1939. This dormitory, a men's dormitory, and a spacious new dining hall were financed by the sale of revenue bonds in the sum of $287,000, to match a PWA grant of $234,-405. The women's dormitory, facing northward upon the court described above, was of Georgian style similar to Alderman Dormitory, but with pleasing differences in detail. The architectural firm was Atwood and Weeks, with A. C. Nash consulting architect; the contracting firm, T. W. Poe and Son. The building has 69 rooms and 25,250 square feet of floor space, and contains 411,680 cubic feet. Named McIver Dormitory for Charles Duncan McIver, founder of the Woman's College at Greensboro, this building, including furnishings, was erected at a cost of $140,231.29.

Three other dormitories, including the third women's dormitory, and extensive additions to the Carolina Inn, were provided for in similar fashion. The sale of revenue bonds in the sum of $386,000 to supplement a PWA grant of $315,805, was authorized by the Executive Committee of the Board of Trustees on November 18, 1938. The third women's dormitory, facing west upon the open quadrangle, was named Kenan Dormitory after Mrs. Henry M. (Mary Lily Kenan) Flagler, donor of the $2,000,000 Kenan Foundation for Distinguished Professors. The architectural firm was Atwood and Weeks, with A. C. Nash consulting architect; the contracting firm, Muirhead Construction Company. This dormitory has 82 rooms and 29,-709 square feet of floor space, and contains 534,390 cubic feet. The cost, including furnishings, was $199,000.

The men's dormitory, a constituent part of the project included with McIver Dormitory, was selected to fill out the east end of a quadrangle, of which the west end was left open along the old Raleigh Road. This building, completed in 1938, was named Stacy Dormitory after Marvin Hendrix Stacy, class of 1902, Professor of Mathematics, Dean of the College of Arts and Sciences, and Chairman of the Faculty of the University from the death of Edward Kidder Graham from influenza in

1918 until his own death from the same disease in 1919. It is a three-storey building, architecturally harmonizing with the four other buildings enclosing the court; and accommodates 110 students. The architectural firm was Atwood and Weeks; A. C. Nash, consulting architect; contractor, V. P. Loftis. The building has 61 rooms and 17,700 square feet of floor space, and contains 280,000 cubic feet. The total cost, including furnishings, was $104,914.

The two men's dormitories, constituent parts of the project included with Kenan Dormitory, were: Whitehead Dormitory, named for Dr. Richard Henry Whitehead, Dean of the Medical School, and Alexander Dormitory, named for Dr. Eben Alexander, head of the Greek Department and Dean of the College of Liberal Arts. These two buildings were completed, respectively, in September and October, 1939. The former was built for medical and graduate students, and stands on the lot at the corner of Columbia and McCauley streets. The latter is located south of the tennis courts, near the old Raleigh Road; and is placed parallel to Lewis Dormitory. It is a brick building three storeys high, and accommodates 110 students. The architect of Whitehead Dormitory was George Watts Carr, the contracting firm, Muirhead Construction Company. It has 81 rooms and 22,850 square feet of floor space, and contains 308,600 cubic feet. It is a brick building three storeys high, and was built at a cost, including furnishings, of $122,384.78. For Alexander Dormitory, the architectural firm was Atwood and Weeks, with A. C. Nash as consulting architect; and the contractor was H. L. Coble. It has 71 rooms and 21,750 square feet of floor space, and contains 338,690 cubic feet. It was built at a cost, including furnishings, of $115,578.69.

The new dining hall, already mentioned above, was completed in January, 1940. The location, at the western extremity of Emerson Field, was dictated by the consideration that a Commons or student cafeteria and restaurant combined should be of easy access to most of the dormitories, classroom buildings, and the Library. The rapid growth of the student body rendered Swain Hall, which accommodated only 500, signally inadequate; and with the erection of the new dining hall, Swain Hall was given up as Commons and converted into an office building. The new dining hall, a brick building of extreme simplicity, one storey high with a basement, was named Lenoir Hall after General William Lenoir, first President of the Board of Trustees. It seats 1,300 people, and has a capacity of 10,000 meals a day, which is three times the capacity of Swain Hall. The architectural firm was Atwood and Weeks, consulting architect, A. C. Nash; and the contractor was A. H. Guion. The building has 34,925 square feet of floor space; and contains 1,006,500 cubic feet. The total cost of the building, including equipment, was $276,426.63.

The additions to the Carolina Inn, mentioned above, which were made in 1939, greatly enhance the appearance of the building-area along the Pittsboro Road south of the Inn. The small wooden Inn Cafeteria was removed to make way for the handsome new red brick improvements. Facing upon Pittsboro Road and upon an open court along that road are: brick buildings containing a total of 15 two-room and three-room apartments for married graduate students; an extension of the Carolina Inn including 42 hotel bedrooms, a Faculty clubroom, a cafeteria with a seating capacity of 200, and quarters for the Alumni Office. The architect was George Watts Carr; consulting architect, A. C. Nash; the contracting firms were Muirhead Construction Company and V. P. Loftis. The total cost of these improvements was $262,972.99.

The next large development in building construction was marked by several novelties. By this time, zoning according to technical classification had become acknowledged, if not accepted, in principle. With the establishment of the Department of Public Health in 1936, the overcrowded Caldwell Hall was patently outgrown; and a massive new building was needed, to provide adequate quarters for the expanding School of Medicine, within which was included the Department of Public Health. A new area was now opened, to allow for expansion in the fields of applied science and in reasonable access to Venable Hall, housing the Department of Chemistry, and Phillips Hall, housing the Departments of Mathematics and Physics. The area happily chosen for this comprehensive expansion lay south of the Raleigh Road and east of the Pittsboro Road. The financial projects for the erection of these two buildings, as well as for other improvements, were nonself-liquidating. The opening of the new area, the practical confirmation of the zoning principle, and the nature of the financing were all novelties of a crucial character, making a new chapter in the history of Campus development. With this step the old Campus was recognized as too restricted an area for free University expansion; and a vast new area south of the old Campus was definitively thrown open for wise use and legitimate exploitation.

On May 3, 1937, President Graham and Controller Woollen were authorized by the Executive Committee of the Board of Trustees to file an application on behalf of the University to the United States for a loan and grant-in-aid in financing the construction of a Public Health and Medical Building and a Clinical Annex. The state appropriated $226,000, the government granted $184,000, to cover the costs of construction. The addition to the Infirmary was completed in May, the new medical building in July, 1939.[5] The spacious and imposing-looking Medical Building, five storeys high and built of brick, is located beyond the Chapel Hill High School, then standing and since burned, but on the opposite (east) side of the Pittsboro Road. The Division of Public Health occupies the ground floor; and the other floors are occupied as follows: first (main) floor, the Charles E. Kistler Memorial Library, administrative offices, and the laboratories and quarters of the Department of Pathology; second floor, an auditorium seating 182, and the Departments of Pharmacology and Physiology; third floor, the Departments of Anatomy and Biological Chemistry; fourth floor, air-conditioned animal quarters, additional research laboratories, rooms for scientific equipment, and storage. The architectural firm was Atwood and Weeks; consulting architect, A. C. Nash; and the contractor, V. P. Loftis, of Charlotte. The building has 188 rooms and 79,650 square feet of floor space, and contains 1,142,-000 cubic feet. The cost of the building was $380,982.02.[6]

In view of the pressing need for additional classrooms and space for new activities, it was decided by the Executive Committee of the Board of Trustees, on November 18, 1938, not to

5. *T. M.*, 1931-1938, pp. 222, 246-47, 248, 264.
6. *Alumni Review*, XXVIII (1938-1939), 99.

house the Department of Zoology in a remodeled Caldwell Hall, after it was vacated by the School of Medicine, but to erect a new building for Zoology. That part of the funds allocated to Caldwell Hall from the P.W.A. grant of 1938 would be used to aid in financing the construction of additions, alterations, and repairs to Bynum Gymnasium, Alumni Building, Gerrard Hall, and Caldwell Hall. This amendment was accepted by the national government on April 10, 1939. The total sum provided for these changes was $437,000, of which the government supplied $196,-000 and the State $241,000.[7] The building for Zoology, named Wilson Hall after the late Henry Van Peters Wilson, head of the Department of Zoology, was admirably placed upon a bold, rounded eminence overlooking the triangle, two sides of which are arcs formed by the intersections of the Raleigh Road, which bifurcates at this point, with the Pittsboro Road. This four-storey structure, built of red brick, has 100 rooms and 30,425 square feet of floor space, and contains 525,000 cubic feet. The architectural firm was Atwood and Weeks; consulting architect, A. C. Nash; the contractor, James I. Barnes. The cost of this building, completed during the academic year 1939-1940, was $187,234.63.[8]

In summary, the greatest material expansion at the least proportionate cost to the State in any similar period of the University's history took place during the years 1935-1941. Thirteen great new buildings, risen as if at the rubbing of Aladdin's lamp, together with handsome additions and extensive remodeling, astounded the graduates of 1935 returning after 1941. The number of buildings, on and off the University Campus, had increased from 53 to 66; and their valuation had increased by $3,500,000, during that period. Yet of this total expenditure, the State of North Carolina contributed the comparatively small percentage of about 19.6—a total of only $697,000. *Mirabile dictu et visu!* Thanks a million, almost three million, to the New Deal, PWA, F. D. R. and F. P. G.!

7. *T. M.*, 1931-1938, pp. 274 ff.
8. Consult "Dedication of the Wilson Zoological Laboratory," *Journal Elisha Mitchell Scientific Society*, LVIII (1942), 1-15. The alterations, renovations, and remodeling of Bynum Gymnasium, Alumni Building, Gerrard Hall, and Caldwell Hall are considered elsewhere in this work.

28

UNIVERSITY SERVICES; THE IMPACT OF WORLD WAR II

I N THE CONTEMPORARY ERA, with its innumerable instrumentalities for individual and mass protection, public health safeguards, scientific sanitation, continental campaigns against prevalent plagues, elaborate technics for the treatment of all forms of disease, it is well-nigh impossible to realize the semi-barbaric conditions under which people generally lived and were willing to live, even down to the last quarter of the nineteenth century. At the University slightly more than half a century ago (September, 1894), illumination was obtained exclusively by means of kerosene lamps and tallow candles; water supply, baths, urinals, closets and sewerage for the entire University, numbering some 425 students and 20 Faculty members, had been installed for only six months; and the dormitory rooms were heated with open fireplaces, the fuel being almost exclusively wood. In winter the roads were inconceivably dreadful, often being hub-deep in mud and almost impassable; and even the public streets of the village were often from 6 to 12 inches deep in gluey red clay mud, with large pools of standing water at intervals. The modern era in Chapel Hill may almost be said to have been symbolically inaugurated with the importation of the first automobile by the late Edward Vernon Howell, who came here in 1897 to found and head the Department of Pharmacy. The story of the vicissitudes experienced by that car and the terror it inspired in horses, mules, and humans, would furnish the material for a minor epic on the birth-pangs of the present age of scientific gimcracks, gadgets, and gremlins.

During the first half-century of the University's history, the provisions for the disposal of waste from the human body were crude, primitive, and unhygienic. A Committee on Sanitary Arrangements in the 1880's occupied itself with these problems and effected some improvement in living conditions.[1]

1. *T. M.*, 1883-1891, p. 259. Report of the Committee on Sanitary Arrangements by Paul C. Cameron, August 26, 1886. Battle states that

Not until several years after the re-opening of the University in 1875 was any effort made by the administrative authorities to supply facilities for the disposal of human waste. About 1880 one "comfort house," to the south of the rock wall, some 50 yards north of the present University Library, was erected by the University authorities; and in the second half of the decade several more were constructed in the same locality. After a time, the students, for sanitary reasons, burned the largest of these structures; and not long afterwards the University authorities condemned the remainder. It was about the year 1887 that several small connected brick structures, each approximately 30 by 40 feet in dimensions, were erected on or near the same site; and these "relief stations," as they were denominated by the students, were patronized until the establishment in 1893-1894 of the college water system, with urinals, closets, showers, and sewerage in the University buildings.[2]

At this same time sanitary facilities were installed in the basement of Smith Hall, then used as the college library. The entrance to these conveniences was in the south wall of the building, at the southwest corner; and one descended by a few stone steps to a corridor running the length of the building (east and west), which was divided by a board partition down the center. South of the partition was a series of individual toilets; and to its north were: a long slate trough for communal use, half a dozen showers, and several bath tubs.[3]

water closets, presumably of a primitive character, were "introduced in 1887"; but no water was laid on in any college building except the Chemical Laboratory, until 1892. Battle, II, 365, 570.

2. Statement of the late Judge R. W. Winston, quoted in Link, p. 130; Love, pp. 3-4; Battle, II, 181, 365, 570, 571. These brick "relief stations" remained standing until comparatively recent years. Presumably these are the structures euphemistically described by Battle as "water closets."

3. For authoritative information regarding these sanitary facilities, now imperfectly remembered by the writer, he is indebted to Dr. William de B. MacNider, a boy of twelve when they were installed. An earlier effort made by the late Professor Walter D. Toy, then recently returned from Paris, to introduce open public conveniences of the French variety was thwarted by a brilliant pun perpetrated by the late President George T. Winston. In 1877 the State established in Smith Hall an Agricultural Experiment Station, occupying four rooms. This station was transferred to Raleigh in 1881. After the burning of Person Hall (interior)

As early as 1890 President Battle, who was much concerned over the danger of disease and epidemic from unhygienic disposal, recommended that the Trustees petition the legislature for $5,000 to install an adequate water system; but no report was made by the committee appointed for that purpose.[4] On May 31, 1892, the Visiting Committee reiterated President Battle's plea; and on June 11, 1892, the Trustees finally appointed a Committee on Water Supply, with Dr. Richard H. Lewis of Raleigh as chairman, and authorized this committee to carry out President Battle's recommendation. A well supplying about 1,500 gallons of water daily was dug at a cost of $1,500; and water was pumped by steam into two capacious iron storage tanks in the attic of the South Building; but this was not immediately used, as the funds, some $4,000, needed to install the requisite facilities, were not then available.[5] In March, 1893, the Trustees decided to erect a water plant, and the contract was awarded to S. W. Holman and Company of Durham. Work now proceeded steadily, the water plant was completed shortly after September 13, 1893, and on February 23, 1894, President Winston announced that the arrangements for water supply, baths, urinals, closets, and sewerage had been carried out. The cost of the waterworks, with installation of facilities, amounted to $5,500.[6]

The steady increase in student attendance and the installation of an electrical plant in 1895 soon rendered the small water system of 1894 entirely inadequate. After repeated representations by President Alderman and the Trustees' petition, March 1,

---

in 1881, the Chemistry Department was transferred to the basement of Smith Hall, where it functioned most unsatisfactorily in the cramped quarters until late 1886, when removal was made to the "new" Chemical Laboratory in the renovated Person Hall.

4. *T. M.*, 1883-1891, p. 453. February 20, 1890. *T. M.*, 1891-1898. April 1, 1891.

5. *T. M.*, 1891-1898, p. 176. October 1, 1892. The facilities needed were pipes in great number, and apparatus for 10 water closets, 4 shower baths, 4 urinals, 1 wash stand, and 1 slop sink. See also Battle, II, 570-71. To supplement the inadequate water supply, a second well was sunk. These wells were located: one near the southwest corner of Old West, the other to the south of the present site of Phillips Hall.

6. *T. M.*, 1891-1898, pp. 247, 249, 293.

1897, to the legislature for relief, the latter body made the first direct grant to the University for enlarging the physical plant. The amount allotted was $7,500, specifically for a suitable system of waterworks. The engineer reported that this sum was far too small for the purpose expressed; and on the recommendation of President Alderman, considerable sums were borrowed from several of the University's endowed funds. A further appropriation of $5,000 was made by the legislature in 1901; and on January 16, 1902, President Venable announced that, at a cost of about $12,000, the new waterworks and sewerage system had been completed.[7]

Within five years time the growing pains of the University were again registered in a water system found to be quite inadequate to meet rapidly expanding needs. It is amusing to recall that, in the opening year of the present century, the Trustee Committee on Sanitary Conditions came to the defence of the century-old mode of heating the dormitories with wood in open fireplaces. This system of heating had been criticised as antiquated, inconvenient, expensive, and, for severe weather, notoriously ineffective. President Venable, on scientific and economic grounds, was opposed to a vaunted Spartan simplicity which guaranteed discomfort in periods of bleak weather, and energetically recommended the installation of a hot water heating plant. At the request of a committee of the Trustees, Professor Joshua Walker Gore, head of the Physics Department and an expert in all matters pertaining to electric lighting, heating and water systems, studied plants at other institutions; and estimated the cost of a suitable plant for this University to be $30,000, the annual income from which would amount to approximately

7. *Ibid.*, pp. 520, 570, 663; 1898-1904, pp. 34, 313. See President Alderman's reports for 1897 and 1898. The reservoir held 50,000 gallons and the filter could purify 25,000 gallons daily. Analyses of the water were made at frequent intervals, and the water shed was inspected monthly. *T. M.*, 1904-1916, p. 209. The stand pipe, located north of the present site of Swain Hall, towered 80 feet above the Campus, which it adjoined. The pumping station, which contained one small gasoline engine, was located on Bowlin's Creek, north of the village. The water was filtered through a steel filter, filled with sand and charcoal. This filter was located to the south of the old power plant which stood on the site of the present east wing of Phillips Hall.

$2,850. By means of sums borrowed from several of the University's invested funds, the plant was erected in 1901 on the present site of Phillips Hall; and the central heating system which was put in operation on October 25, 1901, gave general satisfaction. The plant supplied heat and electricity for fourteen buildings on the Campus.[8] Pursuant to strong recommendations by the Visiting Committee of the Board of Trustees, June 3, 1907, and President Venable's report of 1909, the Executive Committee on March 9, 1909, authorized the President to increase the Power Plant, using funds from the appropriation made by the General Assembly. During 1910 sundry changes in the plant were made, at a cost of $27,557.07.[9] Within less than a decade, sad to relate, the inadequacy of the plant was demonstrated. In 1914 serious damage to the power plant boiler room was sustained during a heavy storm. Repairs were quickly made; but two years later, as will be seen, it became necessary to replace the existing plant with an enlarged and improved establishment.[10]

As early as June, 1895, the Stygian darkness of the hallways of the dormitories, with stairways offering hazards to life and limb, was reported on with high disfavor by the Visiting Committee of the Trustees in the following language: "The broad highway of progress is illuminated by brilliant electric lights and we must march thereon abreast of the foremost." Through

8. *T. M.*, 1898-1904, pp. 171, 229, 281-83, 305-7, 313-63. Dr. R. H. Lewis of Raleigh was chairman of the Trustees' committee which, on February 5, 1901, recommended the installation of a steam-heating plant of the "direct-indirect" type, and the appointment of Professor Gore to examine systems elsewhere and to submit estimates. See Link, pp. 136-39. In a sketch of Professor Gore, Professor Collier Cobb states: "At the University of North Carolina he has been wholly responsible for the electric light plant and in large measure for the heating and water plants. He was one of the prime movers for the investment of endowment funds in these and other improvements, which are sources of revenue to the University. . . . He has developed a strong course of electricity at the University, and as Dean of the Department [School] of Applied Science, he is aiding in the upbuilding of an institution to meet the growing needs of the South." *N. C. B. H.*, V, 107-9.

9. *T. M.*, 1904-1916, pp. 139-40, 209, 312. In 1909 the University was using from three to four times as much water as it had employed eight years earlier.

10. *Ibid.*, pp. 209, 409.

sums drawn largely from the Francis Jones Smith Fund an electric plant, with extensions into the village, was erected and in successful operation by the end of the summer of 1895.[11] Six years later, the electric plant was enlarged and connected with the new heating plant, at a cost of $500. In 1912, owing to the erection of six new buildings, the lighting plant was extended, at a cost of approximately $1,690.[12]

On January 27, 1916, President Graham presented to the Trustees the report of Business Manager Woollen recommending the erection of a new power plant to take care of the needs of the expanding University. During the preceding seven years four new buildings had been built to accommodate the 400 new students. Double pumping necessitated by filtered water had been installed and 24-hour service became essential. The committee, appointed by the Executive Committee of the Trustees, reported that the Council of State had unanimously approved the borrowing of the funds, not to exceed $30,000, necessary to build a power plant adequate to supply the University's needs. The cost of such a plant was estimated by Business Manager Woollen and Professor P. H. Daggett of the Physics Department, at $42,000; and the Executive Committee voted such expenditure, the balance above $30,000 to be raised from escheats and any unexpended portion of the $20,000 appropriated by the legislature of 1913. In 1916-1917 the new plant, contrary to the recommendation that it be located some distance from the Campus, was erected some 50 yards south of present Phillips Hall.[13]

11. *T. M.*, 1891-1898, pp. 456, 462, 466-67. The cost of the plant was in the neighborhood of $8,000. In 1885 Mary Ruffin Smith bequeathed to the University a plantation of some 1,500 acres in Chatham County; and the proceeds of the sale constituted the Francis Jones Smith Fund, so named for her brother, a member of the class of 1837.

12. *T. M.*, 1898-1904, p. 299; 1904-1916, pp. 208, 384.

13. Actually the new power plant was paid for out of the 1917 legislative appropriation of $500,000. Extensions to the plant, at a cost of about $5,750, were made in 1920. *T. M.*, 1904-1916, pp. 548-49, 555, 573; 1917-1924, pp. 88, 227. The committee, appointed by the Executive Committee of the Trustees to investigate the situation regarding a new power plant, consisted of John Manning, John W. Graham, Victor S. Bryant, and William P. Bynum. In the power plant erected in 1916-1917 was installed a steam turbine of 500 H. P., with a capacity of 25,000 gallons

By 1922 considerable sums, totaling slightly more than $43,-700, were expended for sanitary equipment in the old dormitories, alterations on the power house, the installation of sewage disposal plant, emergency water supply, additional baths and lockers, emergency steam line, fire protection, and other items.[14]

Expenditures on a like scale for power, water, light, heating, and sewerage continued during this era of prosperity and expansion. For 1925 the budget included filter plant and water supply, $22,800; heating expansion, $33,700; and storm sewer No. 3, $2,000. The permanent improvement program, offered by President Chase, June 24, 1926, contained estimated figures, as follows: Sanitary Engineering Laboratory $20,000, water shed and storage $100,000, and Campus mains and drainage, $52,000.[15] Large plans and generous estimates for extensions of heating plant, addition of new boilers, laying of mains, permanent storage for water supply, and land for the reservoir on Morgan's Creek were drawn up for the new biennium, totaling projected expenditures of some $160,000.[16]

---

per hour, in the building now occupied by the storeroom of the Buildings Department headquarters. A few years later, this turbine having become inadequate, power was furnished the University by the Southern Power Company until 1925, at which time a new terbine of 750 H. P. was installed. This equipment was employed until 1939, when the present power plant was constructed.

14. *T. M.*, 1917-1924, pp. 203-4, 367, 421, 466-67. The first sewage disposal plant, which was built in Battle Park in 1921, did not work with entire satisfaction; but it continued to be used for a number of the University buildings until the present disposal plant was built on Strowd's Creek in 1925. The estimated costs of the expansion of the power plant down to Commencement, 1922, were: boiler and piping changes in the power house, $19,000; and revamping the heating system, $40,000. Link, p. 200. For reports of estimated cost of improvements and actual expenditures to January 1, 1924, consult *T. M.*, 1917-1924, p. 447; 1924-1930, pp. 22-25. The report of John Sprunt Hill, April 19, 1923, gave the following estimated costs: permanent water supply, $120,000; sewers, heating and lighting extensions, $115,000.

15. *T. M.*, 1924-1930, pp. 292-93.

16. *Ibid.*, pp. 386, 414, 485-86; 1931-1939, p. 5. In 1925 the new Filter Plant, designed to filter 1,000,000 gallons of water every 24 hours, was built at the rear and to the east of Phillips Hall. It was designed by Atwood and Nash, University architects, and constructed by T. C. Thompson and Brothers, University construction contractors. The new water supply was brought by a 12-inch iron main from Morgan's Creek at a

In 1932 the University purchased the land and began the construction of a dam at the junction of Morgan's and Price's creeks, to impound a lake to furnish a water supply for the University, and the citizens of Chapel Hill, Carrboro, and the surrounding area. This concrete dam is 35 feet high and 260 feet long. The lake covers an area of approximately 220 acres and holds 600,-000,000 gallons of water. From this lake water was pumped through one 12-inch cast iron pipe to the new Filter Plant; and in 1943 a second 12-inch line was laid parallel to the former line, to afford additional capacity for the town of Chapel Hill. Since the Filter Plant was built and the dam constructed, the University has run additional water lines throughout the community to take care of the needs of the University and the village.[17]

Prior to 1925, the office of the University Consolidated Service Plants was located in two small rooms in the basement of Alumni Building. "All the Campus buildings were fed by overhead pole line construction. The lines were in deplorable condition. All the outside lights on the Campus were on poles—with a switch on each pole. It was the duty of the night watchman to go around and cut on the lights each evening!"[18] In that same year the University purchased from the Strowd Motor Company at a cost of $35,000, the large building on Franklin Street, then used as a garage, which the University Service Plants now occupies. It contains 26 rooms and has 11,000 square feet of floor space. The total cost of the building and extensive repairs and renovation, gave a grand total of approximately $46,875. The U. C. S. P. moved into the new quarters in February, 1926; and in 1940-41 the office of the University Laundry was transferred from the plant to this building. In 1925 the University acquired

point about three miles west of Chapel Hill. In 1939 the capacity of the Filter Plant was increased 50 per cent. A new Filter Plant, with a capacity of 3,000,000 gallons of filtered water every 24 hours, is now contemplated; and it will be located on the road leading from Carrboro to University Lake about one-half mile from Carrboro, on a 15-acre tract of land purchased in September, 1947 from A. D. Barnes.

17. Data concerning the lake and the laundry (see *infra*) were supplied by J. S. Bennett, Supervisor of Operations.

18. Sketch, fully illustrated, of the history of the University Consolidated Service Plants, Christmas, 1932.

the old plant of the Chapel Hill Telephone Company and turned it over to the U. C. S. P. for operation. Two years later a new plant was built on Rosemary Street, and a new switchboard, carrying 500 lines, was installed. The old switchboard could not be permanently repaired, as the manufacturer had long since gone out of business. It is amusing to recall the ingenious devices to which Mr. Rush, the manager, was compelled to resort, in order to keep the switchboard in action. "He found that the only solution for repairing breakdowns on the board was chewing gum. So a visitor to the exchange might have seen Miss Leigh and Miss Gooch busily chewing gum, while Mr. Rush applied it, as needed, to the board"! This board was in an old frame building on Henderson Street, which was torn down about the year 1927.

At the beginning of the third decade of the present century, the University entered a new field in the establishment of a laundry. For a century and a quarter, the students were entirely dependent upon manual laundering. In the early days they sent their clothes to their parents' homes, often long distances, to be washed and ironed and returned to Chapel Hill; or else, in later years, depended exclusively upon the services of local Negro washerwomen. The conditions in the humble homes of the colored people were often far from sanitary; and thereby disagreeable diseases were disseminated throughout the college population. The rapidly increasing student enrollment revealed a shortage of colored laborers, which eventually became acute. In order to provide adequate and sanitary laundry service for students, faculty, and townspeople, the University took the necessary steps.[19] This new departure was recommended on January 27, 1920, by the Committee on the Development of University Property. It was decided to erect, near the old Power Plant, a structure now known as the Buildings Department and to install a modern laundry. This building was completed in 1921, at a cost of approximately $25,000.[20]

19. The late H. McG. Wagstaff, Professor of History, by a forceful presentation of the need for a laundry, before a committee of the Trustees, meeting in Chapel Hill, was largely responsible for its establishment.

20. *T. M.*, 1917-1924, pp. 227, 239.

Within four years, chiefly owing to the growth of student attendance and increased demands on the part of townspeople, it was found that a greatly enlarged and improved laundry was needed. A location some distance from the Campus was indicated as desirable, as so many of the colored laborers who passed across the Campus several times daily were women. The new laundry was located on the south side of West Cameron Avenue, about half a mile from the former site. This building, erected in 1925, contained 445,400 cubic feet, and cost $17,500; and the machinery installed cost $16,000. Some of the old machines from the first laundry were transferred to the new laundry, and are still in use. The architectural firm was Atwood and Weeks, the contracting firm, T. C. Thompson and Brothers. Since 1925 the building has been twice enlarged, with corresponding increases in equipment and operatives. During the location here of the Pre-Flight School and the Naval R. O. T. C., it was necessary to run two shifts with 162 employes.[21]

The full story of printing and the press in the University and Chapel Hill yet remains to be told, and deserves far more detailed treatment than the exigencies of space here permit.[22] There was an excellent printing establishment in Chapel Hill during the 1850's, when James Martin Henderson published the *Chapel Hill Literary Gazette*, of which he was editor, and printed pamphlets, catalogues, and monographs for the University. In February, 1893, the University Press was incorporated by five members of the Faculty: John Manning, F. P. Venable, J. W.

21. In 1921, when the first laundry went into operation under the direction of G. H. Paulson, 30 employes were required. The present laundry hires 132 employes on only one shift, and picks up laundry at two-week intervals. Repairs on the laundry during the period 1921-1929 amounted to $140.96, old laundry; $1,563.47, new laundry building. A greatly enlarged and improved plant is planned for the near future. Mr. J. S. Bennett, Supervisor of Operations, supplied essential data on the laundry.

22. As these lines are being written, the University of North Carolina Press is celebrating its twenty-fifth anniversary, March 12, 1947. Its story lies outside the scope of the present volume. On August 1, 1899, a motion was passed by the Trustees and referred to the Finance Committee, authorizing the University to buy the interest of the University Printery ("University Press," incorporated February, 1893). *T. M.*, 1898-1904, p. 109. On December 31, 1899, the University purchased the "University Press" for $2,000.

DRESS PARADE OF N. R. O. T. C. IN KENAN STADIUM

REVIEW OF N. R. O. T. C. AND PRE-FLIGHT CADETS
IN KENAN STADIUM

Gore, R. H. Whitehead, and Collier Cobb. Two months later an editor, probably Professor Cobb, managing editor, in the *North Carolina University Magazine* vigorously advocated the establishment of a University Press, either by the University authorities or by a group of alumni. The pressing need for a print shop was occasioned by the world-wide circulation of the *Journal* of the Elisha Mitchell Scientific Society founded in 1884, the establishment in 1893 of the Philological Society which looked forward to issuing and publishing a journal of its own, and the student demand for a college newspaper devoted primarily to covering athletic events. The first issue of the student newspaper, *The Tar Heel*, appeared on February 23, 1893. The primary purpose of "The University Press," as it was somewhat ambitiously called, was to engage in commercial printing and to issue the official publications and journals of the University.

In 1896 the University began to issue the *Record*, containing the President's Report, Catalogue, and other official publications. In rapid succession began to appear other publications: the *James Sprunt Historical Monographs* (1900), the *North Carolina Journal of Law* (1904), *Studies in Philology* (1906), the *North Carolina High School Bulletin* (1910), and the *News Letter* (1914). In addition, various types of job work were handled by the University Press: stationery for the University departments and schools, library call slips, handbills, programs and posters announcing University lectures, concerts, and official occasions of all sorts.

On June 4, 1901, the Board of Visitors, who had made an inspection of the University plant on May 9 preceding, reported to the full meeting of the Board of Trustees the urgent need of additional space for the Department of Pharmacy, in the New West Building wherein it was then domiciled. Since its establishment in 1893, the University Press had occupied three adjoining rooms on the first floor, north side, in New West. In their recommendation, signed by Lindsay Patterson, John W. Fries, and Richard H. Lewis, that the University Press be provided with a building of its own "near the electric power plant," the Board of Visitors further stated: "The continuance of the printing press in the present quarters menaces the safety of the building, and its destruction by fire would most likely be accompanied by the loss of the portraits that adorn the walls of the Dialectic Society, many of which could never be replaced." On July 20, 1901, the Executive Committee of the Trustees voted to lend the University, from the Francis Jones Smith Fund, the sum of $500 "to enlarge the electric plant," part of the enlargement furnishing "a home for the University Press." During the eight years' sojourn in New West, the foremen of the University Press, in succession, were: Charles Abernethy, later member of Congress; Baylus Cade, a retired Baptist minister from Virginia; Zachariah T. Broughton, brother of the distinguished Baptist educator of Raleigh, Rev. Needham Broughton; William Henry Thompson, who founded the *Chapel Hill News;* Eric A. Abernethy, later University Physician; Claude Abernethy, later a physician of Raleigh; Evander McIver, later a physician of Jonesboro; and Isham King, subsequently a member of the Durham printing firm of Christian and King.[23] Faculty supervisors of the first University Press were: F. P. Venable, J. W. Gore, H. F. Linscott, Walter D. Toy, Collier Cobb, and Samuel May.

To house the University Press, which was taken over by the University in 1901, a one-storey brick building, with one large room and a smaller one with lower floor level, was erected just east of the old Power Plant somewhere within the present site of the east wing of Phillips Hall, the University Filter Plant, and the Public Health Laboratory. Professors Gore and Cobb were in charge of the establishment, the latter being active manager. For several years the press was carried on by professional printers, after which it was conducted exclusively by students

23. Consult Louis R. Wilson, *Library Resources and the Philological Club, 1901-1932* (Chapel Hill, 1943), pp. 16-17, and "Foreword," *Books from Chapel Hill* (University of North Carolina Press, 1946); *The Daily Tar Heel,* fiftieth anniversary issue, February 23, 1947; editorial by Collier Cobb, *U.N.C.M.,* April, 1893, pp. 221-22; "University Press," editorial in Golden Jubilee Double Number, *U.N.C.M.,* March-April, 1894, p. 360; *T. M., 1898-1904,* p. 293; *E. C. T. M.,* 1898-1904, July 20, 1901, p. 299; R. W. Madry, "University Printshop falls before Progress," *News and Observer* (Raleigh), July 26, 1925. For helpful information regarding the first University Press, and of the staff of thirteen, of which she was a member, the writer is indebted to Mrs. Samuel J. Brockwell (*née* Fannie Suggs) of Chapel Hill.

until August, 1913, when Zebulon V. Council, one of the founders of the *Durham Morning Herald* and an expert printer and journalist, leased the press from the University and took charge. "In one corner," says Dr. J. Burton Linker, now Professor of Mathematics in this institution, who worked there for four years (1914-1918), "sat the old Babcock cylinder press, and nearby was a small job press. The motor power to run these presses was furnished by a small and not very reliable steam engine using live steam from the adjacent power plant. This steam engine was far from silent; and when it was running and accompanied by the antiquated cylinder press the passer-by on Cameron Avenue did not need to be told that *The Tar Heel* had gone to press."

In characteristic style, Professor Oscar J. Coffin, head of the School of Journalism here, amusingly describes conditions during his college days (1905-1909):

There were two cases of 11-point type for the *Tar Heel*, some long primer for the *Carolina Magazine*, a case or so of German type with umlauts and an equal amount of French accented. Well do I recall the two cases of 10-point italics from which I drew names of bones in a syllabus prepared by Dr. Charles Mangum. There was Greek type, too, for examination questions—I recall nobody in my day save Herb Gunter and one tramp printer who could handle it. I never reached a height beyond that one syllabus, printed in 22-em measure and the *Tar Heel* in 13 ems and next to no thin spaces for the "point."

We printers were paid by the manager by the 1,000 ems. . . . The chairman of the board of directors in my day was Professor Collier Cobb, who dropped by ever and anon—in his perpetual good humor so far as I ever heard save for one news-story written by me as editor of the *Tar Heel* and set up into type by me as compositor, which he pied and for whose distribution he later paid at the suggestion of manager C. W. Gunter.

A good printer, such as the Gunter boys, Isham King, afterwards of Christian and King, S. R. Winters, and Nixon Plummer, later Washington correspondents, and A. L. M. (Lee) Wiggins, recently president of the American Bankers Association, made perhaps as much as thirty cents an hour and on "fat takes" maybe as high as thirty-five or forty cents. But run-of-the-mill compositors like me were hard put to it to realize fifteen cents for sixty minutes of hard labor.

Many students owe their college education to this print shop for providing a means of earning their expenses as they studied at the University. For example, Dr. W. Critz George, now Professor of Anatomy, School of Medicine here, says: "I virtually supported myself by work at the print shop during my first three years in the University. During my senior year I was editor-in-chief of the *University Magazine* and did not have much time that I could devote to remunerative employment. However, some months I not only assembled the copy for the *Magazine* but assisted with setting the type, read the proof, corrected the type, ran it through the press and occasionally helped with mailing it to the subscribers." Another member of the Faculty, Dr. Preston H. Epps, now Professor of Greek here, ran the press, especially the small one; and amusingly relates: "No one of us working there could arrange the plates for any small pamphlet or the like in the larger frame so that when the 24 pages were printed on the large sheet they would be in numerical order when it was folded, except one old printer. And he could arrange them correctly even when he was so inebriated, as he frequently was, that we would have to support him while he did it."

From interesting reminiscences written for this work by A. L. M. Wiggins, class of 1913, manager of the University Print Shop for three years (1911-1913), and now Under Secretary of the United States Treasury, some passages are quoted:

"In the fall of 1912, when we undertook to start the engine for the first time that fall, it was impossible to get it to go. We finally decided that the gasoline tank out in the yard that fed the engine had become filled with water during the summer. We, therefore, pumped it out on the ground. Fortunately, Mr. Charles T. Woollen, Business Manager of the University, was present and supervised the pumping out. We then undertook to make a test to determine whether the liquid was gasoline or water by putting some of the liquid on a shingle, to which I applied a match. It failed to burn and this confirmed our opinion that it was water. In throwing the burning match to one side, however, it landed in a pool of the liquid, with the result of an immediate explosion, which set fire to the eaves of the buildings

—the Print Shop and the Power House. The Fire Department was called out and before the flames were extinguished, there was a damage of something over $2,000 to the building. . . .

"In those days, there were many tramp printers. It was an unwritten rule than any tramp printer who appeared in a print shop must be given a job. It was also the code that they were to be paid in cash every night when they left. The reason being that one never knew whether the tramp printer would turn up the following day or not. . . .

"A tramp printer turned up one day, unshaven and disreputable looking. His bleary eyes told the story—as was usual with tramp printers. I was impressed by his courtly manner and rich English accent. He was given a job. He had nothing to say, but answered all inquiries in monosyllables.

"After two or three days, he became a little more friendly and I made an interesting discovery. He was an Englishman and a graduate of Oxford University. He had been an actor on the stage in London. He was a Shakespearean scholar and a man of wide cultural knowledge. He was a tramp at heart. For many years he had roamed the world with circuses and at odd times followed the trade of printer.

"One afternoon after the work was over, a few of us drew him out and under our encouragement and request, he played a number of scenes from Shakespeare, taking all the parts. It was an electrifying performance with impeccable diction. He went through scene after scene of Shakespearean plays, casting himself into the different characters. Following this, he quoted many of the classics of poetry with dramatic fervor.

"One morning he failed to return. He had responded to the call of the tramp that was in his heart."[24]

When the east wing was added to Phillips Hall in 1925, the shop was moved to the Kluttz Building on Franklin Street; and has since, as his own business, been conducted by Mr. Council there, and later at his present location in the basement of the Strowd Building. Meantime the University authorities, who had failed to supply the University Press with adequate machinery,

24. A. L. M. Wiggins, Washington, D. C., May 5, 1947, to the author.

equipment, and type, discovered that the volume of publication had increased beyond the capacity of the press's facilities. "Confronted with the necessity of issuing its publications in more attractive formats than could be insured through the printery, which was operated principally by a supervising printer with the aid of student assistants," writes Dr. Louis R. Wilson, "the University placed many of its publications in the hands of printers located in the State and, in 1922, provided for the establishment of the University of North Carolina Press."[25]

In conclusion, it is desirable to list a considerable number of structures belonging to the University which are located either on or near the Campus. Outside the scope of the present work are the Morehead Planetarium, the two new dormitories now in process of construction, and the twenty-eight wooden buildings now going up all over the Campus, to provide desperately needed offices and classrooms necessitated by the large influx of new students, principally G. I.'s. The latter buildings are dismantled structures from Camp Forrest, Tullahoma, Tennessee, which were transported to Chapel Hill and are being put up at Government expense for the use of the University for two years without rental charge.

In order here are comments on several of the structures owned by the University. The Puckett house, which stands on the north side of Franklin Street and faces the entrance of Battle Lane, is the residence of Chancellor R. B. House and family. The lot on which the house stands was bought by one Puckett from John Craig in 1817. Professor Denison Olmsted purchased

25. Louis R. Wilson, "Foreword," *Books from Chapel Hill*. After the establishment of the University of North Carolina Press in 1922, the name "University Press," which the printshop had borne for ten years, was changed to "University Printery." From 1912-1913 on, because of the inferior facilities of the "University Press," a number of the University's publications were printed elsewhere—Durham, Raleigh, Baltimore, Menasha, and, in the case of one doctoral dissertation, Heidelberg—although bearing the imprint "The University Press." During the years 1918-1922 Dr. Wilson wrote a number of editorials in the *Alumni Review* vigorously advocating the establishment of a University Press. Assistance in preparing this account of the printery, officially entitled the University Press, was obtained from R. W. Madry, Oscar J. Coffin, Zebulon V. Council, J. Burton Linker, W. Critz George, Preston H. Epps, and A. L. M. Wiggins.

the lot, and probably a house which had been erected upon it, in 1820; and two years later, on leaving the University to accept a position at Yale, he sold it to the University. In 1934-1935 this residence was reconditioned at a cost of $4,000; and repairs during the period 1936-1939 cost $1,088. The Archer House, used as a woman's dormitory and located on the east side of Columbia Street almost midway of the block, was purchased at a cost of $16,800 of Mrs. F. G. Archer by the University in 1921, and renovated in 1924 at a cost of $22,800. The Health Office, located in the northwest corner of the Campus, was erected by the D. K. E. fraternity in the early 1890's and purchased by the University some thirty years later (1923).

Below is given an official list of structures, chiefly residences, now (March, 1947) owned by the University, in which are included several of the buildings already mentioned and described. These buildings are listed as "University Rental Property."

TYPE OF BUILDING	ADDRESS
Telephone Exchange Building	207 E. Rosemary St.
University Service Plants Building	134 E. Franklin St.
University Service Plants Building	136 E. Franklin St.
Residence	118 University Dr.
Residence	508 Pittsboro St.
Residence	113 University Dr.
Residence	115 W. University Dr.
Residence	505 Pittsboro St.
Residence	200 Wilson Court
Residence	202 Wilson Court
Residence	206 Wilson Court
Residence	208 Wilson Court
Residence	210 Wilson Court
Residence	212 Wilson Court
Residence	503 Cameron Ave.
Residence	412 E. Rosemary St.
Residence	500 E. Rosemary St.
Residence	120 S. Boundary St.
Residence	118 S. Boundary St.
Residence	524 Park Place
Residence	522 Hooper Lane

TYPE OF BUILDING	ADDRESS
Residence	601 Park Place
Residence	603 Park Place
Residence	607 Park Place
Residence	611 Park Place
Residence	605 Park Place
Residence	113 Park Place
Fraternity House	Frat Row (Evergreen House)
House used as storage space	House back of Fowler's Food Store
Residence	219 Pittsboro St.
Residence	215 W. University Dr.
Residence	509 North St.
Residence	410 E. Franklin St.
Residence	611 E. Franklin St.
Residence	405 Pittsboro St.

The impact of World War II upon the University and the coming of a Pre-Flight School to Chapel Hill are recorded in the erection of a number of buildings upon the Campus. These structures have now become an integral part of the University plant. They are identified with the Pre-Flight School, and R. O. T. C. and V-12 programs.

Pre-Flight training for Naval Aviation is the brain child of Captain Tom Hamilton. In 1941, prior to the entrance of this country into World War II, the decision was made by the Navy Department that a new type of training was necessary for Navy Fliers.[26] In the spring of 1942 four Pre-Flight Schools were

26. One major division of the Pre-Flight training program for Naval Aviation was designated a Pre-Flight Area. This Area was planned to have four major divisions:
1. Academic, dealing with mathematics, navigation, naval history, plane recognition, and allied subjects.
2. Military conduct, close order drill, ordnance.
3. Physical training in swimming, boxing, wrestling, hand-to-hand, gymnastics and tumbling, mass exercise and physical fitness testing.
4. Sports program, competition by platoons and battalions in all sports that constitute the physical training program.
The purpose of this training area was to make men physically fit, develop endurance, aggressiveness and confidence through competition and thus

established by the Navy Department. The University of North Carolina was selected as the location for one of these schools, both because of the admirable facilities and the rationale for the choice advanced by Controller W. D. Carmichael, Jr. It was agreed that the University would supply facilities for housing and feeding and a program for 1,875 Navy Pre-Flight cadets. This made necessary the renovation, at heavy cost, of ten dormitories in the upper and lower quadrangles, additions to Lenoir Dining Hall and the Gymnasium, and the building of a new hospital, Navy Hall, and a new athletic field. The University of North Carolina made a great constructive contribution to the conduct of World War II through the ability to supply adequate facilities and personnel for assisting in the task of implementing the Navy Pre-Flight program.

The United States Navy also maintained on the Campus R. O. T. C. and V-12 units. Buildings, both permanent and temporary, were erected to afford facilities for the execution of these programs.

Below are listed the principal structures erected upon the Campus for aiding in the effective conduct of the war:

Barracks 1 and 2, 1942; Navy Hall, used as social quarters for cadets, containing 157,130 cubic feet with 7,940 square feet of floor space, 1942, which now bears the name of the Navy Hall Monogram Club; Naval R.O.T.C. Armory, containing 683,100 cubic feet with 15,930 square feet of floor space, Archie Davis, architect, 1942; Canteen ("Scuttlebut"), containing 7,300 cubic feet with 500 square feet of floor space, Archie Davis, architect, 1943; Infirmary, since taken over by the University as college

---

give them command of the fundamental tools that make pilots. Personnel for conducting the program was trained in a school of four weeks duration; four classes were trained at Annapolis and eleven at the University of North Carolina. The men admitted to the school were well trained experts from the schools and colleges of the United States. The Navy Pre-Flight program, hitherto carried on as an extra phase of training, is the first direct attempt to relate, as an integral part of a program, athletics and physical education to the training of men for military service.

For the above data the writer is largely indebted to Professor Guy B. Phillips who served efficiently during World War II as Director of the College for War Training here.

infirmary, containing 445,800 cubic feet with 34,360 square feet of floor space, Atwood and Weeks, architectural firm, 1942.[27]

The estimated value of all University property, as of June 31, 1945, is $15,520,840. All capital additions to the University plant since that date, including buildings formerly owned by the United States Navy, new buildings and services, bring the over-all estimated value of University property, as of April 1, 1947, to the figure $17,000,000.[28]

27. The data regarding the Naval Pre-Flight School, Naval R. O. T. C., and V-12 program were furnished by Professor Guy B. Phillips and Mr. P. L. Burch.
28. These figures were supplied by Mr. L. B. Rogerson, University Research Officer.

29

COLLEGE ATHLETICS AND FACILITIES
FOR SPORTS: 1905-1945

THE MARKED GROWTH of interest in athletic sports, stimulated by the building of the handsome Bynum Gymnasium and the urgent need for additional space compelled by the organization of class teams, made the establishment of new playing fields inevitable. Through the initiative of Dr. R. B. Lawson, physical director, a spacious field known as Class Field was laid off in 1905. It covered a large part of the area known as the Upper Quadrangle of dormitories, where Mangum and Ruffin now stand. This field was used as a practice ground for class football teams; and upon this area were located six tennis courts. About this same time, 1906, Dr. Lawson secured a basketball rule book, mastered the intricacies of this superb game, and introduced it to his classes. Interest in basketball quickly spread over the Campus; and to cater to it Dr. Lawson built an outdoor court just west of Bynum Gymnasium, and started on its triumphant way here one of the finest of modern sports.

After Bynum Gymnasium was erected, the old athletic field, which had been shifted southeastward toward the Raleigh Road, was found to be too restricted. Indeed, it had long been realized that a relocation was unavoidable because of the too close proximity of the field to the college buildings. Accordingly, during the academic year 1907-1908, a new field was laid off covering somewhat the same area as, although considerably smaller than, that now covered by Emerson Field. A small wooden "grandstand" seating about 150 spectators, extremely simple in structure and far from "grand" in appearance, was erected in the northeast corner of the field. The front of the grandstand was some 60 feet behind the home plate; and as it was covered with wire netting only to the height of some 10 feet, a favorite sport for the occupants was catching foul balls which surmounted the barrier.[1] There were only rude wooden "bleachers,"

1. This field with grandstand and the class field with 6 tennis courts appear clearly on the photogravure published by W. T. Littig & Co., 15

with a parallel wooden fence in front, in addition to the small grandstand, for the seating of spectators; and the throng along the fence was usually at least three deep.

The growth in number of intercollegiate contests, the increasing desire to have these contests on the home grounds of the contestants, and the building of good roads which gave rise to a constantly enlarging throng of spectators, all combined to stress the need for an athletic stadium at Chapel Hill. So eager were the students for a stadium that the graduating class, at the 1912 Commencement, contrary to the usual custom of making a gift at the time, voluntarily voted upon themselves a tax of $5 per man for four consecutive years, the total to be added to other sums, raised in this or other manner, for the creation of a suitable and worthy athletic park. Professor M. C. S. Noble interested himself in the matter of realizing the students' desires; and it was rumored that a native of Chapel Hill, who had amassed a fortune as the "Bromo Seltzer King," was lending a sympathetic ear to student yearning. On January 26, 1915, President Edward Kidder Graham announced, amid clamors of enthusiasm, that Captain Isaac Emerson, '79, of Baltimore, had provided funds for a new athletic field, to be built during the coming year. All shared President Graham's expressed view that this handsome gift would meet a great need and evoke universal satisfaction. On January 27, 1916, President Graham announced the completion of the new athletic park, to be called Emerson Field, for the accommodation of baseball, football, and track athletics. The new field measured 600 by 250 feet. A 10-foot wooden fence, later replaced by a post and woven wire fence reinforced by a thick hedge, enclosed a football field, a baseball field, and a quarter-mile running track, 22 feet wide. There were two concrete stands, each 172 feet long, the two accommodating a total of 3,000 spectators. Captain Emerson's gift was the sum of $25,-000; and the field and stands then appeared ample in proportions

---

William Street, New York, in 1907. See reproduction in this book. This photogravure is reproduced in the college annual, *Yackety Yack*, 1908, between pages 134 and 135. In his report to the Trustees, October 12, 1908, President Venable states that during the preceding year a new athletic field had been added, at the cost of $1,000, and that more tennis courts had been built. Battle, II, 684.

to meet all reasonable needs. The stands were originally skeleton structures, supported by concrete pillars, but shortly after erection, the eastern stand was fitted out with showers and lockers for both home and visiting teams. Five years later the west stand also was bricked in, providing showers, toilets, and dressing equipment rooms, as well as a ticket office. Prior to this time, the football players dressed at Bynum Gymnasium. With the steady increase in crowds from year to year, it became necessary to erect large temporary wooden stands, one on the south side, and one at each end of the football field. The straightaway part of the cinder track, it is interesting to recall, extended beyond the wooden enclosure, the starting point for races being about twenty feet south of the southwest corner of Bingham Hall.[2]

For the expansion and development program, covering the years 1923-1924, the legislature provided the sum of $1,668,000. Among the items provided for were: $50,000, earmarked for exercise and recreation grounds; and $40,000 for a physical training building.[3] In the report of expenditures by the Building Committee, January, 1924, occur the following: Indoor Athletic Court, $54,482.45; Tennis Courts, $16,611.47; New Athletic Field, $3,937.78; and Playing Field, $2,302.30. The "new athletic field" which had already been roughly cleared and used by Freshman baseball and football teams in the early twenties, was known as Freshman Field. This covered an area east of Emerson Field, north of the Raleigh highway, west of the town cemetery, and south of the present site of Alexander Hall. This site was the logical choice for such a field as it lies in the southeastern sector, and is adjacent to both Emerson Field and to the then prospective site of a great gymnasium. This field was put in first-class condition, and used by Freshman teams until 1938, when it was turned over to the women for their use in athletic sports. Since 1942, with the coming of the Pre-Flight School, it has borne the name Alexander Field, in conformity with the terminology employed by the Navy, because of its proximity to Alexander Hall. It has served as an intramural field for both civilian and Navy students. Two new dormitories for men are

2. *T. M.*, 1904-1916, pp. 486, 527; Link, p. 163.
3. *T. M.*, 1917-1924, p. 447.

now being constructed on this field. In 1923 the "indoor athletic court," because of the materials used in its construction slangily termed by the students the "Tin Can," was purchased from the Blard-Knox Company of Pittsburgh, Pennsylvania. A standard industrial type building, of steel framework and sheet metal exterior, this structure is 300 feet by 110 feet. Supporting columns inside allow 60 feet of clear space down the center, and are spaced 25 feet from either outside wall. From 1923 until 1938 this building served as the University's main arena for indoor sports. The clear space down the center provided for basketball courts, wrestling area, boxing rings, and an indoor tennis court. Space back of the columns was utilized for an indoor track; and when important matches and contests were held, temporary portable stands were erected for spectators.[4] In the business manager's report for 1923-1924, the construction of an additional recreational field, an indoor field, and forty tennis courts are mentioned as accomplished facts.[5]

Emerson Field perfectly illustrates the inability, indeed futility, of attempting to make adequate provision for the internal stresses and expansive pressure of the contemporary university. Thrown open for football play in the autumn of 1916, Emerson Field was soon found entirely incapable of meeting the demands of the sports-loving public. "By 1921 the number of spectators at the football games exhausted the capacity of all wooden stands that could be built in convenient range of the field, and thereafter thousands of prospective spectators had to be turned away." Five years later, necessity for action became imperative.

Analysis of the situation led to the conclusion that two fields were needed: one for football and the other for baseball and track. Preliminary plans for raising funds on a large scale were discussed and outlined by eighteen alumni, who met at Washington Duke Hotel, Durham, May 24, 1926. The committee formed to present the need and a plan of action to the alumni consisted of Robert Lassiter, chairman, Foy Roberson, secretary, Kemp P. Lewis, L. P. McLendon, J. L. Morehead, and G. W.

4. Data on the University's athletic facilities, supplied by Vernon Crook (typescript).

5. *T. M.*, 1924-1930, p. 42. See Chapter 24.

Hill. This committee at once issued a prospectus of a stadium and a plan of financing it, and within three months had raised about $28,000. When the matter was brought to the attention of William Rand Kenan, Jr., who was contemplating establishing a memorial of some sort to his parents, he expressed the desire to build the stadium, while courteously deferring to the committee in regard to the original plan. His offer was immediately accepted, and on November 13, 1926, after visiting and approving the site, Mr. Kenan formally announced the gift of $275,-000 to erect a stadium of 24,000 seating capacity. In a pamphlet, issued at the time of the dedication of the Kenan Memorial Stadium, November 24, 1927, occurs the following description:

In a natural valley, about two thousand feet from the center of the campus of the University of North Carolina and just above the spot long known as the Meeting of the Waters, there is a natural amphitheatre, easily approached by paths that follow the lie of the land. The brook that flows through this valley has cut a ravine so that the floor of the stream is level and smooth and the banks rise with equal steepness on either side. . . . The object of the designers was to adapt the structure to the natural forest and stream beauty of the location.

Accordingly the brook has been led through a concrete culvert and above it the ground has been built up to form the playing field. The sides of the hills have been hollowed out to give space for the oval lines of the seat banks on either side of the field. The valley has been left open to the west and only partially closed by the field house to the east, so that its lines remain intact and blend with those of the stadium. The forest surrounding the ravine has been preserved; the stadium terrace and planting have been designed to blend with it. And the paths to the stadium wind through the forest and over bridges of stone to the brink of the valley from which, beginning at the level of the rim, the stadium drops away in smoothly curving lines to the field below.[6]

6. *Kenan Memorial Stadium* (Chapel Hill, 1927). This pamphlet includes the resolutions of the Board of Trustees, January 25, 1927, a detailed description, and the reproduction of a water-color painting of the stadium as viewed from the air. The playing field, which was built up with cinders and gravel, drained with tiling, and covered with soil, runs roughly east and west. The field house, a two-story structure of brick covered with stucco, stands at the east end of the field. At the western end is a gateway which is used, not as an entrance for spectators, but for the use of processions. The stadium was designed by Atwood and Nash, and built by T. C. Thompson and Company.

In the course of construction, it was found that the original gift of $275,000 would not cover the cost of both stadium and field house. On January 17, 1928, President Chase announced a supplementary gift by Mr. Kenan of $28,000 for an adequate field house; and one week later the Building Committee announced the completion of the Kenan Memorial Stadium.[7] The connections of Mr. Kenan's family with the founding of the University are extraordinarily close. His great-great-grandfather, James Kenan, was one of the members of the first Board of Trustees; and his great-great-grandfather on the maternal side, Christopher Barbee, donated 221 acres, or about one-fifth of the land then donated, for the Campus of the University. A graduate of the class of 1894, William Rand Kenan, Jr. was a brilliant student, a fine athlete, and a participant in all phases of college life. "By his discovery of carbide in 1893, he laid a foundation for success in chemistry, engineering, and building that was sure and rapid. . . . In railway transportation, gas lighting, water and electric power, hotel and real estate operation, he has become one of the financial and industrial leaders of his generation."[8]

The next important forward step in the development of athletic facilities, which was the culmination of long-continued efforts to develop track athletics and intramural sports, was taken during the period of 1933-1935 through the inauguration of the New Deal. Government programs and projects, designated in abbreviated style CWA, PWA, and ERA, made possible the execution of comprehensive plans for University expansion. Included in these plans were: a great physical education building, an intramural field of large proportions for practice and exercise in various forms of outdoor sport, and a field and stadium for track athletics. In 1933 work was begun on these various projects, the funds being secured with the support of the Civil Works Administration. A stadium seating 7,000 persons and a field for track athletics, on a level almost 100 feet below the Raleigh highway, were constructed to the southeast of the present site of Woollen Gymnasium, in a natural valley surrounded on south and west by dense forests of oak, pine, and hickory.

7. *T. M.*, 1924-1930, pp. 352, 356-57.
8. *Kenan Memorial Stadium.*

KESSING POOL

Commander Oliver Owen Kessing, first Commanding Officer of the
Pre-Flight School at the University, was largely responsible for the
building of this pool. Put into operation in August, 1943, it is 150 feet
long, 49 feet wide, and has a depth of 12 feet at the deepest point.

AERIAL VIEW OF KENAN MEMORIAL STADIUM

The gift of William Rand Kenan, Jr., the stadium, erected in 1927, has a seating capacity of 24,000. The field house, also the gift of Mr. Kenan, can be seen in right foreground.

The quarter-mile cinder track, with a 220-yard initial straight-away course, is 30 feet wide, and of first-class construction. With the completion of this track, the cinder track on and beyond Emerson Field, to the westward, was abandoned. Emerson Field was then reconditioned for baseball, with a new and better orientation of the diamond. On May 18, 1936, Dean of Administration R. B. House presented to the Executive Committee of the Trustees a recommendation, on the part of the Student Athletic Council, the Monogram Club, and the Faculty Advisory Committee, carrying the endorsement of President Graham and himself, that the new track field be named "Fetzer Field" in appreciation of the faithful and highly effective service, in promoting track athletics over many years (1921-1936), of Robert A. Fetzer and of his contribution to the high standards of sportsmanship on the Carolina Campus. This well-merited recognition was conferred by the Executive Committee. During this same period the projected new intramural field, south of the Raleigh Road, east of the present site of Woollen Gymnasium, and north of Fetzer Field was constructed. Both the area and the facilities have been greatly extended since the coming of the Pre-Flight School in 1942.

As early as 1924, the need for a new gymnasium to meet the rapid expansion of the student body was apparent. In the program for the following three years, presented by President Chase on September 30, 1924, one of the major objectives was a new gymnasium. In his report for 1923-1924, Business Manager Woollen declared that a physical education building was a need which must soon be met.[9] Two years later, June 24, 1926, President Chase in his report mentions four primary needs, in the following order: Library, two dormitories, gymnasium to cost $350,000, and a classroom building; and two years later again, September 18, 1928, John Sprunt Hill, speaking for the Building Committee of the Trustees, presented a program totaling $1,823,500, of which the three principal items were: a medical building, a school of education, and a physical education building, the last to cost $400,000. With each successive estimate, the figure for a gymnasium had risen until in 1928 the cost was

9. *T. M.*, 1924-1930, pp. 42, 67.

set at sixteen times the cost of the Bynum Gymnasium which was adequate, when built, for a student body of some 600. With the erection of the Tin Can, all indoor sports events were transferred thither (1924) from Bynum; but this only partially relieved the congestion. For more than a decade before the erection of Woollen Gymnasium, the pool in Bynum Gymnasium remained unused because unsanitary, there being no filters or circulating pumps. As there was no usable swimming pool in Chapel Hill, students had to seek swimming facilities in Durham or elsewhere. The balcony, constructed for an indoor race track, in time became unsafe; and although it continued to be used as a gallery for spectators, eventually it had to be condemned even for that purpose. From 1924 until its abandonment as a gymnasium, Bynum Gymnasium was used only for gymnastics and for required Freshman physical education. The construction of the intramural field and Fetzer Field solved the problem for outdoor sports; but the Tin Can was hopelessly inadequate in size to meet the needs of the student body, as well as having no heating system for winter sports.

A physical education building, more than adequate for all needs in the matter of size and facilities, and an indoor, sanitary swimming pool were needs too acute and pressing to be longer ignored. Under the zoning concept, which had never been lost sight of by the authorities concerned with athletics, it was clear that such a building must occupy a central position in relation to the University's athletics. The facilities in 1938 consisted of ten intramural fields, forty-two tennis courts, two baseball diamonds, two practice football fields, one football stadium, and one building 120 feet by 300 feet. The best location for the proposed physical education building was clearly the site chosen; and the estimated cost, without equipment, was approximately $500,000.

The means for realizing these hopes was afforded by the aid of PWA funds, supplemented by a revenue bond issue authorized by the Trustees of the University. A grant, totaling 45% of the whole cost, would be made by the national government; and the remaining 55% would be financed in some way by the University. Two major objectives were advanced, namely, to meet the requirements of the athletes and to supply adequate living accommodations for the women students. The total cost of construction of a physical education building and a women's dormitory, as submitted by Controller Woollen to the Trustees, November 6, 1936, was $629,100. As $122,000 had already been subscribed, a revenue bond issue for $225,000 would provide for the balance. This plan was adopted by the Trustees, the rate of interest being set at 4%.[10] Mr. and Mrs. James E. Millis of High Point, N. C., contributed funds to equip the gymnasium with lockers, in memory of their son, William Brooks Millis, '38.[11]

Immediately to the west of the gymnasium, and built as an integral part of it, is the swimming pool, funds for which were contributed by Mrs. Bowman Gray, Gordon Gray, and Bowman Gray, Jr., of Winston-Salem, N. C. It was given the name, the "Bowman Gray Memorial Pool" in honor of the husband and father, respectively, of the donors. The combined cost of gymnasium and swimming pool was $646,000, none of which came from state appropriation. The structure has three general units: the Head House or main front wing, the Gymnasium wing, and the pool; and is built of brick and steel. The Head House, three storeys high, measures 174 feet by 53 feet. The main gymnasium floor, of hardwood, is 250 feet long by 150 feet wide; and provides simultaneous accommodations for two basketball courts 94 feet by 40 feet, 4 basketball courts 65 feet by 45 feet, and 3 one-wall handball courts 18 feet by 34 feet. The swimming pool over-all is 206 feet 10½ inches long by 82 feet 5 inches wide and 17 feet deep. The pool itself is 55 feet by 165 feet, with a minimum depth of 3 feet and a maximum depth of 10 feet, and a capacity of 300,000 gallons of water. A charming effect is created by the tiled decks and walls, with aquamarine as the predominant color; and white tile only is used in the pool itself. The architectural firm was Atwood and Weeks of Durham, the contracting firm was the J. A. Jones Construction Company of Charlotte. On June 3, 1938, the Trustees voted

10. *T. M.*, 1931-1938, insert between pages 216 and 217. For fuller details of the financing, which do not concern us here, consult Link, pp. 257-59.
11. Link, p. 261.

that the new gymnasium be given the name "Woollen Gymnasium" in honor of Charles T. Woollen for his continued and energetic labors to make it possible.[12] The facilities afforded by the complete physical education building and swimming pool are both adequate and ample for present indoor gymnastics; and the buildings, taken as a whole, are among the finest and most substantial to be found on any university campus in the world. They symbolize the fostering care of the University's alumni for the physical well-being of the students, just as a great library typifies the concern of the State for the intellectual development of her youth.

A handsome gymnasium for women, with all adequate facilities for indoor exercise, was completed in 1943. It is located just to the south of Woollen Gymnasium. The architects were Atwood and Weeks, the contractor R. K. Steward. The building has 15,247 square feet of floor space, and contains 277.900 cubic feet. The estimated cost of the building was $84,000.

The Bowman Gray Pool, first opened in April, 1938, the Woollen Gymnasium, and the other indoor and outdoor athletic and physical education facilities, were factors largely instrumental in the selection of the University of North Carolina as the site of one of the four United States Navy Pre-Flight Schools. The first Pre-Flight cadets arrived in Chapel Hill in May, 1942; and by the following September, the peak enrollment of nearly 2,000 was reached. The Pre-Flight program placed strong emphasis on swimming as a survival activity. As many as thirty-five per cent of some incoming aviation contingents could not "swim a lick." In the elaborate training pro-

12. Consult R. A. Fetzer and Oliver K. Cornwell, "The New Gymnasium at the University of North Carolina," *The American School and University—1940* (New York, American School Publishing Corporation, 1940), 265-71; also *Proceedings of the College Physical Education Association*, Forty-Second Annual Meeting, Chicago, December 28-30, 1938, pp. 22-23. Cf. also *Alumni Review*, XXV (1936), 127; "New Gymnasium and Pool near Completion," XXVI (1937), 91, 103. The comprehensive and elaborate facilities of Woollen Gymnasium are fully detailed in these publications. The gymnasium and pool were completed and in use in September, 1938. In 1940, when the Fetzer-Cornwell article, "The New Gymnasium, etc.," appeared, the enrollment of the University of North Carolina was 3,508 students; 3,102 men, 406 women.

gram, the fundamental purpose was to give the cadet a better chance to save his life, and the lives of his comrades, in case of accident.

Early in the history of the school Commander Oliver Owen Kessing, first Commanding Officer of the Pre-Flight School here, recognized the imperative need for outdoor swimming facilities. He fathered the practical program for the school; and four months after the arrival of the first cadets, construction of the new pool was begun. It is 150 feet in length, with 7 lanes, each 7 feet wide. At the shallow end the pool has a depth of 4, and at the deep end a depth of 12, feet. Approximately 400,000 gallons of water are required to fill the pool; and the water is purified 3 times every 24 hours. The entire pool and all surrounding decks are ceramic tile. On three sides the decks are 15 feet wide; and at the deep end there is a 20-foot-wide deck.

This pool was put in operation in August, 1943. It was fittingly named by the Board of Trustees in honor of Commander Kessing, richly decorated for his activities at Tulagi, Bougainville, and Ulithi in the South Pacific, and characteristically known as "scrappy Kessing" for his fighting and hard-hitting qualities. The Kessing Pool, which is placed at an acute angle to the southern side of Woollen Gymnasium, was dedicated with appropriate ceremonies on the evening of June 22, 1945. In an appreciation of the fighting commander, Controller William D. Carmichael, Jr., observed: "All his life a man of God's great outdoors, he loves the water, the air, the sky, the sun, and the stars. . . . There is even appropriate symbolism in the pool's chlorine salt, for 'Scrappy' Kessing is the saltiest of all salts—the salt of the earth." [13]

13. See booklet, *Kessing Pool*, issued at the time of the pool's dedication, and containing articles by W. D. Carmichael, Jr. and O. K. Cornwell. Consult also the *Cloudbuster*, Vol. III, No. 40 (1945), 1; No. 41, 3. The architects of Kessing Pool were Atwood and Weeks, the contractor, Roberts Filter Company.

30

CAMPUS ARCHITECTURE: SURVEY
AND PROSPECT

I T WAS the opinion of the Committee on Grounds and Buildings that, in view of the strange and chequered architectural
evolution of the Campus, the many varying styles, the complex problems of location, and imminent vast expansion of the
University, some general study of all these factors, together with
a critical analysis of looming future issues, should be prepared
for the present volume by the gifted and artistic University
architect, Arthur C. Nash. Follows Mr. Nash's arresting and
provocative study.

"Like most of the older American institutions of learning, the
University of North Carolina has been handicapped by the lack
of a comprehensive 'Campus Plan,' yet, to be fair, we must give
the University's founding fathers credit, at least, for having
made a good start.

"Tradition has it that when the site was selected for the first
building—later to be known as 'Old East'—that building was
intended to serve only as one wing of a much more important
two-winged, central building, and that the central building with
its two wings was to face toward the East. As Dr. Kemp P.
Battle once stated (in an address entitled, "History of the Buildings of the University of North Carolina"[1]) 'just as the Capitols
at Washington and Raleigh were faced, under the influence of
orientalization.' But, as we also learn from Dr. Battle, this idea
was soon abandoned in favor of 'a quadrangle' with an open
side facing northward, 'probably at the suggestion of Dr. Caldwell and Prof. Harris, who were educated at Princeton.'

"Thus it came about that the nucleus of a formal plan—the
South Building flanked by Old East and Old West—was established upon a north-south axis. Just how Person Hall (originally
used as a chapel and actually built before Old West was com-

1. This address was delivered in Gerrard Hall on University Day,
1883.

pleted) was intended to fit into the finished composition remains a mystery to this day. A good start, however, was made toward a suitable and dignified plan; though, for many years thereafter it was not clear which was regarded as the more important direction for Campus expansion, the north-south axis or an east-west expansion along Cameron Avenue (extended) with flanking buildings casually placed, after the manner of a village street. At the end of the pre-Civil War period the 'village street' idea quite definitely was in the ascendant.

"All who draw inspiration from the history of the University's early struggle, should be grateful to the Trustees for their decision to retain this group of pioneer buildings—now happily rebuilt with fire-proof interior construction, and grateful too that the University has such an honestly expressed architectural style to fall back upon, deeply rooted as it is in the traditions of her past. Come what may in her future architectural development, she is reasonably certain that Old East, the South Building, and Old West will endure, bearing witness to the Spartan spirit of those early days, as well as to the fundamentally correct taste then current.

"In the post-Civil War period, and up to 1920, the year in which the great building expansion of the University began, not only did the east-west expansion along Cameron Avenue continue, but for the first time since 1848[2] additional construction took place on the North Campus. For, it was within that span of years that Alumni Hall, the Carnegie Library (now Hill Music Hall), and the Battle-Vance-Pettigrew dormitory group were built. Standards of taste, in architecture, were at a low ebb during the greater portion of that period. Between 1860 and 1920 most of our older American colleges and universities were blown about by every wind of architectural doctrine. Harvard, Yale, Princeton, and many of the lesser institutions of learning throughout the land have, among their buildings, ample evidence to prove it. Nor did the University of North Carolina wholly escape this blight; witness the Collegiate Gothic and grey pressed-brick intrusions upon her (Pseudo-) Classic groves!

"The year 1920 marked a turning point in the architectural

2. The date at which Old West was actually completed.

development of the University. For, in that year for the first time in the institution's history, steps were taken to eliminate the haphazard element from the location of Campus buildings, and from the style of architecture in which they were to be designed.

"A distinguished firm of architects was engaged to act as consultants; and a local architectural and engineering organization was installed, with an office on the Campus.[3] These men, at that time, were faced with at least three possible solutions of the 'expansion problem':

1. To develop the North Campus, while retaining all of the existing buildings.

2. To develop the North Campus after 'scrapping' certain of its existing buildings that were admittedly out of key in design, or out of position with regard to accepted standards of architectural grouping.

3. To abandon all idea of expansion in the North Campus area, and to make a fresh start, *southward*.

Solution No. 1 could have resulted in little better than a mongrel-appearing compromise. Solution No. 2 was wrecked upon a solid rock of opposition to the razing of *any* building that could possibly be utilized. Solution No. 3, offering as it did untrammeled space for expansion, was the one selected.

"Here was an opportunity, at last, for the University to develop, and, it is to be hoped complete, at least one centrally situated Campus area according to a previously conceived, orderly design in plan and in elevation. Apparently, all concerned agreed that the new buildings in the South Campus area should conform to the 'Colonial' style. So, for the first time in its history, the University consciously adopted an 'official' style of architecture for its future buildings. These decisions and this South Campus Plan now hold promise for a greater measure of unity of design in the University's future quadrangles and other groups of buildings.

"As the term 'Colonial' as applied to architecture is, at best, rather vague, it would be well for me to make clear what I

3. McKim, Mead, and White, of New York, consulting architects; the T. C. Atwood Organization installed, locally, as architects and engineers.

mean it to include, in the course of this discussion of Campus architecture. One generally accepted definition of 'Colonial' is: 'Architecture such as prevailed in the British settlements of North America previous to the Revolution. It was chiefly a modification of the English Georgian style.' There is still another way in which the term 'Colonial Architecture' currently is used by architects and by the general public; that is, to make it include not only exact replicas of original buildings dating from that period, but, also, to have it include buildings whose only claim to the 'Colonial' label is that they have their roots, so to speak, in Colonial soil; or, are carried out, with more or less success, in the Colonial tradition. This latter definition is one that I make use of in the present discussion. I make it inclusive, not only of buildings constructed within the strictly Colonial time-bracket, but, also, of post-Revolution buildings of the so-called 'Late Colonial' or 'Greek Revival' period; and even of modern buildings carried out in a Colonial manner. Talbot Hamlin, in his *The American Spirit in Architecture*, refers to one particularly successful modern design as 'a modern example of Colonial Re-Creation.'

"It is generally recognized that, because of the practical requirements of modern collegiate buildings, it is unreasonable to expect that literal copies of Colonial originals could adequately meet those requirements. In those days, there were no gymnasium buildings, no highly specialized laboratory buildings, no library buildings (having anything like the complex requirements of such buildings today); and the scientific lighting of classroom buildings was unheard of. Therefore, where the Colonial style is adopted for the buildings of a modern university, literal copying of old models must, to a large extent, give way to a re-interpretation, or 're-creation' of that kind of architecture.

"Under the influence of McKim, Mead, and White, the University's Consulting Architects, development of the Campus Plan took an important step forward. It was now assured of a dominant central motive—the cross-shaped South Campus 'Quadrangle'—carried out with dignity, and with grace of architectural composition. About this central feature, smaller groups or quadrangles could, in future, take their appropriate places without detracting from it. We have already seen several dormitory groups successfully placed, as 'satellites' to this central motive; and several groups of other kinds started, or projected.

"So far, so good. However, judging by the amount of expansion that has taken place in other state universities, it is fair to assume that the University of North Carolina will in time cover vastly more territory than at present. To keep pace with such a huge prospective expansion, the Plan should have an even more extended central motive. Architecturally, it would be possible to develop one along the present north-south axis, reaching all the way from Franklin Street to the woods behind the Library, in point of size capable of holding its own, no matter how great the ultimate over-all expansion of the University Plan might be.

"It can, quite plausibly, be said that the North and South Campus areas, as they are at present planned, actually *do form* such a continuous central feature. To my way of thinking, this is but partly true. For, as long as the North Campus remains in its present sub-standard condition, no true architectural unity or harmony with the more carefully planned South Campus will exist. In other words, in order to make this extended motive effective, the North Campus must be re-planned—particularly so in its Mid-Section. After all, the North Campus is not the University's back yard. It is, or should be its *front yard;* and, as such, should be shown as much honor and respect, if not more, than any other portion of the Campus.

"In connection with the Franklin Street front of the North Campus, which actually is the 'front entrance' to the University grounds, it might be well to remember that, when the Trustees approved the design and the site of the Graham Memorial Building, it was with the understanding that ultimately the Battle-Vance-Pettigrew dormitory group was to be replaced by a building exactly matching the (fully completed) Graham Memorial. Their object, of course, was to obtain a balanced architectural effect at this gateway to the University.

"In other words, the official plan, as approved by the Trustees calls for a building similar in design, symmetrically placed opposite the Graham Memorial. Combined with a certain amount of re-vamping of present grades, the completion of these twin buildings at the 'portal' of the University ought considerably to improve the architectural 'morale' of the whole North Campus.

"Even though the Franklin Street front were remodelled to form a balanced composition, the Mid-Section would still remain as an unsolved problem. For over twenty years, this section combined with Old East, Old West, and the South Building, has served the purpose of a sort of historical museum of the University's architecture. As such, it undoubtedly gave satisfaction to many of the older alumni, who in undergraduate days had acquired a quite understandable sentiment for the North Campus, just as it was, regardless of any of its architectural shortcomings. But, from a perspective of over twenty years, and at a time when the University begins to feel the need of a more intensive use of this space, perhaps what we formerly took for sentiment, may turn out to have been little else than sentimentality!

"After all, have we not, here, a double duty; full measure of respect for the past, as well as responsibility in regard to the future? Posterity may be more lenient toward mistakes made through ignorance, than toward those which, in a more architecturally enlightened period, were caused by a sort of oversentimental conservatism. The feeling that the middle portion of the North Campus could greatly benefit by remodelling is by no means confined to the present. There is evidence that, over 25 years ago, efforts were made in that direction.

"Shortly before the 1920 Expansion—if I am informed correctly—one or more sketch-plans had been made for such remodelling; and ingenious efforts at unifying the divergent architectural styles in that area were evolved. But, the task appeared so hopeless, due to the fact that no demolition of old buildings was, at that time, even to be thought of, that, when McKim, Mead, and White appeared on the scene, they gave up any attempt to expand in that direction.

"Ingenious compromises can still be worked out for the unification of that part of the Campus; but, it is to be hoped that nothing whatever will be attempted there, until such time as it can be carried out in an untrammeled and proper way. That part of the University grounds is far too important to the successful development of the 'Campus Plan' to be cluttered with make-shifts or compromises! It will take courage to perform the major surgery which that Mid-Section of the North Campus requires for its future architectural health. When that pitch of courage has been attained—and I have faith that it will be—the best available architectural talent should be called in, to re-plan that area in keeping both with old Campus tradition and with existing practical needs.[4]

"In connection with such re-study, attention might appropriately be given to the east and west flanking areas, where, as is well known, there is a considerable amount of wasted space. Almost certainly, efficient planning of this space would require the removal of one or more obsolescent buildings.

"Any future planning must be vitally concerned with questions of 'zoning.' In earlier days, when the plan was small, zoning though desirable was not strictly necessary. Now, however, in this time of great expansion, the need for the grouping of buildings into zones has become acute. Credit for introducing the zoning theory here, is, in large measure, due to Dr. John M. Booker, who for many years has given it his untiring support. That his efforts have already borne fruit is evidenced by the fact that there are now well defined zones for men's dormitories, women's dormitories, and athletic activities; and, (partially developed or in prospect) zones for Arts and Letters, Science, and Fine Arts. The group assigned to Arts and Letters appropriately will be housed in buildings near the Library. The Science Zone— inclusive of a proposed 'Science Quadrangle' in the South-West

4. Though Person Hall, which is but one storey in height and presents only a narrow facade towards the central North Campus area, would hardly be adequate as a center motive for this Mid-Section, it could conceivably *be moved southward* a short distance, and then be made to serve as a wing of a much more important center building (a balancing wing, like Person Hall to be added at the other end). In this way that valuable "heirloom," Person Hall, could be retained; and, it might be that its type of architectural detail could be taken as the keynote for the new buildings above mentioned. This suggestion is offered merely as an illustration of the kind of radical remodelling that I have in mind. It is not intended to be endorsed as my preferred solution of this problem. Further study would doubtless bring to light several solutions equally as good or much better.

Campus area—will extend all the way to the Public Health-Medical School group, and will include this at one end, as well as Phillips Hall at the other. Various other zones and sub-zones will, of course, evolve as time goes on. May the zoning tradition, started so successfully by Dr. Booker, be carried on with the enthusiasm it so well deserves!

"By expanding along pre-established lines, the University now has an excellent opportunity to avoid much of the confusion that characterized its growth in the past, and to thus insure for itself an orderly architectural future. In connection with such future growth, I should venture to place first in order of importance, the *completion of the unbuilt portions* of the cross-shaped South Campus group accurately to match the corresponding *completed portions*. Second in importance, I should place *official recognition* (if this might be possible) of the fact that the North Campus group—hitherto grossly 'mis-planned'— *must be re-planned* in keeping with the dignity and honor of its position as the *main approach to the University grounds*. It does not make much difference when the actual remodelling takes place, provided that a carefully studied plan is prepared in advance—as a safeguard against a possible spur-of-the-moment decision to place new construction there, regardless of its effect upon the over-all composition. Upon these two fundamentals, above mentioned, rests the ultimate success of the Campus Plan, involving as it does a *unified dominant central motive* about which *satellite groups* are to be placed, in appropriate zones.

"Space does not permit of a complete survey of future projects for which provision has been made or soon will be made on the expanding plan; but I will comment briefly upon a few: All indications point to the approaching need of additional dormitories for women, as well as for men. As 'elbow room' for women's dormitories appears to be rather more limited, let us consider these first. Several years ago, plans were completed for nearly doubling the present capacity of Spencer Hall; therefore, the carrying out of those plans to completion would seem to be a logical first step. After that, what?

"It has recently been suggested that the University-owned land between the Episcopal Church property and the Graham

Memorial Building could appropriately be used for a further expansion of women's dormitories, and that in connection with such expansion, the present Graham Memorial[5] itself could be turned over to the women students as a combined refectory and 'social center.' This arrangement would work out reasonably from a zoning point of view, and also would offer an excellent opportunity for obtaining the most practical use from the Graham Memorial.

"As to additional men's dormitories, a group of three has been planned to occupy the present Women's Athletic Field; and one of these, Alexander Dormitory, has already been constructed. Several other sites are currently under discussion, some of which are of a decidedly controversial nature. This is mainly due to the fact that the selection of any one of those sites would involve the sacrifice of land already serving other important activities or forming an essential part of the Campus landscaping design. The beautiful pine-clad ridge lying north-eastward of the Kenan Stadium would seem to fall into the latter category. While, practically speaking, much can be said in favor of that site, there is little doubt that the presence of dormitories in that grove would have an adverse effect upon the appearance of the Stadium, one of whose principal claims to distinction is its *unobstructed* sylvan setting.

"When the remaining two dormitories, planned for the Women's Athletic Field site, have been completed, a new athletic field for women will become a pressing need—and probably an up-to-date field house into the bargain. New buildings will undoubtedly be required in connection with possible expansion of the Medical and Public Health Departments. The southwest Campus development will involve, first, the transfer of the present Filter Plant, University Carpenter Shop, etc., to new off-campus sites; and then extensive re-grading of that area by way of preparation for the future 'Science Quadrangle' in accordance with the tentative block-plan which has already been made for that project. Until the necessary detailed study has been given to the plan requirements of individual buildings,

5. In its completed form with extensions at either end, as called for in the original plans for this building.

this block-plan will be more useful as a guide, than as a crystallized idea. In fact, an official plan for the University's future growth can best be regarded as a sort of 'Architectural Constitution'—subject to amendments now and then; but of value chiefly as a stabilizing influence, and as a valuable brake upon popular fads and fancies, as they come and go.

"In view of the widespread interest in the architectural style of the University buildings, a short discussion of this subject might be in order.

"One significant fact that we must not lose sight of is that 'The original buildings, unostentatious though they are, were designed in the Colonial manner.' The chances are that there was no debate about it whatever. That was the prevailing architectural idiom of the time, and it was probably followed quite as a matter of course.

"Owing to the almost total lack of architectural embellishments, such as columns, pilasters, ornamental cornices, doorway enrichments, etc., a satisfactory 'sub-classification' of the architectural style of the older buildings is hardly possible. But, in general terms it can be said that contemporaneous, as they are, with such well-known architects of the late eighteenth and early nineteenth centuries as Jefferson, Latrobe, Thornton, Hoban, and Mills, they are definitely more in key with the work of these men than, for example, with the work of Sir Christopher Wren, whose influence has left such a lasting impression upon the architecture of Williamsburg; in other words, they are more in sympathy with late eighteenth and early nineteenth century Colonial than with that of the seventeenth century. The 'Greek Temple' type of building, at present occupied by the Playmakers, is more easily classified, for it shows well-marked characteristics of the so-called 'Greek Revival' period. The fluted columns of its portico are surmounted by carved wooden capitals, in which Indian corn and wheat replace the traditional Greek acanthus leaf motive. They resemble similar freely interpreted column capitals which were designed by Latrobe for use in the interior embellishment of the north wing of the United States Capitol. In a letter written by Latrobe to Thomas Jefferson, November

5, 1816, in reference to these capitals he describes them as 'approaching the Corinthian order and retaining the simplicity of the Clepsydra or Temple of the Winds.' So, we have an interesting connection between these North Carolinian capitals and ancient Greece, via Benjamin Latrobe and the U. S. Capitol.

"When, therefore, we are looking for suitable 'source material' upon which to base present and future Campus architectural detail, the work of these late eighteenth and early nineteenth century architects would appear to be logically appropriate for this purpose. McKim, Mead, and White in their more conspicuous buildings—such as Manning Hall and the new University Library—showed themselves definitely in sympathy with such sources of Colonial Style. On the other hand, their typical classroom buildings, such as Saunders, Murphey, etc., have been designed in a more 'free' interpretation of Colonial. This may well have been due to the rather specialized nature of the plan requirements, which in addition to a normal quota of classrooms called for an unusual number of narrow 'studies' or offices. As this necessitated a correspondingly large number of narrow windows, definitely out of line with Colonial precedent, a less conventional Colonial design for these buildings resulted, quite logically.

"Elsewhere than within the South Campus it would be my hope that, for source material we should stick to eighteenth century (preferably the latter half) and to the Late Colonial, or Greek Revival referred to above. To introduce more strongly-divergent Colonial styles such as 'Williamsburg' into the assorted Campus styles would seem to be inviting more of confusion than now exists. Besides, if Williamsburg models were followed a false impression might thus be given that the founding of the University took place in a much earlier period than actually was the case.

"For off-Campus buildings, or groups, this criticism need not apply, but, when all is said and done, does it not seem rather inappropriate—even for the town of Chapel Hill—to 'go Williamsburg,' when there are such worthy North Carolinian models to follow, among certain of the old buildings of Hillsboro and Newbern? Stony Brook, Long Island, now very much in the

LOOKING EAST ALONG CAMERON AVENUE

At left, old well and Old East; at right, South Building, with Playmakers
Theatre and Carr Building in background.

LOOKING WEST ALONG CAMERON AVENUE

Left foreground, the Playmakers Theatre; left background, South Building; right foreground, Old East.

SOUTH QUADRANGLE, LOOKING NORTH FROM THE LIBRARY

Left, South Building in distance. Right foreground, Bingham Hall, with Murphey Hall beyond.

VIEW OF THE CAMPUS, LOOKING SOUTH ACROSS NORTH QUADRANGLE

At left, Old East; centre background, South Building, the old well, with Gerrard Hall at right.

public eye, has set an excellent example by basing our Colonial 'restoration' upon regional Long Island tradition.

"In spite of the fact that Colonial is at present generally recognized as the logical and natural style for buildings on the University of North Carolina Campus, we begin to hear murmurings against 'slavish' adherence to any style merely because it happens to be 'traditional'! 'Why not be modernistic, up-to-date, "functional"?'[6] 'Why not introduce at least a few examples of 'Modern' style into the Campus groups, and thereby obtain variety and contrast instead of a stodgy monotony of red brick and Indiana limestone?' On the face of it, this is a natural enough series of questions. And it is perfectly true that as the building program expands, there is *real danger* of an effect of monotony. In all sincerity, when I advocate adherence to Colonial tradition in the designing of these buildings, I am not standing up for monotony. I recognize it to be a danger—a very real threat; and one that must be met and overcome by all architects who, in future, design the University's buildings. It is true that monotony can be avoided by the mere trick of introducing an assortment of different styles. Monotony of effect could thus be avoided; but incoherence and inharmony would occupy its place. Unity would have been sacrificed; and unity is admitted to be a basic requirement of good architecture.

"Fortunately, a wide and pleasing variety exists in historic Colonial designs of buildings—in the use of materials, in the choice of mouldings, characteristic roof lines, proportion and shape of windows, etc. A plentifully wide range of varied detail would still exist even within the 'period' limits which I have recommended, i. e., between 1750 and 1860, late enough to ex-

6. The test of any properly designed building is that it should suitably perform the functions for which it was planned. It cannot be classed as "good architecture" unless it is in this sense "functional." But it does not have to resemble a greenhouse (unless it is a greenhouse); nor does it have to look like a factory, when it, in fact, is not a factory, in order to fulfill its function. In fact, "good architecture" must include the function of beauty of form, of proportion, or even the more elusive function of being in good taste—or else it ceases to be "architecture" (in the accepted sense of that word), and is only fit to be classed as "engineering."

clude 'Early American,' and early enough to avoid what came immediately after the 'Late Colonial' or 'Greek Revival.'

"I feel that (even though based upon economy of cost) the tendency to make use of but one kind of brick, and of only one kind of stone has already been carried about far enough (except, of course, in the case of partially completed quadrangles or groups). I should hope that when new groups of dormitories or other buildings are started, resort should be had to the use of a more 'primitive' appearing brick—such as was originally hand-made for the older buildings (Person Hall, for example), with perhaps no limestone trim at all, or, with white marble trim for sills, cornices, etc.; or that other interesting combinations of materials be used.

"Above all, when new groups are started, the University should beware of 'rubber stamp' repetition of its existing buildings; for, that, beyond anything else, is likely to result in monotony. What is highly important, in my opinion, is to obtain as much variety of architectural treatment as is consistent with harmony of style and design; but, without startling contrasts. A good example of such 'restrained' contrast exists in the venerable 'Harvard Yard,' where rather monotonous brick buildings predominate; but where 'University Hall,' a Colonial building of light grey stone stands out in pleasing contrast to its neighboring buildings, thus enhancing the appearance of the entire group. A similar contrast exists here, on the South Campus, where the Library Building finished as it is in limestone stands out among adjacent buildings of brick.

"If the question were asked: 'Why not introduce an occasional building of *completely contrasting style*, for the sake of variety, Modernistic, Gothic, or whatever?', my reply would be: 'There are examples where such violent contrasts get by, but as a rule group unity is destroyed—even though variety may be gained in the process.'

"If Modernistic, Gothic, or any other 'Anti-Colonial' style should, in future, be introduced at the University of North Carolina, let us hope that it would be confined to some separate quadrangles, or to groups not rubbing elbows too closely with buildings of Colonial design.

" 'Unity, Mass, and Coherence' are as essential in architectural composition as they are in literature, or in music. Following that precept, I believe it to be of the utmost importance that all uncompleted groups on the Campus should be carried out in the style in which they were designed. This applies, of course, to the half-completed South Campus group, to the Alexander Dormitory group, and to the two additional buildings proposed for the Wilson Hall group.

"Thus far, I have been stressing the more technical side of Campus Architecture, with special attention centered upon the past, present, and future development of the 'Campus Plan.' Intimately allied both to the Campus Plan and to Campus buildings—and thus deserving of special comment—is the 'landscaping' of the University grounds.

"The University is most fortunate in possessing a Campus site of unusual natural beauty. It is not a dead level, as is the case with the Campus areas of many other institutions, nor is it situated on precipitous terrain, like certain others; but, gently undulating, the lay of the land lends itself naturally to building sites at different levels, which in itself makes for variety of architectural effect.

"Certain noble old trees, reminiscent of the Primeval Forest, lend special dignity to many Campus areas, serving as a fitting background for younger generations of trees, and for many beautiful shrubs set out under the direction of Dr. William C. Coker, whose skill and artistry are in evidence not only in his *magnum opus*, the 'Arboretum,' but throughout the University grounds, where to the handiwork of Nature he has added a grace and charm all his own.[7]

7. Active on the Campus Committee on Grounds and Buildings, of which for many years Dr. Coker was chairman, are other Faculty members, who also have rendered service of outstanding value in connection with the Building Program; notably, Drs. J. M. Booker and Wm. de B. MacNider. Among former members of the committee the late Charles T. Woollen was a tower of strength. The Woollen Gymnasium most fittingly bears his name; for it was due to his painstaking research over a series of years that the basic program for that building was prepared, and to his enthusiastic leadership that it came into existence.

Special thanks are due Messrs. Coker, Booker, and MacNider, three veteran committeemen of over twenty-five years standing, for the enorm-

"In order that there may be continuity in Campus Plan development, it seems to me that the Campus Committee on Grounds and Buildings, or another committee serving a similar purpose, should be given a permanent status; for there will always be need of some such duly authorized group to serve both as a *liaison* between the University and its architects and as a barrier against the possible infiltration of passing architectural fads and fancies, to the ultimate. undoing of the University's long-term architectural policy.

"The Founding Fathers made a good start with the Campus Plan, the members of this committee are carrying on faithfully. If future members maintain with loyalty this sound and worthy tradition, high standards of future Campus Architecture will be assured, at the University of North Carolina."

---

ous amount of constructive work done by them, in cooperation with the University's architects, towards maintaining the architectural standards of the Campus. These men are still doing valuable work on that committee—of which Prof. R. J. M. Hobbs is now chairman—and the entire Committee deserves the gratitude of all concerned for their enthusiastic support of the forthcoming program for post-war expansion.

31

CAMPUS ARCHITECTURE:
A COMMENTARY

A S MIGHT BE EXPECTED, the architectural forms and idioms of the structures upon the Campus of the University of North Carolina reflect the successive phases of its historical development. The features which impress the visitor— amidst a welter of untitivated Colonial, Classic Revival, Tudor, Georgian, Italian Romanesque, and even a touch of Gothic— are not so much the variety and heterogeneity of disparate styles, as the harmonious elements which pull the whole composition together. The original design of the Campus, soundly conceived and executed on broad lines, has in the main been adhered to. Future developments, tending to strengthen and confirm this original concept, are under constant consideration. Modern enlargements of the scope of the curriculum have compelled the introduction of the sound principle of zoning control, in particular for science, fine arts, commerce, and women's dormitories. The beauties of the setting, the gentle declivities and flowing slopes, the broad expanses of lawn, the monumental trees, luxuriant foliage, and lush flowering shrubbery, the hallowing ivy and gracefully decorative ampelopsis—all cooperate to weld the whole into shapes of beauty and magic.

The first buildings, box-like structures built by competent brickmasons and carpenters, must originally have looked in their primitive barrenness, as Lowell said of the early buildings at Harvard, "as if they meant business and nothing more." James Patterson's Old East and William Nichols' Old West (not as we know them today, but quite unadorned, and only two-thirds the present structures in both length and height) were unified by John Close's very simple, gabled and belfried South Building. Under the transforming hands of Davis and of McKim, Mead, and White, they assumed shapes of classic beauty and dignity. And of the whole Campus composition, Schuyler's comment is significant and satisfying: "The buildings of Chapel

Hill 'look as if they meant business' as strictly as the buildings of Harvard. But they are 'placed,' instead of being promiscuously huddled, and they show so much of the comity which those of Harvard conspicuously lack that they have 'something more.' "[1] Person Hall, a miniature chapel erratically placed on the west side of Grand Avenue, in 1837 surrendered its function as the scene of Commencement exercises to William Nichols' and A. J. Davis' Gerrard Hall, suitably placed for the first westward step along the cross-axis down Chatham, later College Street, and since 1875, Cameron Avenue.

The coming of Alexander Jackson Davis, famous American architect with pronounced Gothic leanings, of the New York firm, Town and Davis, was epochal, in leaving the ineffaceable impress of the artist upon every structure which he touched. Instead of attempting to force the Campus composition into an anomalous Gothic mould, he strove with sure artistic instinct to produce harmony and conformity to pattern and to create an impression of unity. Coming at the height of the Neo-Classic Revival, he redeemed the severe plainness of Gerrard Hall by applying to its southern face, as Fiske Kimball happily expresses it, "a handsome portico of four Ionic columns with a temple pediment, of the classic monumentality which Jefferson's example was spreading all down the Piedmont."[2]

Again, in enlarging and remodeling Old East and Old West, Davis imparted to the North Quadrangle its most dominant and salient feature. "On their northern fronts," again to quote Kimball, "tall square piers, like Greek *antae*, were carried the full height of the three stories, the central space only being pierced as one great opening with triple windows between mullions extending its full height."

The masterpiece of Davis' designing was Smith Hall, described in greater detail in another chapter. Originally stuccoed

1. Montgomery Schuyler, "Architecture of American Colleges: The University of North Carolina," *Architectural Record*, XXX (1911), 62-64.

2. Dr. Fiske Kimball, Director, Philadelphia Museum of Art submitted (May 7, 1945) to the author at his request a brief critical survey of, and commentary on, the Campus architecture, which has been freely quoted in the writing of this chapter.

in gray plaster to suggest stone, the building, designed at the height of the Greek Revival, has as its eastern face a portico of the proto-Corinthian type of the Tower of the Winds. Davis gave "at the centre of the front, and between the columns more widely spaced in order to show it to more advantage, the same extension of the principal entrance to the top of the wall" that he imparted to the remodeled north fronts of Old East and Old West.[3]

The completion of the ante-bellum University was effected through the addition of the New East and New West buildings to the original open-quadrangle of Old East, Old West, and South. These structures, severe in linearity and revealing the influence of the Italian villa model, have a somewhat modernistic note. Designed by William Percival, an architect of fifteen years' experience, they conform in general style and appearance with the elementary Colonial "cubic" form of the earlier structures. Fiske Kimball comments: "Plain vertical strips separate the windows of its central mass, with a heavy bracketed cornice, a type of which the popularity was by no means confined to the Hudson River."

The period of almost half a century following the re-opening in 1875 offers little of architectural interest or note. Montgomery Schuyler deftly damns the old Memorial Hall as "illiterate." Alumni Hall, softened and guarded by luxuriant shrubbery, is readily recognized as a scaled-down model of the New York Public Library, weakened by a needless riot of forms, from French to Greek. Bynum Hall represents, in somewhat more austere form, the same trend of a return to Classical types. Carr Dormitory is an uninspired illustration of the Richardsonian influence; and Peabody, if without distinction, at least is well proportioned, with a faint intimation of Italian influence. Caldwell and Davie halls, the Carnegie Library, and Howell Hall fortunately do no violence to the architectural style of the Campus, while offering little or nothing towards its enhancement. The comparative poverty of the University, compelling the employment of architects of inferior inspiration who feebly followed conventional models, "mercifully protected the University, like

3. Schuyler, *op. cit.*

others in the South, from any great intrusion of inharmonious buildings in that period, so lamentable in its babel of romantic eclecticism."

During a twenty-year period at the opening of the present century, a wave of Tudor influence swept over the Campus, leaving in its wake infelicitous evidences of that misguided trend. Mary Ann Smith Building, with well-burnt brick satisfactorily weathered, fortunately lacks the most glaring features of Tudor. The dormitory pile, Battle-Vance-Pettigrew, with diamond-paned oriels and characteristic gargoyles, is forgivable because of façades of the first two. But they can only be thought of as transitional structures, doomed to ultimate supersession by some noble counterpart to a two-winged Graham Memorial of the original plan. Swain Hall is so businesslike as scarcely to justify critical architectural comment. Phillips Hall, overmodernized Tudor, presents some features of "functional" architecture; but it is sharply divergent from general Campus style and demands radical remodeling and reconstruction, with an imposing entrance upon some later-developed zone of science halls.

A totally new era was ushered in at the beginning of the third decade of the present century, with the engagement on April 16, 1920, of the notable firm of architects, McKim, Mead, and White of New York City, as consulting architects.[4] The traditions of the firm, as well as the activating principles, esthetic and architectual, were admirably represented and carried on in the person of the late William Mitchell Kendall. The architects of record, for the University, were the T. C. Atwood organization. Arthur C. Nash began his connection with the University just two years later than did the firm of McKim, Mead, and White, namely in April, 1922. The Atwood organization, during the period of service (1920-1929) of McKim, Mead, and White, made all the working drawings, let the contracts, and supervised the construction. Mr. Kendall, at irregular intervals, visited Chapel Hill; and, as final arbiter in the matter, he critically analysed the designs of the Atwood organization, which were frequently the individual work of the actual designer, A. C. Nash; and modified them to suit his own standards and tastes. For the most part, Mr. Kendall made few adverse criticisms and

4. See Chapter 26.

insisted upon comparatively minor changes. In a brochure recently issued by McKim, Mead, and White, the following quotation from the Foreword is highly significant, as related to the work of that firm as "consulting architects" here:

The importance of establishing and adhering to a general plan, prepared by a competent architect in collaboration with a landscape architect, cannot be overemphasized. Only rarely is a College or University Group conceived and executed all at one time. Usually the buildings are built singly, and often at long time-intervals apart. Without a far-sighted, flexible general plan and a careful control of design, the rapid changes in taste, and inadequate consideration of building locations result far too often in disorganized groups of buildings, varying in style and materials, so characteristic of the average American College. Beautifully arranged groups unified in design and material are the ideal toward which study should be directed.

In regard to style, the firm has favored the Classical tradition, believing that it is not only more in keeping with American precedent, but more flexible, easier to maintain and better suited to our climate and mode of Campus life, than styles derived from the Gothic or Romanesque. But believing the problem of primary importance is to achieve harmony and unity of the group . . . the firm has sought to make the new buildings conform to the older ones.[5]

The opening of the South Quadrangle to monumental development was registered in the erection in 1920-1921, at the northeast corner of the Quadrangle, of Steele Dormitory, by the architect J. A. Salter, with contracting firm Salmon, Shipp and Poe. Following in rapid succession came Saunders (1921), Murphey (1922), Manning (1923), and Bingham (1928) halls. Steele, Saunders, Murphey and Bingham were modernistic adaptations of Georgian architecture, with Italianate reminders in fenestration and false balcony effects. To the east ran a transverse axis bisecting Manning Hall which, with its towering columns and dignified façade, impressively commands a beautiful quadrangle.[6] The impressive portico erected in 1926 on the southern side of South Building, the columns too slender for Ionic, duplicating in style those of Manning Hall, dominates the South Quadrangle at its upper end. At the southwest corner of the intersection of Cameron Avenue and the Raleigh Road arose

5. *Recent Buildings designed for Educational Institutions, by McKim, Mead & White* (1946).
6. Consult Plates XXII and XXIII, *ibid*.

in 1920-1921, forming a spacious and well-disposed quadrangle, the four dormitories, Ruffin, Mangum, Manly, and Grimes. East of the Raleigh Road, opposite this quadrangle was erected in 1924 a group of four dormitories, two on each side of a quadrangle unenclosed at either end: Aycock, Graham, Everett, and Lewis. Notable structures of this era are Graham Memorial (completed in 1931), with impressive lines and beautiful brickwork, though crippled for the lack of the two wings of the original plan; Venable Hall (1924) representing the "functional" type of adapted Georgian; Spencer Hall Dormitory (1924), dignified Georgian in a beautiful setting; and the new Library (1929), which dominates the southern end of the South Quadrangle. This last-named structure, chiefly after the original design of Arthur C. Nash, is regarded by some as the greatest architectural achievement which the Campus can offer, by others as too elaborate in decoration, and too divergent from the characteristic simplicity of prevailing style and tone here.[7] This building, says Fiske Kimball, "continues the great line of Roman-domed libraries in such positions [commanding a quadrangle] at American universities, inaugurated by Jefferson's Rotunda at the University of Virginia and so nobly continued by McKim's at Columbia University and Stanford White's at New York University."[8]

During the period of McKim, Mead, and White's régime as

7. Mr. Nash, to whom principal credit is due for the main features of this structure, suggested the change from a cupola to a dome, and the substitution of limestone for brick. The structure in conspicuous architectural features, he remarked in a letter to the writer (April 23, 1945), "owes its air of charm and distinction to the finishing touches given by Mr. [William Mitchell] Kendall, *at his own draughting board.* Particularly is this true of the dome, with its octagonal substructure surmounted by a beautifully proportioned Colonial balustrade. The portico, pediment, and entrance doors are likewise beautifully proportioned; and, to crown all, Mr. Kendall has made use of just the right amount of ornamentation, perfect in style and scale, and appropriately placed. Fortunately, too, by a special arrangement with McKim, Mead, and White, the University was enabled to have all the 'full-size details' and architectural models turned out by that firm's superbly trained draughting force—all under the careful surveillance of Mr. Kendall."

8. Consult *Recent Buildings Designed for Educational Institutions,* Plates IV, IX, X, XXII, XXIII, XXIV, XXXII, XLIX, LXXIII. Plate IV gives a partial plot plan showing nine buildings on which McKim, Mead, and White were consulting architects.

"consulting architects," the official architects for T. C. Atwood, engineer, were: H. P. Alan Montgomery in the designing of Ruffin, Mangum, Manly, and Grimes dormitories, and Saunders, Murphey, Manning and Bingham halls; and Arthur C. Nash in the designing of Venable Hall, Aycock, Graham, Everett, Lewis, and Stacy dormitories, Spencer Hall (woman's dormitory), Graham Memorial, and Library. McKim, Mead, and White is solely responsible for the Morehead-Patterson Memorial Bell Tower, a modernization of an Italian Romanesque campanile, with conical Gothic roof, and open arcade in a chaste, formal setting of boxwood bushes.

Noteworthy for conservatism and restraint, a refined sense of proportion, a conspicuous feeling for dignity and beauty in harmonious conjunction are the buildings designed by Nash: the Carolina Inn, Kenan Stadium, Playmakers Theatre (a reverent remodeling of A. J. Davis' Smith Hall), and the new Memorial Hall, a total reconstruction, in concept and design, of the old Memorial Hall, the two having almost nothing in common but the site. Later structures of T. C. Atwood, engineer, with H. R. Weeks as architect and A. C. Nash as consulting architect, are: Public Health Medical Building, Woollen Gymnasium and Bowman Gray Swimming Pool, Lenoir Dining Hall; Alderman, Kenan and McIver Women's dormitories; Wilson Hall, Alexander Dormitory, and Women's Gymnasium Unit. The outdoor swimming pool is the exclusive design of Mr. Weeks. For the additions to the Carolina Inn, including the Bryan Apartments, and the Whitehead Dormitory, the architect was George Watts Carr; for the Navy Building and the Hostess House the architect was Archie Davis; and for all these structures A. C. Nash was consulting architect. Particularly noteworthy, from the standpoint of architectural design and appropriate setting, are: the Women's Dormitory Quadrangle in modernized Georgian style (opposite the Arboretum and east of the old Raleigh Road); and the new structures adjacent to and associated with the Carolina Inn. The best qualities of the architects, George Watts Carr and Archie Davis, are revealed in the well-proportioned and excellently conceived structures which they designed.

One might make an interesting study of changes effected in

the appearance of certain structures on the Campus, through architectural modifications and artistic recreations. Mention has been made, for example, of the notable improvements effected in such buildings as Old East, Old West, Gerrard Hall, and Memorial Hall. South Building has undergone various reconstructions, involving among other details the belfry, the doorways, and the noble portico dominating the South Quadrangle. The story of two marked Campus beautifications, one involving the well and the other the north entrance to the South Building, is so interesting that it is given here in the words of Edwin A. Alderman, who became President in 1896.

"In the fall of 1897, if my memory does not fail me, I was possessed with a great desire to add a little beauty (which, after all, is the most practical influence in the world) to the grim, austere dignity of the old Campus at Chapel Hill. Looking out of my window on the first floor of the South Building, I beheld the old well squalid and ramshackled. I determined to tear it down and put something there having beauty. Of course, money with which to do ambitious things was utterly lacking. I had always admired the little round temples which one sees reproduced so often in English Gardens. These were spread over England by the Stuarts under the influence of the French tradition, derived largely from the Temple of Love in the Garden at Versailles. This temple of love was lineally descended—

1. From a Greek shrine
2. From the Tholos at Epidaurus
3. From the Temple of Vesta at Tivoli
4. From the 'Pietro Montorio' by Bramanti.

Our little well is, therefore, a sort of sixth cousin of a Greek shrine, or third cousin of the Temple of Vesta, or second cousin of the Temple at Versailles.

"I was more familiar with the Temple at Versailles. So I found a picture of it and some pictures of round temples in English Gardens derived from it, and took all of these to my ever helpful friend in all practical matters about the University, Professor J. W. Gore, and asked him if we could reproduce it, or something like it, fairly decently at very trifling cost, in wood. He said he thought we could. He then drew, or *had drawn*, a pencil sketch based on the temple at Versailles, in scale for our purposes, took up its building with some nearby lumber company, and lo! the little structure went up, seemed to my eyes well proportioned and now, after the passage of twenty-seven years, has stolen into the hearts of people as beauty in any sort of form has a way of doing, and is also by way of becoming somewhat mythical as to its origin.

"I recall a fine shindy I had with a very distinguished professor who intimated broadly to me that I was foolish to spend money (about $200) for such luxurious gewgaws when so many vital things—sewers, water works, electric fixtures—cried out for improvement. I recall intimating to my distinguished colleague that he would do well to attend to his own 'damn' business, and not only built the little temple, but recklessly begged dear old Gore to reproduce over the main door of the South Building a fine detail of the doorway over Westover, a noble Colonial home on the James. The Westover touch is there still. At the same time I sought some sort of atmosphere by planting vines on the buildings—especially the South and Memorial—which were conscientiously dug up for some time by the colored workmen in their annual and biennial yard raking and grass cutting orgies. The entire riotous expenditure for all these things did not exceed $500.00—a sum to excite the derision and loud scorn of this generation of bond issuers and town builders. It was the day of small things in money matters but of full grown ideas about great permanent aims. The whole well incident, the building of the little Temple, was a pitiful, yet beautiful, illustration of the way Democracy cries out for beauty to give it backbone— spiritual backbone—that will make it so strong that it can and will defy self gratification, mobs and red terrors.

Beauty
Old yet ever New
Eternal Voice
and
Inward Word."[9]

9. Part of a letter from Dr. Alderman, Charlottesville, Virginia, December 16, 1923, to Mrs. Mary Graves Rees of Chapel Hill.

Mr. Eugene Harris, Registrar, a gifted amateur draftsman, drew the design for the well, at Professor Gore's request.[10] Professor Collier Cobb presented for Dr. Alderman's approval a large book carrying a beautiful reproduction of the grand Georgian doorway to William Byrd's "Westover" as a model for the present north entrance of South Building; and the scale-drawing for this was probably also drawn by Mr. Eugene Harris. The old well, an open cylindrical structure with flat conical top, is reproduced in Battle's *Sketches*, as is also the South Building, showing the old doorway as a mere rectangular opening in the wall.[11] Another happy improvement of a Campus building is registered through the well-designed portico on the eastern face of Old East, which is a modern addition.[12]

And so this chronological display of dissolving films, traversing a century and a half, concludes. The continuity reels off to its end. A hurried backward glance at the University's beginnings compels the conclusion that the founding fathers, in the concept of simple colonial buildings on three sides of a small quadrangle, were proceeding in the manner traditional in American colleges from Harvard onward. The stern spirit of pioneer days is reflected in the gaunt simplicity of these early buildings.

Dr. Samuel Eusebius McCorkle said in his dedicatory sermon on the occasion of the laying of the cornerstone of the Old East building, October 12, 1793:

The two English universities [Oxford and Cambridge] have been called the eyes of the nation, the lights of church and state; and prodigious have been their influence both in politics and religion. They have arrived at mature age. Ours is the infant of a day. It is just raising its feeble hands, and stretching them out. The one it holds out to the church, the other to the nation. Let the ministers both of justice and mercy take it by the hand. It will one day, by the patronage of Heaven, reward us all.

The universities of Great Britain—Edinburgh, Oxford, and

10. Letter of Earl P. Holt, class of 1903, whose wife, Eugenia, was a daughter of Eugene Harris, Oak Ridge Institute, April 11, 1946, to Louis Graves.

11. Consult *U. N. C. C.*, facing page 25.

12. Battle, I, facing page 60. This portico should be compared with the two uncovered platforms, with stairways at north and south, placed at the sides of the building.

Cambridge—exercised predominating influence over the early American colleges and universities, in matters not only of studies, but also of architecture and of student control. The rules and ordinances of Queen's College in Mecklenburg County, North Carolina, under the act of incorporation, January 15, 1771, were directed to be modeled upon the "laws and customs of Oxford and Cambridge, or those of the colleges in America." The same might equally have been said of the architectural design of a quadrangle, triple-walled by buildings forming an enclosure, as a sort of prison for the students. The system of proctors and confinement of students within an enclosure was introduced here from the beginning; and Caldwell was the most active and relentless of proctors in keeping the students in order and within the college quadrangle. The very phrase "in quad" survives to this day from the English college custom of regarding the college quadrangle as a place of detention.

The ante-bellum era of architectural development is associated with the names of three professional architects of note, William Nichols, William Percival, and Alexander Jackson Davis. Fiske Kimball commends Percival's happily rationalized use of simple Classic elements, in New East and New West; and affirms that with Davis' enlargement of Old East and Old West, embodying the creation of tall square piers on their northern fronts, the Old Campus gained its most characteristic and striking feature. In adding to Gerrard Hall a handsome portico of four Ionic columns with a temple pediment, Davis redeemed and beautified a building barren in architectural character or elegance. The masterpiece of Campus architecture, Davis' supreme accomplishment, was Smith Hall, the exquisite eastern portico being modeled upon the classic Clepsydra—a structure, as described by Kimball, "with the crystalline form of a porticoed temple—then the ideal of 'cubic architecture'—with heavy columns of free Corinthian type."

For the period, 1875 to 1920, there was no progress, but rather retrogression, in the field of architectural design. No guiding principle was at work, nor any continuity of control. The confusion of styles, the lack of harmony, finally precipitated a crisis. The engagement of the great architectural firm of McKim,

Mead, and White of New York City, and slightly later the acquisition of the services of Arthur C. Nash as consulting architect, registered the University's architectural salvation. The South Quadrangle was opened as natural extension southward along one of the two main axes of the original Campus plan. With the creation of a Committee on Grounds and Buildings, the fixation of colonial as the dominant form of architecture, the conservation of the principle of harmony established, and zoning accepted as both desirable and inevitable, the University may look forward with no little confidence, in matters both educational and architectural, to a new day of progress, expansion, and beautification.

THE COLLEGE WELL, *circa* 1890

Dr. Edwin A. Alderman, who became president of the University in 1896, determined to tear down this "squalid and ramshackled" old well and put in its place something marked by dignity and beauty.

THE OLD WELL TODAY

This structure, built by order of President Alderman, replaced the well shown above, and is, in the words of Dr. Alderman, "a sort of sixth cousin of a Greek shrine, or third cousin of the Temple of Vesta, or second cousin of the Temple at Versailles."

AERIAL VIEW OF THE CAMPUS, LOOKING SOUTH
ALONG GRAND AVENUE

APPENDICES

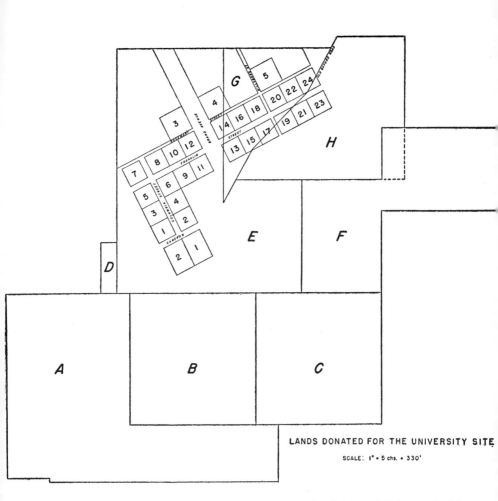

LANDS DONATED FOR THE UNIVERSITY SITE

SCALE: 1" = 5 chs. = 330'

A, donated by Edmund Jones, 200 acres; *B*, donated by John and Solomon P. Morgan (heirs of Mark Morgan, who promised the land), 107 acres; *C*, donated by John Daniel, 107 acres; *D*, donated by James Craig, 5 acres; *E*, donated by Christopher Barbee, 221 acres; *F*, donated by Hardy Morgan, 125 acres; *G*, donated by Benjamin Yeargin, 50 acres; *H*, donated by Hardy Morgan, 80 acres.

The tracts of land shown here are only a part of the total 1,386 acres donated to the University. They are the tracts which "lie on Chapel Hill or adjoining thereto." The numbered lots on either side of Grand Avenue were those marked off for the sale of 1793. For further information about these lots, see Battle, I, pp. 44-48.

Map redrawn by Mrs. Carolyn Bolt from a map by L. J. Phipps based on deeds recorded at the courthouse in Hillsboro. According to the original deeds, the two tracts of land (F and H on this map) donated by Hardy Morgan overlap.

354

MAPS SHOWING DEVELOPMENT
OF UNIVERSITY CAMPUS, 1793-1945.

A The Retreat (1858)

B Second Astronomical
Observatory

C First Gymnasium (1885)

D Dr. Alexander's House

E Second President's House

F Puckett House (now
Chancellor's house) (1822)

G First President's House
(1795)

H Second Infirmary (1895)

1 Old East (1793)

2 Person Hall (1797)

3 South (1798)

4 Gerrard (1822)

5 Old West (1822)

6 Smith (Playmakers) (1851)

7 New East (1857) (1859)

8 New West (1857) (1859)

9 (Old) Memorial Hall
(1885)

10 Alumni (1898)

11 Carr (1899)

12 Smith (Graduate Club)
(1901)

13 Bynum Gymnasium (1904)

14 Y.M.C.A. (1904)

15 Howell Hall (Pharmacy)
(1906)

16 Hill Music Hall (1907)
Auditorium (1930)

17 Infirmary (Abernethy Hall)
(1907)

18 Davie (1908)

18a President's House (1907)

19 Caldwell (1911)

20 Peabody (1912)

21 Battle-Vance-Pettigrew
(1912)

22 Swain (1913)

22a Emerson Stadium (1915)

23 Phillips (1918)

24 Steele (1920)

25 Grimes (1921)

26 Manly (1921)

27 Ruffin (1921)

28 Mangum (1921)

29 Saunders (1922)

29a Archer House (1922)

30 Murphey (1922)

31 Manning (Law) (1923)

32 "Tin Can" (1923)

33 Spencer (co-ed dorm)
(1924)

34 Venable (new chemistry)
(1925)

35 Kenan Stadium (1927)

36 Aycock (1924)

37 Graham (1924)

38 Everett (1928)

39 Lewis (1924)

40 Library (1928)

41 Buildings Department
(1916)

42 Filter Plant (1925)

43 Greenhouse (1926)

44 Memorial Hall (new) (1930)

45 Graham Memorial (1923) (1931)

46 Bingham (1929)

47 Morehead-Patterson Tower (1930)

48 Carolina Inn (built, 1924; given to University, 1935)

49 Alderman Hall (1937)

50 Chas. T. Woollen Gymnasium (1937)

51 Bowman Gray Pool (1937)

52 Medical & Public Health (1938)

53 Stacy Dormitory (1938)

54 Kenan Hall (1939)

55 McIver Hall (1939)

56 Alexander Dormitory (1939)

57 Whitehead Dormitory (1939)

58 Carolina Inn additions (1939)

59 Carolina Inn apartments (1939)

60 Lenoir Hall (1939)

61 Wilson Hall (1939)

62 New Power Plant (1939)

63 New Infirmary (1942)

64 Womens' Gymnasium (1943)

65 Monogram Club (1942)

66 Naval Armory (1942)

67 Greenhouse (1942)

68 Kessing Pool (1943)

69 Institute of Government (built, 1939; became a part of the University, 1942)

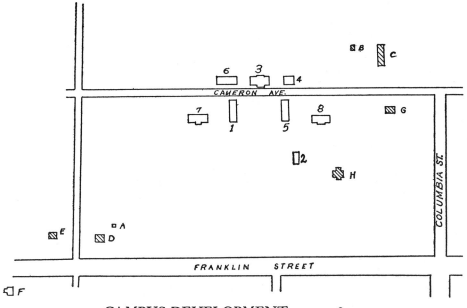

CAMPUS DEVELOPMENT, 1793-1875

Buildings in outline are those erected or acquired by the University during the period 1793-1875; crosshatched buildings, those erected during this period but subsequently torn down. For identification of individual buildings, see legend on pp. 355-56. C, the First Gymnasium and H, the Second Infirmary, although not built until a later period, are pictured on this map. On the next map their sites are occupied by the buildings that replaced them. Map drawn by Grey Culbreth.

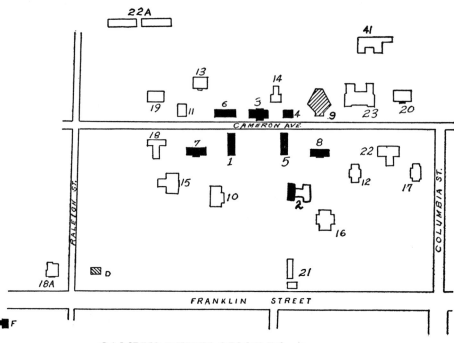

CAMPUS DEVELOPMENT, 1875-1920

Buildings in outline are those erected or acquired by the University during the period 1875-1920; crosshatched buildings, those erected during this period but subsequently torn down; black buildings, those built during an earlier period. For identification of individual buildings, see legend on pp. 355-56. Map drawn by Grey Culbreth.

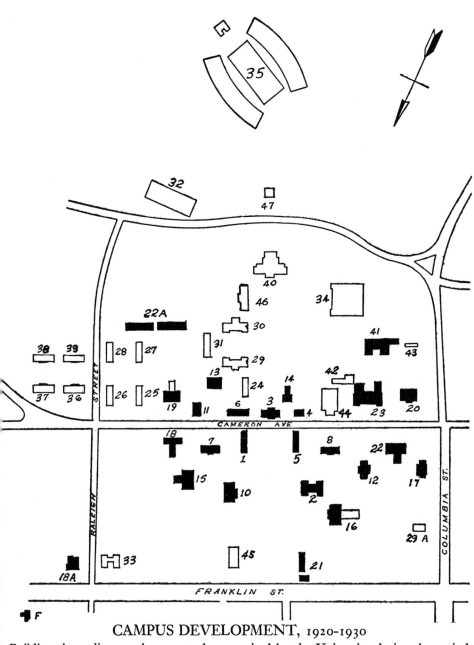

CAMPUS DEVELOPMENT, 1920-1930

Buildings in outline are those erected or acquired by the University during the period 1920-1930; black buildings, those built during an earlier period. For identification of individual buildings, see legend on pp. 355-56. Map drawn by Grey Culbreth.

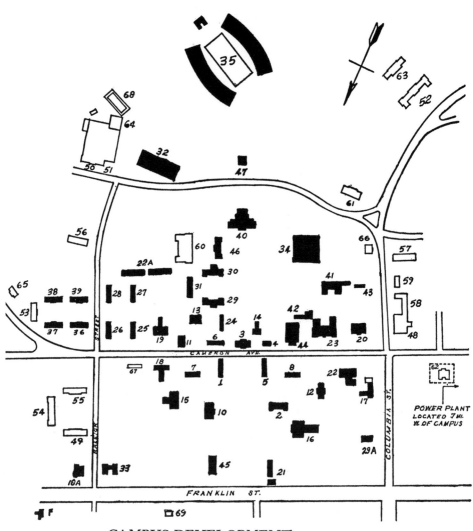

CAMPUS DEVELOPMENT, 1930-1945

Buildings in outline are those erected or acquired by the University during the period 1930-1945; black buildings, those erected during an earlier period. For identification of individual buildings, see legend on pp. 355-56. Map drawn by Grey Culbreth.

BUILDING COMMITTEES

EARLY BUILDINGS

THE TRUSTEES have followed no consistent policy in planning and directing the construction of new buildings. The first buildings were erected under the supervision of special committees of the Trustees. During President Swain's administration he was included in the membership, and the practice of including the president of the University on building committees seems to have been continued thereafter. Only one building—the first Memorial Hall—was erected during President Battle's term and there was none under President Winston, but two were constructed during Alderman's tenure. A different committee was named for each building but the President was a member of both. During President Venable's administration there continued to be a separate committee for each new building constructed, but the University representation was increased. Each committee consisted of several Trustees, the President, and one or more Faculty members, the latter usually being professors whose departments were particularly affected.

TRUSTEE BUILDING COMMITTEES

On June 5, 1917 the University Trustees named John Sprunt Hill, J. Bryan Grimes, and Charles T. Woollen a standing committee to consider what lands adjoining, and in the vicinity of, the University property it would be advisable for the University to purchase, and to report on such lands, with their recommendations, to the Executive Committee.

A few weeks later another committee, with J. Bryan Grimes as chairman, was appointed to cooperate with the University Faculty Committee on Grounds and Buildings in the preparation of plans for the development of the south part of the Campus. Its original membership consisted of J. Bryan Grimes, John Sprunt Hill, and Haywood Parker, but later President H. W. Chase and Charles T. Woollen were added to the committee.

On March 23, 1921 these two committees were consolidated and designated a Building Committee. Two persons were added to the new committee, making its full membership J. Bryan Grimes, (chairman), J. S. Hill, Haywood Parker, George G. Stephens, James A. Gray, H. W. Chase, and C. T. Woollen. In May of that year W. N. Everett and W. C. Coker were made members. After Mr. Grimes' death he was replaced April 19, 1923 by C. F. Harvey. Mr. Hill was made chairman, and he continued to make a semi-annual report until June, 1931.

During the P. W. A. building program there was no special building committee, President Graham making progress reports to the Trustees once or twice a year.

On April 30, 1943 the Trustees voted for the appointment of a Building Commission at each of the three institutions of the Greater University of North Carolina to consist of three Trustees and three members of the Faculty. Governor Cherry designated for the Chapel Hill unit the following: John Sprunt Hill, Chairman, Collier Cobb, Jr., and W. E. Horner for the Trustees; R. J. M. Hobbs, H. G. Baity, and P. W. Wager for the Faculty; and the University administrative officers President Frank P. Graham, Controller William D. Carmichael, Jr., Chancellor Robert B. House, and Business Manager Claude E. Teague. Some months after the appointment of the committee Mr. Hill asked to be relieved of the chairmanship, and he was succeeded by Mr. Cobb.

THE FACULTY COMMITTEE ON GROUNDS AND BUILDINGS

In 1913-14 Acting-President E. K. Graham appointed the Faculty Committee on Grounds and Buildings to study the development of the physical plant of the University. Its first chairman was Dr. W. C. Coker, who served in that capacity from 1913 to 1942. He was succeeded as chairman by Professor R. J. M. Hobbs. The following has been the membership of the committee, with inclusive dates of service, until the end of 1945:

Collier Cobb	1913-1921
William C. Coker	1913-
George Howe	1913-1914
A. S. Wheeler	1914-1930
William de B. MacNider	1918-
John M. Booker	1920-
Howard W. Odum	1921-1943
G. M. Braune	1922-1930
Charles T. Woollen	1922-1938
Herman G. Baity	1934-
Richard J. M. Hobbs	1936-
R. T. Smith	1938-1940
Paul W. Wager	1938-
William D. Carmichael, Jr.	1941-1943
Robert B. House	1942-
William M. Prince	1943-
Claude E. Teague	1943-

Faculty Journal, September 6, 1913.

UNIVERSITY BUILDINGS

THE FOLLOWING LISTS contain the names of the various buildings of the University. The first contains the names of buildings no longer existing.

The information given for each building is as accurate and complete as possible. In some instances the date given is that of the laying of the cornerstone; in others, in which cornerstones were not included, the date is that of the completion of the building. The information concerning architects and builders is fragmentary.

UNIVERSITY BUILDINGS NO LONGER EXISTING

Steward's Hall (north of present Carr Building), 1795; Samuel Hopkins, contractor; Martin Hall, builder; torn down, 1847.

First President's House (where Swain Hall now stands), 1795; Samuel Hopkins, builder; removed, 1913.

Grammar School (on northwest corner of Presbyterian Church lot), 1802; sold, 1832.

Astronomical Observatory (on site of present tennis courts), 1831; built under the direction of President Joseph Caldwell; burned, 1838.

Second Observatory (back of present Phillips Hall on Dr. Mitchell's lot), date not known; torn down about 1900.

The Retreat or First Infirmary (at southwest corner of present Spencer Hall lot), 1858; A. J. Davis, architect; in use as an infirmary until 1891.

Second President's House (on same lot as the present President's House), date not known; burned, 1886.

Alexander House (original Thomas H. Taylor home; on lot now occupied by Spencer Hall), about 1815; torn down, 1924.

Old Gymnasium (between Phillips and Peabody halls), 1885; enlarged and remodeled as Second Commons Hall, 1898; torn down about 1915-16.

Old Memorial Hall (on site of present Memorial Hall), 1885; Samuel Sloan, architect; J. P. Daugherty, builder; torn down, 1930.

First Dissecting House (south of Memorial Hall), 1890.

First Water Works (well, back of Memorial Hall; hydrants, on Campus; bathroom, under Smith Hall), 1893.

First Power Plant (on site of present Phillips Hall), 1901; torn down about 1924.

Second Infirmary (near southwest corner of Hill Hall), 1895; later removed to Columbia Street.

Second Dissecting House (on site of present Venable Hall), erected about 1900; use for this purpose discontinued, 1911.

PRESENT UNIVERSITY BUILDINGS

Old East, 1793; James Patterson, builder; lengthened and third storey added 1824; remodeled, 1848; interior rebuilt with fireproof construction by Atwood and Nash, 1924.

Person Hall; named for Thomas Person, donor; east wing, 1797; Samuel Hopkins, supervisor; central section, 1886; west wing, 1892; remodeled as an art museum by Atwood and Weeks, 1934.

South Building, 1798-1814; begun by Samuel Hopkins, finished by John Close; portico added 1927 by Atwood and Nash, architects. The south portico suggestion was made by A. C. Nash and approved by W. M. Kendall, of McKim, Mead, and White, supervising architects.

Gerrard Hall, 1822-1837; named for Charles Gerrard, donor; William Nichols, architect and builder.

Old West, 1822; William Nichols, supervisor and builder; addition, 1848; interior rebuilt with fireproof construction by Atwood and Nash, 1923.

Smith Hall (Playmakers Theatre), 1851; named for Governor Benjamin Smith, donor; A. J. Davis, architect; John Berry, builder; interior remodeled, 1924; R. K. Smith, donor; Atwood and Nash, architects.

New West, 1859; William Percival, architect; Thomas H. Coates, builder; remodeled, 1926; Atwood and Nash, architects.

New East, 1859; William Percival, architect; Thomas H. Coates, builder; remodeled, 1926; Atwood and Nash, architects.

Alumni Hall, 1898; Frank P. Milburn, architect; Zachary and Zachary, builders.

Carr Building, 1899; General Julian S. Carr, donor; Pearson and Ashe, architects; Zachary and Zachary, builders.

Mary Ann Smith Building, 1901; Mary Ann Smith, donor; Frank P. Milburn, architect; Zachary and Zachary, builders.

Bynum Hall, 1904; named for William Preston Bynum, Jr., grandson of donor, William Preston Bynum; Frank P. Milburn, architect.

Y. M. C. A., 1904; Frank P. Milburn, architect.

Howell Hall, 1906; named for Edward Vernon Howell; Frank P. Milburn, architect; N. Underwood, contractor.

Hill Music Hall (originally Carnegie Library), main part, 1907; Andrew Carnegie, donor; Frank P. Milburn, architect; auditorium added, 1930; John Sprunt Hill family, donors; Atwood and Nash, architects.

Abernethy Hall (originally third University Infirmary), 1907; named for Eric A. Abernethy, long-time University Physician; Frank P. Milburn, architect; addition, 1924; Atwood and Nash, architects; T. C. Thompson and Company, contractors.

Davie Hall, 1908; named for William R. Davie; Frank P. Milburn and Company, architects; N. Underwood, contractor; fireproof addition, 1925; Atwood and Nash, architects.

President's House, 1907; Frank P. Milburn, architect; remodeled, 1929; Atwood and Nash, architects.

First Filter Plant and Storage Reservoir, 1909; W. M. Piatt, engineer.

Caldwell Hall, 1911; named for Joseph Caldwell; Milburn, Heister and Company, architects; I. G. Lawrence, builder.

Peabody Hall, 1912; named for George Peabody, donor; Milburn, Heister and Company, architects; N. Underwood, contractor.

Battle-Vance-Pettigrew, 1912; named for Kemp Plummer Battle, Zebulon Baird Vance, and James Johnston Pettigrew; Milburn, Heister and Company, architects; I. G. Lawrence and Son, contractors.

Swain Hall, 1913; named for David Lowrie Swain; W. B. Barrow, builder; Milburn, Heister and Company, architects; remodeled, 1924; Atwood and Nash, architects.

Emerson Stadium and Athletic Field, 1915; named for Isaac Emerson, donor.

Buildings Department (originally housed Second Power Plant, and in 1921, first University laundry), 1916; Pierce, builder; addition, 1921.

Phillips Hall, 1918; named for James Phillips, Charles Phillips, and William Battle Phillips; C. C. Hook, architect; I. G. Lawrence, builder; wings added, 1925 and 1927.

Steele Dormitory, 1920; named for William Leak Steele; J. A. Salter, architect; Salmon, Shipp, and Poe, contractors.

Laundry, 1925; T. C. Atwood Company, architects; T. C. Thompson and Brothers, contractors; extension, 1944; Atwood and Weeks, architects; Brooks Lumber Company, builders.

Grimes Dormitory, 1921; named for Bryan Grimes; H. P. Alan Montgomery, architect;* T. C. Thompson, contractors.

Manly Dormitory, 1921; named for Matthias E. Manly and Charles Manly; H. P. Alan Montgomery, architect;* T. C. Thompson and Brothers, contractors.

Ruffin Dormitory, 1921; named for Thomas Ruffin and Thomas Ruffin, Jr.; H. P. Alan Montgomery, architect;* T. C. Thompson and Brothers, contractors.

Mangum Dormitory, 1921; named for Willie Person Mangum, Willie Person Mangum, Jr., and Rev. Adolphus Mangum; H. P. Alan Montgomery, architect;* T. C. Thompson and Brothers, contractors.

Archer House, purchased, 1921; remodeled by T. C. Atwood Company.

Murphey Hall, 1922; named for Archibald DeBow Murphey; H. P. Alan Montgomery, architect;* T. C. Thompson and Brothers, contractors.

*McKim, Mead, and White, consulting architects.

Saunders Hall, 1922; named for William Laurence Saunders; H. P. Alan Montgomery, architect;* T. C. Thompson and Brothers, contractors.

Indoor Sports Building (Tin Can), 1923; T. C. Atwood Company, builder.

Manning Hall, 1923; named for John Manning; H. P. Alan Montgomery and Arthur C. Nash, architects;* T. C. Thompson and Brothers, contractors.

Aycock Dormitory, 1924; named for Charles B. Aycock; Atwood and Nash, architects;* T. C. Thompson and Brothers, contractors.

Graham Dormitory, 1924; named for John W. Graham; Atwood and Nash, architects;* T. C. Thompson and Brothers, contractors.

Lewis Dormitory, 1924; named for Richard H. Lewis; Atwood and Nash, architects;* T. C. Thompson and Brothers, contractors.

Spencer Hall, 1924; named for Cornelia Phillips Spencer; Atwood and Nash, architects;* T. C. Thompson and Brothers, contractors.

Carolina Inn, 1924; given to the University in 1935 by John Sprunt Hill and family; A. C. Nash, architect; additions, 1939; George Watts Carr, architect; A. C. Nash, consulting architect.

Venable Hall, 1925; named for Francis P. Venable; Atwood and Nash, architects;* T. C. Thompson and Brothers, contractors.

Present Filter Plant, 1925; Atwood and Nash, architects.

Greenhouse, 1926. George W. Hill, donor.

Kenan Stadium, 1927; William Rand Kenan, Jr., donor; named for William Rand Kenan, Sr., Thomas S. Kenan, and James G. Kenan; Atwood and Nash, architects; T. C. Thompson and Brothers, contractors.

Everett Dormitory, 1928; named for W. N. Everett; Atwood and Nash, architects;* T. C. Thompson and Brothers, contractors.

Library, 1928; Atwood and Nash, architects;* T. C. Thompson and Brothers, contractors.

Bingham Hall, 1929; named for Major Robert Bingham; Atwood and Nash, architects;* H. P. Alan Montgomery, designing architect; T. C. Thompson and Brothers, contractors.

Morehead-Patterson Bell Tower, 1930; named for Morehead and Patterson families; McKim, Mead, and White, architects; T. C. Thompson and Brothers, contractors.

Memorial Hall, 1930; Atwood and Nash, architects; T. C. Thompson and Brothers, contractors.

Graham Memorial, 1931; named for Edward Kidder Graham; Atwood and Nash, architects;* T. C. Thompson and Brothers, contractors.

Fetzer Field, 1933; named for Robert A. Fetzer.

Woollen Gymnasium, 1937; named for Charles T. Woollen; At-

*McKim, Mead, and White, consulting architects.

wood and Weeks, architects;** J. A. Jones Construction Co., contractors.

Bowman Gray Pool, 1937; Mrs. Bowman Gray and children, donors; named for Bowman Gray; Atwood and Weeks, architects;** J. A. Jones Construction Co., contractors.

Alderman Hall, 1937; named for Edwin A. Alderman; Atwood and Weeks, architects;** George W. Kane, contractor.

Medical and Public Health Building, 1938; Atwood and Weeks, architects;** V. P. Loftis, contractor.

Stacy Dormitory, 1938; named for Marvin H. Stacy; Atwood and Weeks, architects;** V. P. Loftis, contractor.

McIver Hall, 1939; named for Charles Duncan McIver; Atwood and Weeks, architects;** T. W. Poe and Son, contractors.

Kenan Hall, 1939; named for Mary Lily Kenan (Mrs. Henry M. Flagler); Atwood and Weeks, architects;** Muirhead Construction Company, contractors.

Alexander Dormitory, 1939; named for Eben Alexander; Atwood and Weeks, architects;** H. L. Coble, contractor.

Whitehead Hall, 1939; named for Richard H. Whitehead; George Watts Carr, architect;** Muirhead Construction Company, contractors.

Carolina Inn Apartments, 1939; George Watts Carr, architect;** Muirhead Construction Company, contractors.

Lenoir Hall, 1939; named for William Lenoir; Atwood and Weeks, architects;** A. H. Guion, contractor.

Wilson Hall, 1939; named for Henry V. Wilson; Atwood and Weeks, architects;** James I. Barnes, contractor.

New Power Plant, 1939; Atwood and Weeks, architects; W. C. Olsen, engineer.

Institute of Government, 1939; Atwood and Weeks, architects; H. F. Mitchell, contractor.

Infirmary (originally Navy Hospital), 1942; Atwood and Weeks, architect;** Muirhead Construction Company, contractors.

Naval Armory, 1942; Archie Davis, architect;** Muirhead Construction Company, contractors.

Greenhouse, 1942; gift of General Education Board.

Monogram Club, 1942; Archie Davis, architect;** T. W. Poe and Son, contractors.

Kessing Pool, 1943; named for Commander Oliver Owen Kessing; Atwood and Weeks, architects; Roberts Filter Company, contractors.

Women's Gymnasium, 1943; Atwood and Weeks, architects;** R. K. Stewart and Son, contractors.

**Arthur C. Nash, consulting architect.

TABULATION OF BUILDINGS ACCORDING TO ARCHITECTS, CONSULTING ARCHITECTS, ETC., 1921-1942

Name of Building	Architect	Consulting Architects	Date of Completion
RUFFIN, MANGUM, MANLY, and GRIMES dormitories	H. P. A. Montgomery*	McKim, Mead, and White	1921
SAUNDERS and MURPHEY halls	H. P. A. Montgomery*	McKim, Mead, and White	1922
MANNING HALL	H. P. A. Montgomery*	McKim, Mead, and White	1923
BINGHAM HALL	Designed by architects above but not built until 1929		
VENABLE HALL	Arthur C. Nash*	McKim, Mead, and White	1925
Five dormitories of the AYCOCK, GRAHAM GROUP	Arthur C. Nash*	McKim, Mead, and White	1924-33
SPENCER HALL, women's dormitory	Arthur C. Nash*	McKim, Mead, and White	1924-25
GRAHAM MEMORIAL	Arthur C. Nash*	McKim, Mead, and White	1931
LIBRARY	Arthur C. Nash*	McKim, Mead, and White	1928
CAROLINA INN	Arthur C. Nash*	(none)	1924
KENAN STADIUM	Arthur C. Nash*	(none)	1927
Remodeling of SMITH HALL as PLAYMAKERS' THEATER	Arthur C. Nash*	(none)	1925
MEMORIAL BELL TOWER	McKim, Mead, and White	(none)	1931
NEW MEMORIAL HALL	Arthur C. Nash*	(none)	1930
WOOLLEN GYM and BOWMAN GRAY SWIMMING POOL	H. R. Weeks*	Arthur C. Nash	1937
MEDICAL and PUBLIC HEALTH BUILDING	H. R. Weeks*	Arthur C. Nash	1938

*T. C. Atwood, engineer.

LENOIR DINING HALL	H. R. Weeks*	Arthur C. Nash	1939
ALDERMAN, KENAN, McIVER, women's dormitories	H. R. Weeks*	Arthur C. Nash	1937-39
WILSON HALL (Zoology)	H. R. Weeks*	Arthur C. Nash	1939
ALEXANDER DORMITORY	H. R. Weeks*	Arthur C. Nash	1939
NEW INFIRMARY	H. R. Weeks*	Arthur C. Nash	1942
WOMEN'S GYM UNIT	H. R. Weeks*	Arthur C. Nash	1943
KESSING POOL	H. R. Weeks*	(none)	1943
Additions to CAROLINA INN, including BRYAN APARTMENTS	Watts Carr	Arthur C. Nash	1939
WHITEHEAD DORMITORY	Watts Carr	Arthur C. Nash	1939
NAVAL ARMORY	Archie Davis	Arthur C. Nash	1942
NAVY HALL (also known as Monogram Club, "Hostess House," and "Officer's Club")	Archie Davis	Arthur C. Nash	1942

*T. C. Atwood, engineer.

INDEX

INDEX

Abernethy, Charles, foreman of University Press, 306.

Abernethy, Claude, foreman of University Press, 306.

Abernethy, Eric A., death of, 178; foreman of University Press, 306; in charge of Summer School students, 178; purchases second Infirmary, 227; University Physician, 178.

Abernethy Hall, 364; for history, *see* Infirmary, third.

Academies in North Carolina, before 1800, 40. *See also* names of academies.

Academy of the Sciences, 40.

Adams, Agatha Boyd, vii.

Agricultural and Mechanical College Land Scrip, transferred to University, 197.

Agricultural Experiment Station, established in Smith Hall, 296; transferred to Raleigh, 296.

Agriculture, theory and practice of, in early curriculum, 40.

Alderman, Edwin Anderson, becomes President of Tulane University, 225; dormitory named for, 289; comment concerning the establishment of the University, 5; introduces coeducation in the University, 289; reconstructs main door of South Building, 349; report to the Trustees on Carr Building, 210; story of the building of the Old Well, 348-49.

Alderman, Mrs. Edwin Anderson, vi.

Alderman Dormitory, 367; history of, 289-90.

Alexander, Eben, dormitory named for, 291; occupies house on Spencer Hall lot, 57; supports student

athletic contests, 253; uses Infirmary as office, 178.

Alexander Dormitory, 367; history of, 291.

Alexander Field, used as intramural field, 317.

Alexander House, 363.

Altitude and azimuth telescope, purchased by Caldwell, 98.

Alumni, efforts to raise funds for gymnasium, 249; meeting of representatives at Chapel Hill, Oct. 2, 1920, 239; meeting at Greensboro, Oct. 11, 1920, 241; meetings organized in campaign for University, 1920, 241.

Alumni Association, committee on raising funds for athletic fields, list of members, 318-19; meeting, 1891, 211; meeting at Commencement, 1905, 256; suggests removal of the remains of W. R. Davie to the Campus, 132.

Alumni Association of Washington, D. C., sponsors Campus beautification, 277.

Alumni Building, 364; cornerstone, contents of, 212; history of, 212; imitation of New York Public Library, 343; Physics Department housed in, 212; remodeled, 90, 294.

Alumni Review, edited by Louis R. Wilson, 238; established, 238; presents case for needs of University, 243; statement from mass meeting of student body, 241; stresses need for development of University, 238.

Alves, Gavin, 12, 13.

Alves, Helen, 12.

Alves, McDowal, 12.

Alves, Walter, 12, 13; donor to University, 30; security for John

called College Street, 122; named for Paul C. Cameron, 201.

Campaign for funds, 1921. *See* North Carolina, University of, campaign for funds, 1921.

Campus, architectural and landscape development of, 133-45; boundaries defined by Trustees, 208; bounds laid off, 53; definition of, v; described by student in 1860, 172; description of in fifties and sixties, 163-64; drawing of preserved in Metropolitan Museum, 131; earliest drawings of, 161-62; eastern boundary of, 121; "Grand Avenue," 54; highways through, 23; once called the Grove, 60; original dimensions of, 54; "ornamental grounds," 53-54; plan for development suggested by Elisha Mitchell, 88-89; plans for development, 90; rock fences on, 123, 125, 164-65.

Campus beautification, appropriation for in 1848, 160; constructive steps toward, 53-63, 129; funds appropriated for, 127. *See also* Coker, W. C. *and* Grounds and Buildings, Committee on.

"Campus Beautiful," pamphlet distributed by Washington Alumni, 277.

Campus development, expenditures prior to Civil War, 166-67; highest point before Civil War, 166-72; inaugurated, 121-32; maps showing, 357-60; new area opened, 292-93; new direction in planning, 234; real beginning of, 133.

Campus plan, 329-31; and University expansion, 275-76; McKim, Mead, and White on importance of, 345; original axes of, 352.

Campus planting, description of, 163-64.

Canteen ("Scuttlebut"), 313.

Captains commanding student military companies, 1861, 181.

Cards, played by students, 113-14.

Carmichael, William D., vi; contributes to renovation of Person Hall, 288.

Carmichael, William D., Jr., on Commodore Kessing, 325; helps secure Pre-Flight School for Chapel Hill, 313.

Carnegie, Andrew, gift for Library, 213.

Carnegie Foundation, contribution from, 280.

Carnegie Library. *See* Library, Carnegie.

Carolina Inn, 23, 366; additions to, 221, 290, 292; designed by Arthur C. Nash, 220; donated by John Sprunt Hill, 220; location of, 107.

Carolina Inn Annex, 23.

Carolina Inn Apartments, 367.

The Carolina Magazine, 240-41.

Carr, George Watts, buildings designed by, 291, 292, 347.

Carr, John Wesley, 195.

Carr, Julian S., contributes to building new dormitory, 210; presents Alumni Building, 212.

Carr Dormitory, 364; architectural style of, 343; history of, 210-11.

Carrboro, 245; railroad station, 112.

Cave, Belfield W., 26.

Cave's Mill, later King's Mill, 26.

Cemetery, enclosure of, 101.

Central Hotel, location of, 219-20; property purchased by University, 229.

Chair of History Fund, 210, 212.

Chamberlain, Mrs. Hope S., vi.

Chambers, Lenoir, 239.

Chapel Hill, bounds laid off, 53; branch railway line built, 176; cemetery, students buried in, 176; climate of, 174; companies in Civil War, 181; described by Swain in 1836, 122; described in *Raleigh Standard* in 1859, 171-72; description of, 28; descrip-

394 INDEX

Military Science, plans for instruction in, 1864, 118.

Mills, Robert, advises Swain on building materials, 129; architect of Washington Monument, 128.

Millis, Mr. and Mrs. James E., contribute to Woollen Gymnasium, 323.

Millis, William Brooks, 323.

"Mineral Springs," location of, 27.

Miss Fannie's Spring, 28.

Mitchell, Elisha, amateur landscape architect, 126; arrives in 1818, 60; as astronomer, 100, 107; as botanist, 126, 269; as bursar, 60, 123; as Superintendent of Buildings and Lands, 60-61, 62, 87, 123, 127, 167, 270; death of, 107, 126; director of Library, 123; directs hard-surfacing of Campus roads, 165; drafts Faculty petition to save Person Hall, 69; letter to Charles Manly concerning Loader's work on Campus, 160; location of laboratory, 52, 107; location of land conveyed to him by Trustees, 125; on need for addition to South Building, 84; plan for Campus expansion, 88-89, 237; pleads for facilities for physical sciences, 83; registers complaint with Trustees against superintendent, 62; takes initiative in laying rock walls, 124; varied activities of, 123.

Mitchell, H. F., Jr., remodels Gerrard Hall, 1938, 90.

Modernistic style, on University of North Carolina Campus, 337.

Momberger, William, drawing of Campus, 162.

Monogram Club, recommends naming track field Fetzer Field, 321.

Monogram Club Building, 313, 367.

Montgomery, H. P. Alan, building architect for Manning, Saunders, Murphey, 277; designer of Ruffin, Mangum, Manly, and Grimes dormitories and Saunders, Murphey, Manning, and Bingham halls, 347.

Moore, Alfred, 9, 13, 14, 98; characterization of, 17; donor to University, 30.

Moore, Bartholomew Figures, 147.

Moore, Dave, 111.

Moore, J. B., 122.

Moore, John W., author of *The Heirs of St. Kilda*, 117.

Morehead, J. L., 318.

Morehead, J. M., (Governor), confers with A. J. Davis on remodeling University buildings, 135; receives Buchanan in Chapel Hill, 170.

Morehead, John Motley, donates Bell Tower, 221-22.

Morehead-Patterson Bell Tower, 366; architectural style of, 347; history of, 222.

Morehead Planetarium, 310.

Morgan, Hardy, land donated by, 354; purchase of lands from, 15.

Morgan, John, land donated by, 354.

Morgan, Mark, 26, 354.

Morgan, Solomon P., 354.

Morgan District, 10.

Morgan's Creek, 23; plants growing near, 265-66; reservoir on, 301; mills on, 26.

Morrill Act, lands allotted to University, 197.

Morrison, Cameron, 243.

Morse, Jedidiah, 8.

Mosely, William Dunn, letter describing Chapel Hill in 1853, 56.

Mott, John R., 251.

Mount Bolus, 245; origin of name, 27.

Mount Mitchell, named for Elisha Mitchell, 107.

Muirhead Construction Company, remodels Alumni Building, 212.

Murfreesborough, Tennessee, negotiations for sale of University lands, 206-7.

406 INDEX

Taylor, Thomas H., location of former home, 279; location of store, 57; owner of house on Spencer Hall lot, 57; reappointed Superintendent, 62; services as Superintendent of property and financial concerns prove unsatisfactory, 60.
Taylor, Tyre C., editor of *Carolina Magazine*, 1920, 240.
Teague, C. E., vi.
Telescopes, in ·first Observatory, 98, 102-3.
"Temple of Folly," epithet applied to Main Hall, 74. *See also* South Building.
Tennessee lands, increased in value by westward emigration, 206; sale of, 72, 81, 84, 135; Legislature confirms land warrants, 207.
Tenney, John B., conducts dining room in Steward's Hall, 52.
Tenney, Oregon, owner of plantation near Chapel Hill, 27.
Tennis, introduced in Chapel Hill, 251; courts of University, 252.
Thompson, Henry, contractor for President's House, 46.
Thompson, Henry C., runs boarding house in Chapel Hill, 57.
Thompson, Jacob, accompanies President Buchanan to Chapel Hill, 169; address in Chapel Hill, tribute to Doctor Caldwell, 169-70; Secretary of the Interior, 168; speaks in Gerrard Hall, 91.
Thompson, T. C., and Brothers, contractors for remodeling of New East and New West, 153.
Thompson, Will H., quotation from, 173.
Thompson, William Henry, foreman of University Press, 306; founder of *Chapel Hill News*, 306.
Thornton, Mary L., vii.
Thyatira, location of McCorkle's school, 54.
Thyatira Presbyterian Church, 6.

"Tin can." *See* Athletic Court, indoor.
Totten, H. R., botanical observations of, 269.
Tourgée, Albion W., and Negro education in North Carolina, 194.
Town, Ithiel, consulted on University buildings, 129; partner of Alexander Jackson Davis, 88, 133.
Toy, Walter D., efforts to improve sanitary facilities, 296; Faculty supervisor of University Press, 306.
Track team, first, wins Southern championship, 252.
Transit instrument, in first Observatory, 104; purchase recommended by President Caldwell, 97.
Transylvania Company, purchases lands from Cherokees, 86.
The Triangle, in Battle Park, 28.
Triassic sea, depression east of Chapel Hill, 25.
Trimble, Ralph M., drawings of first Astronomical Observatory, 102, 103.
Troy, Matthew, teacher in Preparatory School, 43.
Trustees, and athletic contests, 109, 253; and early curriculum, 39-40, 42; and Main Building, 73, 74-75, 78, 81; and sale of University lands and property, 44, 63, 87, 122, 197; appoint a steward, 47; appoint a superintendent of the property and financial concerns of the University, 60; appoint committee in charge of University lands, 206-7; appoint committee on water supply, 297; appoint committee to employ an architect, 150; appoint committee to examine legal status of Gerrard's will, 87; appoint committee to investigate funds of University, 77; appoint committee to memoralize the General Assem-